MODERNISM LONDON STYLE

Rather than relying on provocative mannerisms or fractures, the architectural wealth of London's Art Deco is the product of a shared tradition of construction and style, through which one can trace an orientation towards the familiar, consideration for surrounding buildings and an integration into its cultural and historical context. Drawing on England's classical traditions, a formal canon arose and was slowly and continually advanced. Despite novel ideas of space and material, its fundamental attitude always remained intact; no disintegration into single parts, much less a so-called dissolution of architecture, took place. Thus the characteristic feature of Art Deco is its long, yet constant evolution of its sculptural physicality.

For this reason, in this photographic series, morphological character and façade as formal expressions of building volume lie in the foreground, and with them architecture as a sculptural object: the initially rigidly geometric, primarily flat façades and volumes gradually loosen up, break up, and begin to oscillate; from clear and unified compositions more complex ones develop, finally melting into harmoniously flowing free-forms.

In documenting this play of forms, harsh sunlight is the greatest aid. For only through the effects of light and shade do the sculptural force and spatial depth of this architecture stand out.

Der architektonische Reichtum des Londoner Art déco basiert nicht auf provozierenden Manierismen und Brüchen; vielmehr ist eine gemeinsame Bau- und Stiltradition durch Orientierung am Gewohnten, Rücksichtnahme auf die Bauten der Umgebung und die Eingliederung in ihren kulturellen und historischen Kontext spürbar. So hat sich ein formaler Kanon, der bis in die klassizistische Tradition Englands zurückreicht, erhalten und dennoch langsam und kontinuierlich weiterentwickelt. Trotz neuer Raumvorstellungen und Materialien bleibt diese Grundhaltung immer bestehen; ein Zerfall in Einzelteile, gar eine sogenannte Auflösung der Architektur, findet nicht statt. So ist die langsame, aber stetige Evolution der skulpturalen Körperlichkeit das charakteristischste Merkmal des Art déco.

Aus diesem Grund stehen in der folgenden Serie die Volumetrie und die Fassade als formale Ausdrücke des Baukörpers und damit die Architektur als skulpturales Objekt im Vordergrund: Die anfänglich streng geometrischen, primär flachen Fassaden und Volumen spielen sich frei, brechen auf, beginnen zu schwingen; aus den klaren Einheiten entwickeln sich teils komplexe Kompositionen, um schließlich in harmonisch fließenden Freiformen zu verschmelzen.

Bei der Dokumentation dieses Formenspiels ist das harte Sonnenlicht der wichtigste Helfer. Nur durch die Licht- und Schattenwirkung tritt die bildhauerische Kraft und räumliche Tiefe dieser Architektur zutage.

Niels Lehmann

THE
ART DECO HERITAGE

DIE BAUTEN DES
ART DÉCO

MODERNISM LONDON STYLE

NIELS LEHMANN

EDITED BY

HERAUSGEGEBEN VON

CHRISTOPH RAUHUT

HIRMER

MODERN OR MODERNE ?

Adam Caruso

Neoclassicism, stripped classicism, Georgian, neo-Swedish, neo-Dutch, Tudor, Gothic, exoticism, modern, moderne, all of these styles are evident in the architecture of Britain from the first decades of the 20th century. British architecture of this period cannot simply be classified as 'modern' or 'traditional' since many of the leading practitioners adopted a range of styles depending on the programme and the setting of a project. This tendency can be understood as an extension of Victorian eclecticism, with that period's reliance on history being supplemented by an equally enthusiastic engagement with contemporary practice in continental Europe and the United States. However one characterises this time, a time of significant confusion that bears comparison with the architectural Babel of today, many British buildings of the period between the wars could be called Art Deco.

Art Deco is a design style as popular with the general public as it is held in contempt by architects. The smooth forms and glamorous materials that characterise Art Deco were at least as important to the design of interiors, furniture, clothing and products, as they

MODERN ODER MODERNE ?

Neoclassicism, Stripped Classicism, Georgian, N
Swedish, Neo-Dutch, Tudor, Gothic, Exoticism, Mode
Moderne – all diese Stilrichtungen sind in der britisc
Architektur der ersten Jahrzehnte des 20. Jahrhunderts
entdecken. ›Modern‹ oder ›traditionell‹ wären hier vere
fachende, gar unpassende Kategorien, praktizierten d
viele der führenden Architekten das ganze Spektrum
Stile je nach Programm und Ort. Diese Vorgehensw
scheint an den viktorianischen Eklektizismus anzukn
fen, wobei der vertrauende und vertraute Rückgriff
die Historie von einem gleichermaßen großen Enthusi
mus für die zeitgenössischen Entwicklungen im übri
Europa und in den USA begleitet wurde. Viele Gebä
der Zwischenkriegszeit, deren deutlich erkennbare Ver
sicherung nicht wenig an das architektonische Babel
heute erinnert, besaßen jedoch eine Gemeinsamkeit:
können als ›Art déco‹ bezeichnet werden.

Art déco findet als Stilrichtung ebenso großen A
klang in der Öffentlichkeit wie Ablehnung in der Arc
tektenschaft. So waren abgerundete Formen und m
däne Materialien für Art-Déco-Einrichtungen, -Mö

re to architecture. The prevalence of this style in the riod between the end of the First World War and financial collapse of 1929 coincides with the emer- ıce of a new kind of consumer behaviour, driven by sire, rather than necessity. Unlike neoclassicism, Art ouveau, modernism, and postmodernism, Art Deco is iriously free of intellectual pretensions. Its precious faces are opaque, reflecting no deep inner meanings. is engagement with pure formal pleasure is shared rhaps only by Rococo, another artistic manner that s historically suffered from a mixed reputation. While ıt flowering of formal exuberance in the 18th century s an expression of sensual pleasure in the paintings Antoine Watteau and Jean-Honoré Fragonard, in the ırches of south Germany, Bohemia and Austria it was o a celebration of divine ecstasy. Art Deco, however, only a celebration of carnal pleasure and the rapture capitalism and the free market. 18th century England wed Rococo art with some suspicion, if only for being o French'. By the 20th century, England was predis- sed to the American brashness and exuberance of Art co, which was embraced by the privileged classes of interwar period. Streamlined steamships and equally eamlined houses provide many of the luxurious set- gs for Hercule Poirot to solve murders amongst the d-Atlantic aristocracy **Fig. A**.

Art Deco was the contemporary British architecture the interwar period. That Britain did not experience odernism can be explained by its trajectory as a world wer. During the course of the 19th century, when the wer and reach of the Empire was at its greatest, Brit- architecture was practised with considerable sophis- ation. The work of such diverse figures as Augustus

-Kleider und -Objekte mindestens so prägend wie für die Art-Déco-Architektur. Die Vorherrschaft dieses Stils in der Periode zwischen dem Ende des Ersten Weltkriegs und der Weltwirtschaftskrise von 1929 fällt zusammen mit einem neuen Konsumverhalten – nicht länger Notwendigkeit, sondern Begehren bilden den Antrieb. Anders als der Neo-Klassizismus, der Art nouveau, die Moderne oder die Postmoderne stellt der Art déco jedoch keine intellektuellen Ansprüche. Die edlen Oberflächen sind opak, sie spiegeln keine tiefere Bedeutung wider. Einzig im Rokoko, das eine ähnlich gemischte Rezeption durchlebte, gab es vielleicht eine vergleichbare Freude an der puren Form. Diese Blüte formalen Überschwangs im 18. Jahrhundert war zum einen Ausdruck sinnlichen Vergnügens, etwa in den Gemälden Antonie Watteaus und Jean-Honoré Fragonards, zum anderen Feier göttlicher Ekstase, wie in den süddeutschen, böhmischen und österreichischen Kirchenbauten. Anders der Art déco, der nur körperliches Vergnügen und den Triumph des freien Marktes und Kapitalismus feiert. Die Kunst des Rokoko hatte man im England des 18. Jahrhunderts argwöhnisch betrachtet, weil sie zu ›französisch‹ war. Nun

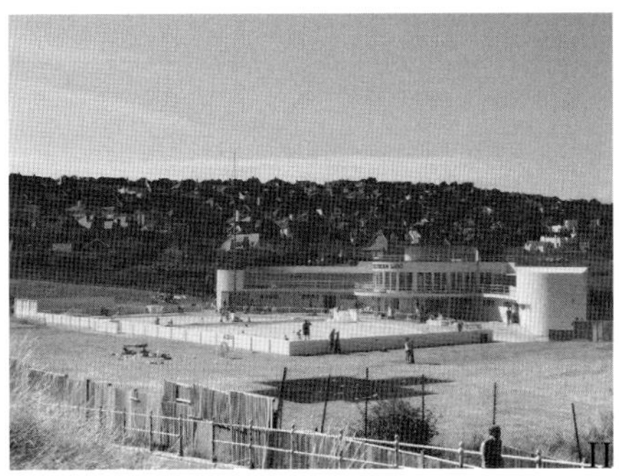

A Lido Saltdean, R.W.H. Jones, 1938

Pugin (1812–1852), William Butterfield (1814–1900), Alfred Waterhouse (1830–1905), Richard Norman Shaw (1831–1912) and Philip Webb (1831–1915) engaged, each in their own manner, with the challenges of new technologies and new typologies in ways that served the interests of their clients at the same time as developing the capacity of the discipline itself to address the 'modern world'. These architects looked to the history of architecture to provide answers for contemporary practice. It was the work of these architects that drew Hermann Muthesius (1861–1927) to Britain for six years on behalf of the Deutscher Werkbund and resulted in his book *Das englische Haus*. It is in this work that one finds the roots of modernism.

By the beginning of the 20th century the British Empire had peaked in size and in influence and with its decline there began a period of consolidation. The necessity to project an imperial identity across the diverse nations of the Empire put a heavy demand on the representational architecture of the colonies, and much British architecture of this period was predictably pompous and historicist. This stasis can be compared with the

im England des 20. Jahrhunderts war die privilegie Gesellschaft der Zwischenkriegszeit fasziniert von c amerikanischen Keckheit und Überschwänglichkeit c Art déco. Stromlinienförmige Dampfschiffe wie Häu boten gleichermaßen die glamouröse Folie, vor der H cule Poirot inmitten der mittelatlantischen Aristokra die Mörder aufspürte **Abb. A**.

Art déco war der zeitgenössische Architektur der Zwischenkriegszeit in England. Dass Großbrita nien die Moderne selbst nicht erlebte, erklärt sich a seinem Weg als Weltmacht. Im 19. Jahrhundert, die Macht und der Einfluss des britischen Empires a größten waren, zeichnete sich die britische Architek durch ein hohes Maß an Selbstsicherheit und Selb verständlichkeit aus. Die Arbeiten solch unterschi licher Persönlichkeiten wie Augustus Pugin (1812–185 William Butterfield (1814–1900), Alfred Waterho (1830–1905), Richard Norman Shaw (1831–1912) u Philip Webb (1831–1915) stellten sich der Herausfor rung neuer Technologien und Typologien, wobei sie s wohl die Wünsche ihrer Klienten erfüllten als auch Fähigkeit ihrer eigenen Disziplin aufzeigten, die ›mod ne Welt‹ zu reflektieren. Jene Architekten blickten a die Geschichte der Architektur, um Lösungen für zeitgenössische Praxis zu finden. Ihre Werke veranla ten Hermann Muthesius (1861–1927), im Auftrag Deutschen Werkbundes für sechs Jahre nach Großb tannien zu kommen und das Buch *Das englische Haus* verfassen. Hier liegen die Wurzeln der Moderne.

Zu Beginn des 20. Jahrhunderts hatte das britisc Empire seinen Zenit bereits überschritten, Größe u Einfluss waren rückläufig, es begann ein Zeitabsch der Konsolidierung. So galt es, in den unterschiedlich

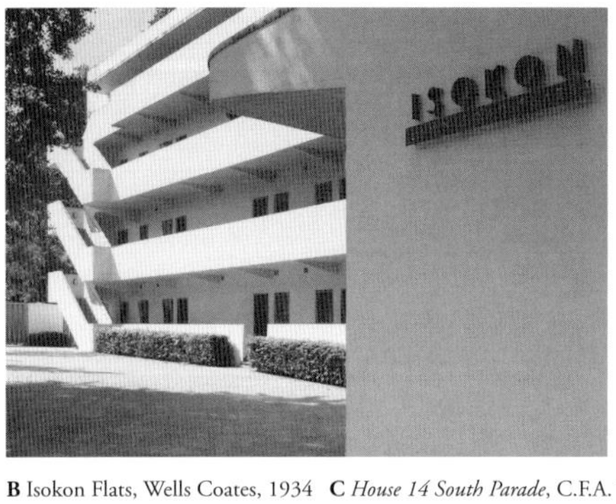

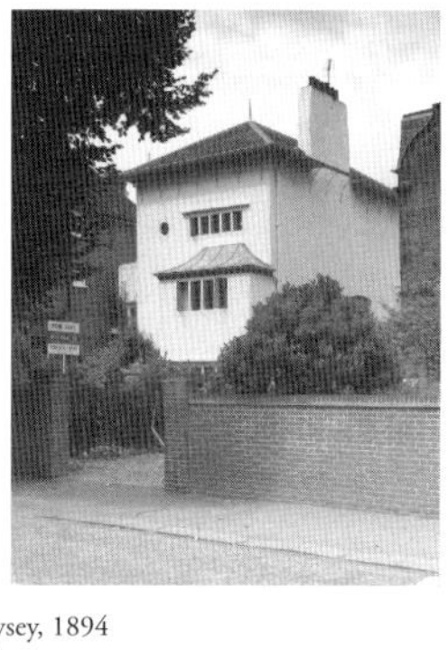

B Isokon Flats, Wells Coates, 1934 **C** *House 14 South Parade*, C.F.A. Voysey, 1894

namism that characterised the social and political uations in France, in the Weimar Republic, in Austria l in the Soviet Union; places where modernism took d and brightly flourished before burning out. The British buildings from the period that could be con-ered modern, say Amyas Connell's High and Over 31), Wells Coates' Isokon (1934) **Fig. B** or Berthold betkin's Highpoint (1935) suffer from their isolation. at all of these buildings were designed by expatriates gests that the language of modernism, and its associ-d social polemic, were exported rather than native to British context. The British architectural discourse that time was dominated by the influence of Sweden, Netherlands and the United States, countries whose hitecture had been, until recently, greatly influenced 19th-century Britain, an influence that abruptly nged direction by the turn of the century. Whilst dernists practising in Britain would claim an inter-ionalism for their work, more 'traditional' architects, o were every bit as well travelled and engaged in the ernational scene, were trying to make work that was temporary at the same time as extending the line-of an 'English' architecture as articulated by John skin and the formidable legacy of the 19th century.

In his essay 'The British Contemporaries of Frank yd Wright' John Summerson makes an instructive nparison between Wright (1867–1959), whose work l personal charisma served as a central impetus to the elopment of European modernism, and architects of same generation in Britain. Although architects like win Lutyens, and to a lesser degree C.F.A. Voysey . **C**, carried the influence of Arts and Crafts archi-ture into the 20th century, only the work of Charles

Nationen des Empires eine gemeinsame Identität zu etablieren, was insbesondere über die Repräsentationsbauten in den Kolonien geschehen sollte. Es erstaunt kaum, dass die britische Architektur jener Zeit meist pompös und geschichtsträchtig war. Diese Stagnationsphase verhielt sich konträr zur gleichzeitigen sozialen und politischen Dynamik in Frankreich, der Weimarer Republik, Österreich und der Sowjetunion – Orte, an denen die Moderne Fuß fasste und eine großartige Blütezeit erlebte, bevor sie zusammenbrach. Die wenigen britischen Gebäude, die als modern bezeichnet werden können, wie Amyas Connells High and Over (1931), Wells Coates' Isokon (1934) **Abb. B** oder Berthold Lubetkins Highpoint (1935), stehen isoliert da. Da sie alle von Immigranten errichtet wurden, liegt die Vermutung nahe, dass die Sprache der Moderne und die mit ihr einhergehende soziale Polemik von außen eingebracht wurden und nicht in Großbritannien selbst wurzelten. Der britische Architekturdiskurs jener Zeit war bestimmt durch Einflüsse aus Schweden, den Niederlanden und den USA – Länder, deren Architektur durch das Großbritannien des 19. Jahrhunderts geprägt worden war, bevor um die Jahrhundertwende plötzlich der umgekehrte Weg eingeschlagen wurde. Während aber die Modernisten in Großbritannien ihre Arbeit als ›international‹ propagierten, versuchten die eher ›traditionellen‹ Architekten, die genauso weitgereist und in der internationalen Szene involviert waren, Gebäude zu bauen, die dem Zeitgeist entsprachen und zugleich in der Tradition einer ›englischen‹ Architektur standen, wie sie John Ruskin formuliert hatte und die das großartige Erbe des 19. Jahrhunderts war.

In seinem Essay *The British Contemporaries of Frank Lloyd Wright* zieht John Summerson einen aufschluss-

Rennie Mackintosh (1868–1928) was material in the development of a modernist architecture. It could be said that both Mackintosh and Wright benefitted from being at a geographical distance from the centres of fin-de-siècle architecture, from Vienna, Paris and Brussels. Their work displays a certain abstraction that is informed by a robust and Gaelic quality, something that moderates and simplifies the extreme formal elaboration of the contemporary *jugendstil* architecture.

Other key figures of this generation were John James Joass (1868–1952) and Charles Holden (1875–1960), architects who built more than Mackintosh, but were not as well known internationally, and whose work cannot be said to have had a consequential relationship to the development of modernism. Early works by these architects, the Royal Insurance Office on Piccadilly by Joass (1909) and Holden's British Medical Association Building on the Strand (1908), have impressive Portland stone façades organised with the taut, nervous energy of what was then known as Neo-Mannerism. By the late 1920s Holden was working for the Underground Electric Railways Company of London (UERL), initially

reichen Vergleich zwischen Wright (1867–1959), der
seinen Werken und seinem Charisma die Entwickl
der europäischen Moderne stark beeinflusste, und Arc
tekten seiner Generation in Großbritannien. Obwohl
chitekten wie Edwin Lutyens und, in geringerem Ma
C.F.A. Voysey **Abb. C** die Arts-and-Crafts-Architek
ins 20. Jahrhundert überführten, war es allein das W
von Charles Rennie Mackintosh (1868–1928), das ei
grundlegenden Beitrag zur Entstehung einer moder
Architektur bildete. Es scheint, als ob Mackintosh
auch Wright von ihrer geografischen Distanz zu
Zentren der Fin-de-Siècle-Architektur Wien, Paris
Brüssel profitierten. Ihre Arbeit zeigt ein gewisses
an Abstraktion, das an eine typisch gälische Robust
anknüpft, und so den starken formalen Ausdruck des
gendstils mäßigt und vereinfacht.

Andere wichtige Figuren jener Generation wa
John James Joass (1868–1952) und Charles Hol
(1875–1960). Beide Architekten bauten zwar mehr
Mackintosh, waren aber international weniger bekan
Ihre Arbeiten scheinen keine wirkliche Einflussgröße
der Entwicklung der Moderne darzustellen. Ihre frü

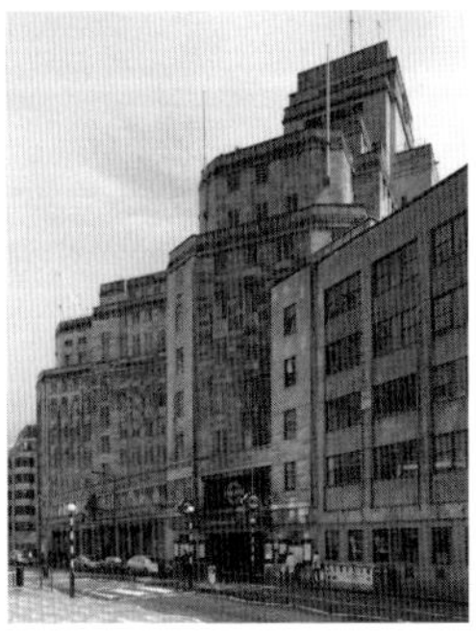

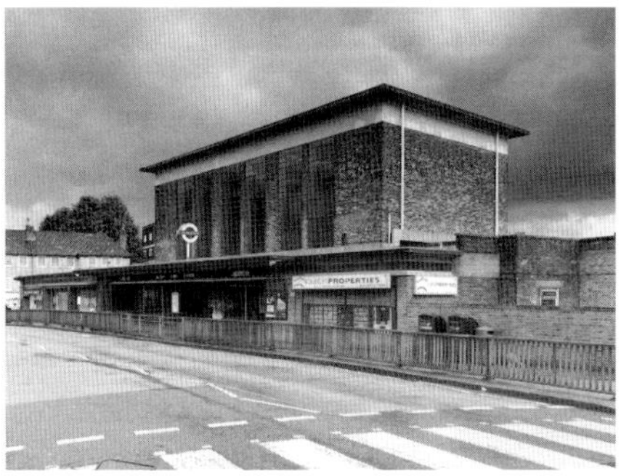

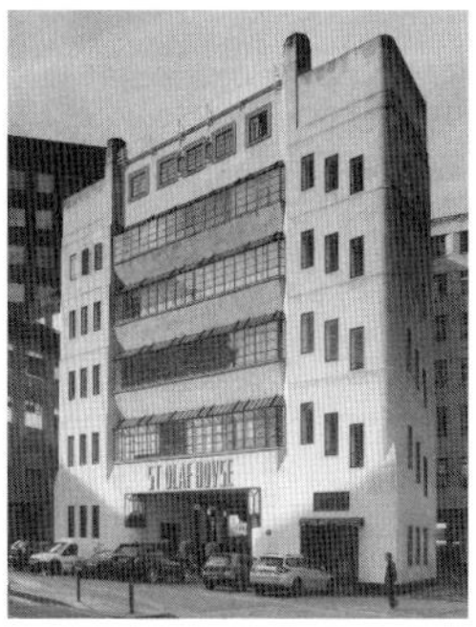

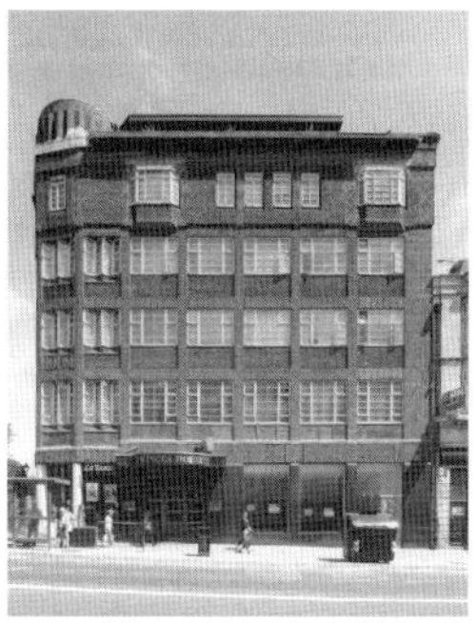

D Broadway House, Charles Holden, 1929 **E** Acton Town Tube Station, Charles Holden, 1933 **F** St Olaf House, H.S. Goodhart-Rendel, 1931 **G** Princes House, H.S. Goodhart-Rendel, 1936

their headquarters building at 55 Broadway (1929) ;. **D**, and eventually on the major extensions to the rthern, District and Piccadilly lines **Fig. E**. 55 Broad- y, with its stepped profile rising from a plinth that ows the perimeter of the site, bears some relationship Manhattan's setback architecture of the same period, eference accentuated by the Portland stone cladding l the vertical organisation of its windows. Holden's igns for the underground, informed by an extensive ernational tour of contemporary architecture with UERL's formidable general manager Frank Pick, are most lasting legacy. Their carefully judged material priety, brick and concrete for the suburban stations, vertine and brass for central stations like Piccadilly cus, allied with consistently well judged references to numental precedents, are as satisfying and intelligent ay as when they were built. However, their language educed classicism is clearly derived from continental dels, most specifically Gunnar Asplund's work of the 20s.

The other significant architect of this generation was S. Goodhart-Rendel (1887–1959). His best-known lding is St Olaf House (1931) **Fig. F** on the Thames in thwark. Its landward façade is an indescribable mix of dernist elements, such as the four strips of horizontal el glazing, and historical references, such as the sym- trical and emphatically monumental stair towers. The ade is clad in Portland stone which is tightly skin-like, also has a battered profile like a castle. This façade omewhere between the AEG-Turbinenfabrik (1909) Peter Behrens and the Fagus-Werk (1913) by Walter opius. Princes House (1936) in Brighton **Fig. G**, also Goodhart-Rendel, exhibits a textile-like handling of

Werke, wie Joass' Royal Insurance Office (1909) oder Holden's British Medical Association Building (1908), verfügen über eindrucksvolle Fassaden aus Portlandstein, deren straffe und doch nervöse Dynamik man damals als Neo-Manierismus bezeichnete. Gegen Ende der 1920er Jahre arbeitete Holden für die Underground Electric Railways Company of London (UERL), errichtete erst 1929 ihre Hauptverwaltung am Broadway 55 **Abb. D** und später die ausgedehnten Erweiterungsbauten der Northern, District und Piccadilly Line **Abb. E**. Die Hauptverwaltung, deren abgetreppter Umriss auf einem Sockelgeschoss sitzt, das den Grundstücksgrenzen folgt, zeigt einige Verwandtschaft zu der zeitgleichen *Setback*-Architektur Manhattans. Diese Referenz wird durch den Portlandstein als Fassadenmaterial und die vertikale Organisation der Fenster noch verstärkt. Holdens beständigstes Erbe sind die Underground-Stationen, für deren Entwürfe er auf einer Reise zur internationalen zeitgenössischen Architektur, zusammen mit dem durchaus anspruchsvollen Generaldirektor der UERL Frank Pick, Eindrücke sammelte. Heute wie damals beeindruckend und von kluger Überlegung zeugend sind die stets passenden Anleihen bei historischen Baudenkmalen sowie die unterschied-lichen Materialitäten: Beton und Backstein für die Stationen der Vorstädte und Travertin und Messing für die Stationen der Innenstadt wie Picadilly Circus. Jedoch ist ihre Architektursprache eines gemäßigten Neo-Klassizismus deutlich von kontinentaleuropäischen Vorbildern abgeleitet, insbesondere von Gunnar Asplunds Arbeiten aus den 1920er Jahren.

Der andere bedeutsame Architekt jener Zeit war H.S. Goodhart-Rendel (1887–1959). St Olaf House (1931) **Abb. F** an der Themse in Southwark ist sein bekanntestes

brickwork in its façades that is at odds with the flat handling of this material in English Georgian architecture. This use of brick is also distinct from an Arts and Crafts sensibility, which more strongly emphasises the structural image of wall and arch, an expression that refers to a Ruskinian ethic of handcraft. Both of these buildings betray a continental influence, the stripped monumental classicism of H.P. Berlage **Fig. H**, the Hanseatic brick architecture of Fritz Höger, but without the heroic scale and without the benefit of the grand urban gesture. These buildings impress with the small-scale *décorative* articulation that organises and elaborates their façades. Goodhart-Rendel was a contemporary of W.M. Dudok (1884–1974), but one cannot claim that his œuvre had the same coherence or international significance as that of the City Architect of Hilversum.

The degree to which a building is modern is no longer a relevant question. Perhaps we should reconsider a more 19th-century definition of the 'modern', as an art that emerges naturally from present circumstances, that is a mirror held up to the monumental as well as to the everyday. The contemporary architectural discourse

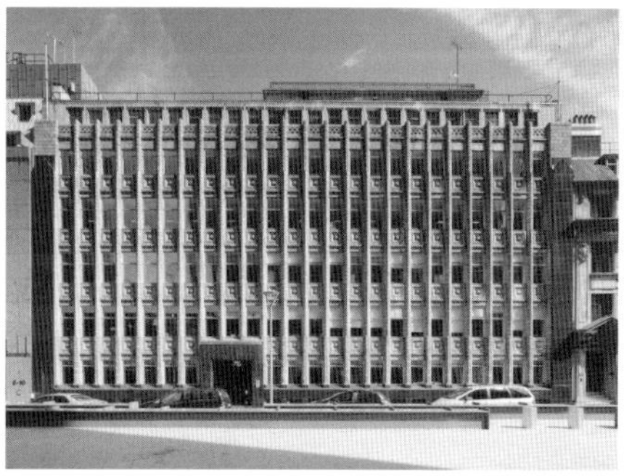

H Holland House, H.P. Berlage, 1916

Werk. Die landseitige Fassade ist ein unbeschreiblic Mix moderner Elemente, wie der vier horizontalen Fe terbänder mit Stahlrahmen, und historischer Refer zen, wie der symmetrischen und betont monumenta Treppentürme. Die Fassade ist von einer dünnen H aus Portlandstein überzogen, ihr Umriss jedoch abges wie bei einer Burg. Sie ähnelt einerseits der Turbinenf rik der AEG (1909) von Peter Behrens, andererseits d Fagus-Werk (1913) von Walter Gropius. Das ebenfalls Goodhart-Rendel erbaute Princes House (1936) in Bri ton **Abb. G** zeigt einen fast textilen Umgang mit Ba stein in der Fassade, der sich deutlich von den flächi Backsteinfassaden des englischen *Georgian* absetzt. S Umgang mit Backstein widerspricht auch dem Emp den der Arts-and-Crafts-Bewegung, die das konstr tive Bild von Tragen und Lasten – eine Referenz an Ruskin'sche Handwerksethik – viel stärker betonte. Be Gebäude lassen einen kontinentalen Einfluss erken – den enthüllten, monumentalen Klassizismus von H Berlage **Abb. H** und die hanseatische Backsteinarchi tur von Fritz Höger –, jedoch fehlt ihnen der herois Maßstab und die adäquate große urbane Geste. Sie be drucken durch eine kleinmaßstäbliche dekorative Ar tektursprache in der Gliederung und Gestaltung der F saden. Goodhart-Rendel war ein Zeitgenosse von W. Dudok (1884–1974), jedoch kann man nicht behaup dass sein Œuvre dieselbe Kohärenz oder dieselbe inter tionale Bedeutung hatte wie das Werk des Hilversu Stadtarchitekten.

Wie modern ein Gebäude ist, ist heutzutage keine levante Frage mehr. Vielleicht aber sollten wir eine an 19. Jahrhundert anknüpfende Definition neu bedenk ›Modern‹ als Begriff für eine Kunst, die sich auf sel

tinues to ponder abstract and non-architectural mat- like globalisation and technology. Instead of build- new modernisms in response to the formidable chal- ges of contemporary practice, we would do better to ow the example of 19th-century architects and look what the history of our discipline can tell us about here and the now. The original rhetoric of an early h-century building, or its lack of any rhetorical justi- tion, is much less important than a building's actual sical presence and its ongoing engagement with the . As difficult as it is to precisely define the Art Deco itecture of London, there exists a considerable legacy uildings that exhibit certain features of modernism, nout being modernist, that have a spirit of invention is at odds with the pompous structures of late Em- . These buildings are worthy of our attention. It is ause of their thematic ambiguity and formal eclecti- n that they are especially relevant to the complexities he 21st century.

graphy (selection) Verwendete Literatur (Auswahl)

, Gavin (ed): Britain in the Thirties, issue of: Architectural Design 49 (1979), No 10/11.

erson, John: 'The British Contemporaries of Frank Lloyd Wright', in: The Unromantic and other Essays. London, 1990, pp. 235–244.

verständliche Weise aus dem Gegenwärtigen ergibt, die sowohl das Monumentale wie auch das Alltägliche widerspiegelt. Der zeitgenössische architektonische Diskurs versenkt sich weiterhin in abstrakten und nicht-architektonischen Themen wie Globalisierung und Technologie. Anstatt als Antwort auf die enormen Herausforderungen der gegenwärtigen Praxis neue Modernen zu formulieren, sollten wir lieber dem Beispiel der Architekten des 19. Jahrhunderts folgen und schauen, was uns die Geschichte unserer Disziplin für das Hier und Jetzt lehren kann. Viel wichtiger als die ursprüngliche Rhetorik eines Gebäudes des frühen 20. Jahrhunderts oder das Fehlen einer rhetorischen Rechtfertigung ist die heutige physische Präsenz eines Gebäudes und sein fortwährender Dialog mit der Stadt. So schwierig es ist, die Art-Déco-Architektur von London präzise zu definieren, so existiert doch ein beachtliches Erbe an Gebäuden, die gewisse Merkmale der Moderne aufzeigen, ohne jedoch modern zu sein, die ein Erfindungsgeist umgibt, der nicht zu den pompösen Bauwerken des späten Empires passt. Diese Gebäude verdienen unsere Aufmerksamkeit. In ihrer thematischen Uneindeutigkeit und ihrem formalen Eklektizismus sind sie von hoher Relevanz für die Komplexitäten des 21. Jahrhunderts. Übersetzung: Christoph Rauhut

THE PHOTOGRAPHIC DOCUMENTATION OF AN ARCHITECTURAL MOVEMENT – A CONTRADICTORY ENDEAVOUR ?

Christoph Rauhut

Illuminating, far fetched or odd: why would you photograph the entire built output of an architectural movement and bring it together in a book?

In short, this book places the building itself in the foreground, as still being the most important task of architecture. The photographs document an architectural legacy, one which continues to shape London and England. They are meant to enthuse an interested readership, including architects, for the wealth of forms and design ideas as well as the physical presence of the Art Deco buildings. The book is a reference work, made with reverence for an architecture of great quality.

And yet, in preparing a photographic record, more fundamental questions arise: first of all, how does one define the boundaries of the built production of an architectural movement? Furthermore, in which order should the buildings be presented? And finally, what is the significance of architectural photography as the medium for a visual record? The following remarks represent first theses – as English Art Deco was a proposition for an architectural spirit for the metropolis of London in the 1920s.

DIE FOTOGRAFISCHE DOKUMENTATION EINER ARCHITEKTURBEWEGUNG – EIN WIDERSPRÜCHLICHES VORHABEN ?

Erhellend, abwegig oder kurios: Die ganze Bau
produktion einer architektonischen Bewegung abzuf
grafieren und in ein Buch zu stecken – weshalb ein
ches Unterfangen?

Verkürzt: Dieses Buch rückt das gebaute Objek
immer noch wichtigste Aufgabe der Architektur in
Vordergrund. Die Fotografien sind die Dokumenta
eines architektonischen Erbes, das London und Engl
noch heute prägt. Sie wollen den interessierten Leser
Architekten für den formalen Reichtum, die gestal
sche Idee und die physische Präsenz der Gebäude des
déco begeistern. Das Buch ist Referenz für und Reve
an eine qualitätvolle Architektur(bewegung).

Die Ausarbeitung einer fotografischen Dokume
tion stellt jedoch grundsätzlichere Fragen: Zualler
wie definiert und grenzt man die Bautenproduktion e
architektonischen Bewegung ein? Und weiter, in wel
Anordnung präsentiert man die Gebäude? Und letzt
was bedeutet Architekturfotografie als Mittel in e
visuellen Dokumentation? Folgende Anmerkungen
erste Thesen – so wie der englische Art déco Vorsc

e drawing of boundaries,
l the fiction of completeness

To group different buildings together according to, instance, architectural style is an occasionally contra- tory undertaking. Pevsner pointedly illustrated this blem, in describing a particular building, '[whose] per- ality can be called Gothic, Gothic Revival, or Gothic vival Revived, or just English.'[1] The challenge here is to ne distinct groups for buildings to be ordered, to draw ndaries where before none existed.

Several different models and approaches are possible: search for the bizarre and the unknown has, for in- nce, been the dominant tendency for recent volumes architecture photography – books such as Frédéric aubin's *Cosmic Communist Constructions Photographed*[2] Philipp Meuser's *Architekturführer Pjöngjang*[3] are then sidered to be up-to-date witnesses of history by such sites as *Spiegel Online*.[4] The interest in the media for forgotten, the prohibited and the kinky in these cases rlaps with the idea of documentation. However, instead drawing attention to the bizarre or the extraordinary, book is directed towards a magnificent body of work, eritage that is the result of a particular architectural ition.

The expression of such an architectural position is a nmonly recognised formal canon – according to the the- hat emerged in the 18th century with the beginnings rt history. The focus on predominantly formal aspects nin a temporal framework makes it possible to define a rete area. This strategy of isolation, principally aimed he definition of styles, has remained the most popular erlying concept for writing the history of architecture, continues to shape the history of architectural ideas.

für einen architektonischen Geist der Metropole London in den 1920er Jahren war.

Das Festlegen von Grenzen und die Fiktion der Vollständigkeit

Gebäude unterschiedlichen Gruppen wie beispielsweise architektonischen Stilen zuzuordnen, ist ein mitunter widersprüchliches Unterfangen. Nikolaus Pevsner pointierte dieses Problem wie folgt: »The personality [of this building] can be called Gothic, Gothic Revival, or Gothic Revival Revived, or just English.«[1] Die Herausforderung ist, unterschiedliche Gruppen zu definieren, diesen Objekte zuzuordnen und Grenzen zu ziehen, wo vorher keine waren.

Verschiedenste Modelle und Ansätze sind möglich: So dominiert zum Beispiel in jüngster Zeit in Architekturbildbänden die Suche nach dem Skurrilen und Unbekannten – Bücher wie Frédéric Chaubins *Cosmic Communist Constructions Photographed*[2] oder Philipp Meusers *Architekturführer Pjöngjang*[3] werden dann auf Webseiten wie *Spiegel Online* als tagesaktuelle Zeugnisse der Zeitgeschichte besprochen.[4] Das mediale Interesse für das Vergessene, Verbotene, Verkorkste deckt sich in diesen Fällen mit der Thematik der Dokumentationen. Vorliegendes Buch will den Blick jedoch nicht auf das Skurrile oder Besondere lenken, sondern auf die hohe Qualität eines großartigen Erbes, das Produkt einer architektonischen Haltung war.

Ausdruck einer solchen architektonischen Haltung ist ein gemeinsam anerkannter, formaler Kanon – so die These, die im 18. Jahrhundert mit den Anfängen der Kunstgeschichte aufkommt. Die Fokussierung auf zumeist formale Gesichtspunkte in einem zeitlichen Rahmen erlaubt

At the beginning of the 21st century, a period in which we are encountering a digital utopia of limitlessness, the question of selection and isolation is emphatically a contemporary one. Evidently the model of architectural styles remains the strongest when defining groups of buildings: almost every architectural image on *Flickr*, the market leader in image-hosting sites, is labelled in such a way.

That productive uses and dangerous one-sidedness lie close together with this approach, however, was revealed with particular concision in the 20th century. It was then that the strategy of art-historical isolation was used most effectively for the (propagandistic) attempts to define architecture and architectures. To give one example, whereas the book Vincent J. Scully published in 1955, *The Shingle Style*,[5] which grew out of his doctoral thesis, made a long architectural tradition 'tangible' for the first time, and so brought it within the discourse **Fig. A**, *The International Style* exhibition of 1932 not only reduced the contemporary production of buildings to a handful of early works, but also led with hindsight to an all too one-sided reception of the breadth of architecture at the beginning

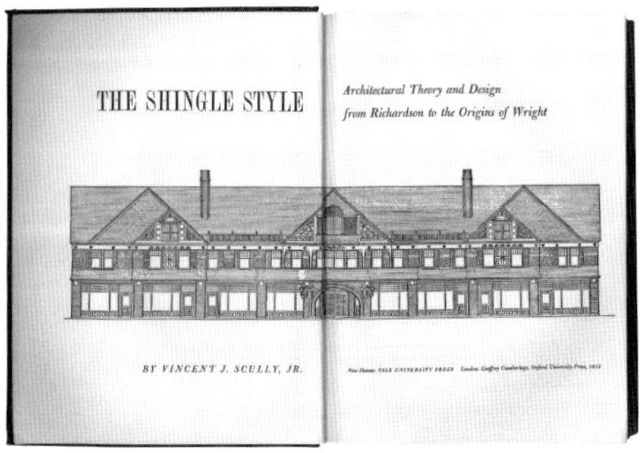

A Inside cover page / Innentitel: Scully, The Shingle Style, 1955

es, ein abgeschlossenes Feld zu definieren. Diese Strat der Eingrenzung, prinzipiell auf das Festlegen von St zielend, bleib seitdem das populärste Konzept der Ar tekturgeschichtsschreibung und prägte fortan unsere chitektonische Begriffsgeschichte.

Die Frage des Auswählens und Eingrenzens ist rade im beginnenden 21. Jahrhundert, in dem wir digitalen Utopie der Grenzenlosigkeit ausgesetzt s und angesichts der Masse von Informationen, Bild und Bits dringlichst nach den Parametern unserer In mationsauswahl suchen, eine vehement zeitgenössis Augenscheinlich bleibt das Modell architekturgeschi licher Stile bei der Festlegung von Gebäudegruppen Stärkste: Fast jedes Architekturbild beim marktbest menden Imagehoster *Flickr* hat eine solche Zuordnur

Dass bei diesem Ansatz jedoch produktiver Nut und gefährliche Einseitigkeit eng beisammen liegen, z te sich in besonderer Prägnanz im 20. Jahrhundert dem die Strategie der kunstgeschichtlichen Eingrenz aufs Effektivste für die (propagandistischen) Versuche Definition von Architektur und Architekturen gen wurde: Während zum Beispiel das aus seiner Disserta hervorgegangene Buch *The Shingle Style* **Abb. A** von V cent J. Scully 1955 eine eigentlich lange Architekturtr tion erstmals ›greifbar‹ machte und so in den Diskurs brachte,[5] reduzierte die Ausstellung *The International S* von 1932 die zeitgenössische Bautenproduktion nicht auf wenige Inkunabeln, sondern führte aus langer S auch zu einer allzu einseitigen Rezeption der Vielfalt Architektur des beginnenden 20. Jahrhunderts. Noch mer populäre und weit verbreitete Kennzeichnungen ›Die andere Moderne‹, ›Die traditionelle Moderne‹ ›Antimoderne Moderne‹ verweisen darauf, wie tief

he 20th century. Still-popular and widely used terms ı as 'the other modernism', 'traditional modernism' 'antimodern modernism' indicate how deep the shock he supposed modernism was, and still is. If, in the 21st ury, a book adheres to such an approach to writing one should be aware of the pitfalls and potentials.

One of the greatest potentials in the drawing of the ts of such a record lies in the fiction of completeness. s implies, really, that all the buildings can be fully wn, and that we might draw irrefutable conclusions – this book also tries to play that card. Yet completeness its bedfellow absoluteness are impossible to attain: our (art-historical) conceptual consensus provides us ı inexact and time-bound lines of separation, precise ndaries and divisions cannot be drawn conclusively; eover, we can never claim that we know all buildings, only admit the existence of the 'etceteras'[6] – the criti- and knowledgeable reader might for these reasons find ies missing in our inventory.

form-groups and the judgement of relatedness

Any presentation of a group of objects needs an order. ırsory glance into books on architecture discloses some sibilities for buildings: the chronological sequence ap- rs to be the most popular method. Architects' mon- ıphs, overviews of architectural history, as well as ıitectural manifestoes are mostly structured along e lines. Ordering according to size is another possi- y. Size defines the beginning and end points equally isely as each object can be assigned an exact place in sequence; everything appears comparable and under- dable **Fig. B**. Amongst architects themselves, sort- buildings according to function is hugely popular;

Schock der angeblichen Moderne saß und immer noch sitzt. Hält ein Buch im 21. Jahrhundert an einem solchen Zuschreibungsmodell fest, sollte man sich der Gefahren und Potenziale bewusst sein.

Eines der größten Potenziale beim Festlegen der Grenzen einer Dokumentation liegt in der Fiktion der Vollständigkeit. Impliziert diese doch, dass wir alle Objekte kennen und wir uns ein endgültiges Bild machen können – auch dieses Buch versucht jene Karte auszuspielen. Und doch ist eine Vollständigkeit und eine damit verknüpfte Absolutheit nicht zu erreichen: Unsere (kunstgeschichtlichen) Begriffskonsense geben ungenaue und zeitgebundene Trennlinien vor, genaue Grenzen und Abgrenzungen sind nicht endgültig zu ziehen; und auch können wir niemals behaupten, alle Objekte zu kennen, sondern nur die Existenz des »Undsoweiters« eingestehen[6] – der kritische und kundige Leser möge aus diesen Gründen fehlende oder auch überzählige Gebäude finden.

Von Formengruppen und (Wahl-)Verwandschaften

Präsentationen von Objekten bedürfen einer Anordnung. Der Blick in Architekturbücher offenbart einige solcher Möglichkeiten für Gebäude: Die chronologische Reihe scheint die populistischste Methode zu sein. Architektenmonografien, Überblickswerke zur Baugeschichte und auch Architekten-Manifeste sind zumeist so gegliedert. Die Anordnung nach Größe ist eine weitere Möglichkeit. Die Größe definiert Anfangs- und Endpunkt ebenso genau, wie jedes andere Objekt einen exakten Platz in der Reihe zugewiesen bekommt; alles scheint vergleichbar und nachvollziehbar **Abb. B**. Unter Architekten höchst beliebt ist eine Sortierfolge nach Gebäudefunktionen; im *Handbuch der Architektur* finden wir sogar Ställe für

in the *Handbuch der Architektur* we even find categories for barns for working horses, horses for breeding and horses for riding, as well as aquaria **Fig. C** and archives. And in books that address local and regional building traditions, the material is often structured according to the dictate of the site: house number, street and place being the essential parameters.

Though the selection of an ordering method is already an evaluative and interpretive step, it is a common feature of the approaches described above that their implementation can be carried out (relatively) objectively. However there are also possible ordering sequences that are based on the judgement of an ordering individual – the order and representation is then the overlay of subjective and objective judgements.

Architects and architecture theorists have returned again and again to the natural sciences, in particular biology, to select from their repertoire of concepts, often more richly developed, for use in their own work. Typical of such an overlay of subjective and objective judgements is a classic work in biology (and also art theory), within which categories such as systematic and didactic, artistic and

Arbeits-, Zucht- und Luxuspferde, Aquarien **Abb. C** u

Archive als Kategorien. Und in Büchern der Denkr

pflege oder jenen, die sich den lokalen und region

Bautraditionen zuwenden, gilt für die Gliederung des

terials häufig das Diktat der Lage: Hausnummer, St

und Ort sind dann die entscheidenden Parameter.

Ist die Auswahl einer Anordnungsmethode bereits

wertender und interpretierender Schritt, eint die besch

benen Ansätze, dass ihre Umsetzung (relativ) objektiv

folgt. Jedoch gibt es auch Möglichkeiten der Sortierfo

die auf dem Urteil eines ordnenden Individuums basi

– die Anordnung und Präsentation ist dann Überlager

subjektiver und objektiver Entscheidungen.

Architekten und Architekturtheoretiker haben

fach auf die Naturwissenschaften und insbesondere

Biologie zurückgegriffen, um für die eigene Arbeit

meist besser beschriebenen Konzepte jener Felder zu

zen. Exemplarisch für eine Überlagerung subjektiver

objektiver Entscheidungen ist ein historischer Klass

der Biologie, aber auch der Kunsttheorie – vermen

sich in ihm doch Kategorien wie systematisch und dic

tisch, künstlerisch und assoziativ zu einer ganz eige

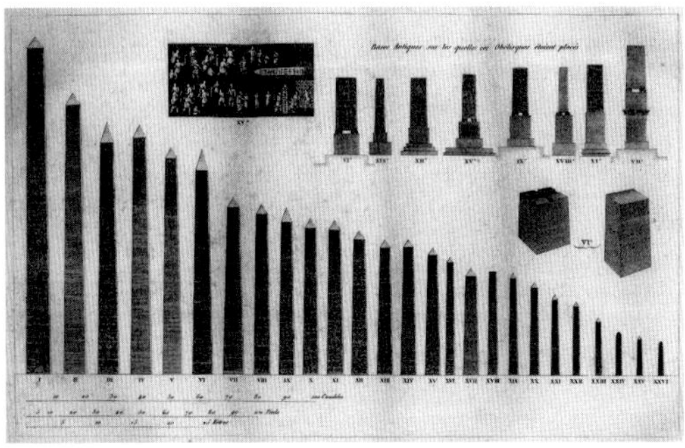

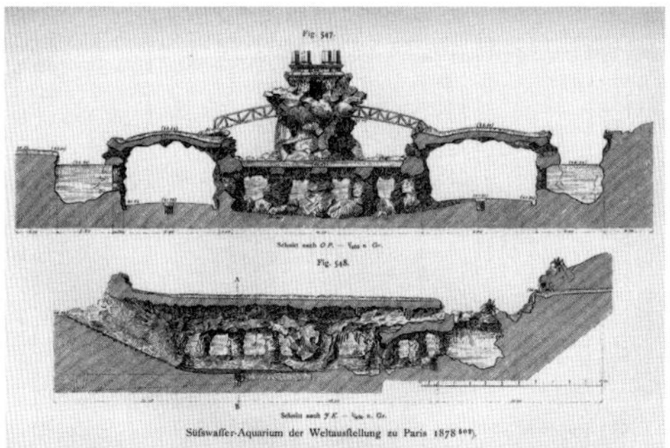

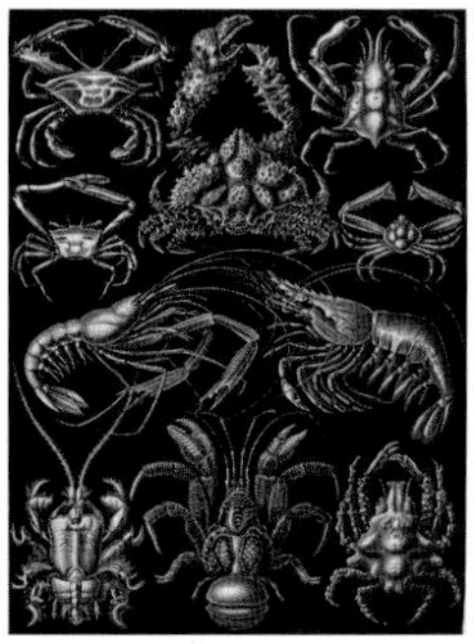

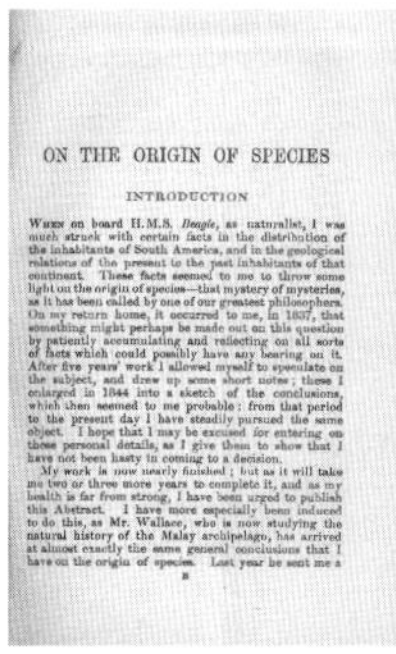

B Obelisks / Obelisken: Rondelet, Kunst zu bauen, 1833–36 **C** Aquarium: Handbuch der Architektur, Vol. / Bd. 6-4-6, 1893 **D** Decapoda: Haeckel, Kunstformen der Natur, 1899–1904 **E** Darwin, On the Origin of Species, 1907 [1859]

ociative, are blended to form an entirely unique meth- characteristically neither subjective nor objective.[7]

In this manner Ernst Haeckel's *Kunstformen der ur* uses both figural-formal and scientific criteria for construction of an ordering system.[8] To present this, eckel put 'thousands of figures [from zoology], which had drawn during scientific expeditions in nature', a 'systematic order'[9]: he grouped the objects accord- to their form and geometry into so-called 'form- ups' **Fig. D**, which were in turn arranged into an over- ning system. This approach is largely analogous to the cept of evolution, which had begun to unfold from beginning of the 19th century onwards, and found zenith, almost half a century before Haeckel's work, the publication of Charles Darwin's *On the Origin pecies by Means of Natural Selection* **Fig. E**.[10] Haeckel, ever, did not primarily take up the commonly associ- axiom of 'selection as a factor of progress', focussing e on the aspect of degrees of relatedness, which is also of the theory of evolution: the new entity is (in the n) an agglomerate of already existing and known ele- nts. Consequently, there are life forms which are more ely and those which are more distantly related to one ther, whereby the degree of relatedness depends on de- pment over time.

The ordering of buildings in this book draws on this of thought. It is also assumed here that there are dif- nt degrees of relatedness between the buildings, where e are closely related, and others distantly. From the ciple of relatedness, the ordering sequence is derived: elation to the others each building is given its specific e. The process is neither entirely objective nor entirely ective. For almost identical buildings, the exact se-

bezeichnenderweise weder subjektiven noch objektiven Methode.[7]

So nutzt Ernst Haeckels Werk *Kunstformen der Natur* sowohl gestalterisch-formale als auch wissenschaftliche Kriterien für die Findung einer Anordnungssystematik.[8] Haeckel wählt für die Präsentation von »Tausende[n] von Figuren [aus der Zoologie], die [er] auf [...] wissenschaftlichen Reisen nach der Natur gezeichnet« hat, eine »systematische Ordnung«:[9] Er gruppiert die Objekte nach ihrer Form beziehungsweise Geometrie in sogenannte »Formengruppen« **Abb. D**, die wiederum in eine übergeordnete Systematik eingeordnet werden. Dieser Ansatz knüpft eng an die Denkfigur der Evolution an, die sich seit dem Beginn des 19. Jahrhunderts zu entfalten begann und fast ein halbes Jahrhundert vor Haeckels Werk in Charles Darwins Veröffentlichung *On the Origin of Species by Means of Natural Selection* **Abb. E** einen Höhepunkt gefunden hatte.[10] Haeckel greift jedoch nicht primär das zumeist assoziierte Axiom ›Selektion als Faktor des Fortschritts‹ auf, sondern fokussiert stärker auf den in der Evolutionstheorie ebenfalls inkorporierten Aspekt von Verwandtschaftsgraden: Das Neue ist hierbei zu weiten Teilen eine Zusammenstellung bereits bestehender und bekannter Elemente. Es gibt folglich enger und weiter verwandte Lebewesen, wobei der Verwandtschaftsgrad im Zusammenhang mit einer zeitlichen Entwicklung steht.

Die Anordnung der Gebäude im vorliegenden Buch knüpft an jene Gedanken an: Auch hier wird davon ausgegangen, dass es Verwandtschaftsgrade unterschiedlicher Stärke zwischen den verschiedenen Gebäuden gibt, manche also enger und manche entfernter verwandte Objekte sind. Aus dem Prinzip der Verwandtschaften ergibt sich die Reihenfolge: Im Verhältnis zu den anderen Objekten

quence is ultimately a personal choice of the person sorting them; the more distant relations are more unequivocal. The resulting sequence has a chronological dimension: older buildings are more often found towards the beginning of the book, and the newer towards the end. Hardly surprising, since the evolutionary theory is also a model for historicisation, requiring the temporal component to explain past developments and to allow space for future combinations. For buildings this observation does not always apply, but still remains just as formative: buildings that are more closely related in their forms are usually from contemporary contexts. So perhaps the photographs mirror the 'evolutionary process of a style', as that which is already inherent ultimately develops into an image in our popular perception?

The types of relatedness are critical for the resulting image: volume and form, expression and figure, physiognomy and corporeality are the criteria which Haeckel established on the threshold between biology and art theory, and which are here employed once more – for they can serve the purposes of this undertaking, alongside an evaluation of architectural ideas and intentions.

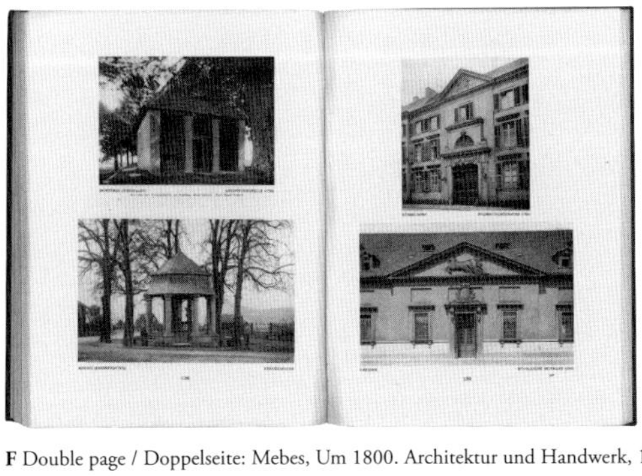

F Double page / Doppelseite: Mebes, Um 1800. Architektur und Handwerk, 1908

erhält jedes Gebäude seinen konkreten Platz. Das Ver
ren ist weder gänzlich objektiv noch gänzlich subje
Bei Gebäuden engen Verwandtschaftsgrads ist die ge
Reihenfolge der Gebäude letztlich personalisierte
scheidung der sortierenden Person; die entfernten
wandtschaften sind fix.

Die entstehende Reihenfolge hat chronologi
Züge: Ältere Gebäude sind eher am Anfang des Buche
finden und jüngere am Ende. Dies ist kaum überrasch
ist doch die Evolutionstheorie auch ein Historisieru
modell: Es bedarf der zeitlichen Komponente, um ver
gene Entwicklungen zu erklären und Raum für zuk
tige Kombinatoriken zu erlauben. Auf Gebäude ist d
Beobachtung zwar nicht eins zu eins zu übertragen, b
aber prägend: Formal enger verwandte Gebäude stam
zumeist aus zeitgleichen Kontexten. Vielleicht spiegeln
Fotografien somit den ›Evolutionsprozess eines Stiles‹
der, in dem sich das anfangs bereits Inhärente schluss
lich zum populären Bild der Wahrnehmung entwicke

Entscheidend für das entstehende Bild ist die Art
Verwandtschaft: Volumetrie und Form, Ausdruck
Gestaltung, Physiognomie und Körperlichkeit sind
Kriterien, die Haeckel an der Grenze zwischen Biol
und Kunsttheorie etabliert hat und die auch hier wi
aufgegriffen werden – können sie doch zur Umsetz
wie Bewertung architektonischer Ideen und Absic
dienen.

Architekturfotografie als visuelles Dokumentationsmedium

Die Rede von einem populären Bild der Wahr
mung weist auf eine weitere Bedingung einer Gebä
dokumentation hin: Architektur kann zwar durch

:hitectural photography as a medium
/isual documentation

As for such images in popular perception, they point further requirement for the documentation of build-s: though architecture can be described through a ltiplicity of concepts, the use of a visual medium is tral to its mediation and communication. Architec-e can hardly be separated from visual means of repre-cation – not only in designing, but also in illustrating buildings themselves.[11]

Any documentation of a building consequently ails a choice of a visual medium, whether drawing, del, photography, visualisation, animation, etc. Out :hese, the most popular medium for architectural umentation, in the 20th century and also at the be-ning of the 21st, is photography.

In his influential essay 'The Work of Art in the Age Mechanical Reproduction',[12] Walter Benjamin named uirements of the medium, which also appear to serve xplanations for the success of photography in docu-ating architecture: as a form of documentation made g the eye, photography is clearly distinguishable ts execution from earlier media, such as drawings, ch are made using the hand. The visual production cess of photography leads to an altered perception of representation – in this case, of the architecture – ough the viewer, which can, in summary, be des-ed as more 'direct'; drawing for instance being a e strongly regimented medium of representation.[13] Benjamin's view, photography as a form of representa- is aimed at a wider public, and simplifies direct ac- to the medium – qualities which echo the aims of book.

Vielzahl von Begrifflichkeiten beschrieben werden, die Benutzung eines visuellen Mediums ist jedoch zentral in Vermittlung und Kommunikation. Architektur ist kaum von bildlichen Präsentationen zu trennen – nicht nur im Entwurf, sondern auch in der Veranschaulichung des gebauten Objektes.[11]

Eine Dokumentation eines Gebäudes ist folglich auch die Wahl eines visuellen Mediums: Zeichnung, Modell, Fotografie, Visualisierung, Animation etc. Aus jener Auswahl ist das populärste Medium für die architektonische Dokumentation im 20. und auch beginnenden 21. Jahrhundert die Fotografie.

Walter Benjamin nannte in seinem einflussreichen Aufsatz *Das Kunstwerk im Zeitalter seiner technischen Reproduzierbarkeit*[12] Bedingungen des Mediums, die auch Erklärungen für den Erfolg der dokumentierenden Architekturfotografie zu sein scheinen: Als mit dem Auge erstellte Dokumentation kann die Fotografie deutlich von den vormals gebräuchlichen Medien, wie die von Hand erstellte Zeichnung, in ihrer Machart unterschieden werden. Jener visuelle Produktionsprozess führt zu einer veränderten Wahrnehmung der Darstellung – hier der Architektur – durch den Betrachter, die verkürzt als ›direkter‹ bezeichnet werden kann; darüber hinaus sei die Zeichnung generell ein stärker codiertes Darstellungsmedium.[13] Als Darstellungsart zielt die Fotografie aus Benjamins Sicht somit auf ein breiteres Publikum und vereinfacht den unmittelbaren Zugang – Eigenschaften, die der Zielsetzung dieses Buches, zu begeistern, entsprechen.

Als Dokumentationsmedium für Gebäude war die Fotografie bereits früh in Gebrauch, so zum Beispiel für die Maßnahmen der Commission des monuments historiques in Frankreich, die in den 1850er Jahren begannen.[14]

Early on, photography was used as a medium for documenting buildings, for example, in the initiatives of the Commission des monuments historiques in France, which began in the 1850s.[14] Still widely eschewed amongst architects at the time, early architectural photography was primarily a product of the academic study of art and the nascent field of historic building conservation, and as such was principally understood as an objective form of documentation. For instance, Paul Mebes' well-known and programmatic work *Um 1800. Architektur und Handwerk im letzten Jahrhundert ihrer traditionellen Entwicklung*[15], which in attempting to create a resurgence of a past epoch relies almost exclusively on the persuasiveness of the much younger technology of photography **Fig. F**, was still confident of this idea of objectivity at the beginning of the 20th century. However, it was quickly shown that architectural photography comes in many forms: at the end of the 19th century, the field was defined increasingly by the two poles of artistic vision and documentary objectivity – one might almost say poetry and positivism,[16] – which in extended form were also present in the 20th century.[17] Architects discovered the medium around the turn of the century. It was a younger generation of architects making these first steps, who, in their 'sales catalogues' – monographs of their own work **Fig. G** – almost entirely replaced drawings with photographs.[18] The architects of classical modernism grasped this moment for propaganda and advertising to such an extent that the polemicists labelled their photography as a replacement for the buildings themselves: as soon as an image of a building was published, it became more important than the object itself.

In der Architektenschaft noch weitgehend abgelehnt,
die frühe Architekturfotografie primär ein Produkt
jungen Kunstwissenschaften und der Anfänge der De
malpflege und wurde deshalb hauptsächlich als obje
ves Dokumentarium verstanden. Paul Mebes' bekan
und programmatisches Werk *Um 1800. Architektur*
Handwerk im letzten Jahrhundert ihrer traditionellen E
wicklung,[15] das im Versuch des Wiederauflebenlass
einer vergangenen Epoche beinahe ausschließlich
die Überzeugungskraft der viel jüngeren Technik
Fotografie vertraut **Abb. F**, war zum Beispiel Anfang
20. Jahrhunderts immer noch von dieser Auffassung
tragen. Dennoch zeigte sich schnell, dass Architek
fotografie nicht gleich Architekturfotografie ist: Im
gehenden 19. Jahrhundert wurde das Feld zunehm
durch die zwei Pole künstlerischer Gestaltungswille
dokumentarische Objektivität – oder überspitzt: Po
und Positivismus[16] – bestimmt, die in erweiterter F
auch im 20. Jahrhundert galten.[17] Zur Jahrhundertw
de entdeckten Architekten das Medium. Schrittmac
war eine junge Architektengeneration, die in ihren
pulär werdenden ›Verkaufskatalogen‹, Monografien
rer eigenen Werke **Abb. G**, die Zeichnung fast gänz
durch die Fotografie ersetzten.[18] Die Architekten
Klassischen Moderne griffen dieses propagierende
werbende Moment in solcher Konsequenz auf, dass
Polemiker sie sogar bezichtigten, die Fotografie sei sc
Ersatz für das Gebäude: Sobald ein Foto des Gebä
publiziert sei, werde jenes wichtiger als das Objekt sel

In der zweiten Hälfte des 20. Jahrhunderts setzte
besondere die Kunst neue Sichtweisen der Architek
fotografie frei. In Kunstwerken wurde vielfach das
kumentarische in Frage gestellt, damit gespielt oder a

In the second half of the 20th century architectural ›tography was liberated, especially by the new ways of ing revealed by art. In works of art, the very idea of the :umentary was questioned, played with, and worked h,[19] for instance in the output of Bernd and Hilla :her, who set objective photography in opposition the concept of the documentary.[20] And in architec- e, photography also became at that time a strategy for uiring knowledge and a means of reflection on the fession.[21] The search for academic rigour expanded polar pair of artistic vision and documentary objec- ty.

The photography of this book avoids links to aca- nic or artistic considerations, attempting instead to n itself with the pragmatic conception of documenta- found in the 19th century, as Robert Sobieszek elo- ntly describes: 'to record travel discoveries, to docu- nt patrimony, to serve the architect for design and motion, to take stock of urban deterioration, demo- on or reconstruction.'[22] At the centre of this are the ldings themselves, which remain the central purpose rchitecture.

y document Art Deco? A perspective

In concluding, let us return to the polemic on the tography of modernist architecture. Photography had erve as a replacement for the buildings themselves, as works of modernism were often made as 'throwaway sumer products'[23]: many buildings developed damage er quickly **Fig. H**, and their construction technique not very robust (a charge that must not be levelled inst the 'modernist' architects alone).[24] In this respect, tography was also a survival strategy.

gearbeitet,[19] beispielsweise in den Arbeiten von Bernd und Hilla Becher, die dem Begriff des Dokumentarischen die objektive Fotografie entgegenstellten.[20] Und auch war die Fotografie in der Architektur zu diesem Zeitpunkt Strategie der Wissensaneignung und Mittel zur Reflexion über die Disziplin geworden.[21] Die Suche nach Wissenschaftlichkeit erweiterte das Polepaar künstlerischer Gestaltungswille und dokumentarische Objektivität.

Die Fotografien in diesem Buch vermeiden ein Anknüpfen an wissenschaftliche oder künstlerische Überlegungen, vielmehr versuchen sie sich an der pragmatisch-dokumentarischen Konzeption des 19. Jahrhunderts zu orientieren, wie sie Robert Sobieszek wortreich und treffend beschrieb: »to record travel discoveries, to document patrimony, to serve the architect for design and promotion, to take stock of urban deterioration, demolition or reconstrcution.«[22] Das gebaute Objekt als wichtigste Zielsetzung der Architektur steht im Vordergrund.

Warum den Art déco dokumentieren? Ein Ausblick

Abschließend sei noch einmal auf die Polemik zur Architekturfotografie der Moderne zurückzukommen.

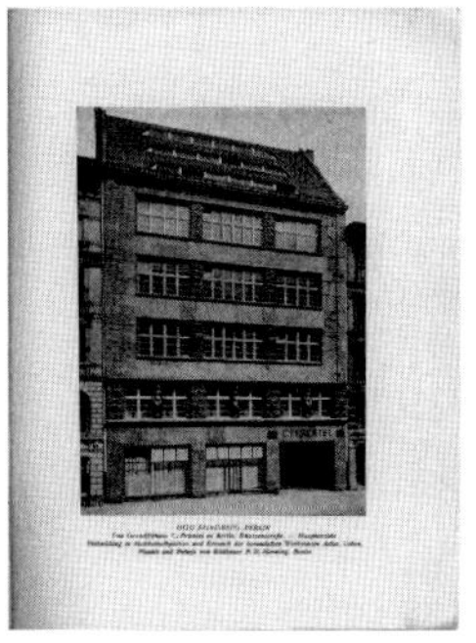

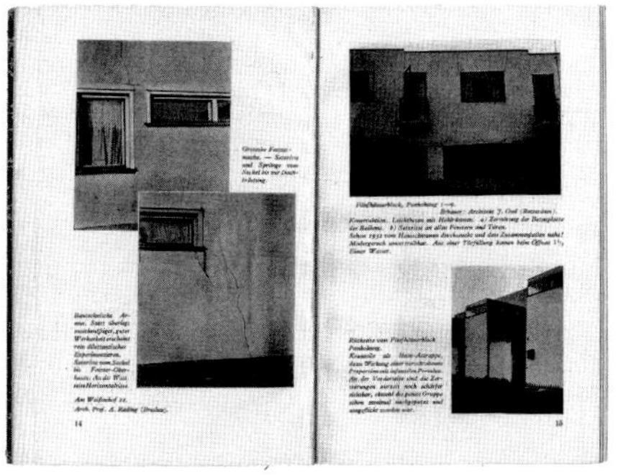

G Page / Seite : Ausgeführte Bauten. Otto Salvisberg, 1914 **H** Double page / Doppelseite: Vincentz, Bausünden und Baugeldvergeudung, 1932

For the buildings in *Modernism London Style,* opposite points of departure apply: until now only a few of the buildings have been photographed or documented; and their construction is typically robust and durable. Though no causal link exists between these two facts, both are important: the construction technique is one guarantor for today's enthusiasm for Art Deco **Fig. I, J**: 'Robustness of form' and 'robustness of material' are two catch phrases, which characterise English architecture in comparison to the historic development of building cultures in other nations, and they also describe the quality of the buildings shown here. 'Robustness of material' means not just England's almost continual use of brick in its constructions,[25] but also the long lines of craft tradition that can be found in other building materials. 'Robustness of form' refers to the long-valued acceptance and gradual transformation of architectural elements in English architecture,[26] as we know for instance from the various architectural revivals, and as clarified here in detail in the photographs. Both factors might serve as explanations for the non-existence of distinctly iconic works of Art Deco: all buildings are of quality. Furthermore, our enthusiasm for English Art

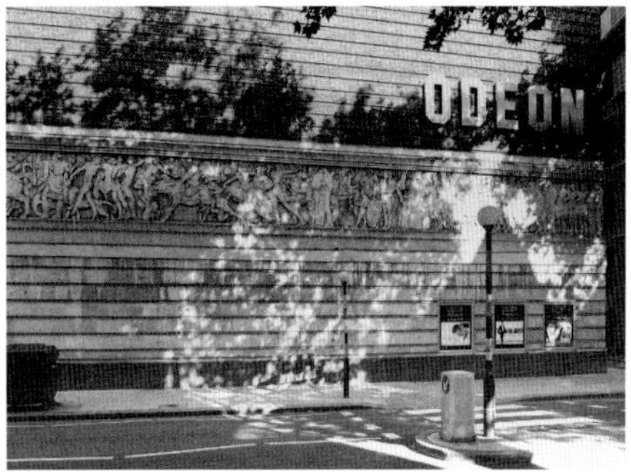

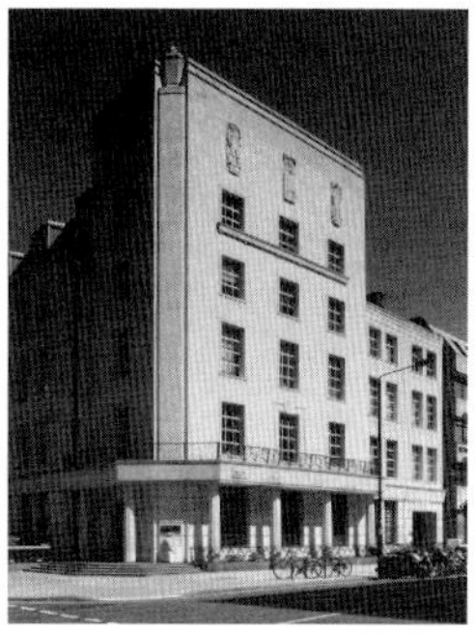

I Saville Theatre, Bennett & Son / Bertie Crewe, 1931 **J** Bentham House, H. & H. Martin Lidbetter, 1958

Ersatz für das Objekt musste die Fotografie auch werd
weil die Inkunabeln der Moderne häufig – überspitz
als »Konsum- und Wegwerfprodukte« angelegt ware
Viele zeigten schnell Bauschäden **Abb. H**, ihre Baute
nik war wenig solide (was aber nicht nur den ›moc
nen‹ Architekten anzulasten war).[24] Die Fotografie
zugleich eine Überlebensstrategie.

Für die Objekte des *Modernism London Style* ge
inverse Ausgangslagen: Fotografiert oder dokument
wurden bislang nur wenige; die typische Bauausf
rung ist solide und beständig. Zwischen beiden F
stellungen besteht kein kausaler Zusammenhang, d
sind beide wichtig: So ist die Bautechnik des Art d
Abb. I, J auch Garant für die heutige Begeisteru
›Formbeständigkeit‹ und ›Materialbeständigkeit‹ s
zwei Schlagworte, die die englische Architektur
Vergleich zu anderen nationalen Baukulturen in il
historischen Entwicklung charakterisieren, und sie
schreiben auch die Qualität der hier gezeigten Gebäu
›Materialbeständigkeit‹ meint nicht nur die fast ko
nuierliche Verwendung von Backstein als Baumate
in Bauten Englands,[25] sondern auch die langen ha
werklichen Traditionslinien, die im Bereich and
Baumaterialien zu finden sind. ›Formbeständigkeit‹
weist auf die lang währende Akzeptanz und nur gra
elle Veränderung architektonischer Elemente in der e
lischen Architektur,[26] wie wir sie etwa aus den Revi
kennen und wie sie auch die vorliegenden Fotogra
im Detail verdeutlichen. Beide Faktoren bedingen m
licherweise das Fehlen wirklicher Inkunabeln des
déco: Alle Gebäude sind qualitätvoll. Der Enthusias
für den englischen Art déco spiegelt somit auch die
kenntnis wider, dass Tradierungen im Bauwesen zu e

:o also mirrors the observation that the passing on of :t traditions in construction leads to long-lasting dis- ıable quality. That no one has photographically docu- ıtend this until now allows us to redress this today and .ttempt to establish these buildings in the canon of an ıitecture of quality. Translation: Philip Shelley

rn, Ian; Pevsner, Nikolaus: Sussex (The Buildings of Britian). Harmondsworth, 1973 (1st 65), p. 457 (commentary on St Leonard's lynchgate in Aldrington).

ubin, Frédéric: Cosmic Communist Constructions Photographed. Cologne, 2011.

ıser, Philipp: Architekturführer Pjöngjang. Berlin, 2011.

ılze, Karin: 'Komm in die Wabe, Genosse!', on: Spiegel Online, 29 January 2011, see: 'www.spiegel.de/kultur/gesellschaft/0,1518,741915,00.html (as of 3 January 2012).

ly, Vincent J.: The Shingle Style. Architectural Theory and Design from Richardson to rigins of Wright. New Haven, 1955.

the impossiblity of completeness from inventories and suchlike, cf. among others: Eco, rto: Die unendliche Liste. Munich, 2009 [orginal italian text Milan 2009], in particular -7, 15–17.

fundamental shift in the concept of objectivity at the end of the 19th century should be cf. in particular: Daston, Lorraine; Galison, Peter: Objektivität. Frankfurt am Main, [English original text New York 2007].

ckel, Ernst: Kunstformen der Natur. Leipzig/Vienna, 1899–1904.

., p. 4.

rwin, Charles: On the Origin of Species by Means of Natural Selection. London, 1859.

in particular here the results of the research programme on Iconic Criticism from the rsity of Basel: Beyer, Andreas; Burioni, Matteo; Grave, Johannes: 'Einleitung. Zum Er- en von Architektur als Bild', in: idem (eds). Das Auge der Architektur. Zur Frage der chkeit in der Baukunst. Munich, 2011, pp. 10–32, in particular pp. 11, 14–15.

njamin, Walter: 'Das Kunstwerk im Zeitalter seiner technischen Reproduzierbarkeit'. an edition 1939 [first French edition 1935], in: idem. Gesammelte Schriften. Band I. furt am Main, 1980, pp. 472–492.

d., pp. 474–475, 480.

wis, Kristina: 'In monumentaler Mission. Frühe Fotografie im Europa des 19. Jahrhun- in: Derenthal, Ludger et al. (eds). Ein neuer Blick. Architekturfotografie aus den Staat- Museen zu Berlin. Türbingen, 2010, pp. 22–25, here p. 23.

bes, Paul (ed): Um 1800. Architektur und Handwerk im letzten Jahrhundert ihrer tradi- en Entwicklung. Munich, 1908.

wis, Kristina: 'Positivismus und Poesie. Architekturfotografie um 1900', in: Derenthal see ref. 14), pp. 33–36.

rticularly worth reading on this subject: Stierli, Martino: 'Fotografische Feldforschung Architektur und Kunst der 1960er Jahre', in: Moravánszky, Ákos; Kirchengast, Albert Experiments. Architektur zwischen Wissenschaft und Kunst (TheorieBau, 2). Berlin, pp. 54–91. Cf. also Daston/Galison 2007 (see ref. 7), pp. 121–200.

ell, Matthias: Das Haus und sein Buch. Basel, 2009, pp. 8–11.

sjak, Andrea: 'Architekturfotografie als Sujet der zeitgenössischen Kunst', in: Derenthal see ref. 14), pp. 71–76, here p. 71.

d., p. 72.

erli 2011 (see ref. 17), p. 70.

bieszek, Robert A.: "This Edifice is Colossal". 19th-Century Architectural Photography. ster, 1986, p. 2.

gler, Karl: 'Substanz oder Zeichen? Über die ungleichartige Lebensdauer von Architek- in: Archimaera (2011), No 4, pp. 9–30, here p. 13.

for example the unfortunate case of the Weissenhof Estate (see the polemic from that here: Vincentz, Curt R.: Bausünden und Baugeldvergeudung. Hannover, 1932) or the lecline of Le Corbusier's Villa Savoy (see the relevant dramatisation by Wolfgang Döring: ktiven einer Architektur. Frankfurt am Main, 1970, pp. 36 37).

: Campbell, James W.P.: Brick. A World History. London, 2003.

: Colloway, Stephen; Powers Alan (eds): The Elements of Style. An Encyclopedia of Do- Architectural Design. 4th ed. London, 2012 (1st ed. 1991).

langfristig lesbaren Qualität führen. Dass sich bislang niemand einer fotografischen Dokumentation angenommen hat, erlaubt uns, dies heute nachzuholen und gleichzeitig zu versuchen, die gebauten Objekte in den Kanon einer qualitätvollen Architektur einzureihen.

1 Nairn, Ian; Pevsner, Nikolaus: Sussex (The Buildings of Britian). Harmondsworth 1973 (1. Aufl. 1965), S. 457 (Kommentar zum Lychgate von St Leonard in Aldrington).

2 Chaubin, Frédéric: Cosmic Communist Constructions Photographed. Köln 2011.

3 Meuser, Philipp: Architekturführer Pjöngjang. Berlin 2011.

4 Schulze, Karin: Komm in die Wabe, Genosse! in: Spiegel Online, 29. Januar 2011, siehe http://www.spiegel.de/kultur/gesellschaft/0,1518,741915,00.html (Abruf 3. Januar 2012).

5 Scully, Vincent J.: The Shingle Style. Architectural Theory and Design from Richardson to the Origins of Wright. New Haven 1955.

6 Zur Unmöglichkeit der Vollständigkeit von Auflistungen und dergleichen, vgl. u.a.: Eco, Umberto: Die unendliche Liste. München 2009 [Italienischer Originaltext Mailand 2009], vor allem S. 5–7, 15–17.

7 Anzumerken ist der grundlegende Wandel des Objektivitätsbegriffs im ausgehenden 19. Jahrhundert. Vgl. hierzu insbesondere: Daston, Lorraine; Galison, Peter: Objektivität. Frankfurt am Main 2007 [Englischer Originaltext New York 2007].

8 Haeckel, Ernst: Kunstformen der Natur. Leipzig/Wien 1899–1904.

9 Ebd., S. 4.

10 Darwin, Charles: On the Origin of Species by Means of Natural Selection. London 1859.

11 Vgl. hierzu insbesondere die Ergebnisse des Forschungsschwerpunkts Bildkritik an der Universität Basel. Siehe: Beyer, Andreas; Burioni, Matteo; Grave, Johannes: Einleitung. Zum Erscheinen von Architektur als Bild, in: Dies. (Hg.): Das Auge der Architektur. Zur Frage der Bildlichkeit in der Baukunst. München 2011, S. 10–32, hier vor allem S. 11, 14–15.

12 Benjamin, Walter: Das Kunstwerk im Zeitalter seiner technischen Reproduzierbarkeit. Deutsche Fassung 1939 [Erste französische Fassung 1935], in: Ders.: Gesammelte Schriften. Band I. Frankfurt am Main 1980, S. 472–492.

13 Ebd., S. 474–475, 480.

14 Lowis, Kristina: In monumentaler Mission. Frühe Fotografie im Europa des 19. Jahrhunderts, in: Derenthal, Ludger u.a. (Hg.): Ein neuer Blick. Architekturfotografie aus den Staatlichen Museen zu Berlin. Türbingen 2010, S. 22–25, hier S. 23.

15 Mebes, Paul (Hg.): Um 1800. Architektur und Handwerk im letzten Jahrhundert ihrer traditionellen Entwicklung. München 1908.

16 Lowis, Kristina: Positivismus und Poesie. Architekturfotografie um 1900, in: Derenthal 2010 (wie Anm. 14), S. 33–36.

17 Besonders lesenswert hierzu: Stierli, Martino: Fotografische Feldforschung in der Architektur und Kunst der 1960er Jahre, in: Moravánszky, Ákos; Kirchengast, Albert (Hg.): Experiments. Architektur zwischen Wissenschaft und Kunst (TheorieBau, 2). Berlin 2011, S. 54–91. Vgl. auch Daston/Galison 2007 (wie Anm. 7), S. 121–200.

18 Noell, Matthias: Das Haus und sein Buch. Basel 2009, S. 8–11.

19 Lesjak, Andrea: Architekturfotografie als Sujet der zeitgenössischen Kunst, in: Derenthal 2010 (wie Anm. 14), S. 71–76, hier S. 71.

20 Ebd., S. 72.

21 Stierli 2011 (wie Anm. 17), S. 70.

22 Sobieszek, Robert A.: »This Edifice is Colossal«. 19th-Century Architectural Photography. Rochester 1986, S. 2.

23 Kegler, Karl: Substanz oder Zeichen? Über die ungleichartige Lebensdauer von Architekturen, in: Archimaera (2011), H. 4, S. 9–30, hier S. 13.

24 Vgl. zum Beispiel die Schadensfälle in der Weißenhofsiedlung (siehe die zeitgenössische Polemik, hier: Vincentz, Curt R.: Bausünden und Baugeldvergeudung. Hannover 1932) oder den schnellen Verfall von Le Corbusiers Villa Savoy (siehe die diesbezogene Zuspitzung von Wolfgang Döring: Perspektiven einer Architektur. Frankfurt am Main 1970, S. 36–37).

25 Vgl.: Campbell, James W.P.: Brick. A World History. London 2003.

26 Vgl.: Colloway, Stephen; Powers Alan (Hg.): The Elements of Style. An Encyclopedia of Domestic Architectural Design. 4. Aufl. London 2012 (1. Aufl. 1991).

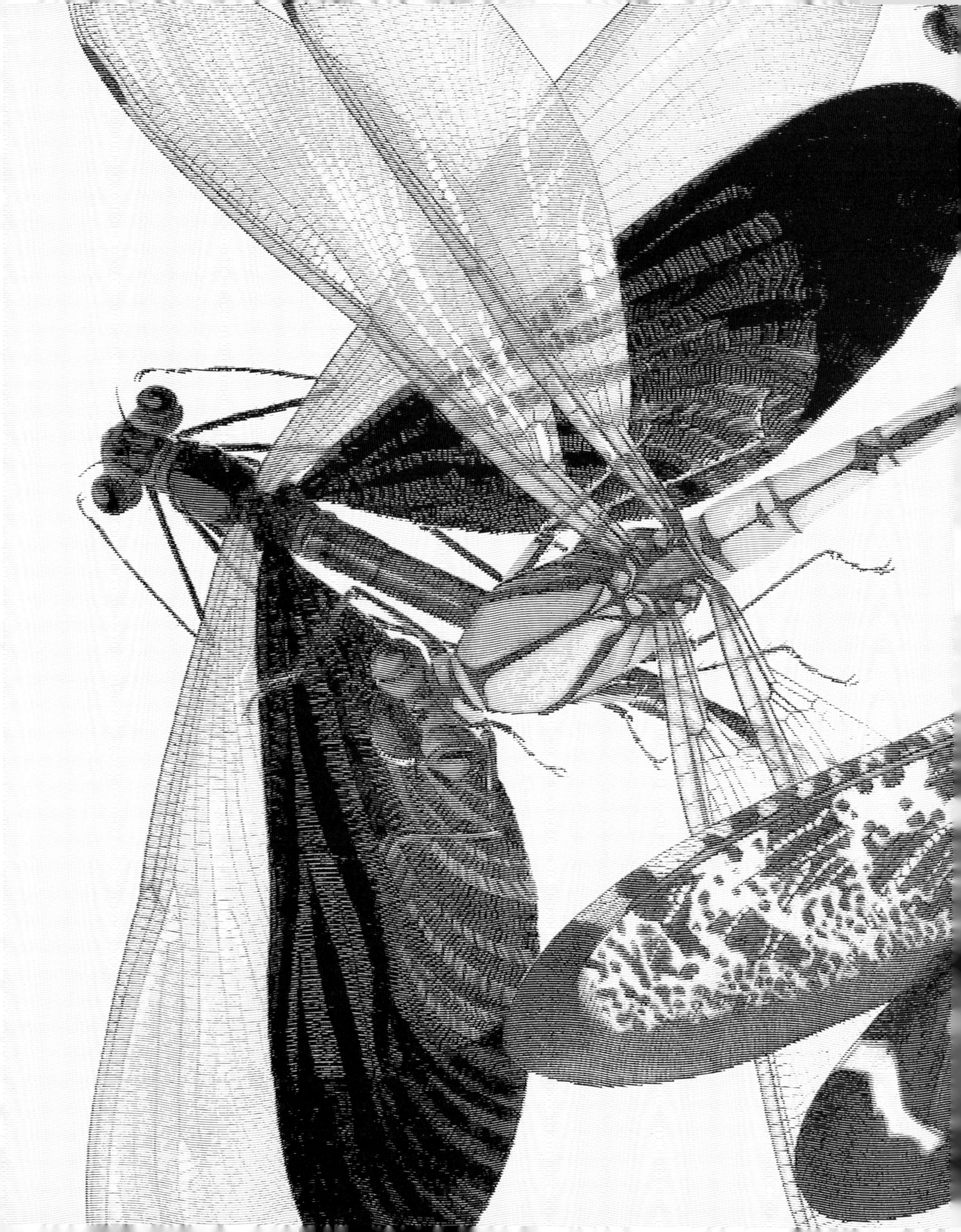

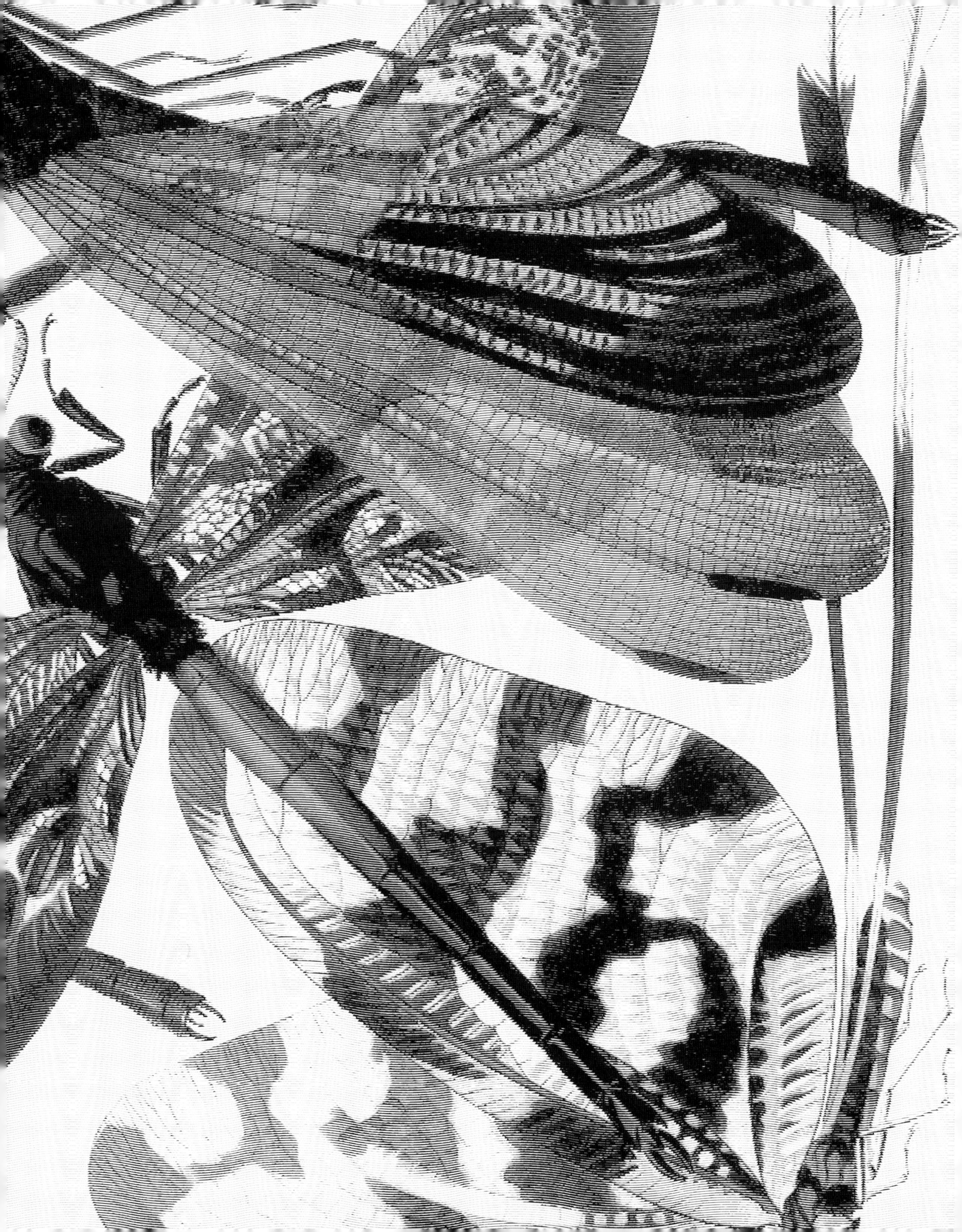

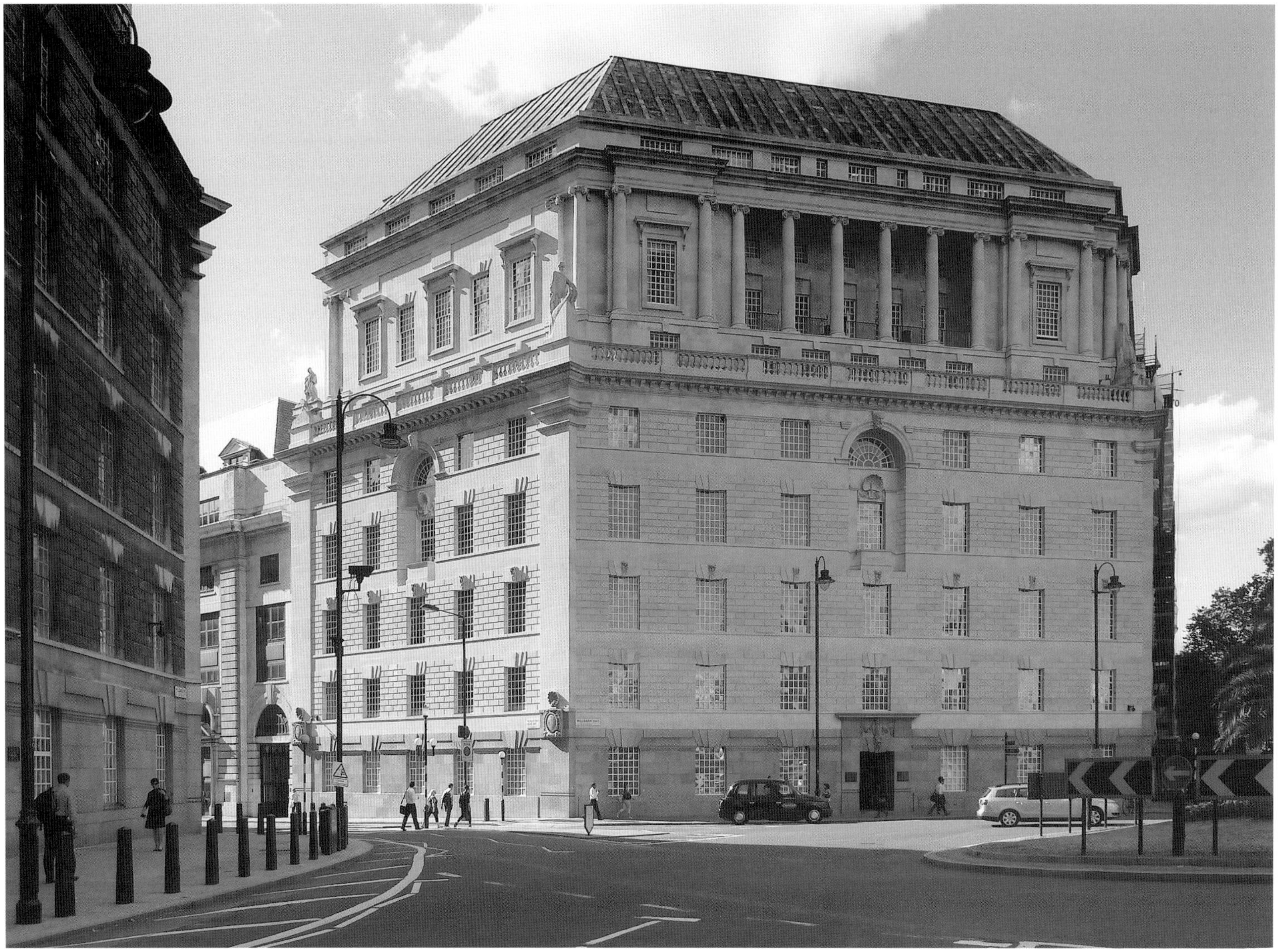

1

3

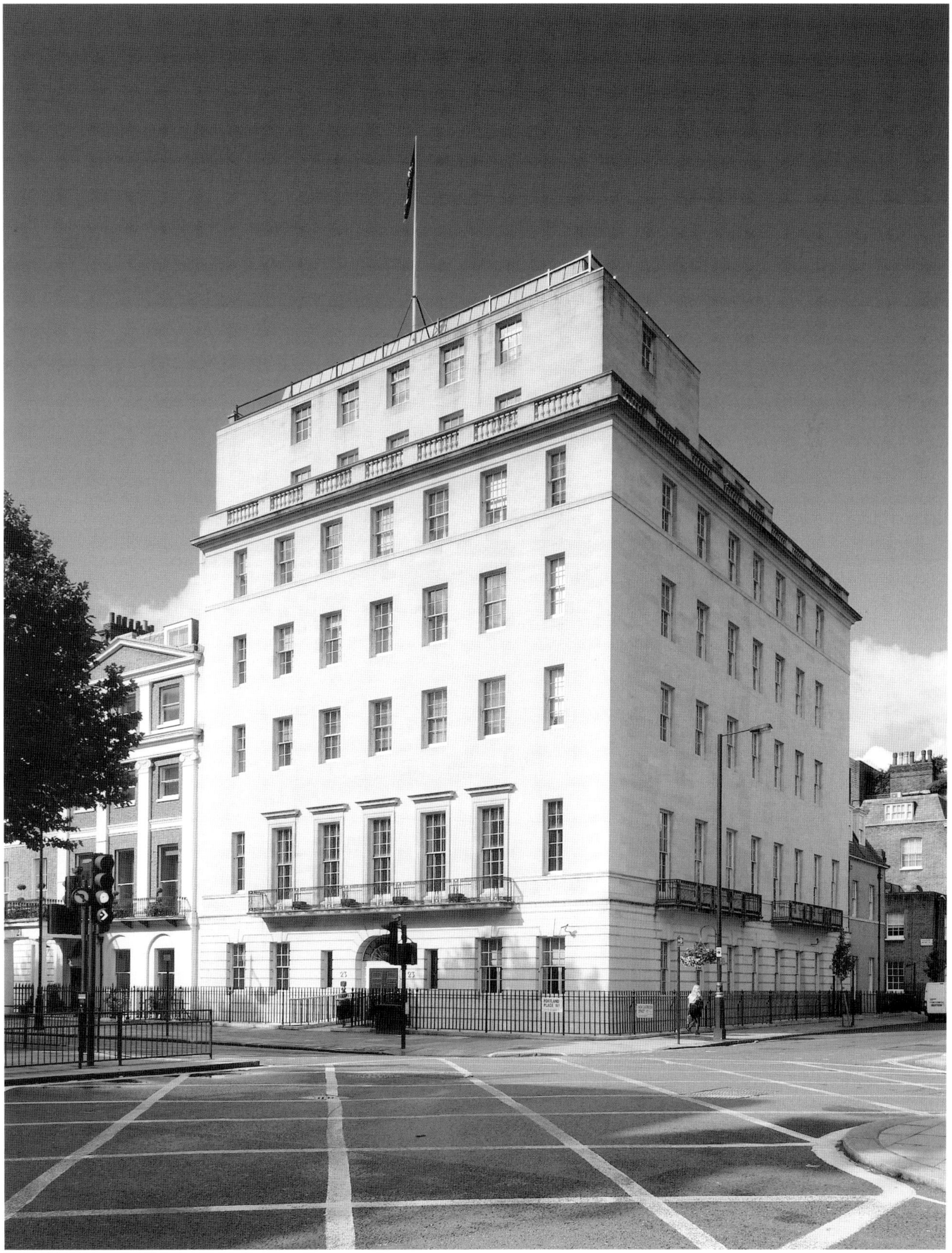

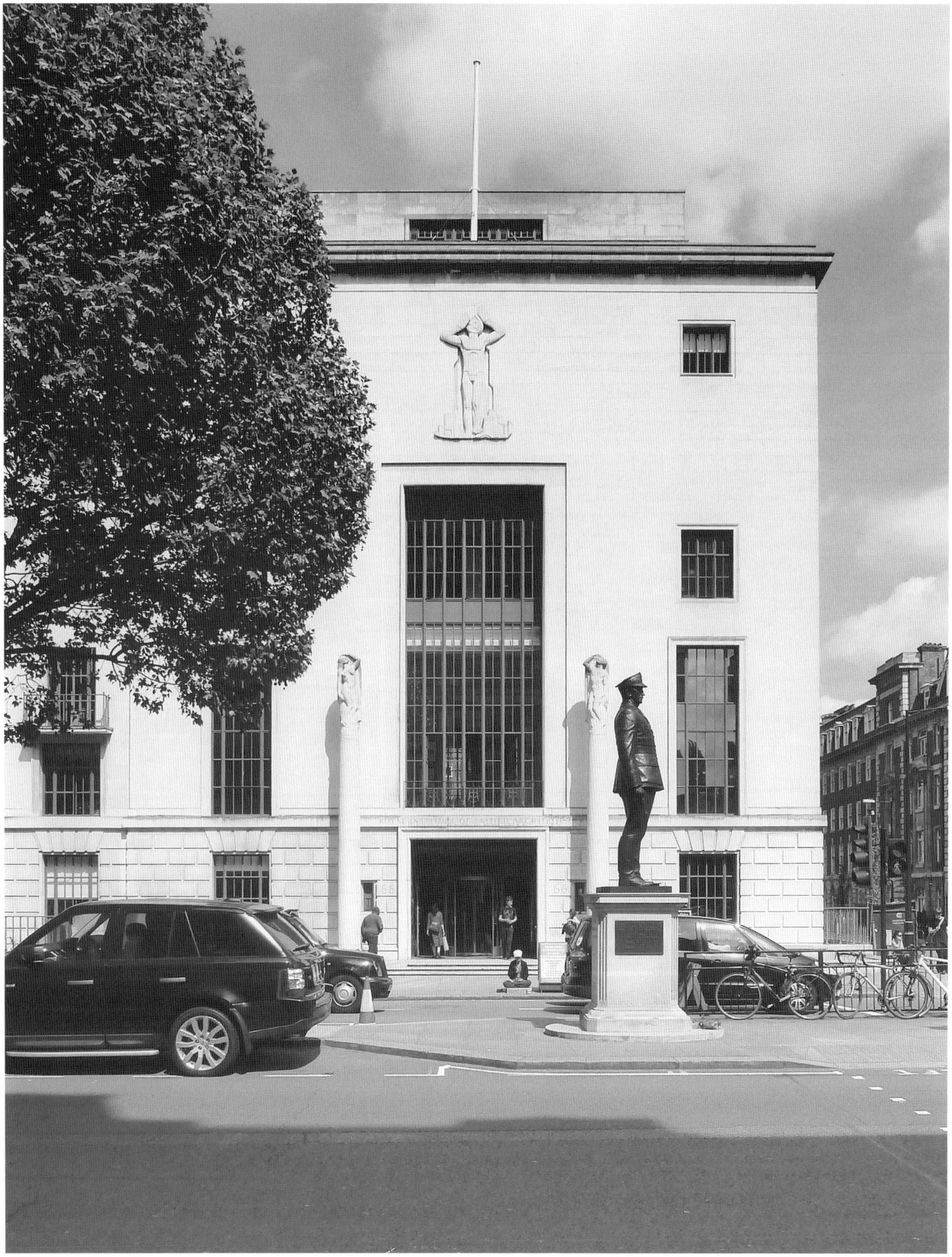

6

6

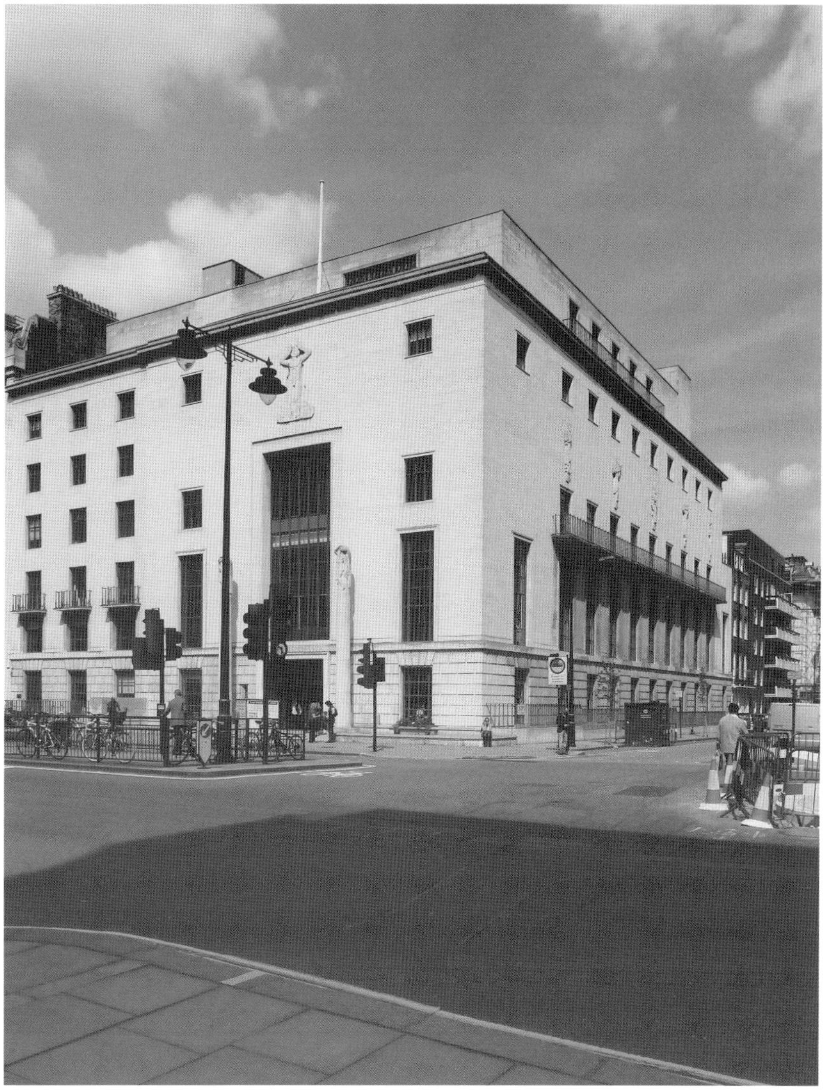

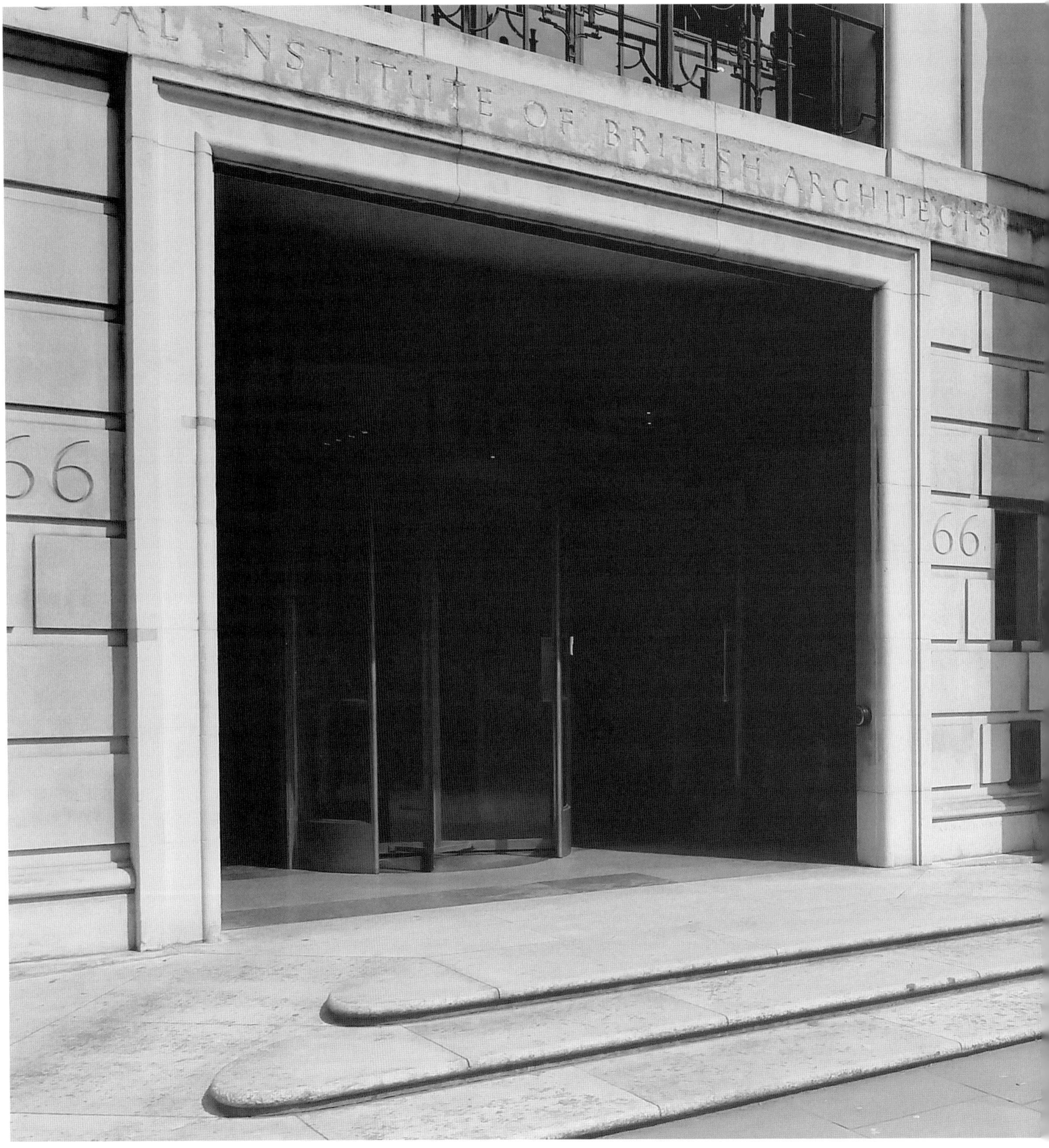
INSTITUTE OF BRITISH ARCHITECTS
66
66

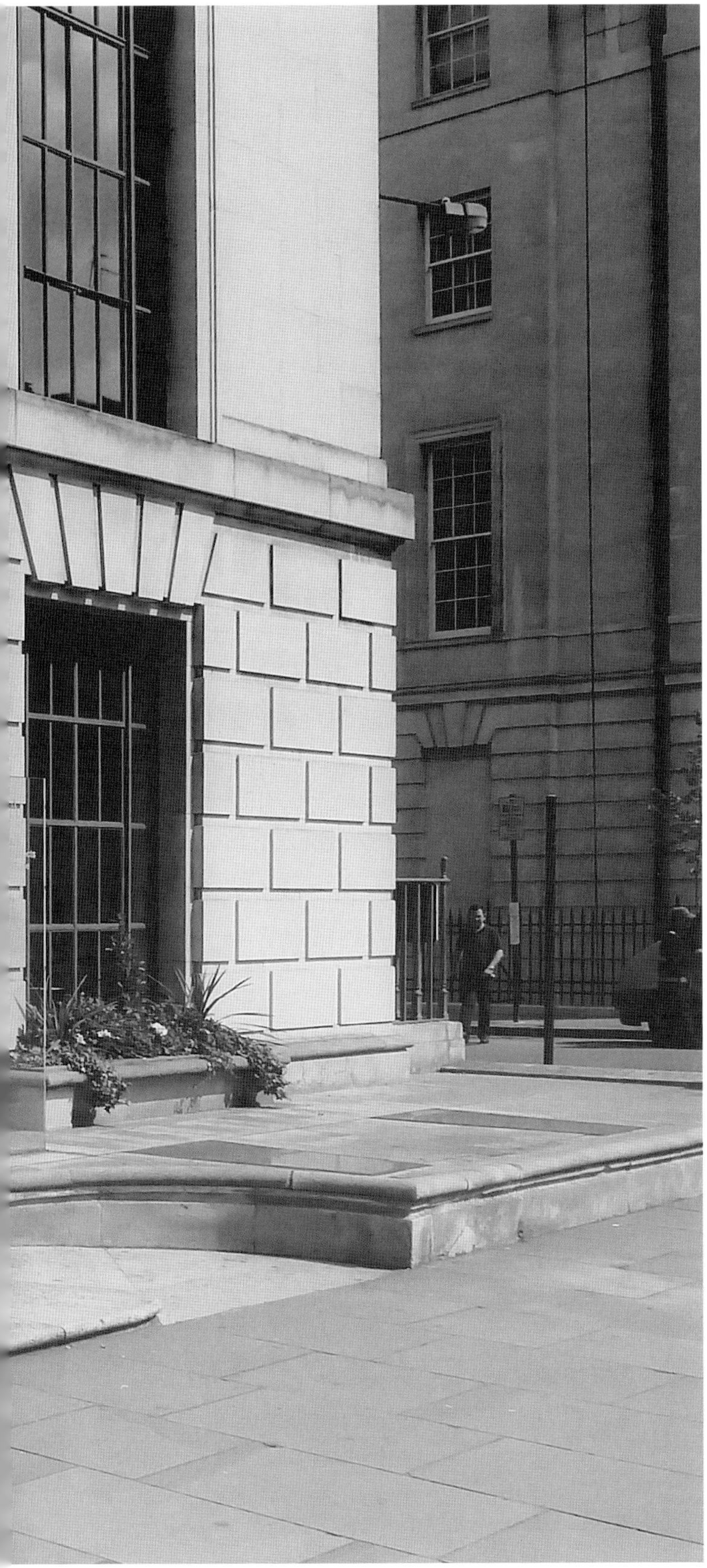

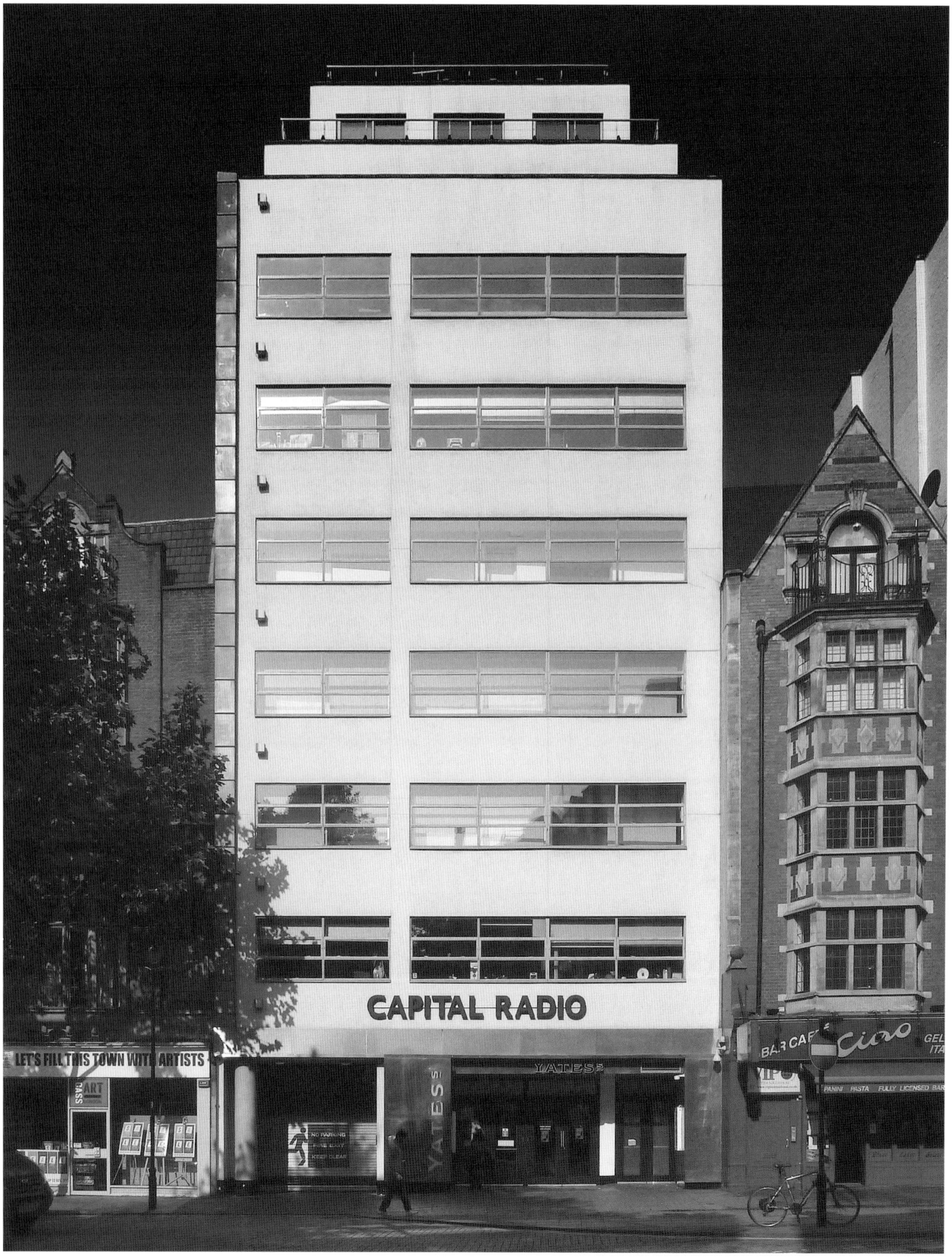
CAPITAL RADIO
LET'S FILL THIS TOWN WITH ARTISTS
YATES'S
BAR CAFE
Ciao
PANINI PASTA FULLY LICENSED BAR

7

8

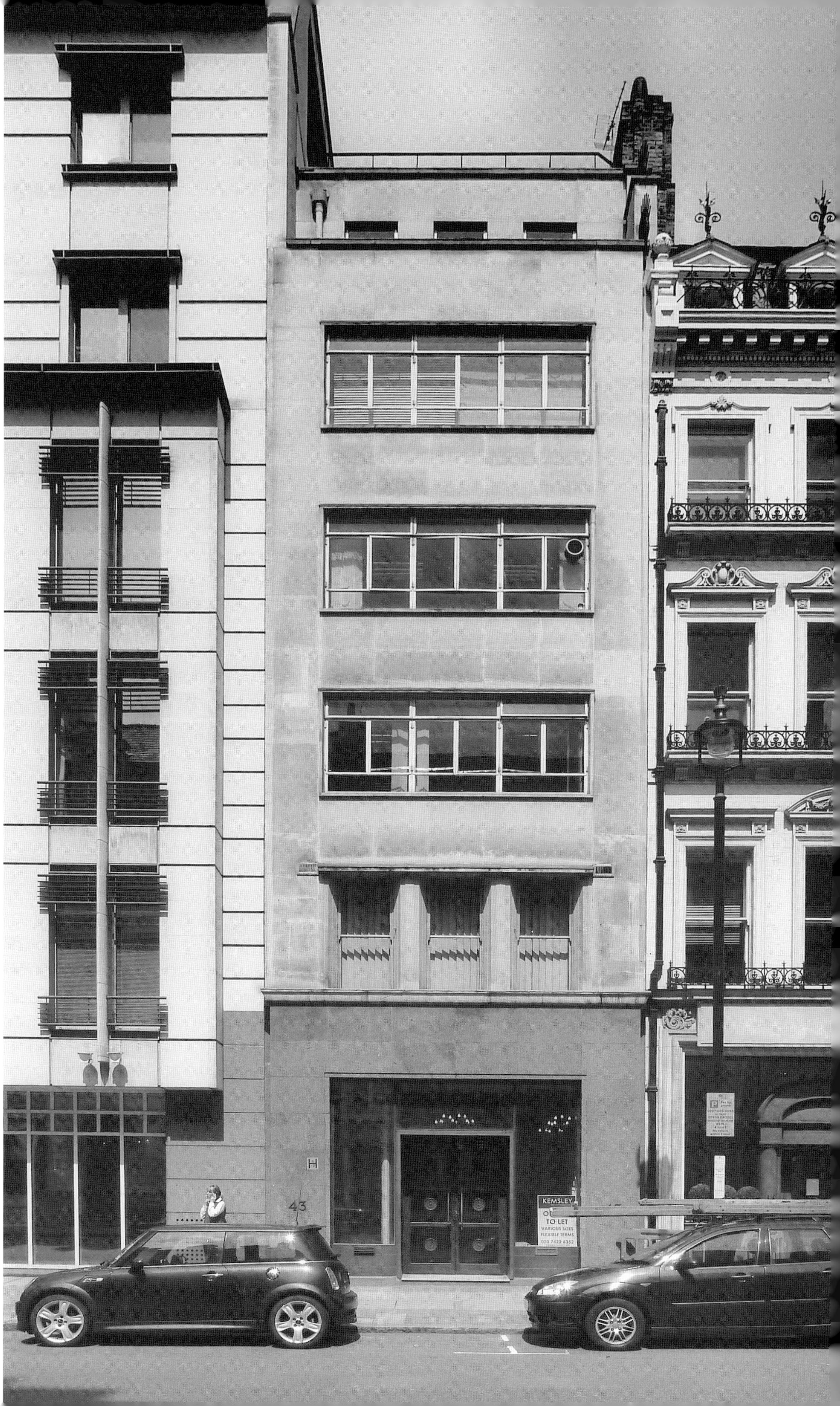

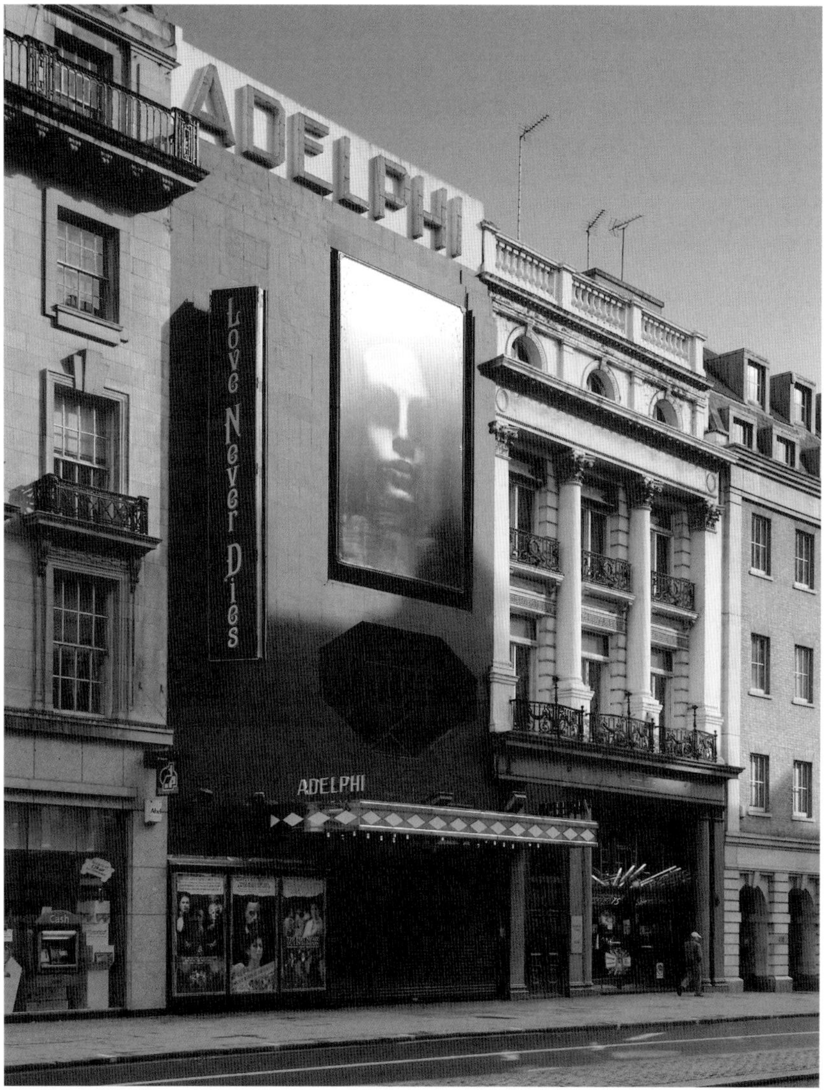

9

10

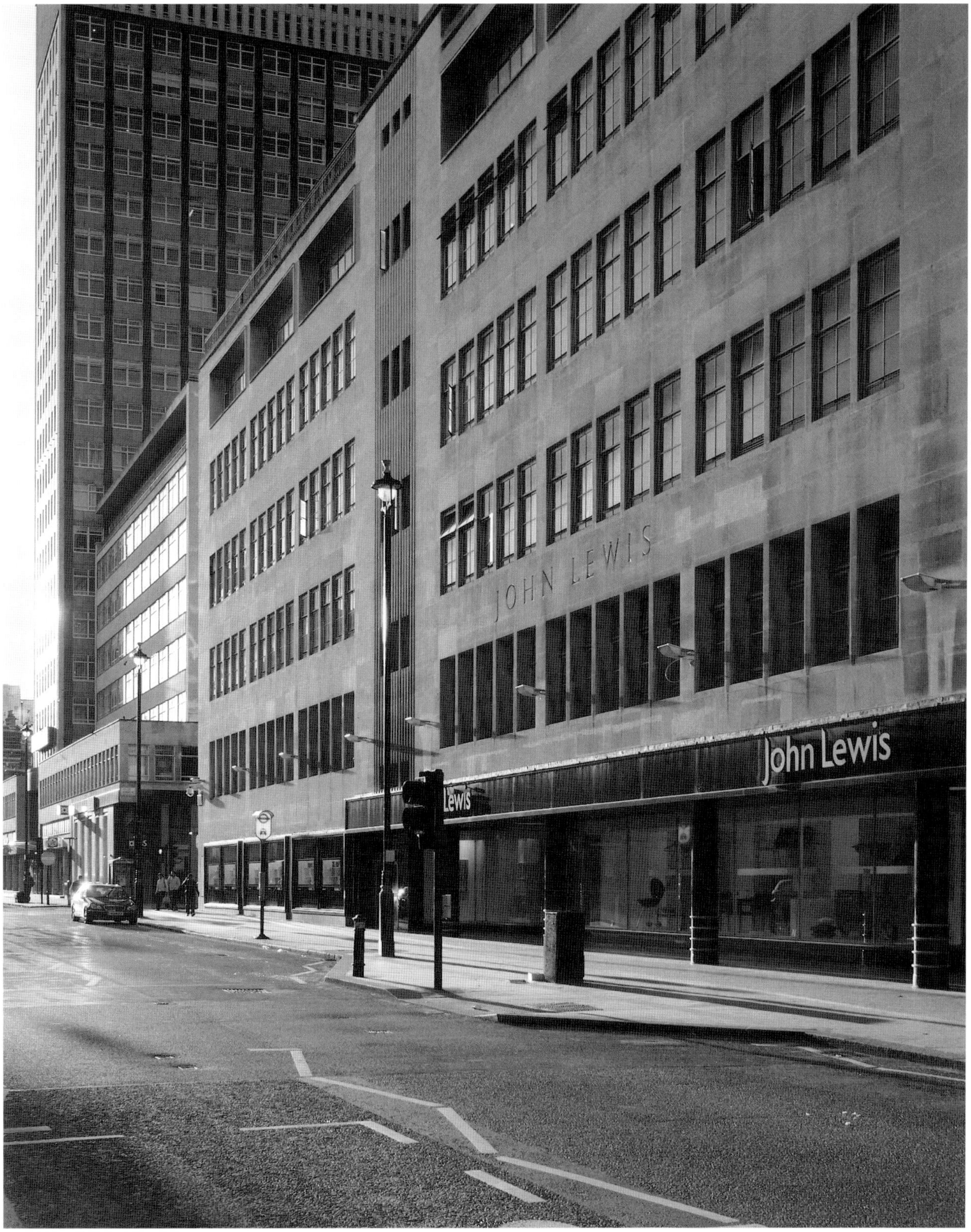

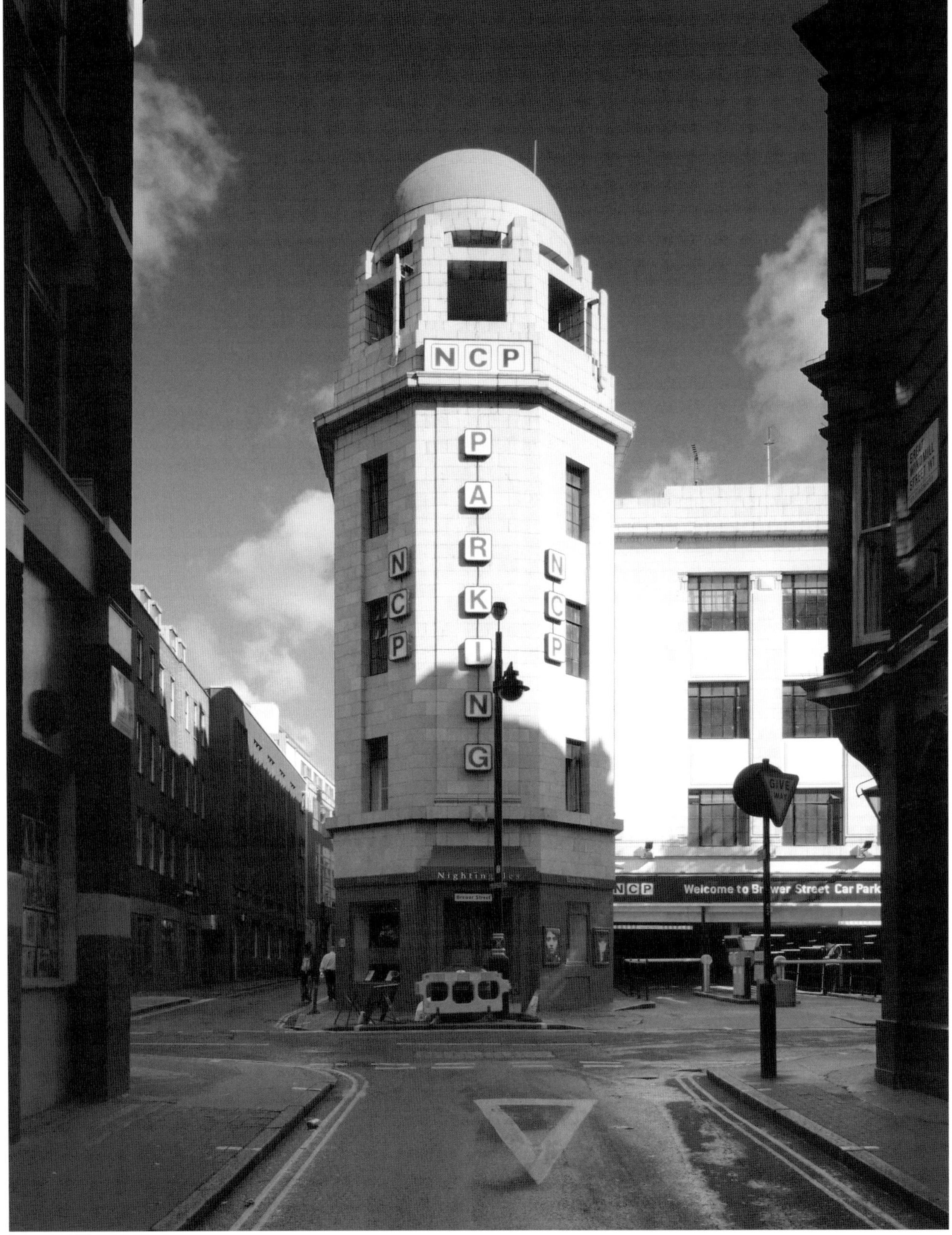
NCP
PARKING
NCP
NCP
GIVE WAY
NCP
Welcome to Br wer Street Car Park

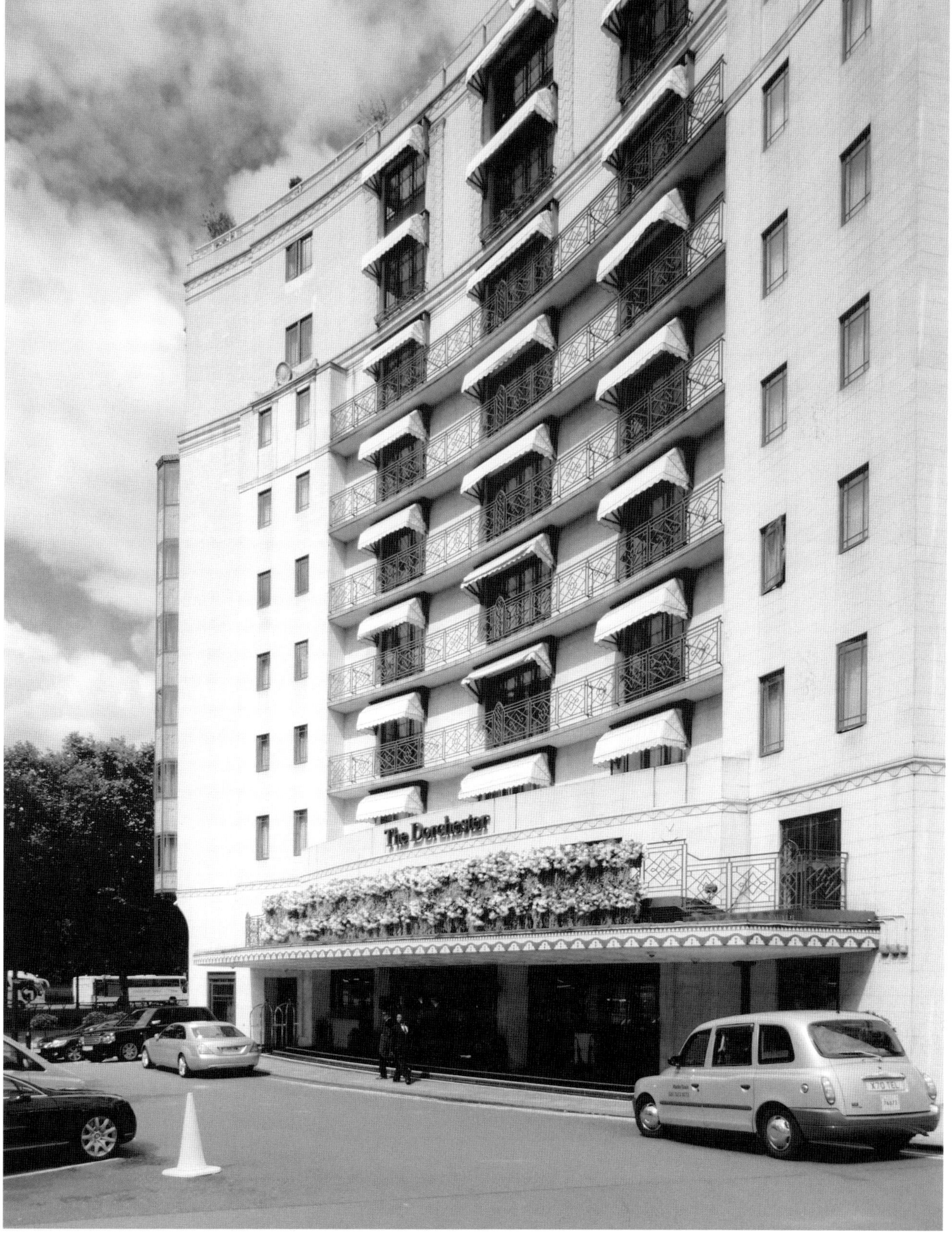
The Dorchester

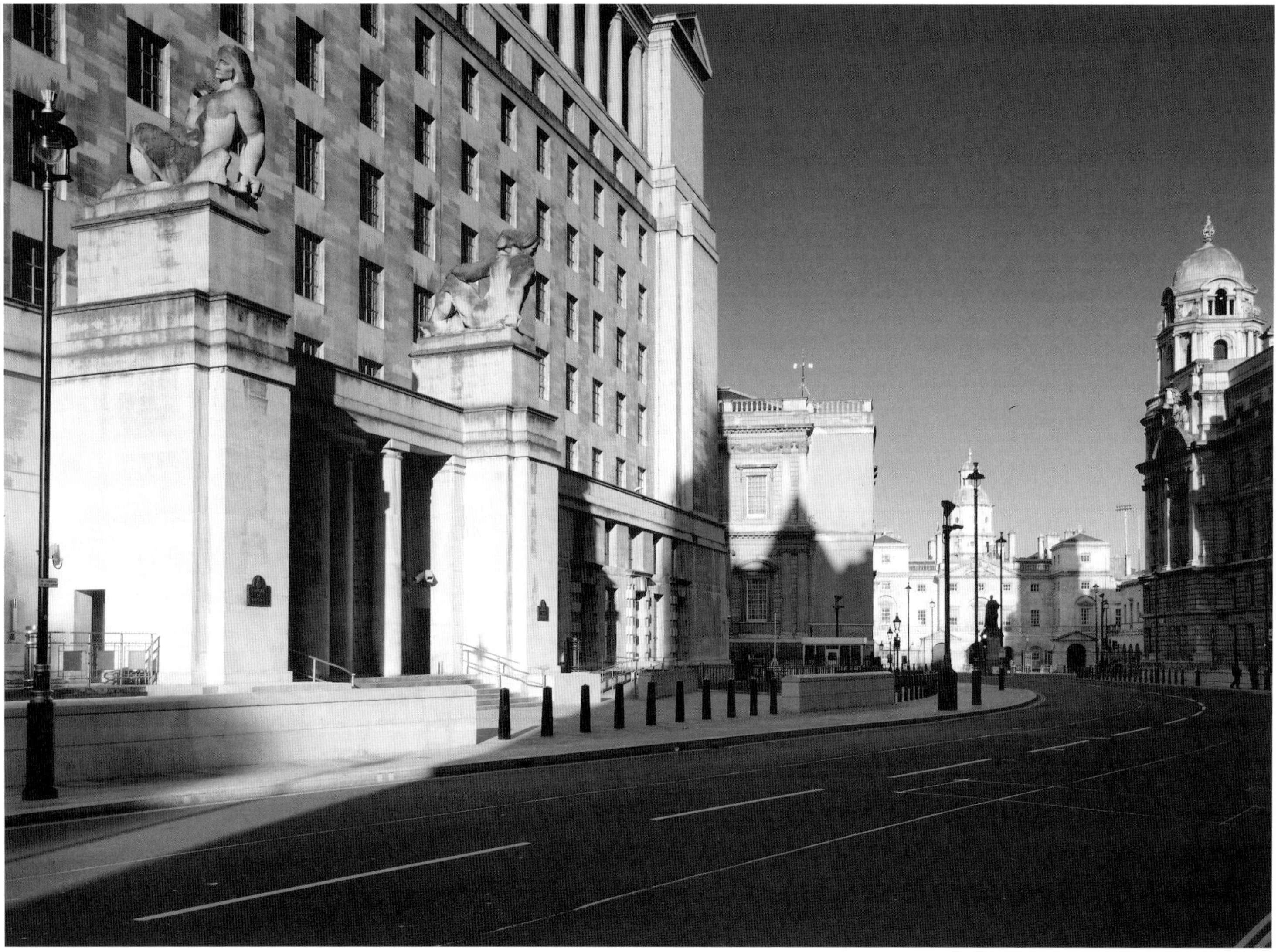

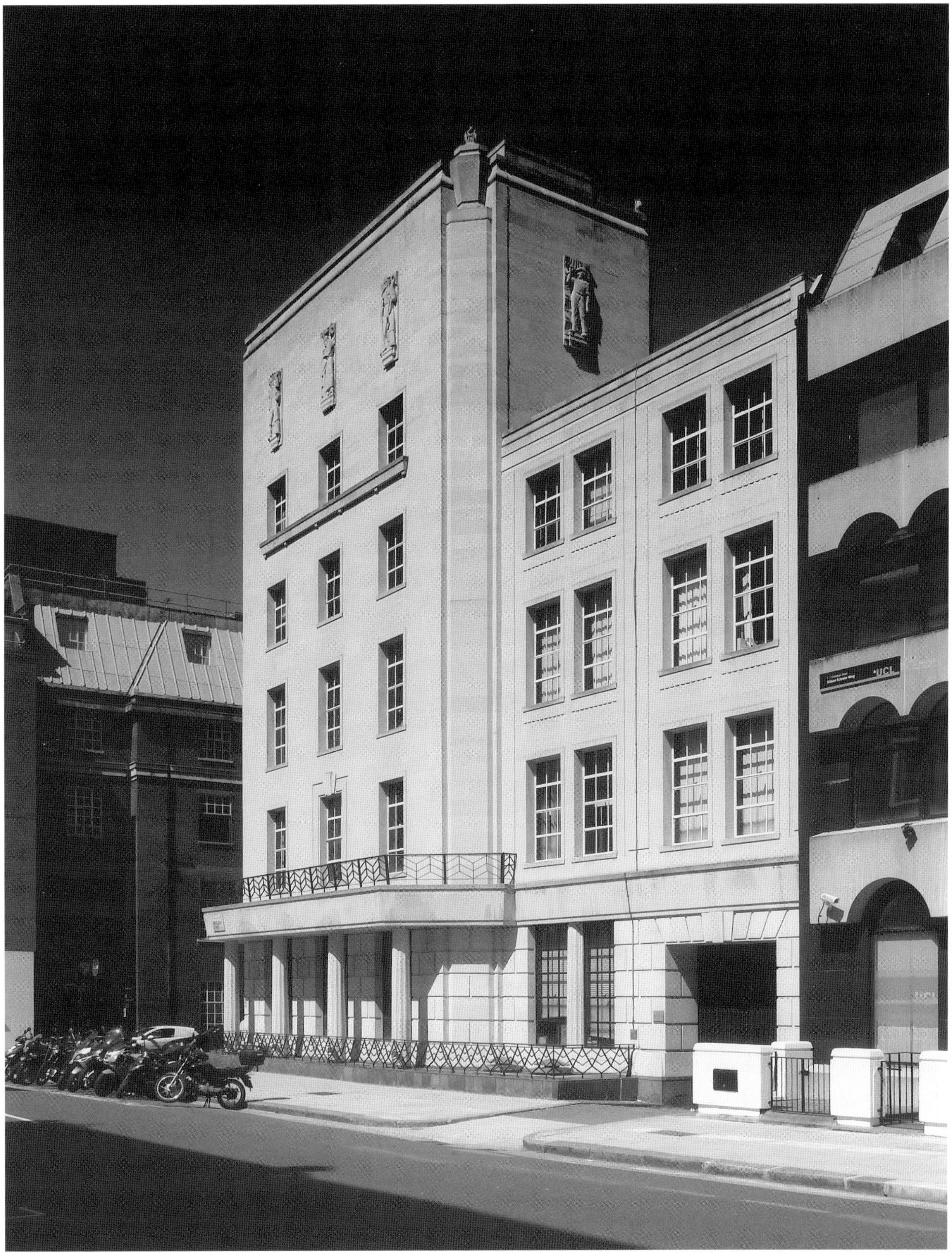
UCL

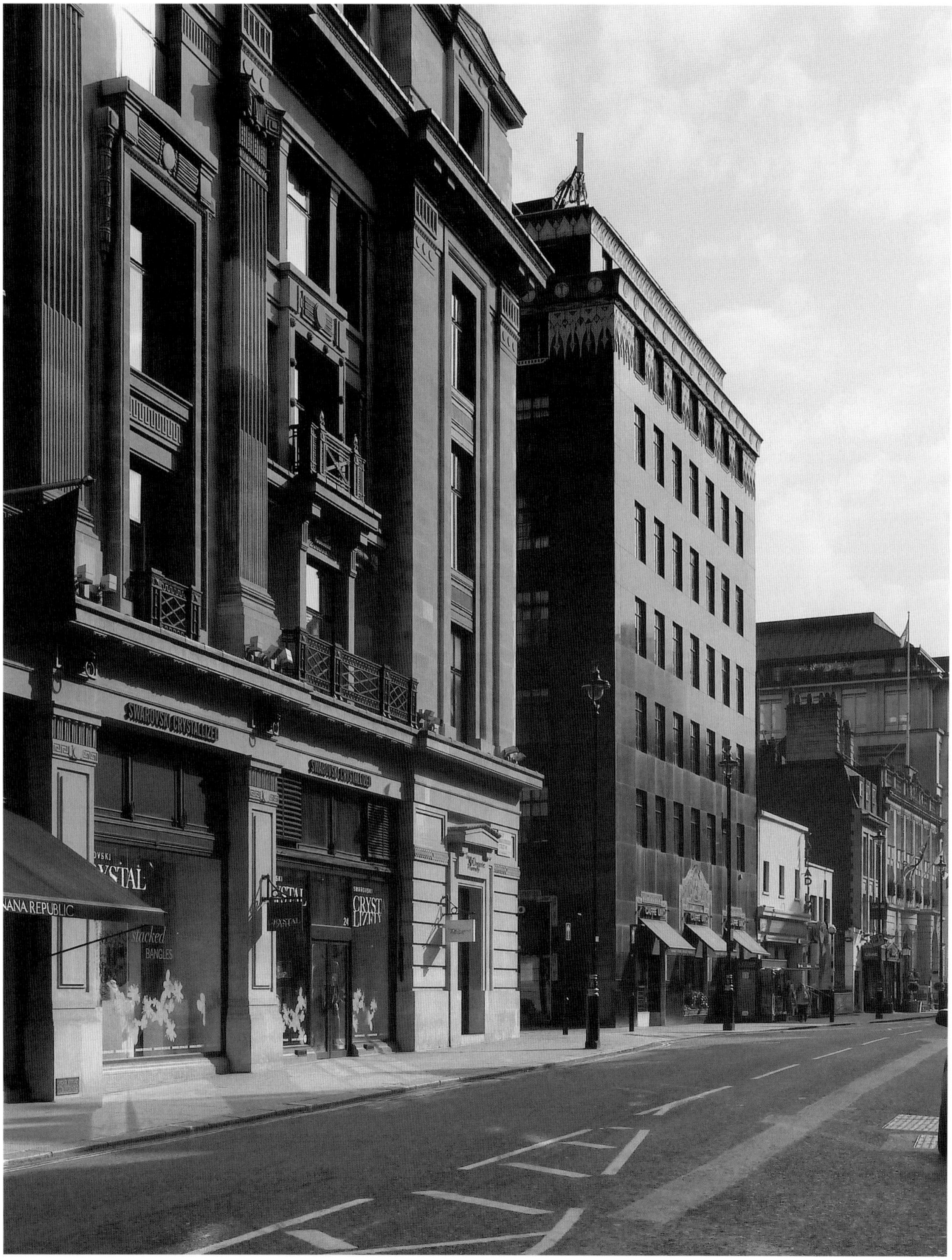
SWAROVSKI CRYSTALLIZED
NANA REPUBLIC
stacked
BANGLES

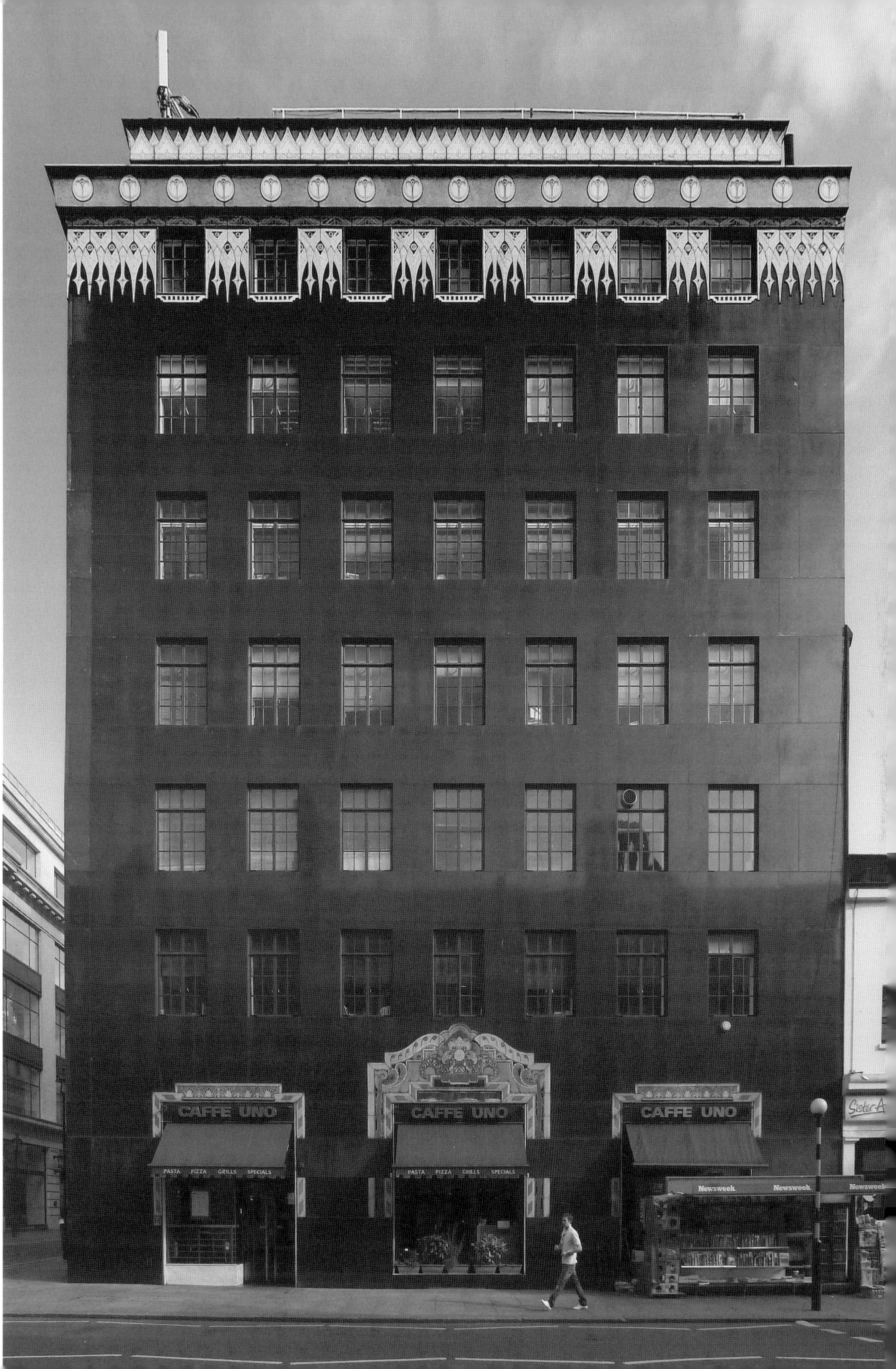
CAFFE UNO
PASTA PIZZA GRILLS SPECIALS
CAFFE UNO
PASTA PIZZA GRILLS SPECIALS
CAFFE UNO
Newsweek
Newsweek
Newsweek

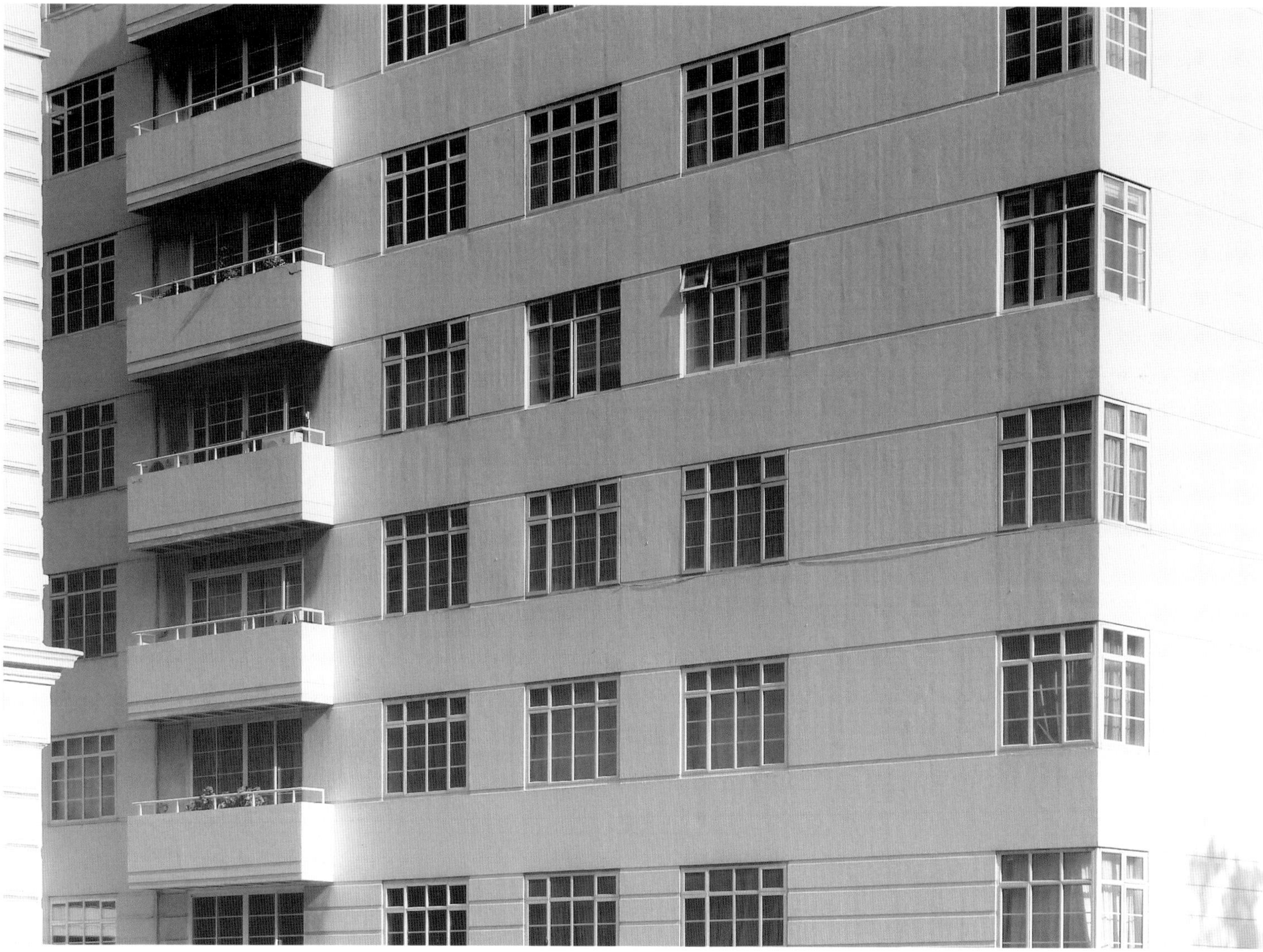

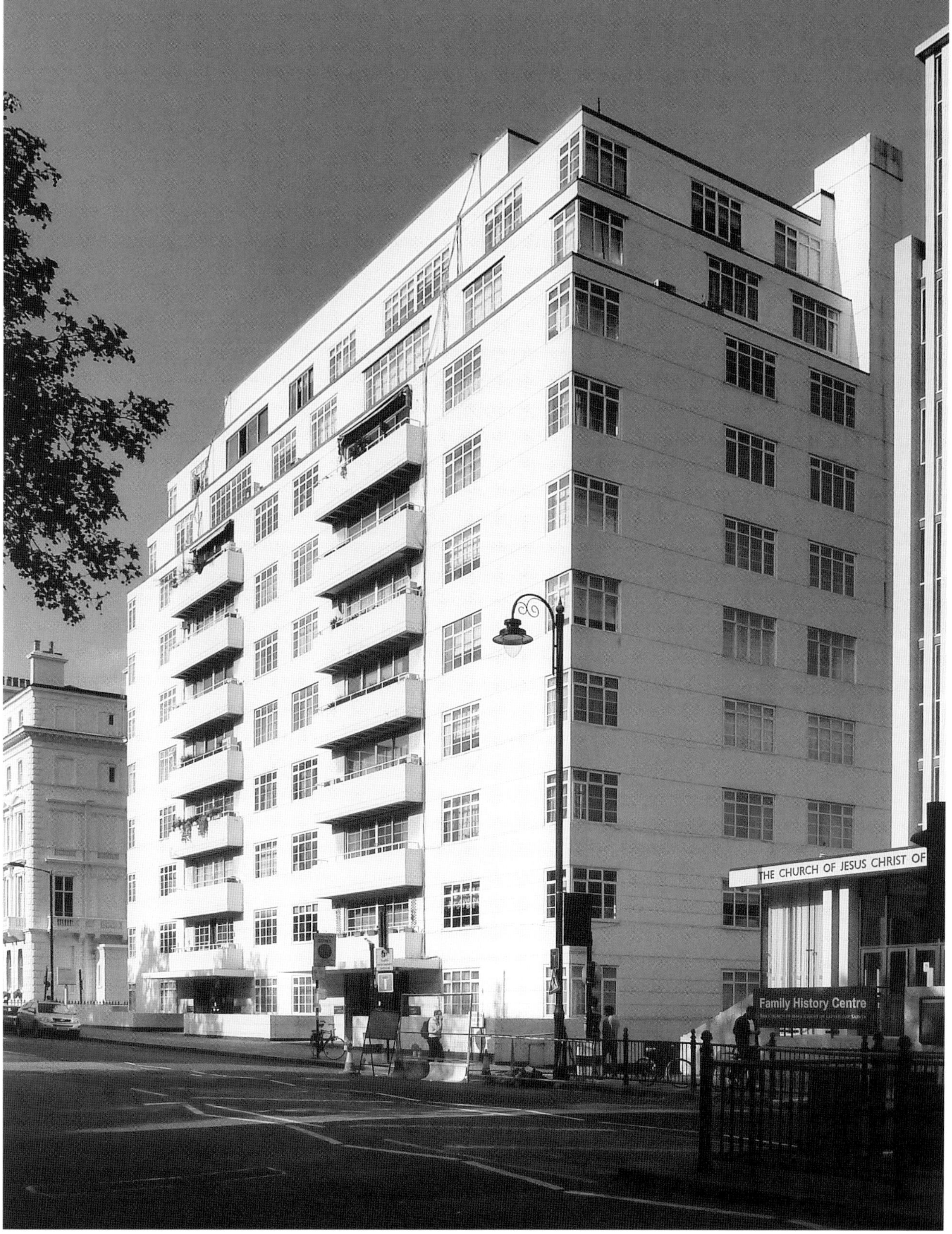
THE CHURCH OF JESUS CHRIST OF
Family History Centre

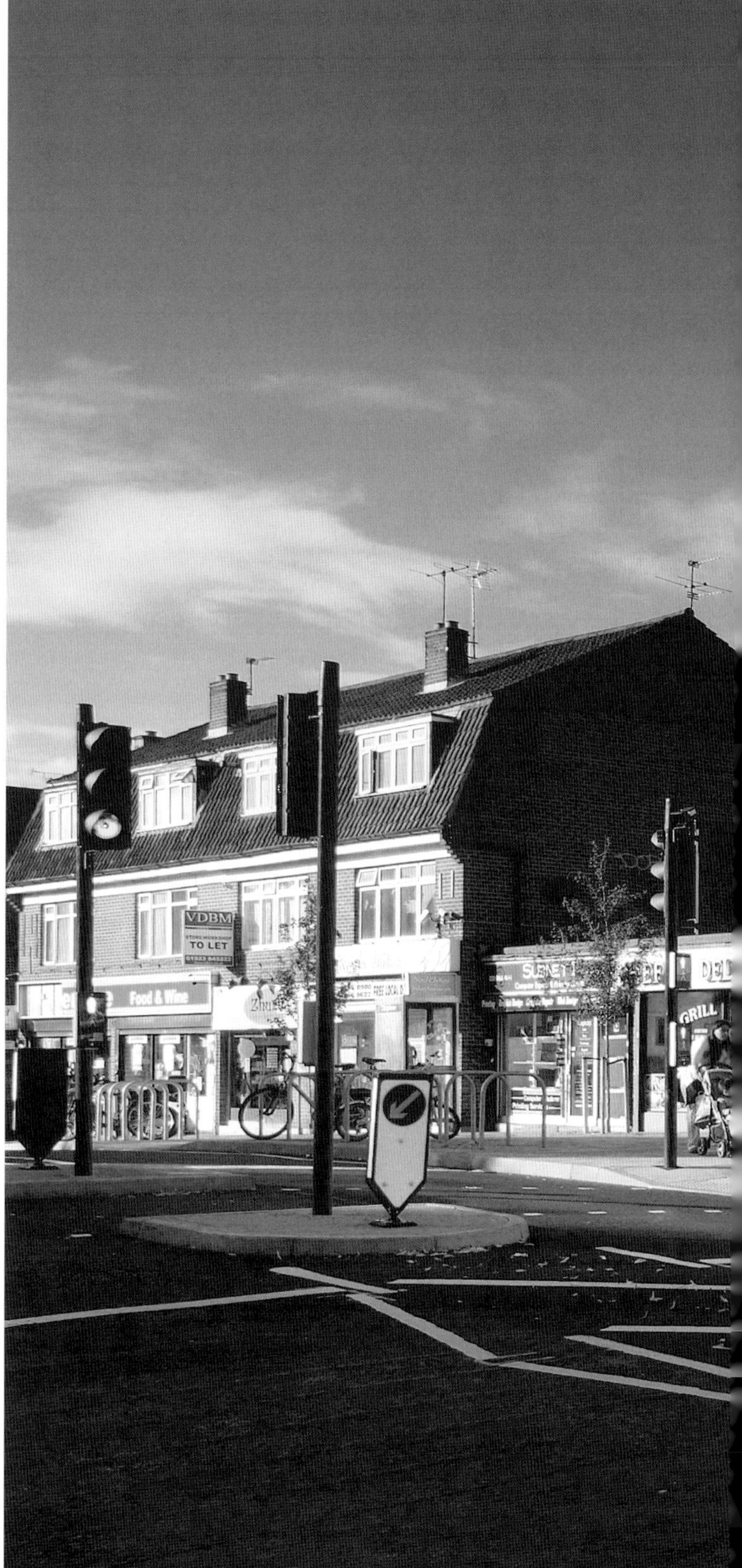
VDBM
TO LET
Food & Wine
GRILL

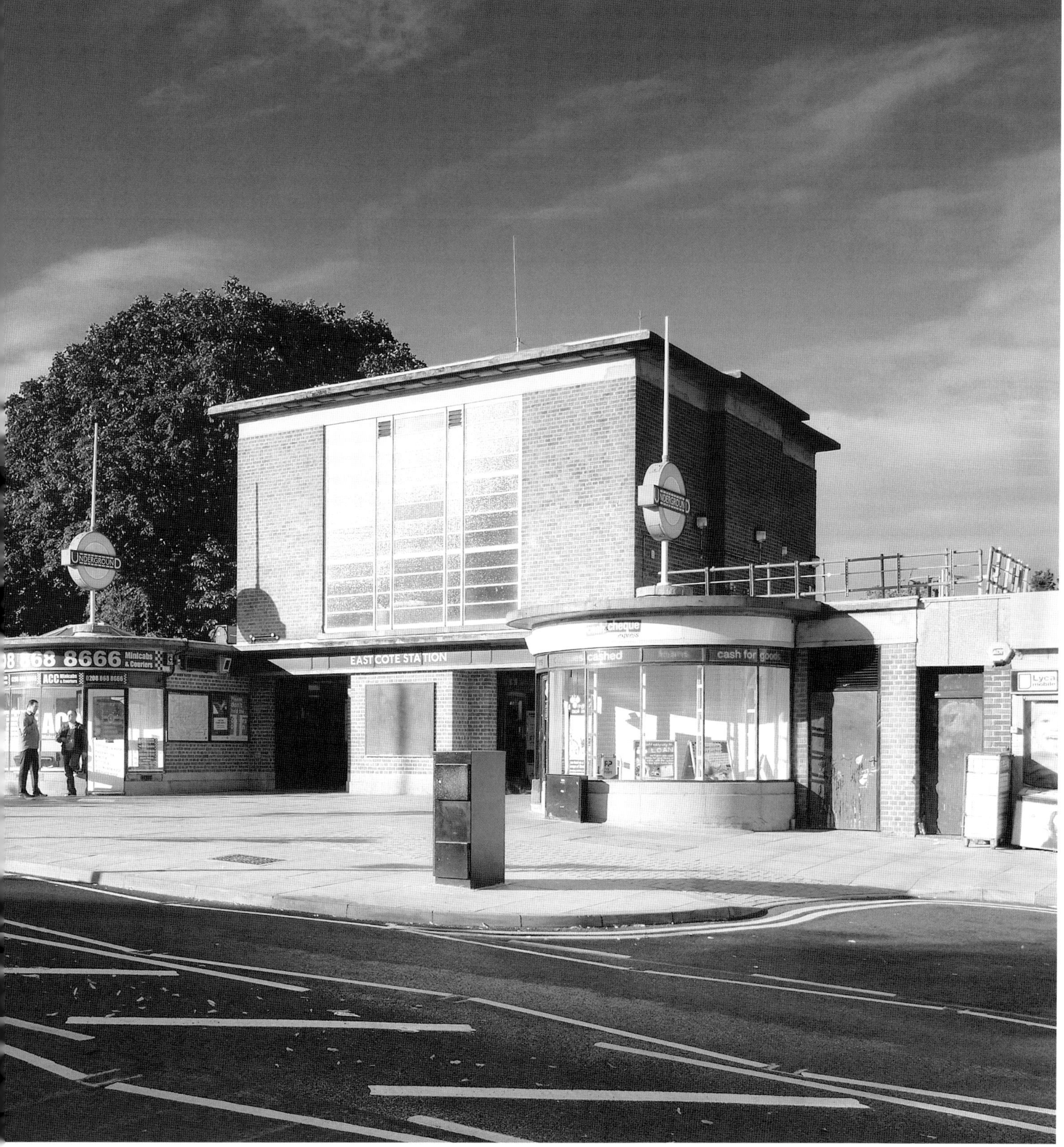
UNDERGROUND
UNDERGROUND
EASTCOTE STATION
Minicabs & Couriers
cheque express
cashed

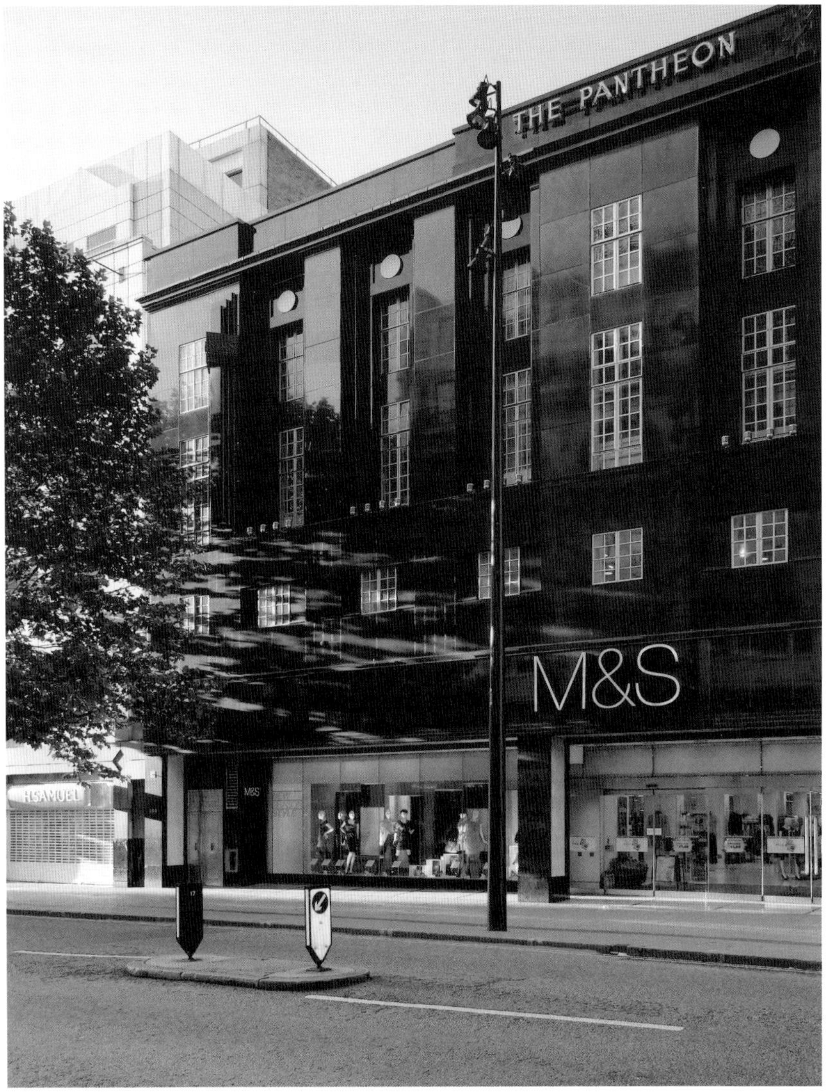
THE PANTHEON
M&S

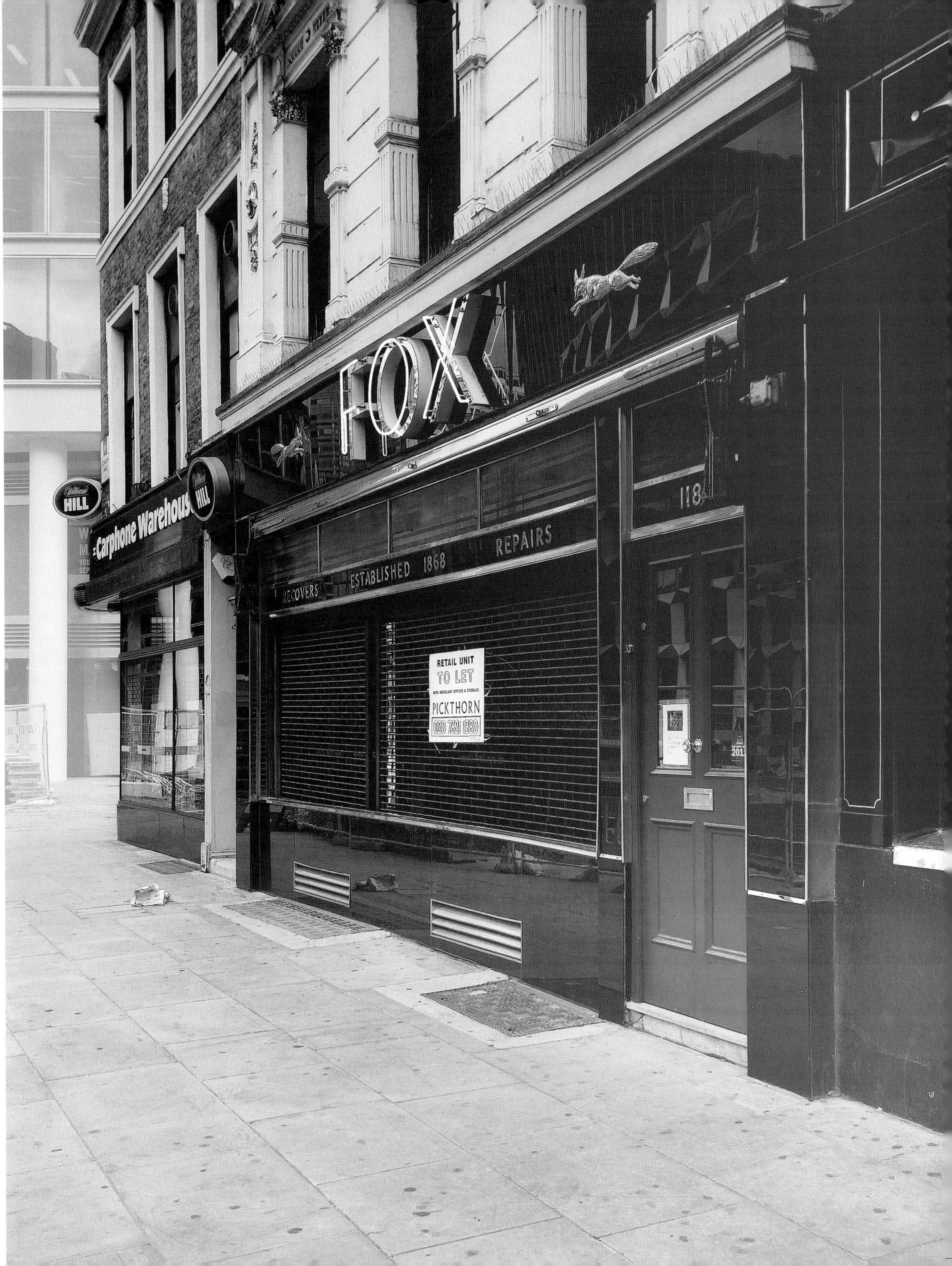
William Hill
Carphone Warehouse
FOX
118
RECOVERS
ESTABLISHED 1868
REPAIRS
RETAIL UNIT
TO LET
PICKTHORN
020 7621 1380

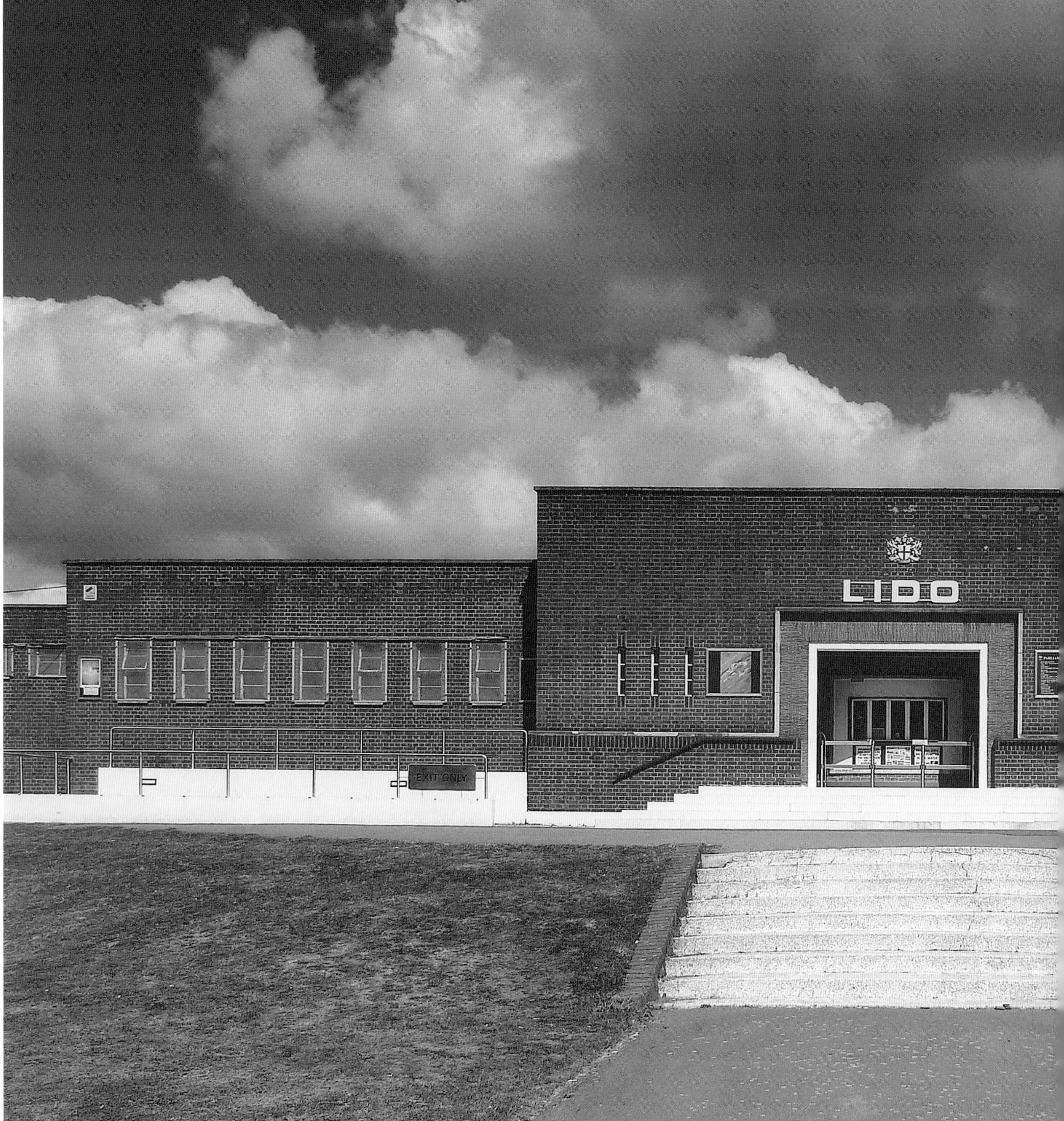
LIDO
EXIT ONLY

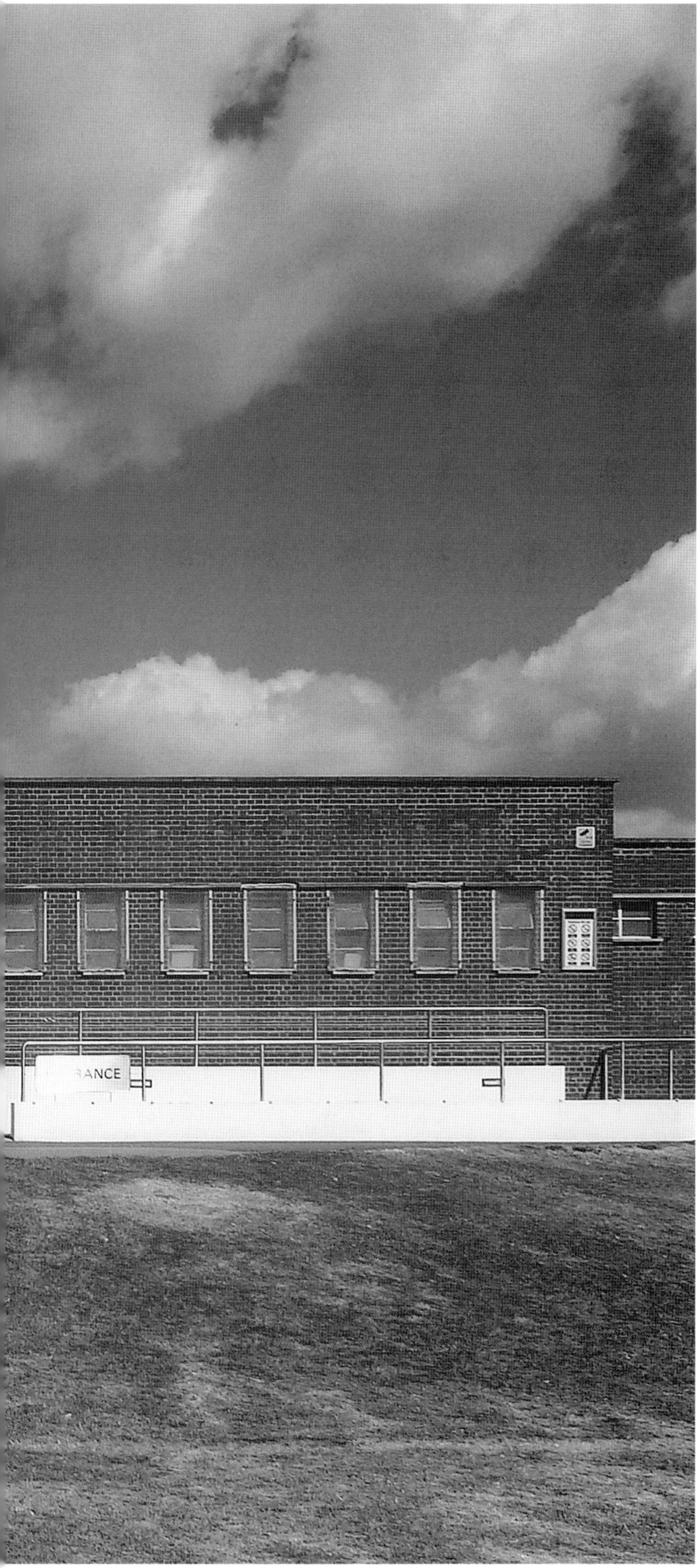
RANCE

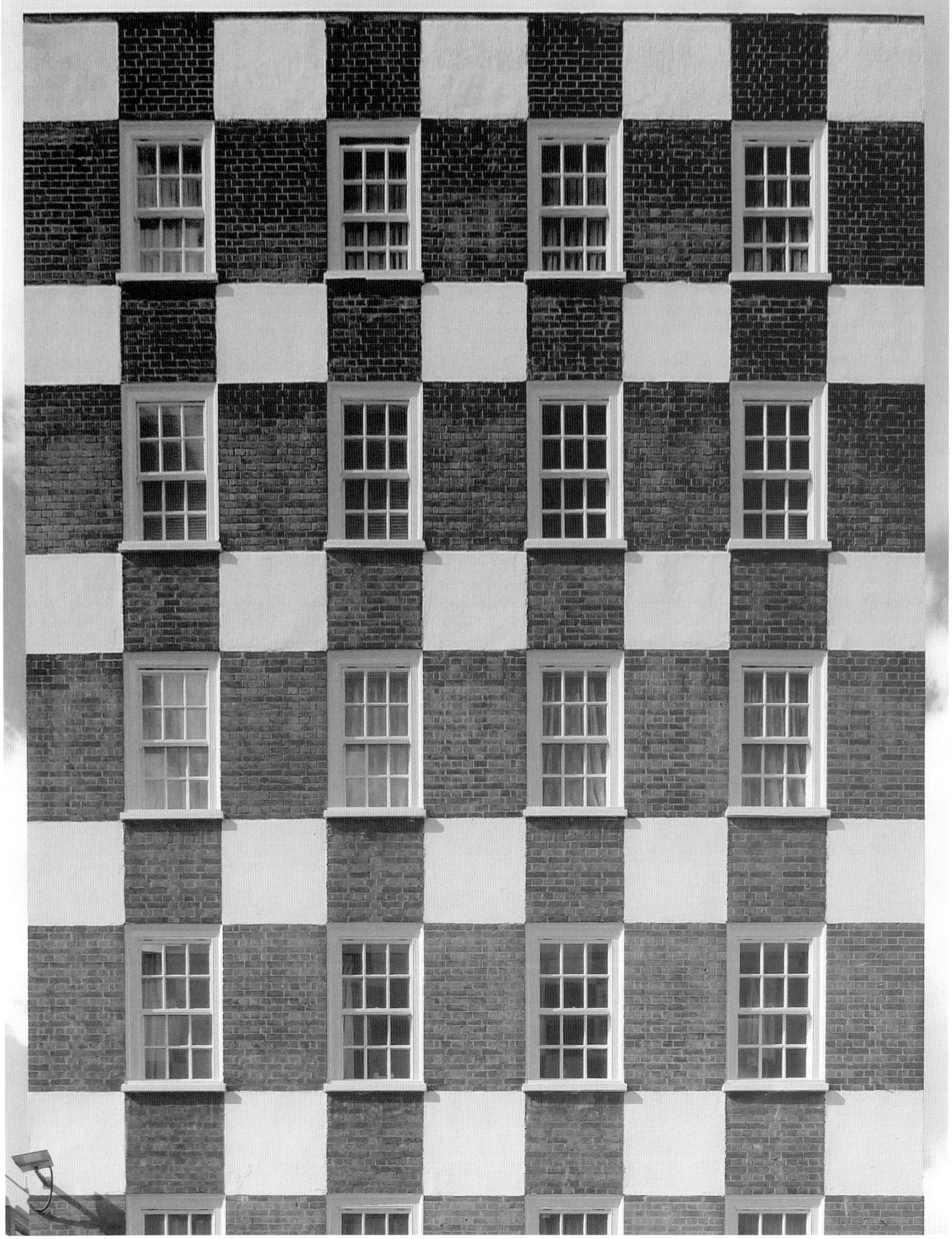

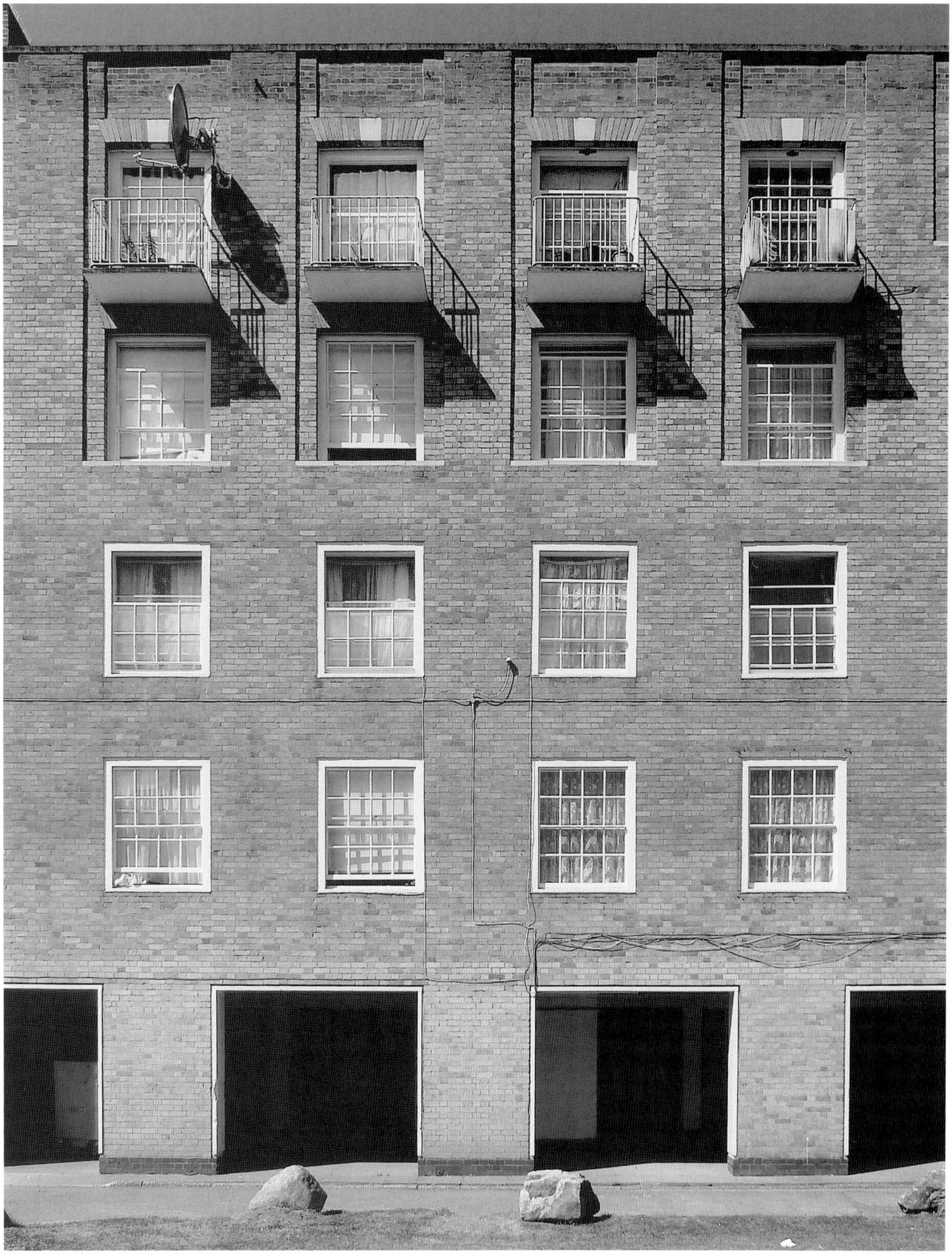

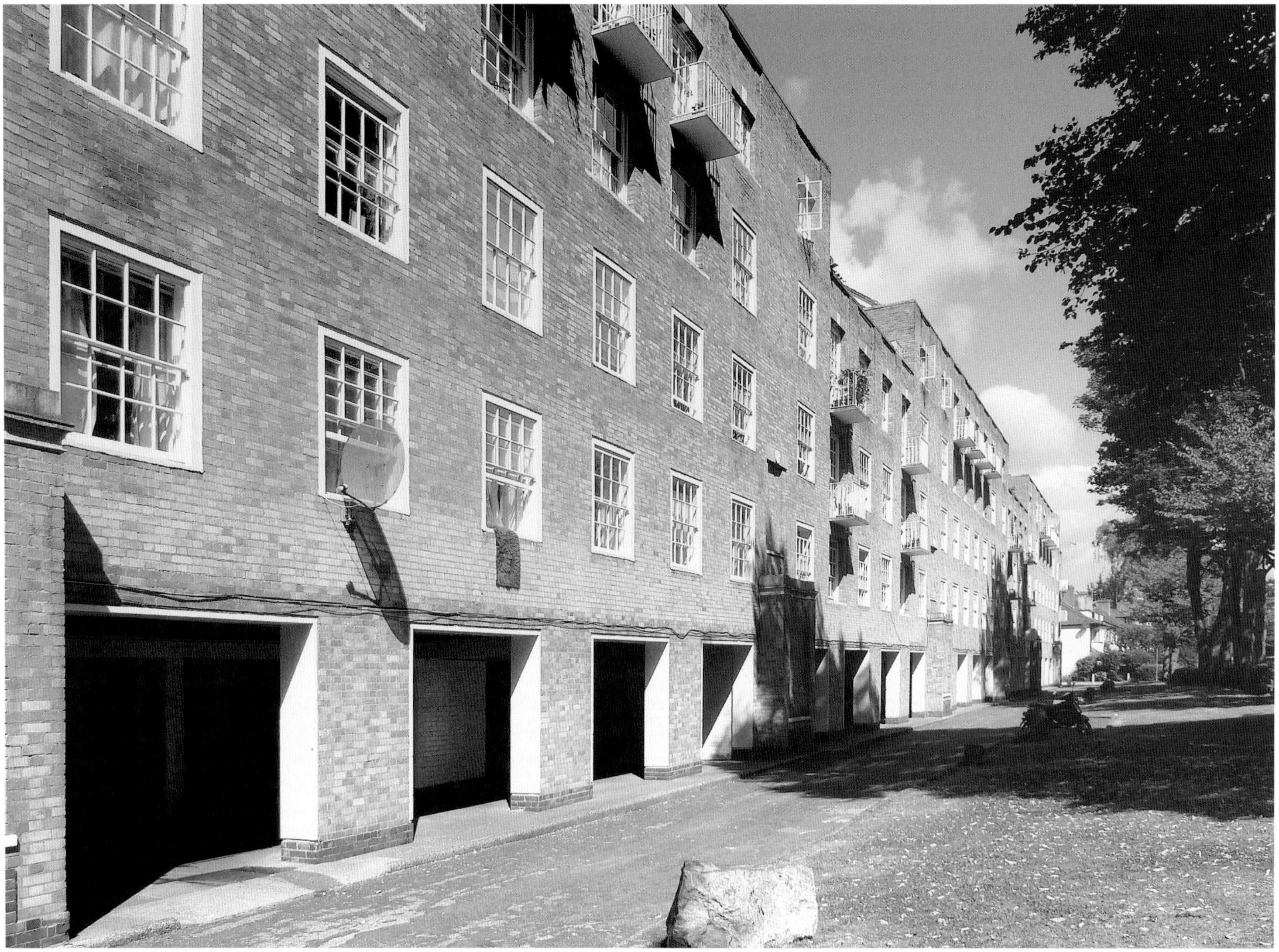

38

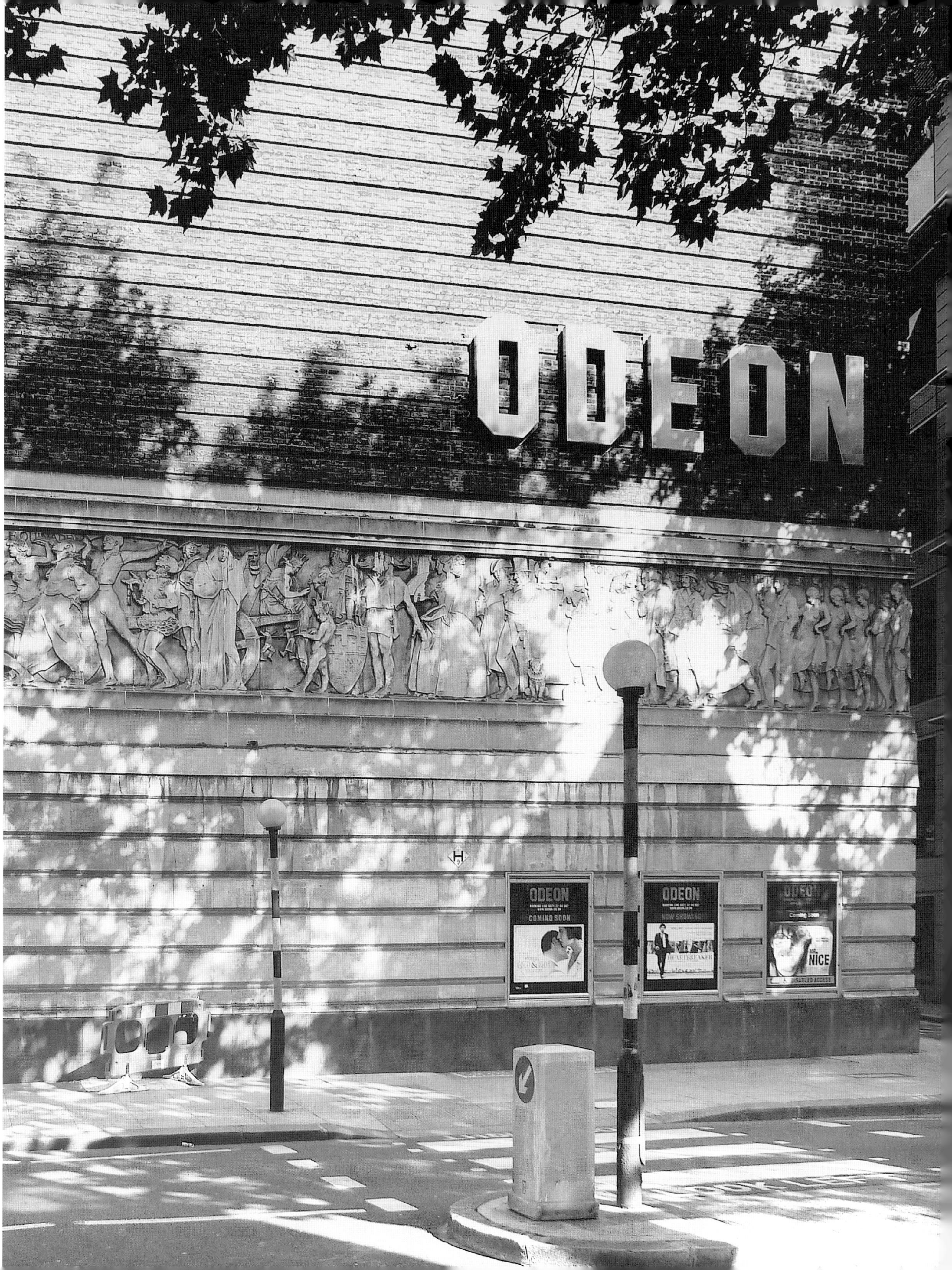
ODEON

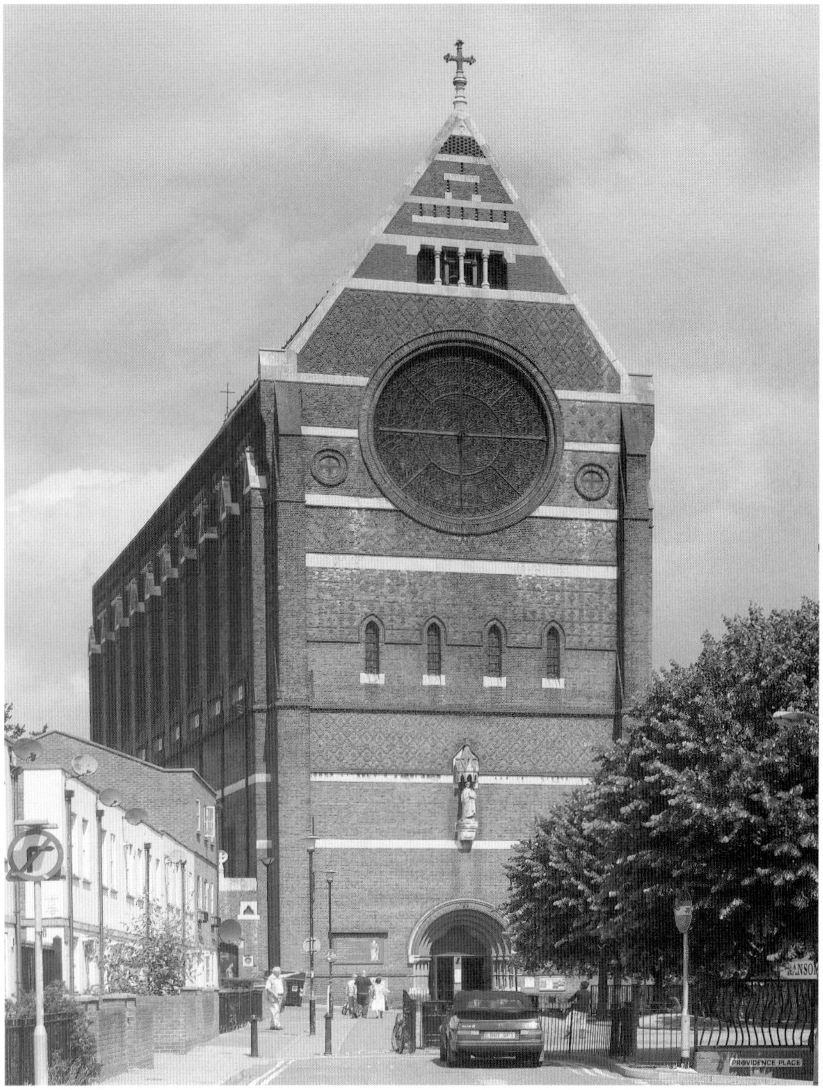
PROVIDENCE PLACE

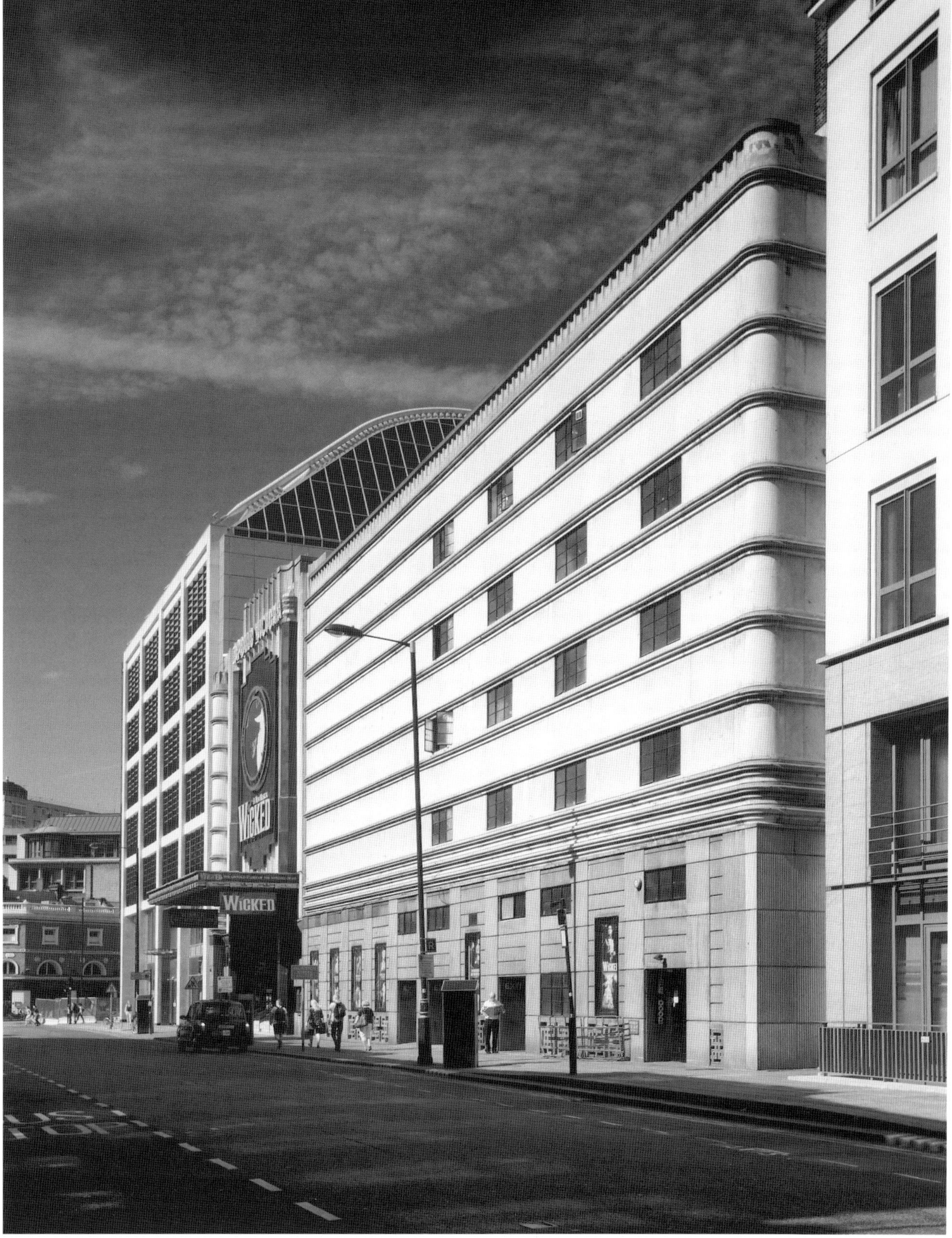
WICKED
WICKED

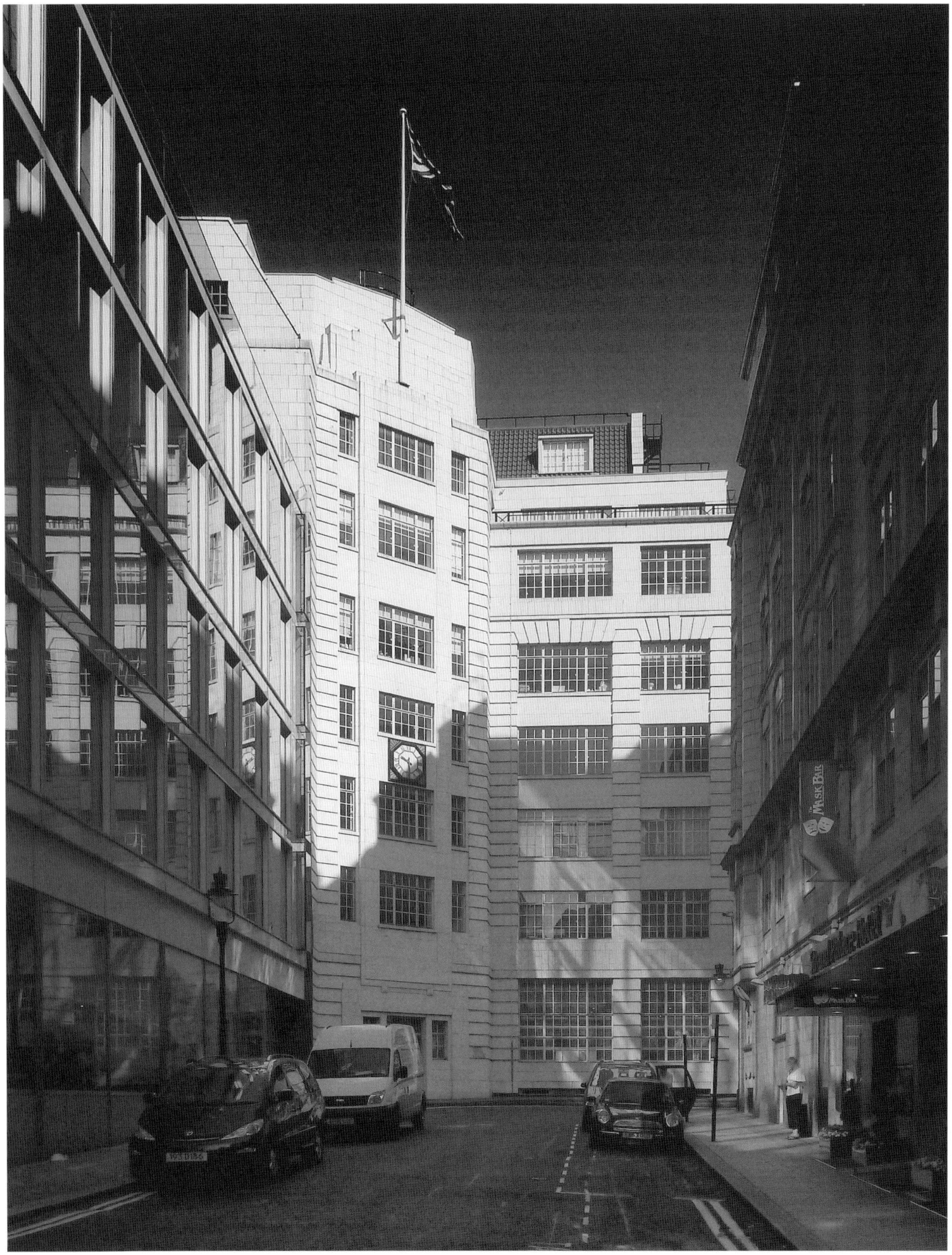
MASK BAR

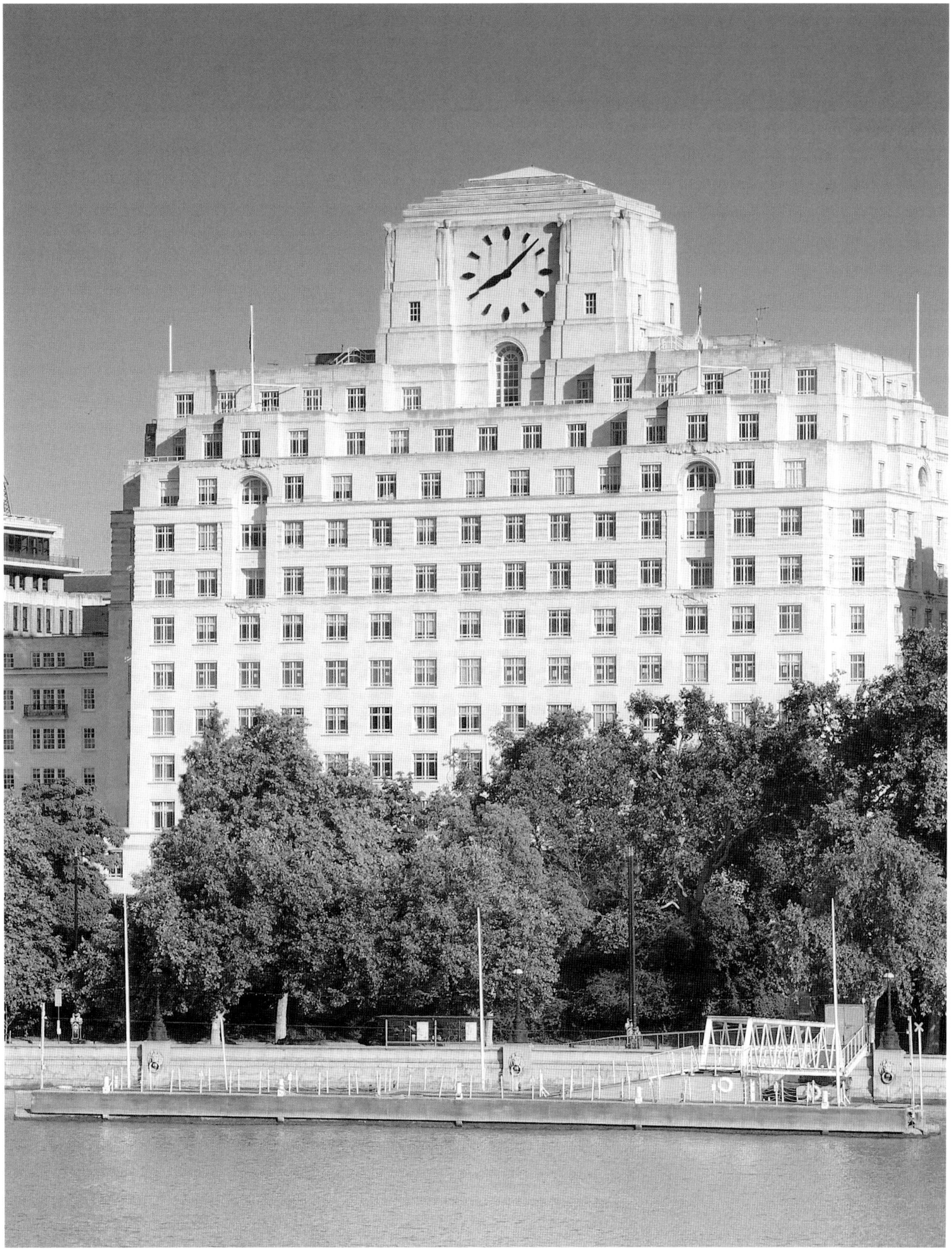

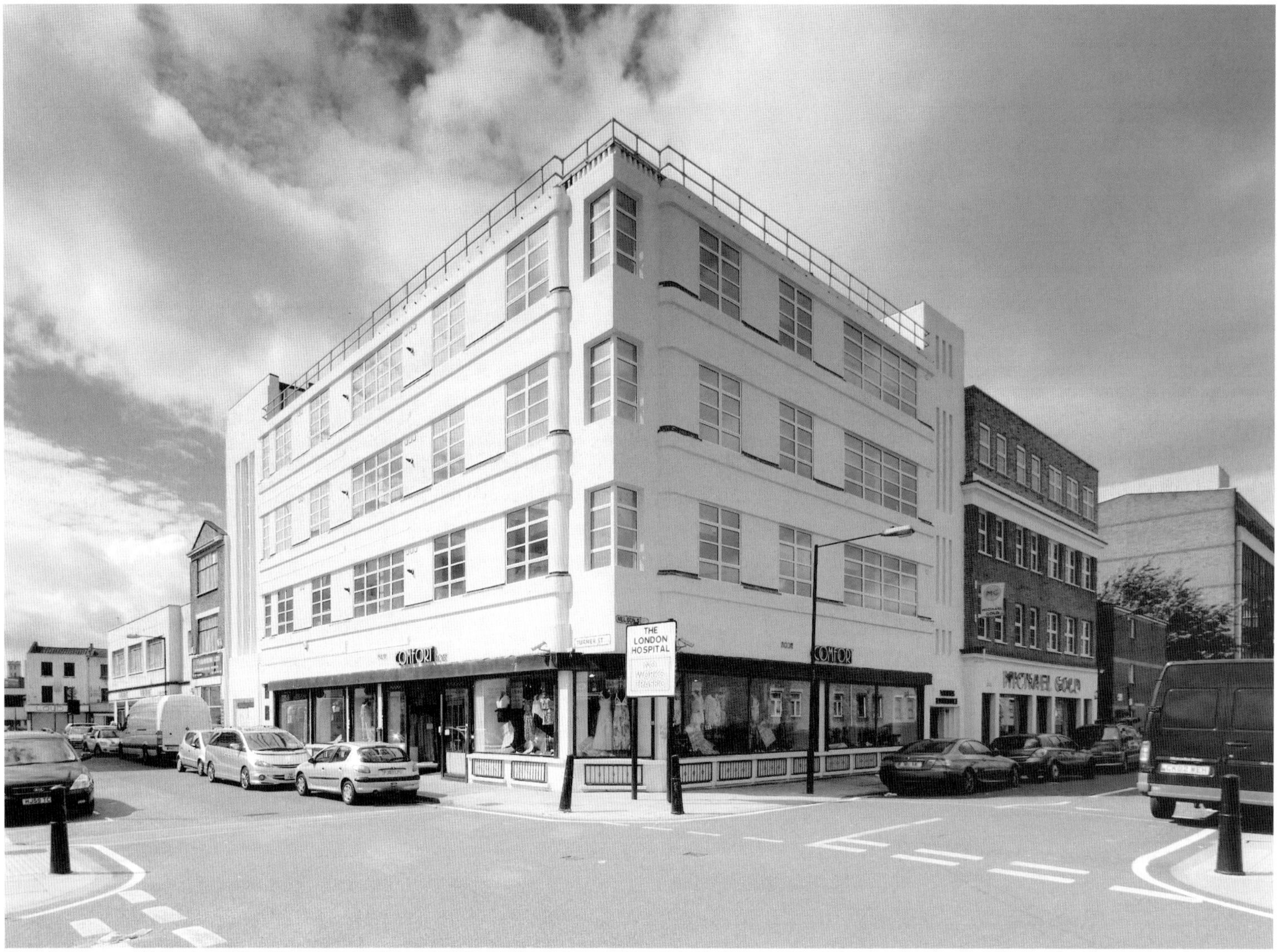
NELSON ST
TURNER ST
THE LONDON HOSPITAL
NO WORKS TRAFFIC
COMFORT
COMFOR

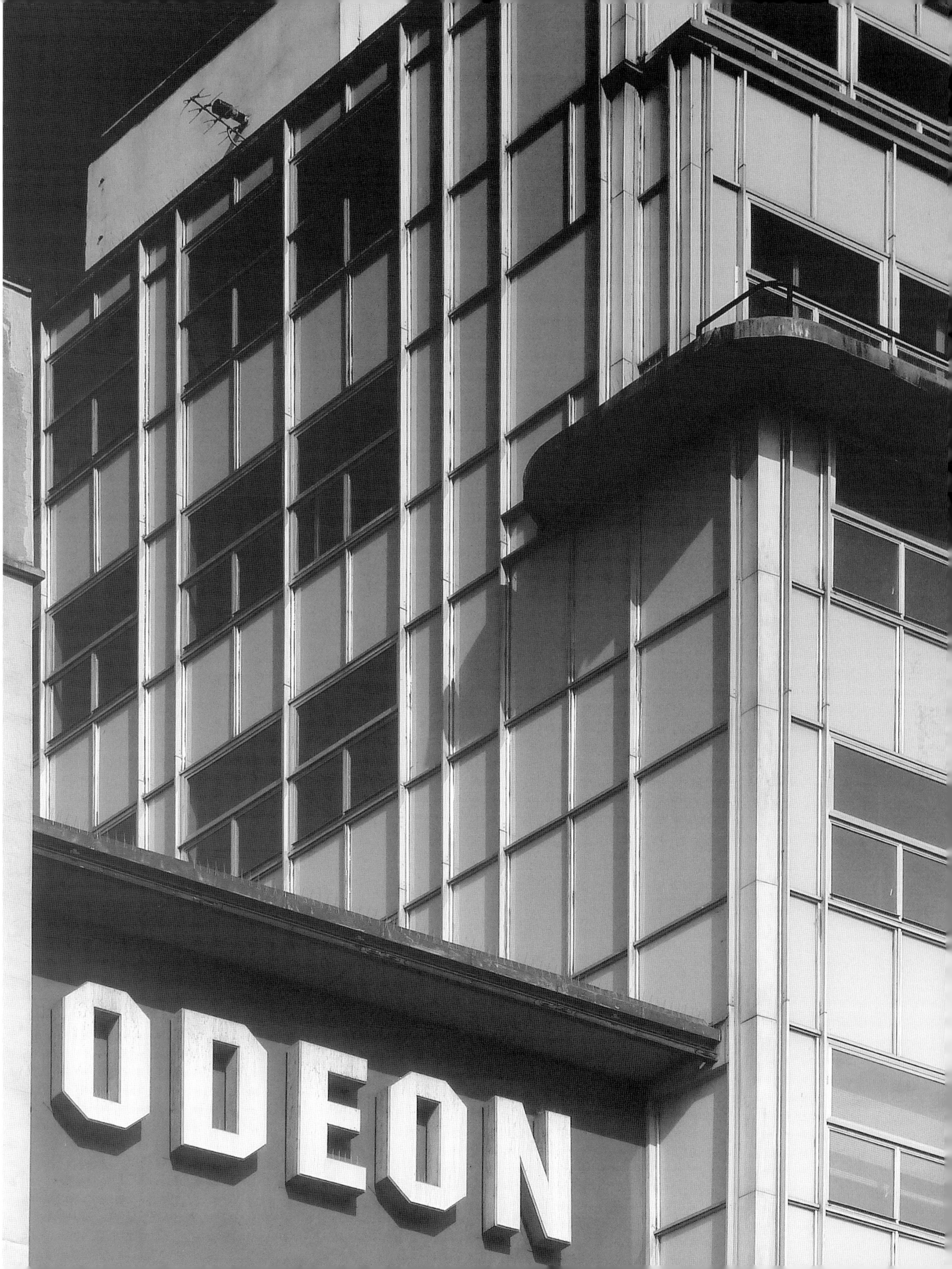
ODEON

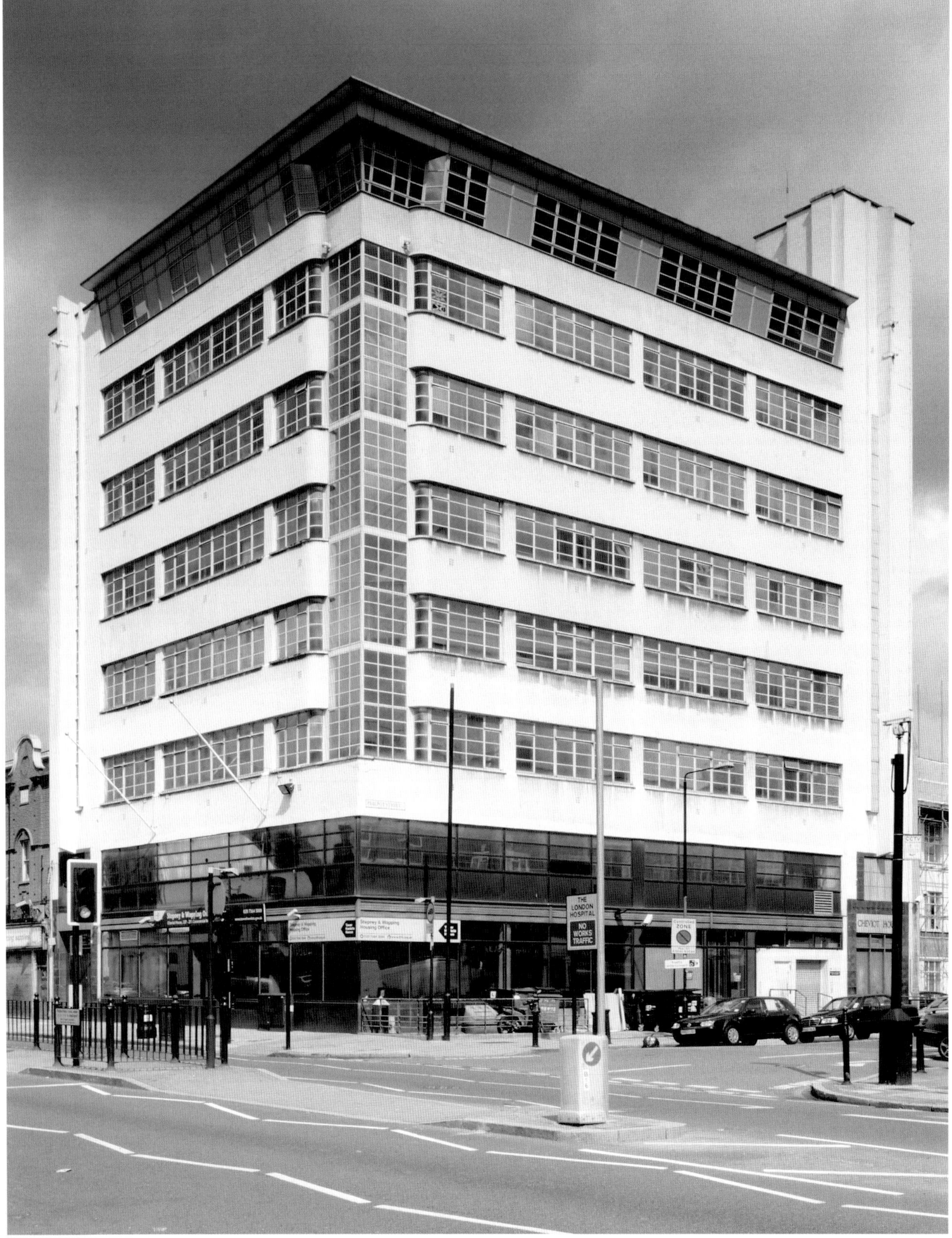
THE LONDON HOSPITAL
NO WORKS TRAFFIC

69

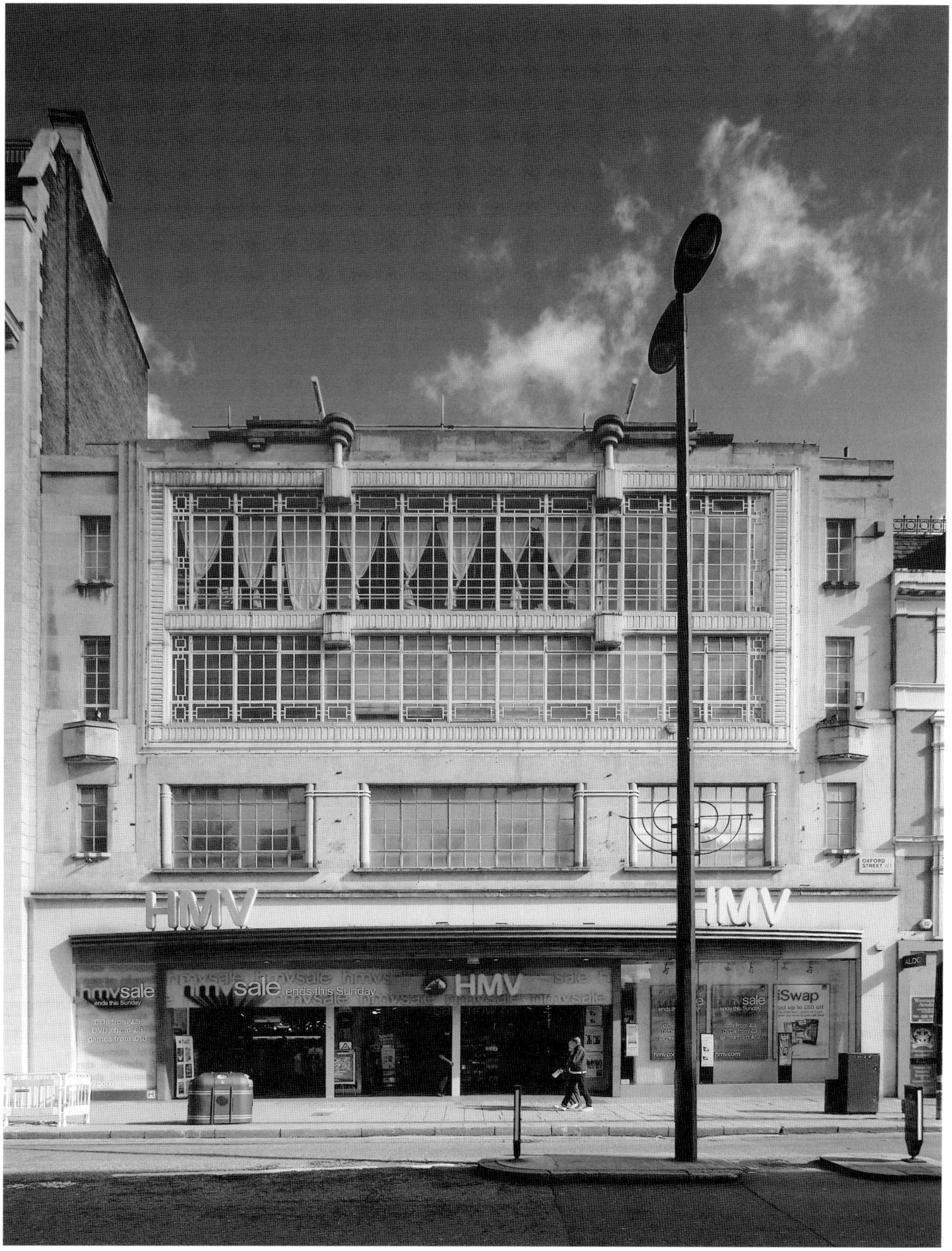
HMV
HMV
hmvsale
ends this Sunday
hmvsale
ends this Sunday
HMV
iSwap
OXFORD
STREET W1

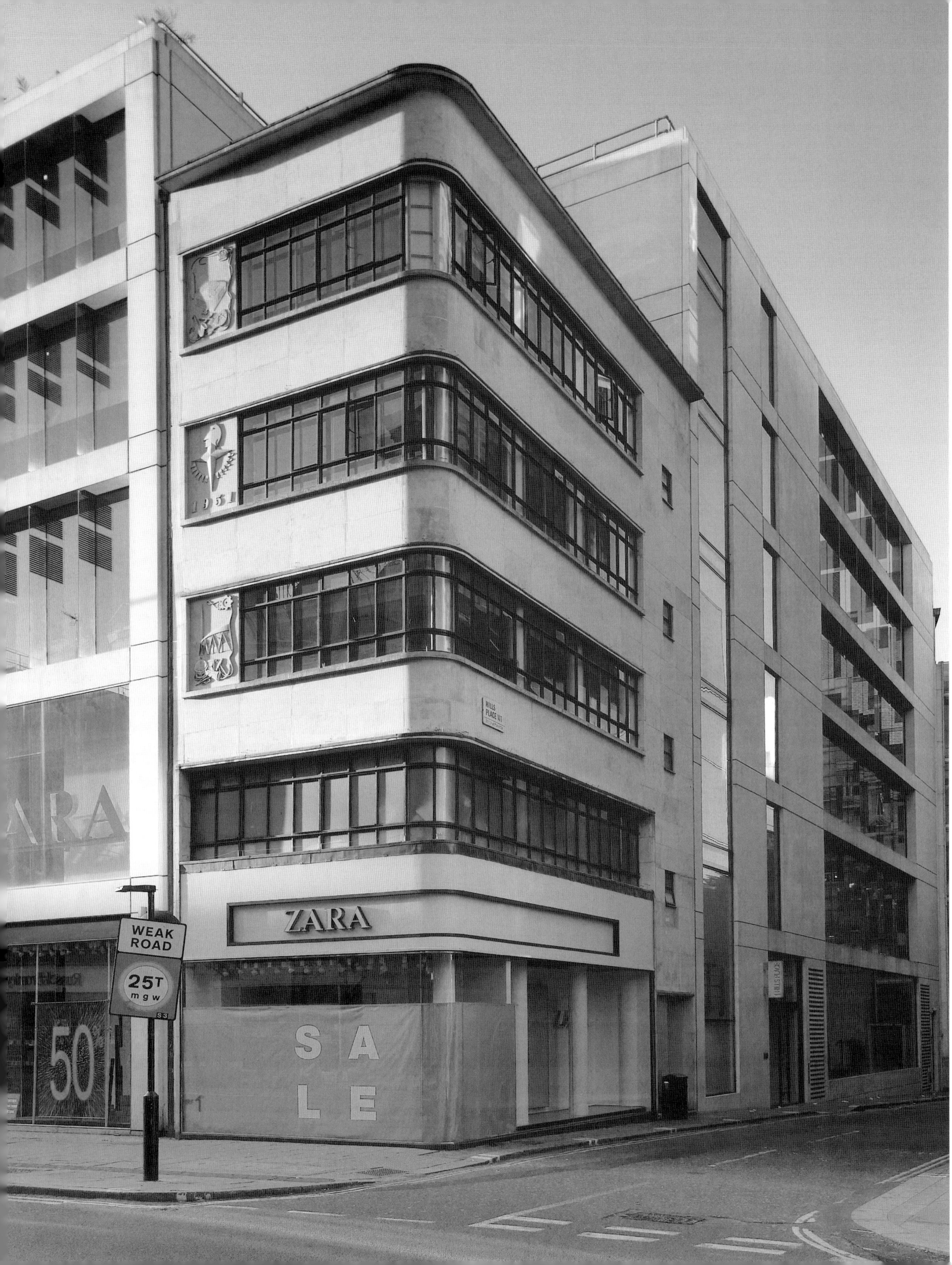
1951
ZARA
WEAK
ROAD
25T
mgw
S A
L E
50

74

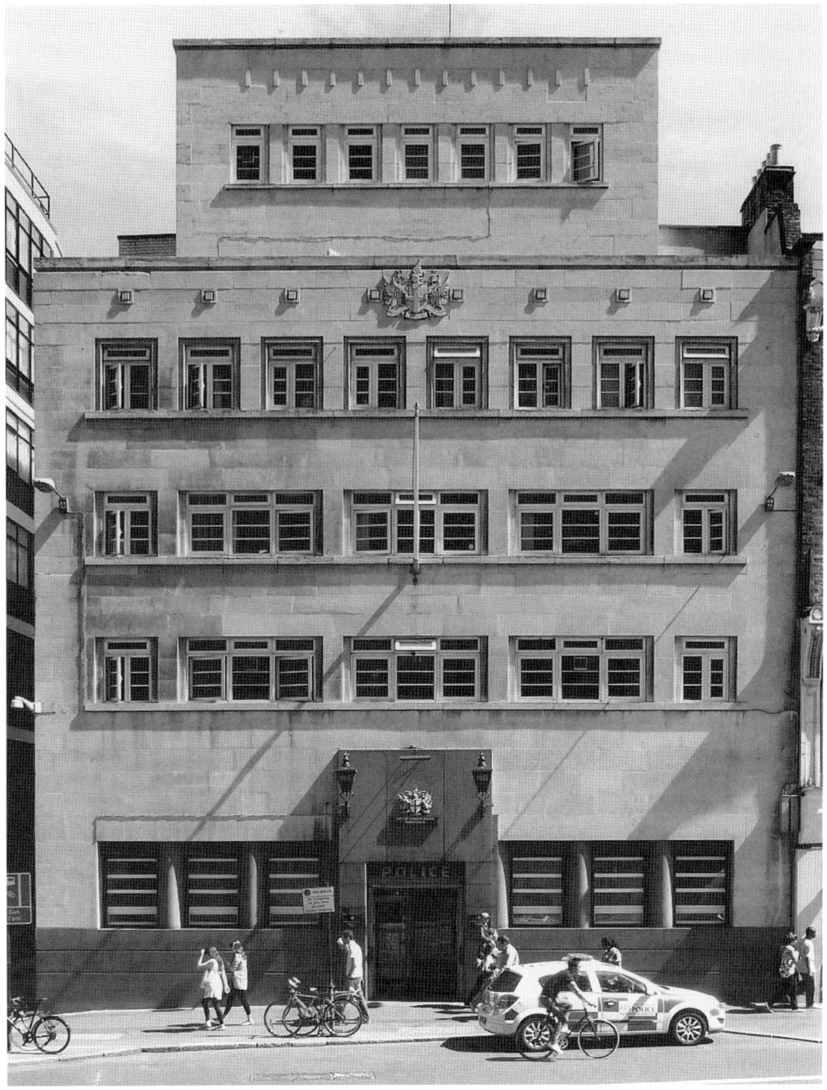

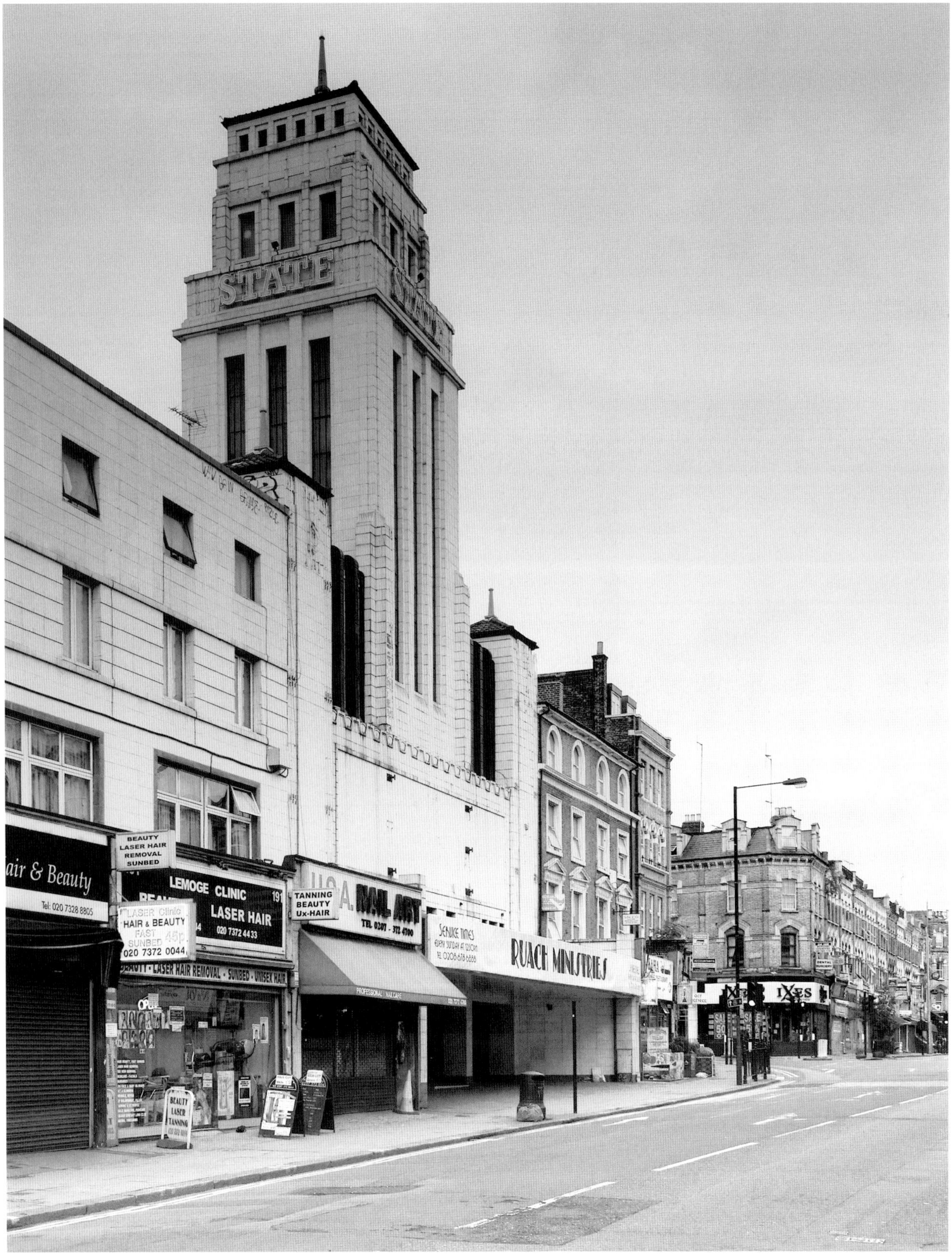
STATE
air & Beauty
Tel: 020 7328 8805
BEAUTY
LASER HAIR
REMOVAL
SUNBED
LEMOGE CLINIC
LASER HAIR
020 7372 4433
LASER Clinic
HAIR & BEAUTY
FAST
SUNBED
45p
020 7372 0044
BEAUTY - LASER HAIR REMOVAL - SUNBED - UNISEX HAIR
TANNING
BEAUTY
Ux-HAIR
RUACH MINISTRIES
IXES

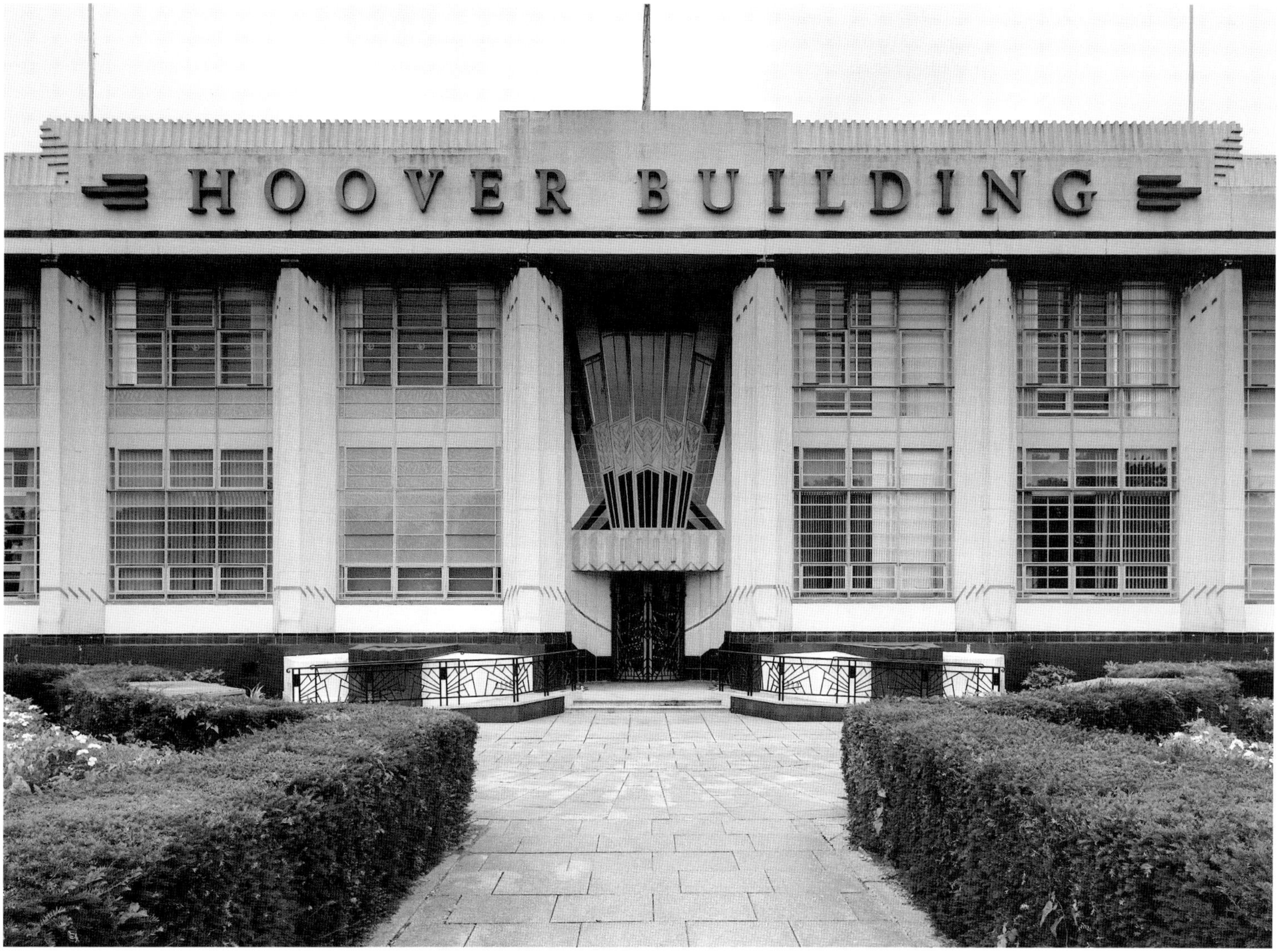
HOOVER BUILDING

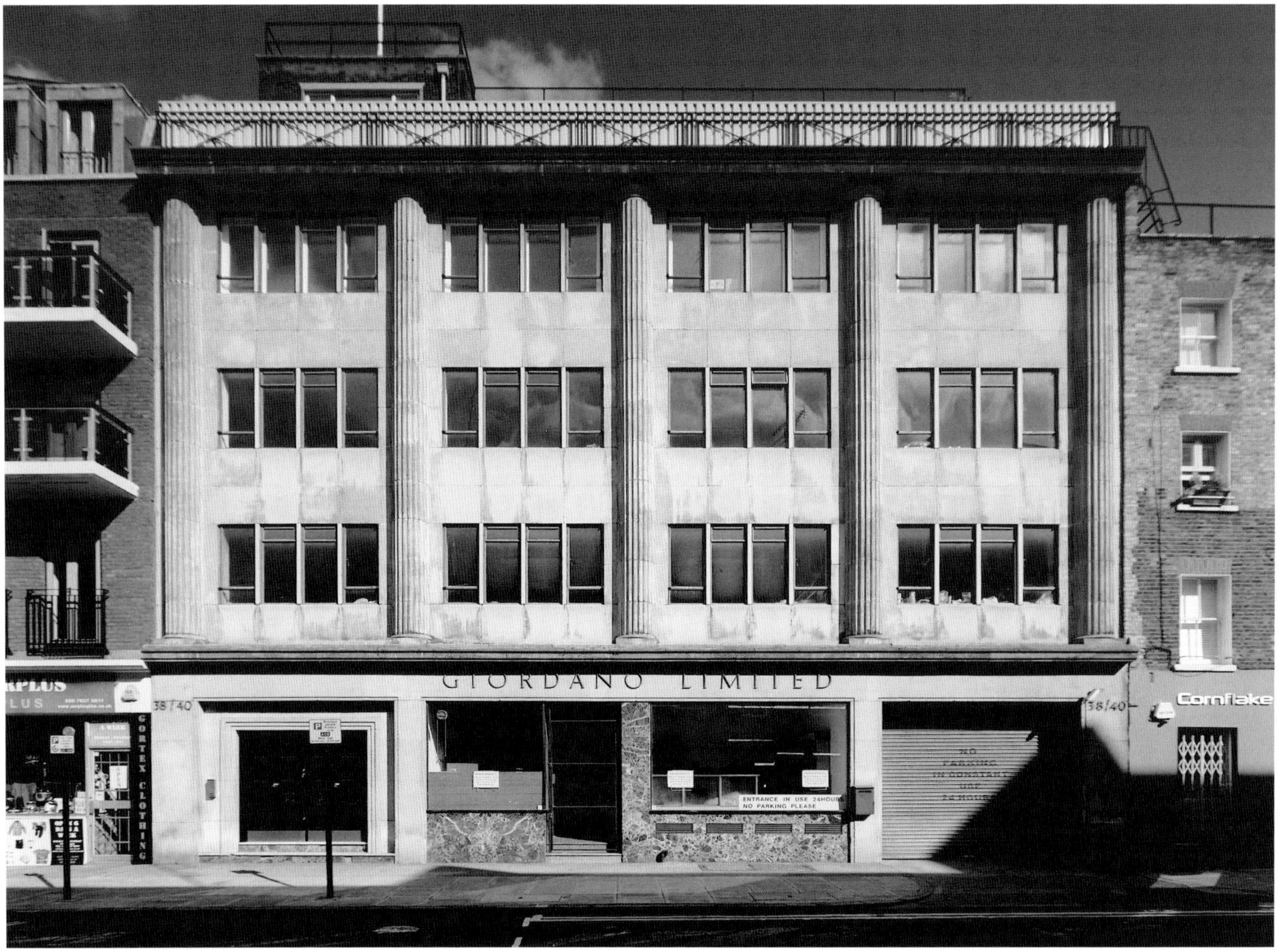
GIORDANO LIMITED
38/40
38/40
GORTEX CLOTHING
ENTRANCE IN USE 24HOURS
NO PARKING PLEASE
Cornflake

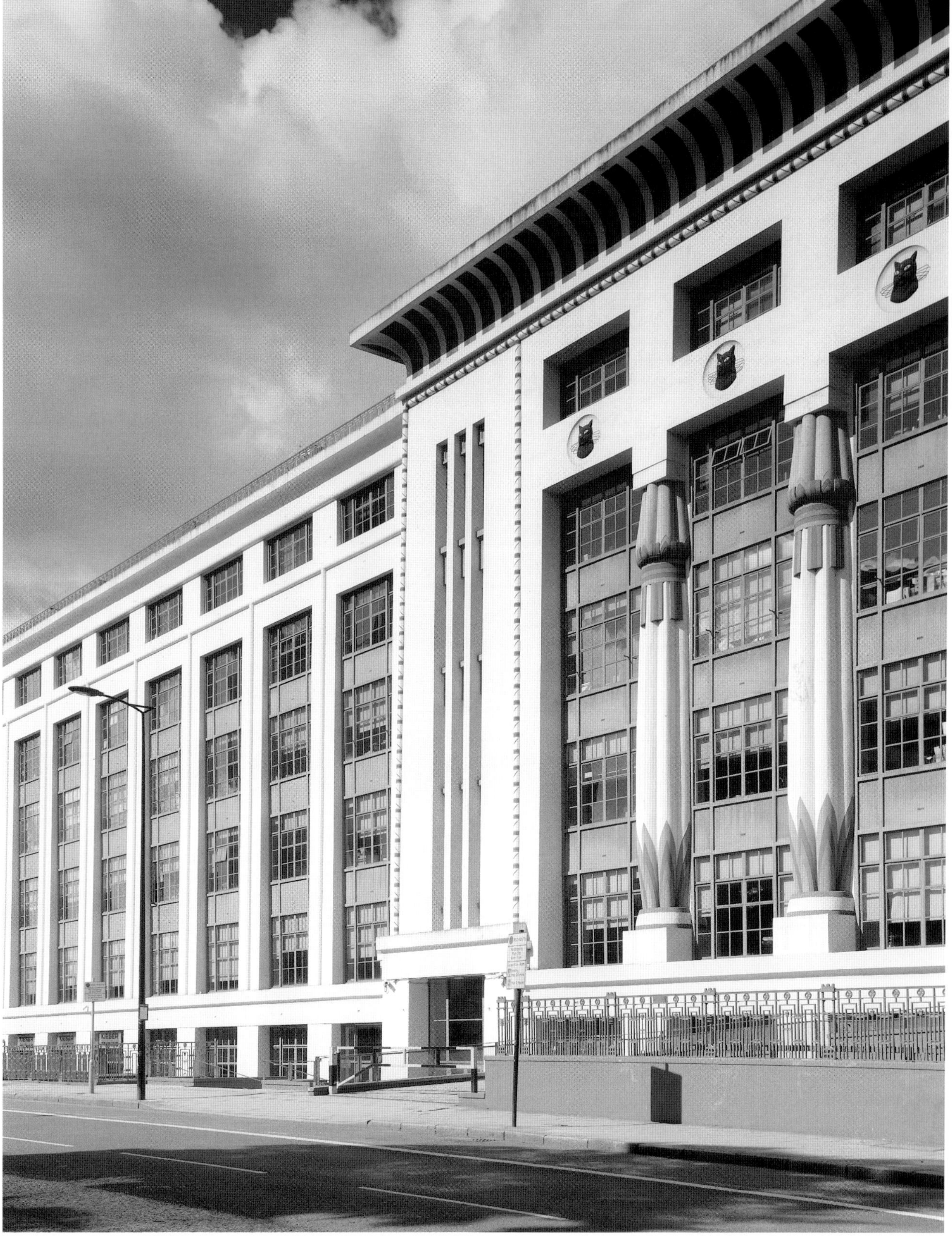

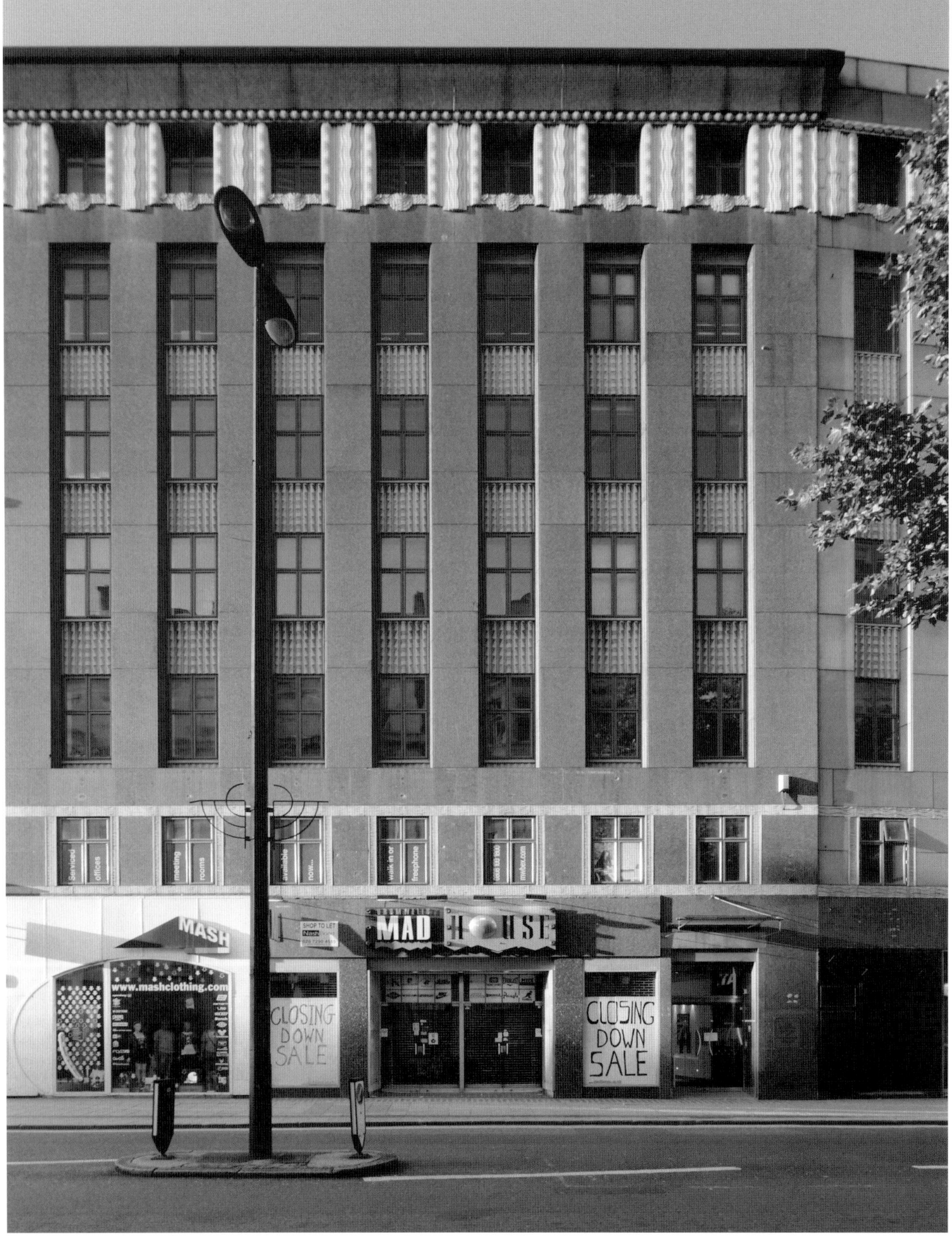
MASH
www.mashclothing.com
CLOSING DOWN SALE
CLOSING DOWN SALE

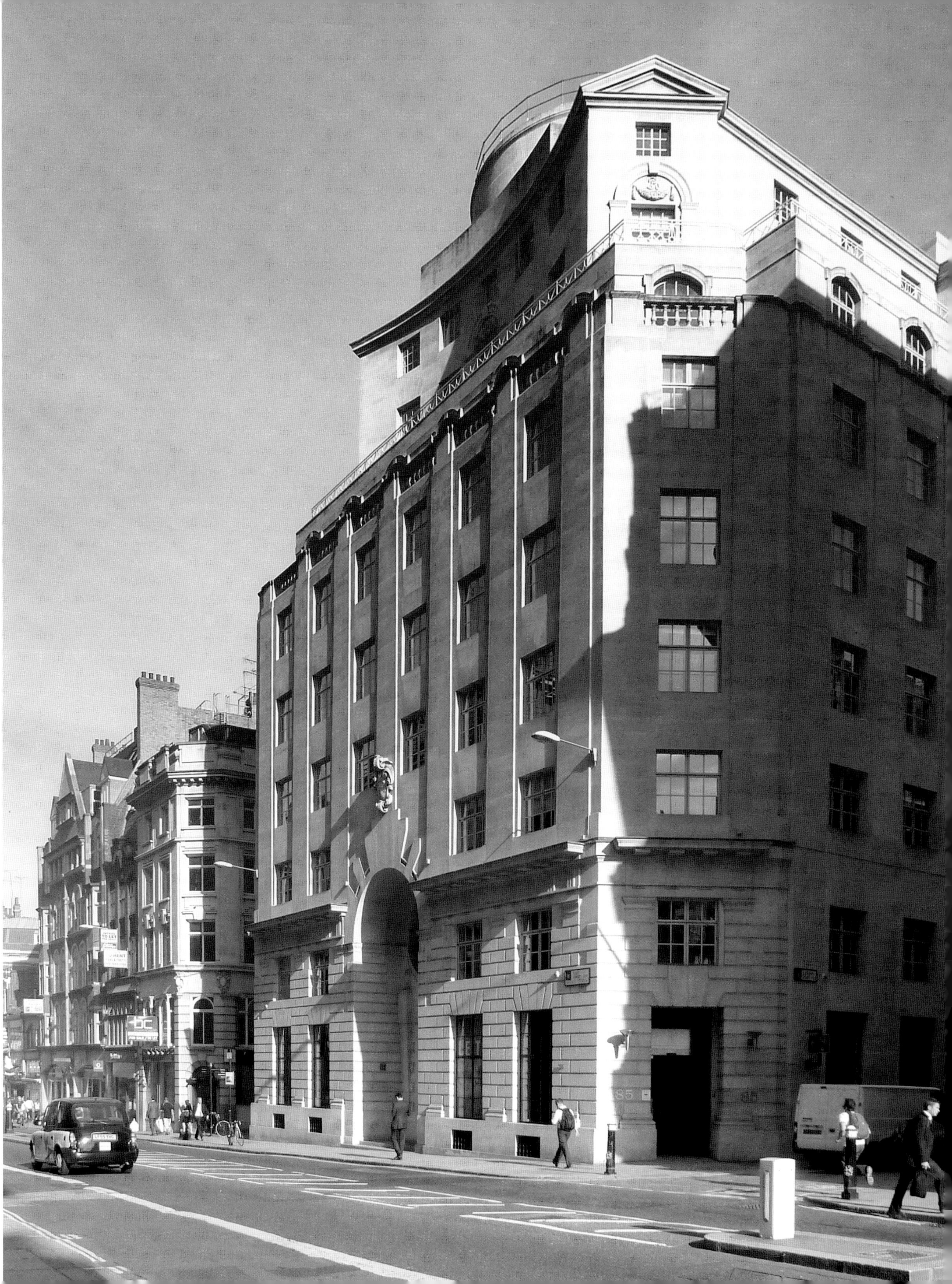

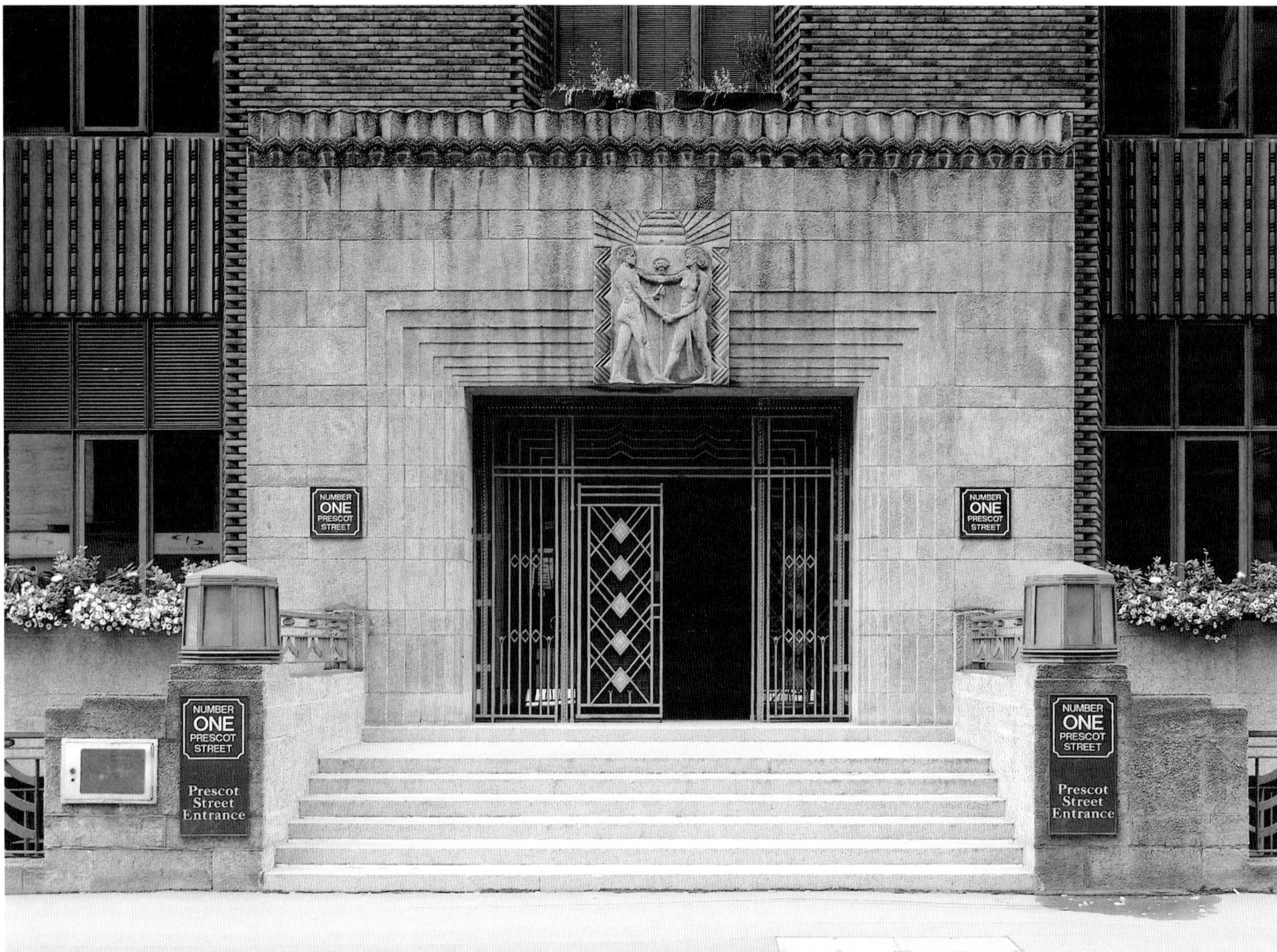
NUMBER
ONE
PRESCOT
STREET
NUMBER
ONE
PRESCOT
STREET
NUMBER
ONE
PRESCOT
STREET
Prescot
Street
Entrance
NUMBER
ONE
PRESCOT
STREET
Prescot
Street
Entrance

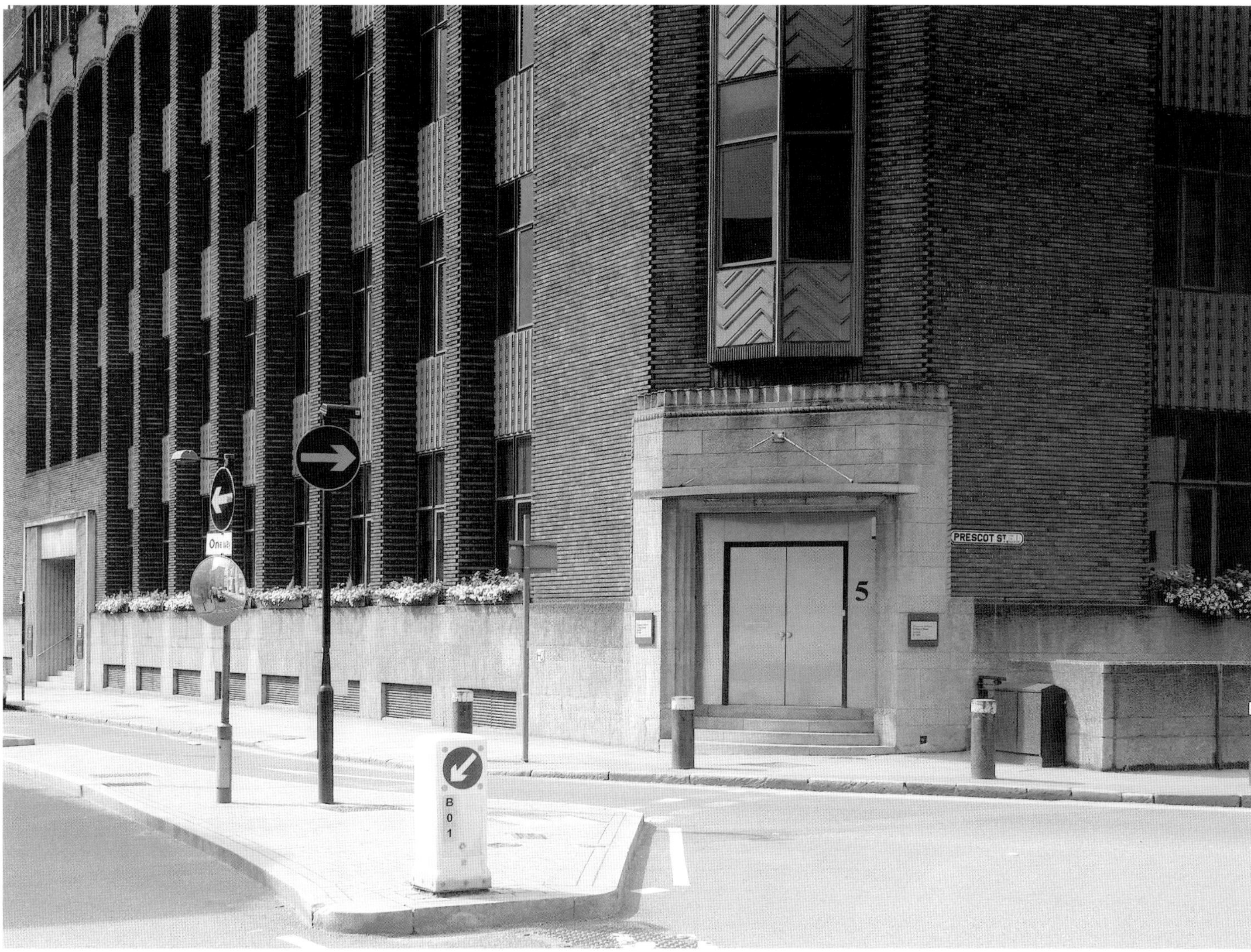
PRESCOT ST
5
B 0 1

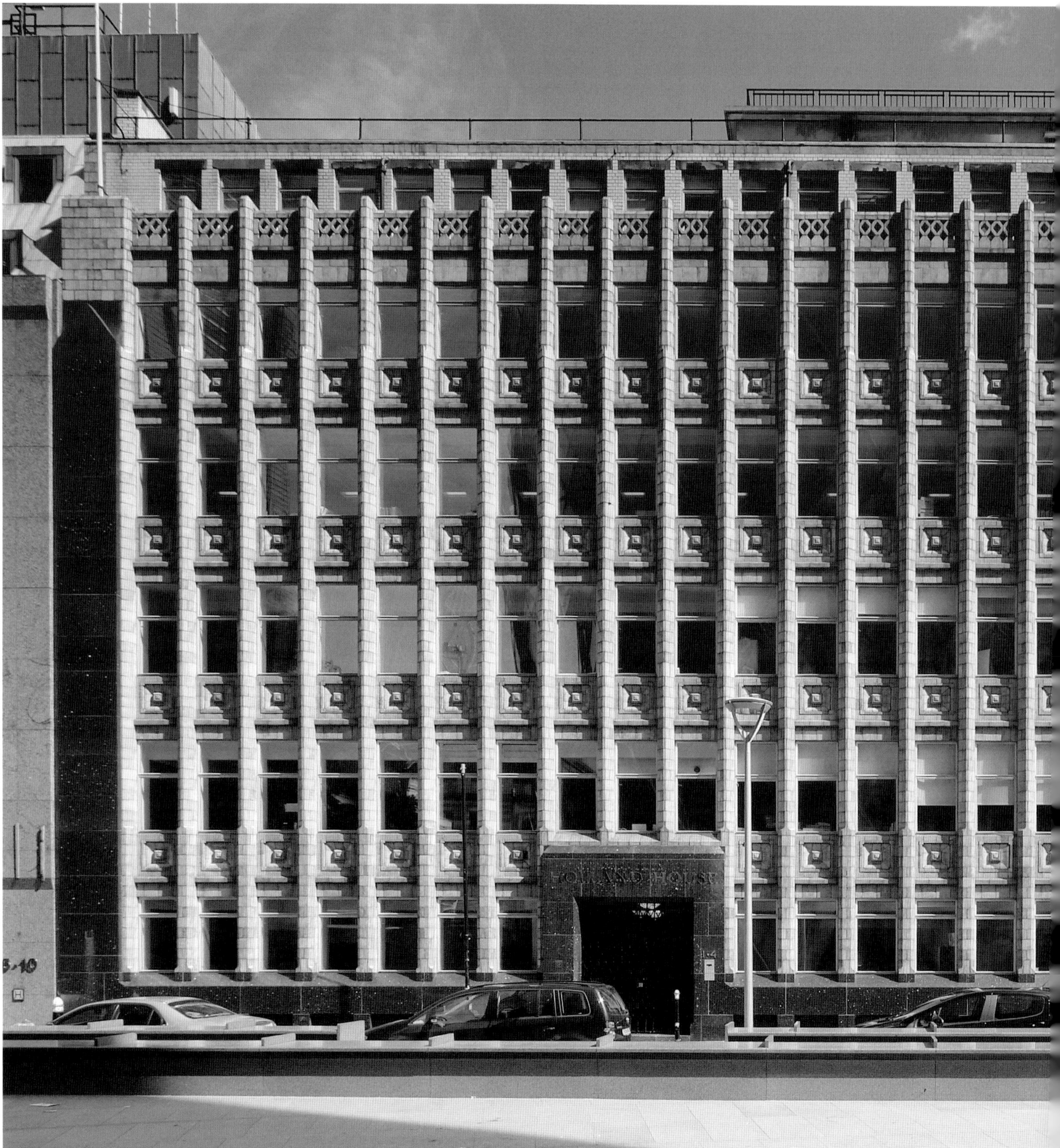

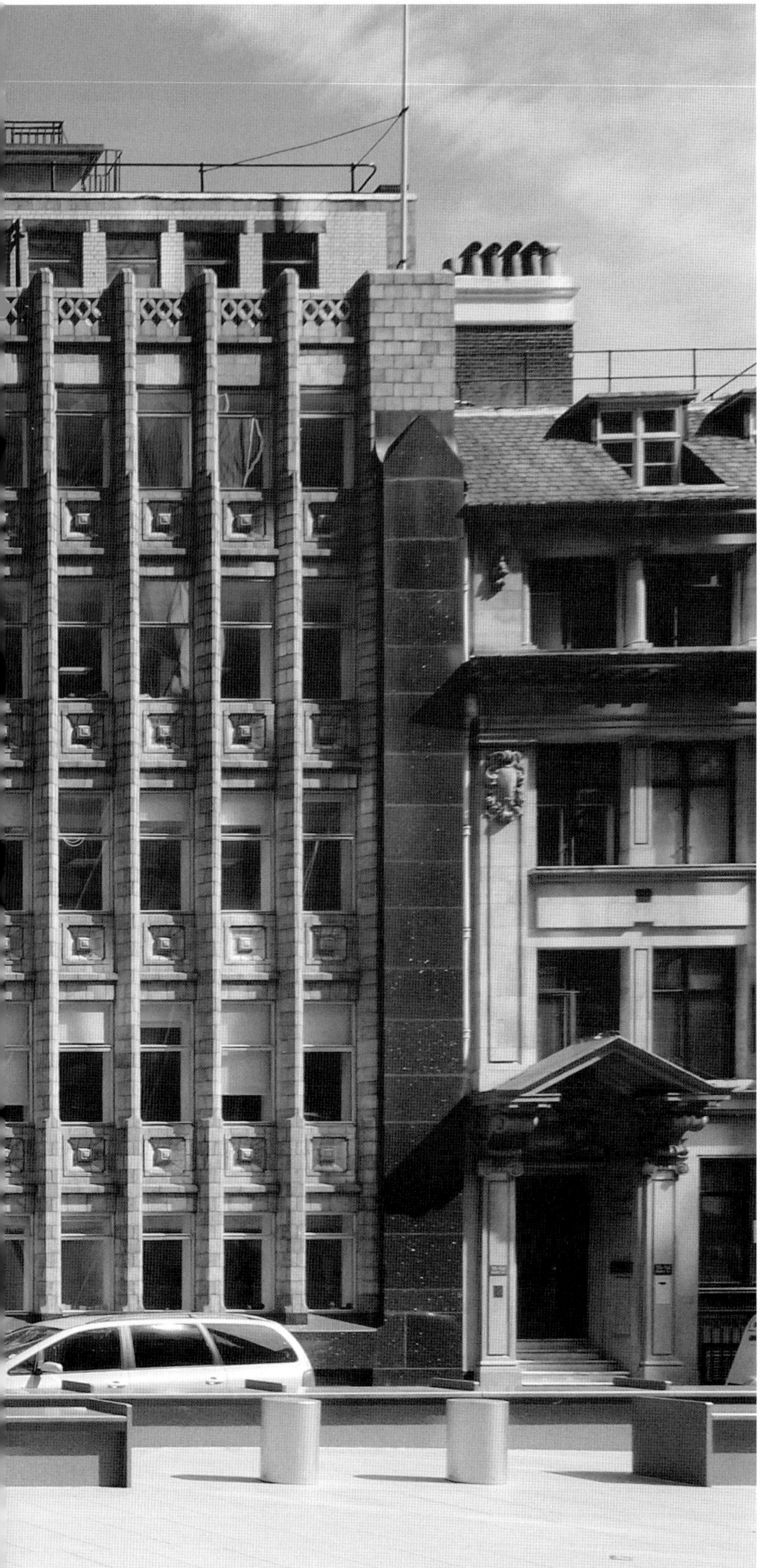

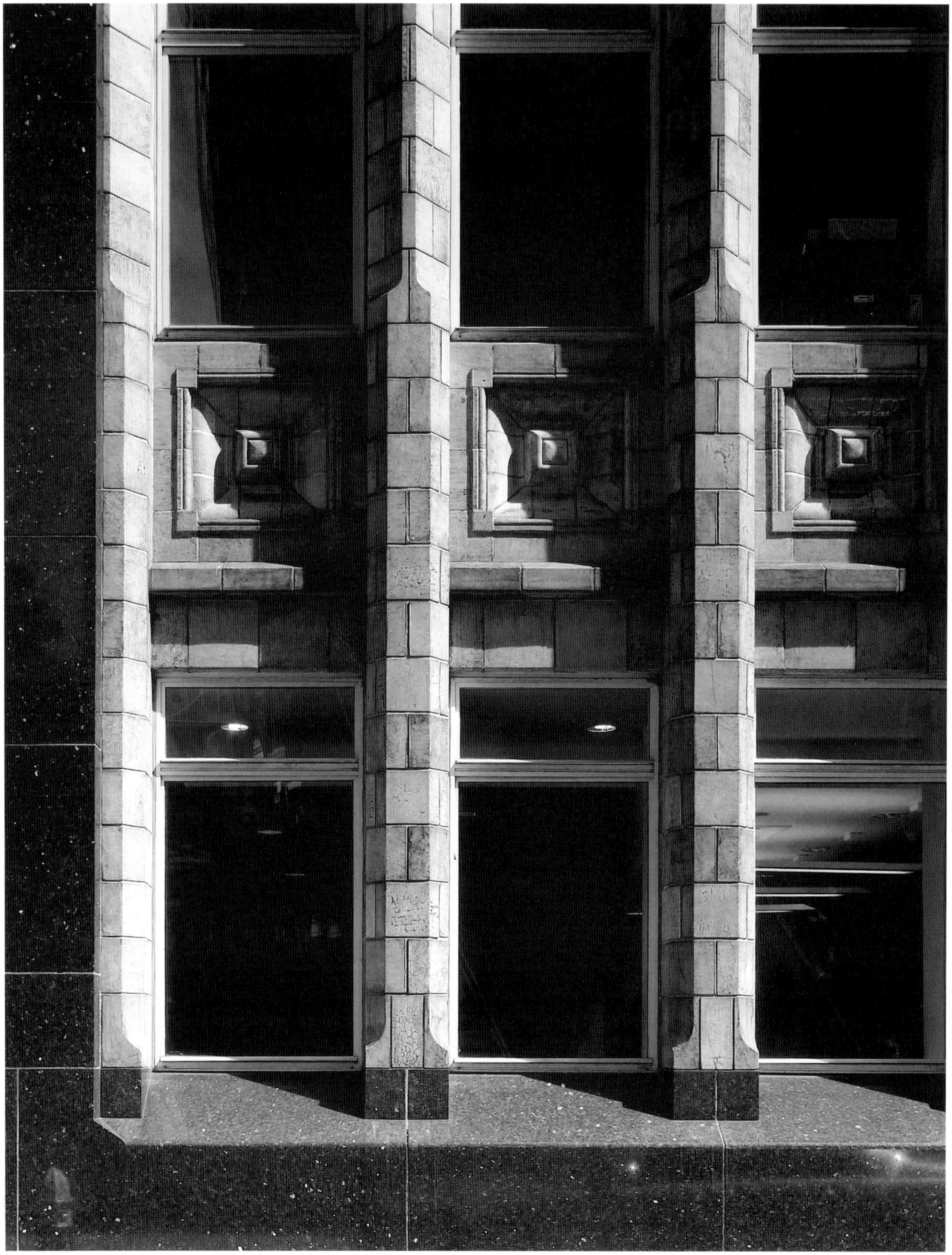

93

93

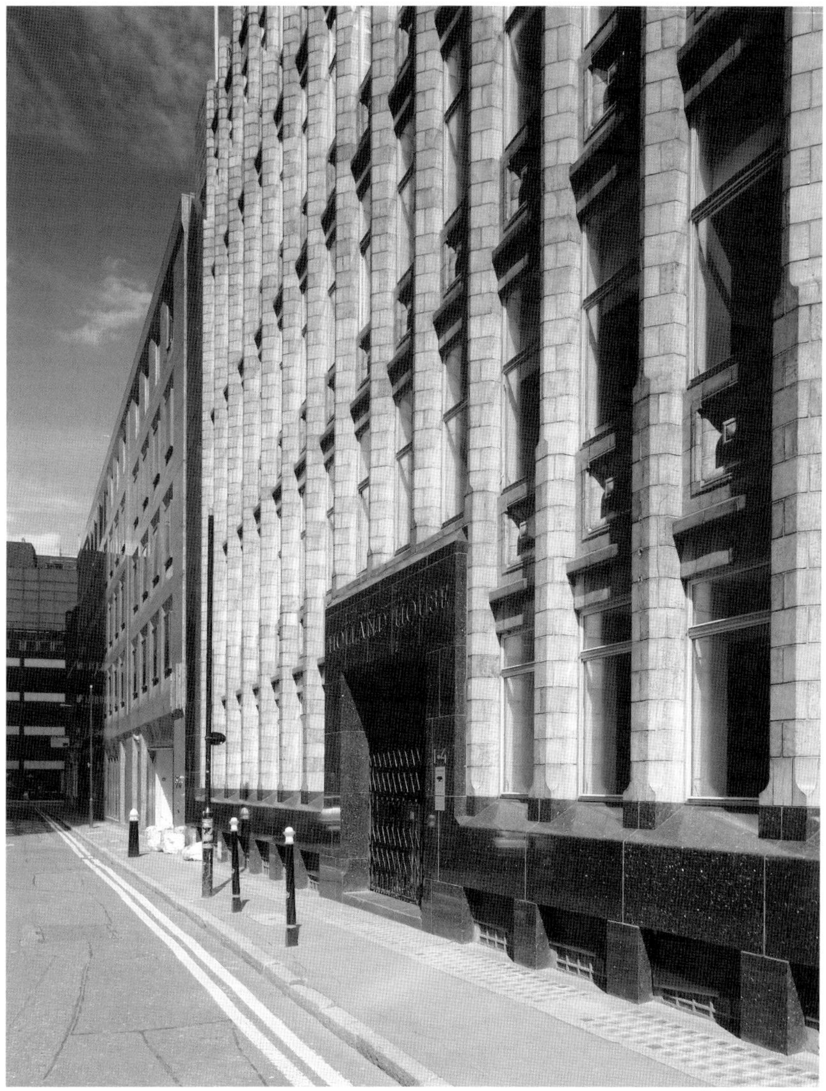

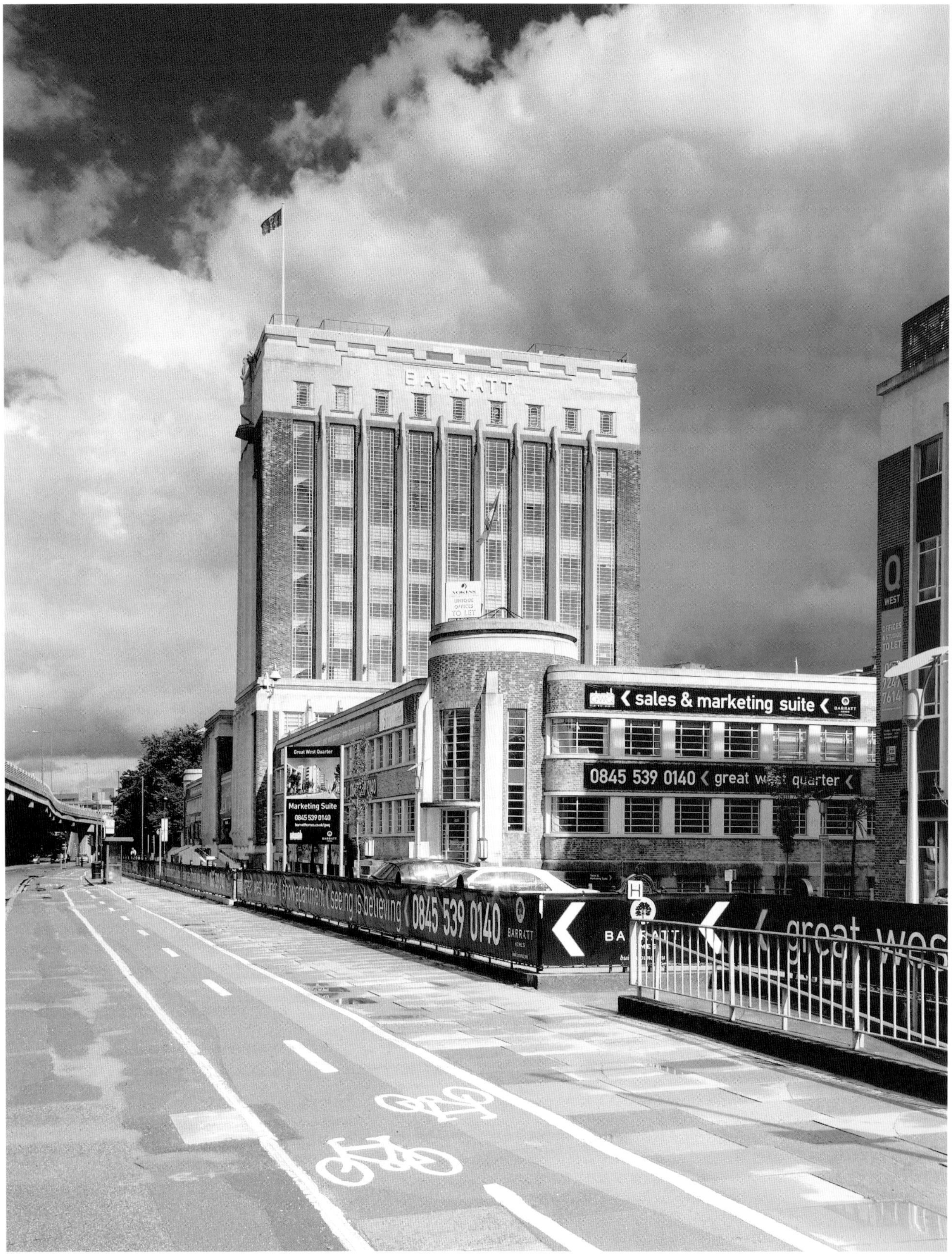
BARRATT
UNIQUE OFFICES TO LET
< sales & marketing suite <
0845 539 0140 < great west quarter <
Great West Quarter
Marketing Suite
0845 539 0140
seeing is believing < 0845 539 0140
Q WEST

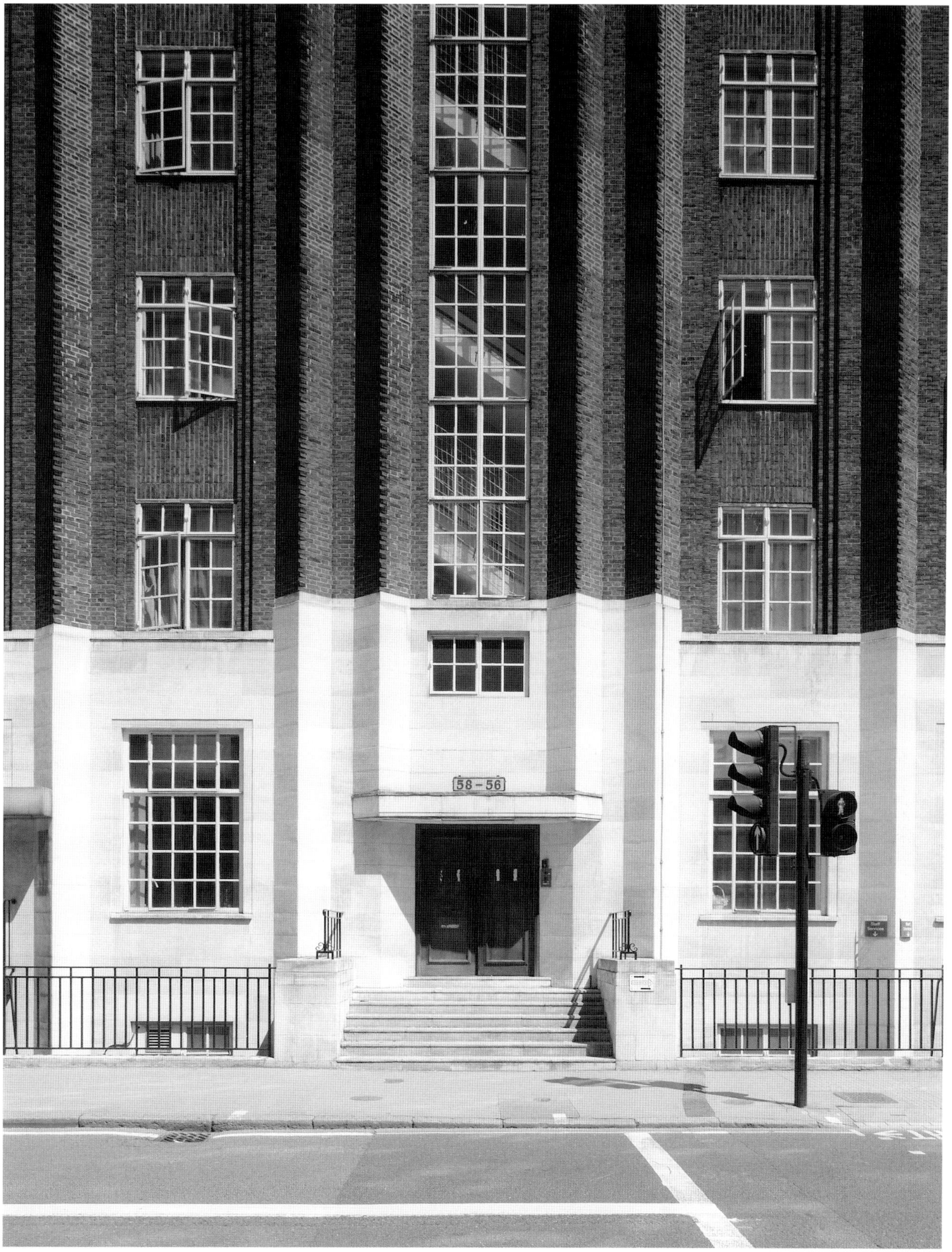
58–56

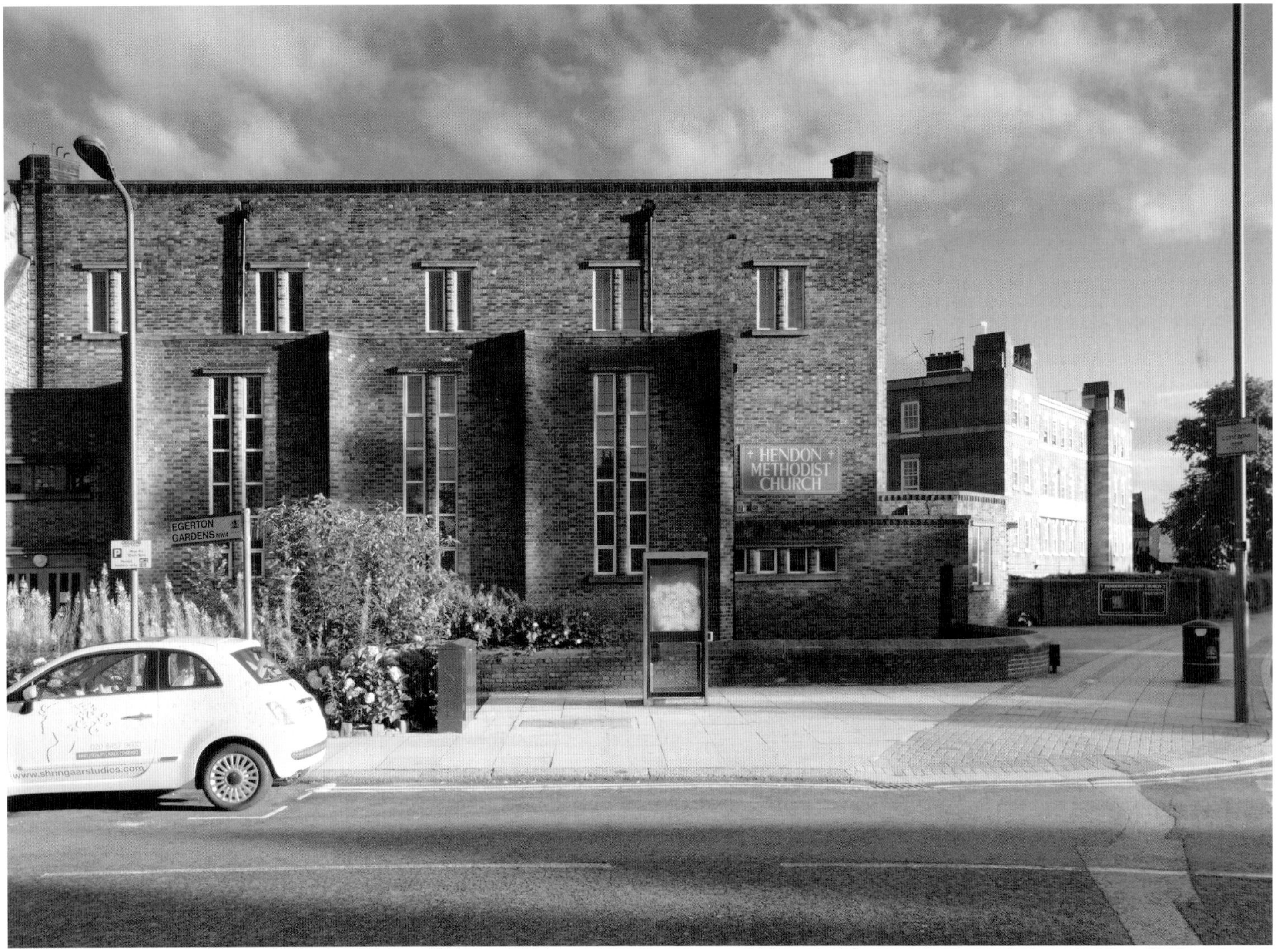
HENDON METHODIST CHURCH
EGERTON GARDENS NW4
www.shringaarstudios.com

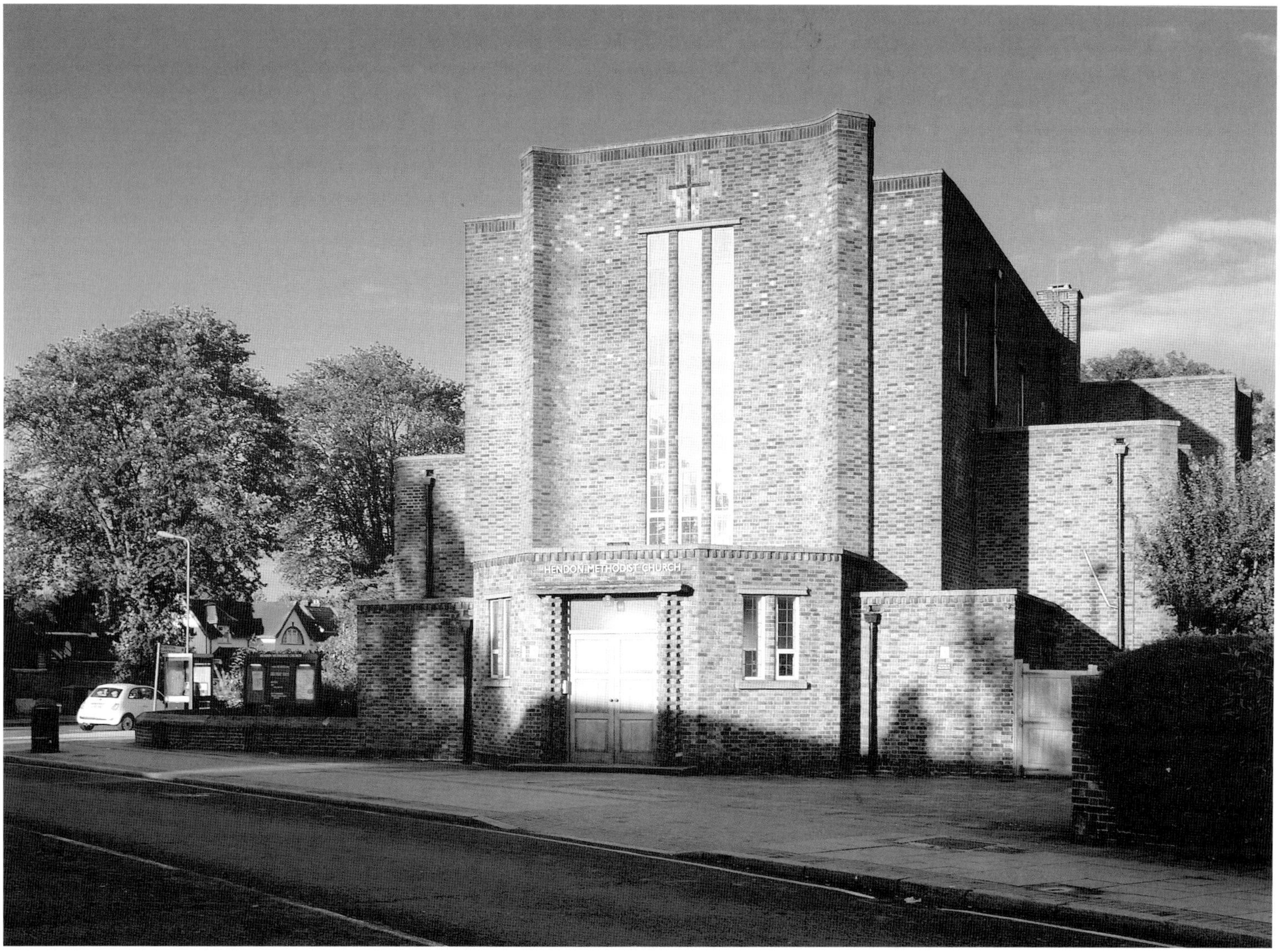
HENDON METHODIST CHURCH

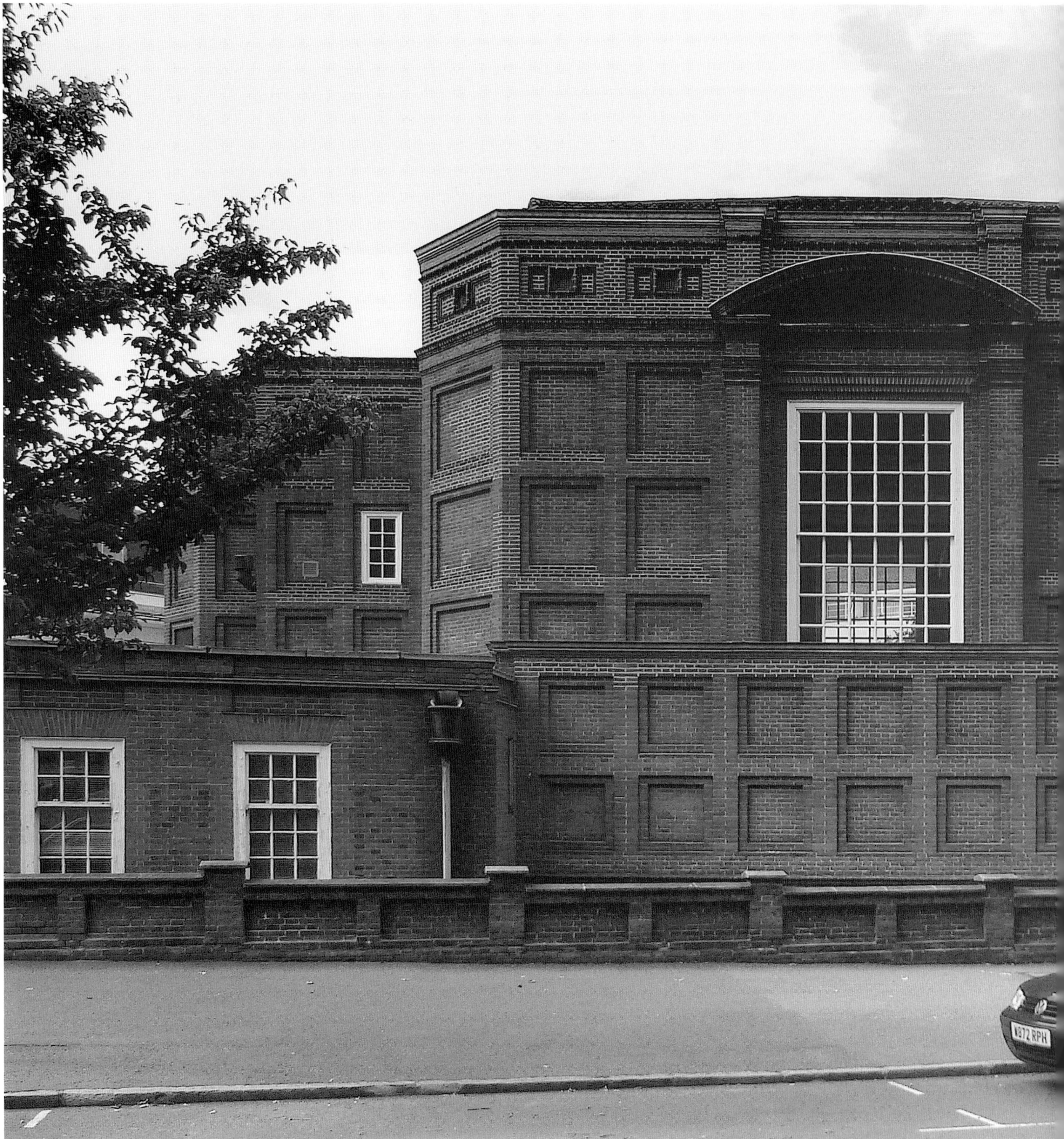

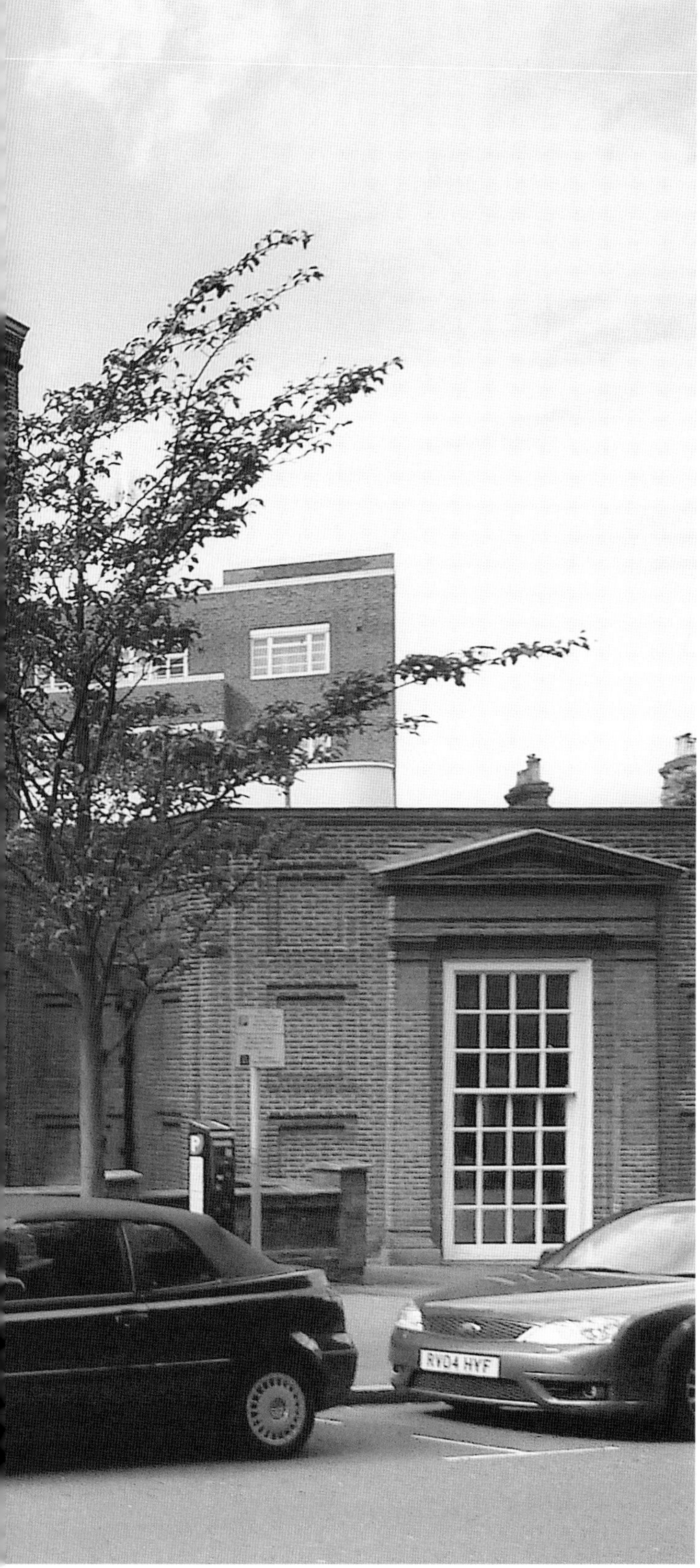

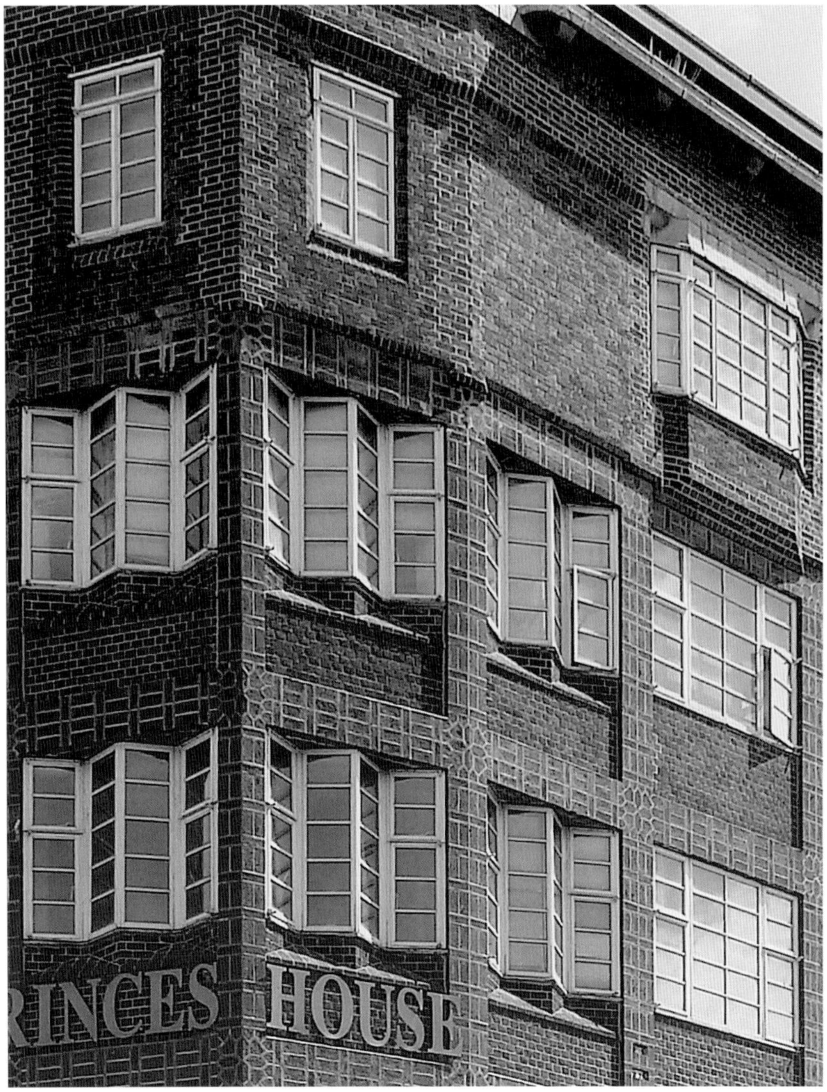
RINCES HOUSE

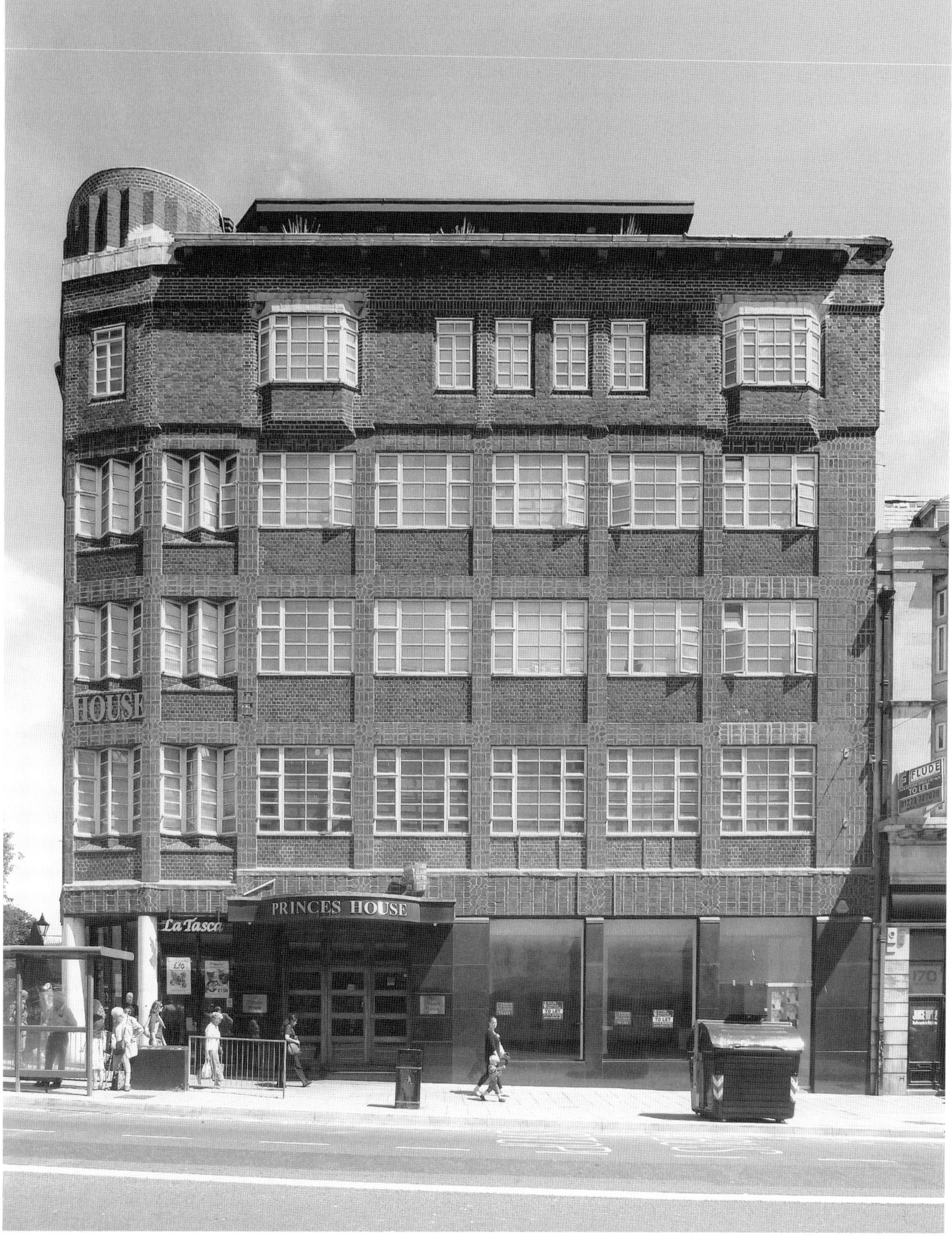
HOUSE
PRINCES HOUSE
La Tasca
FLUDE
TO LET

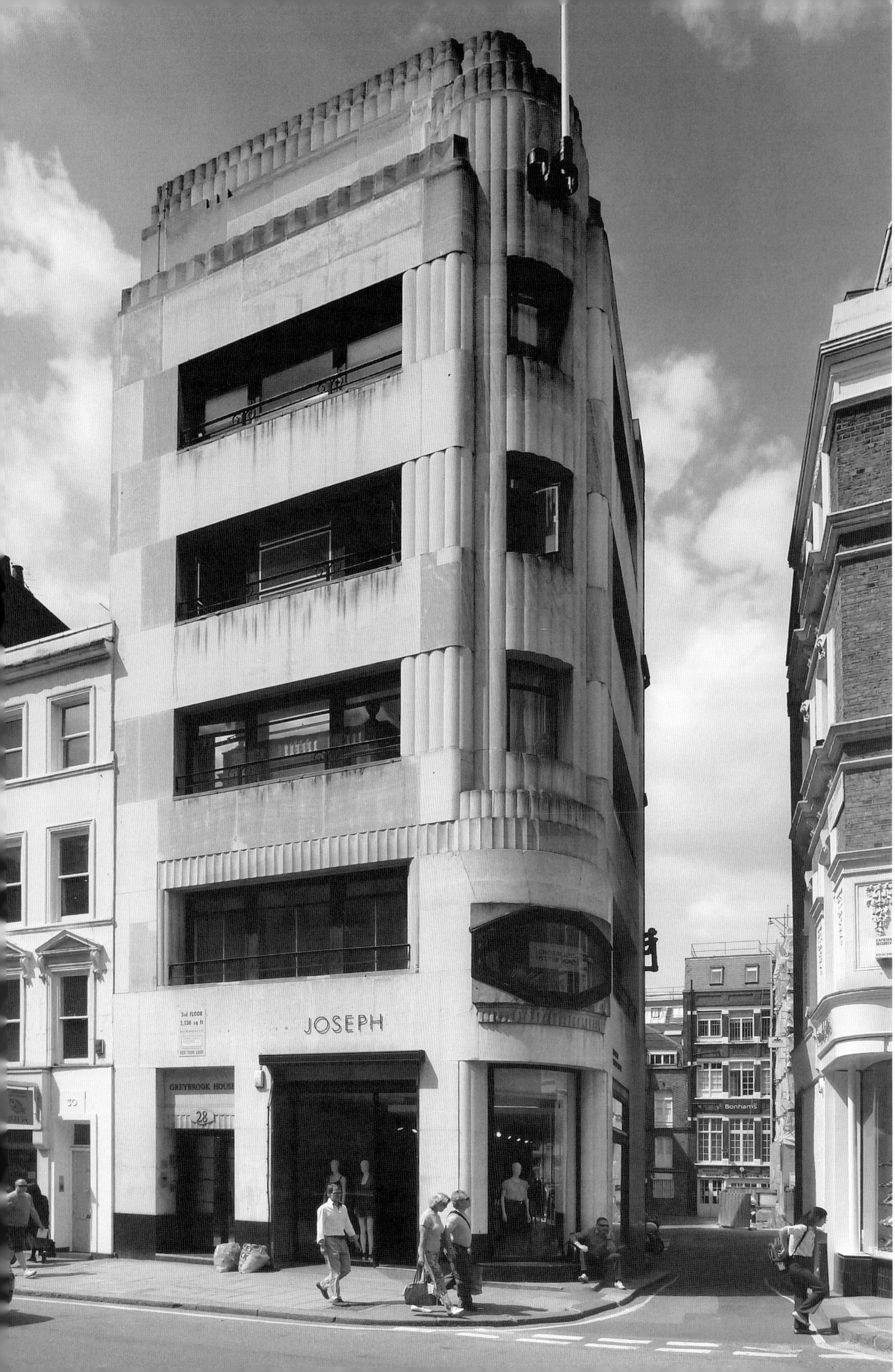
JOSEPH
GREYBROOK HOUSE
28
Bonhams

09

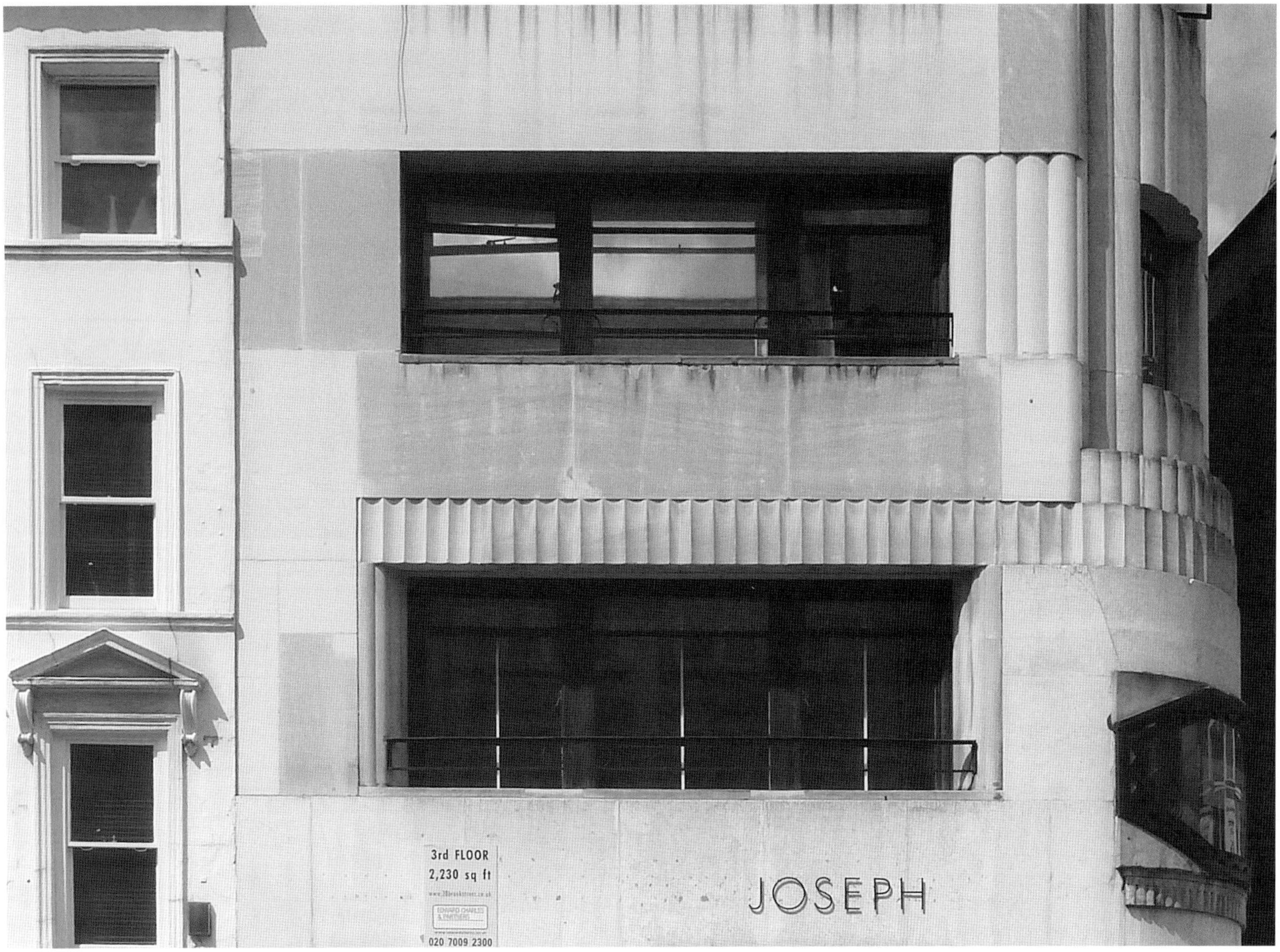

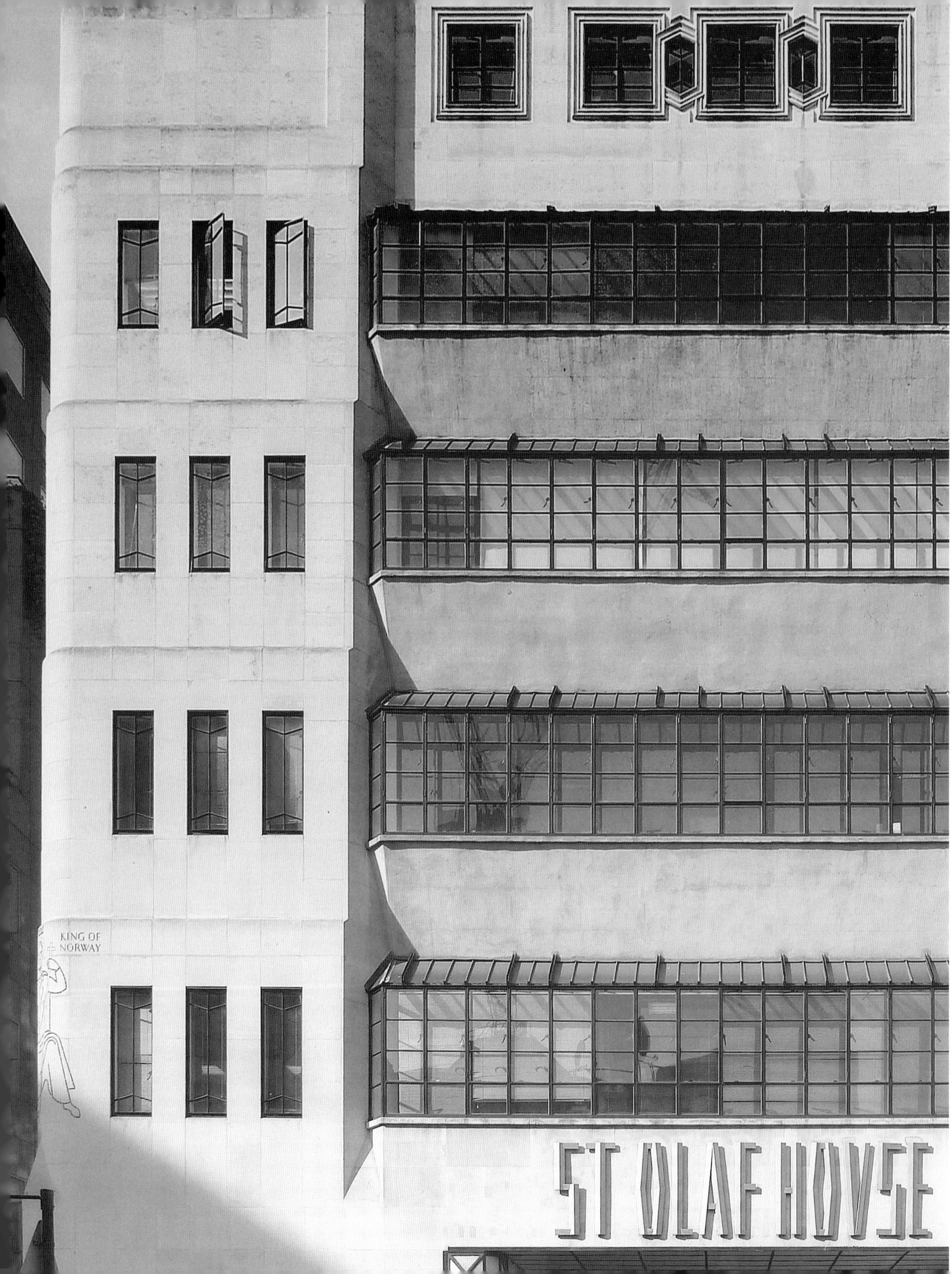

11

113

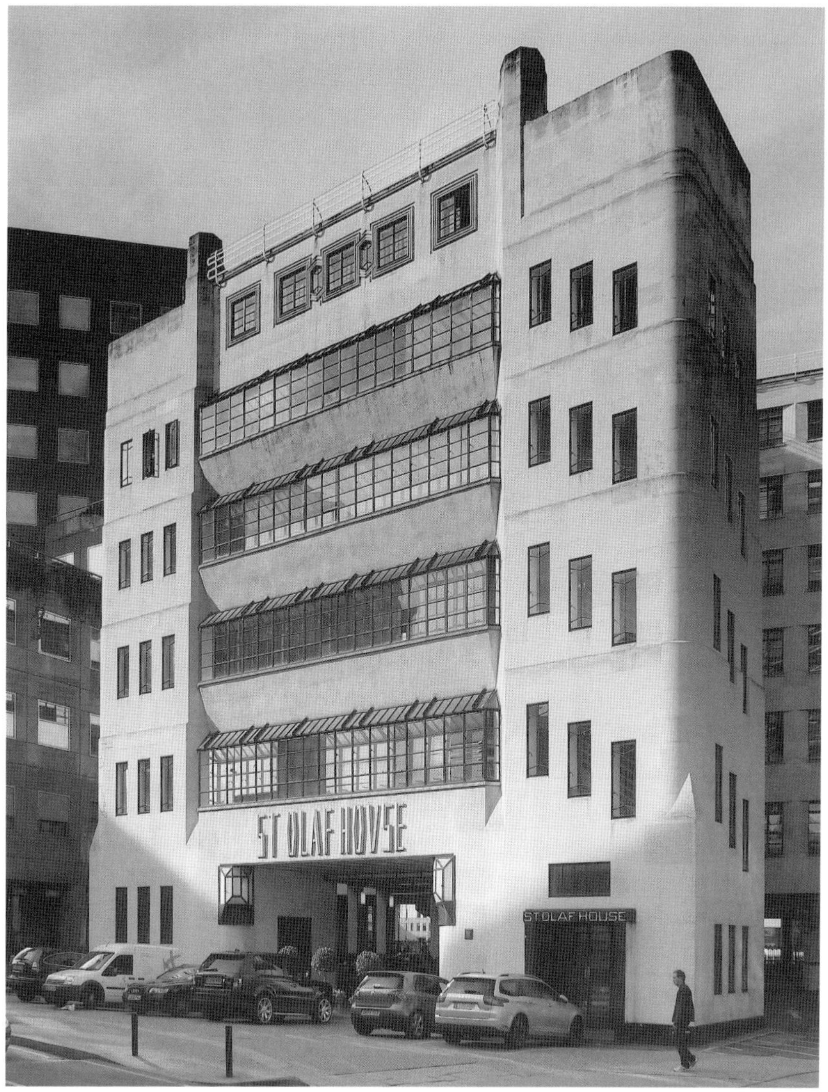

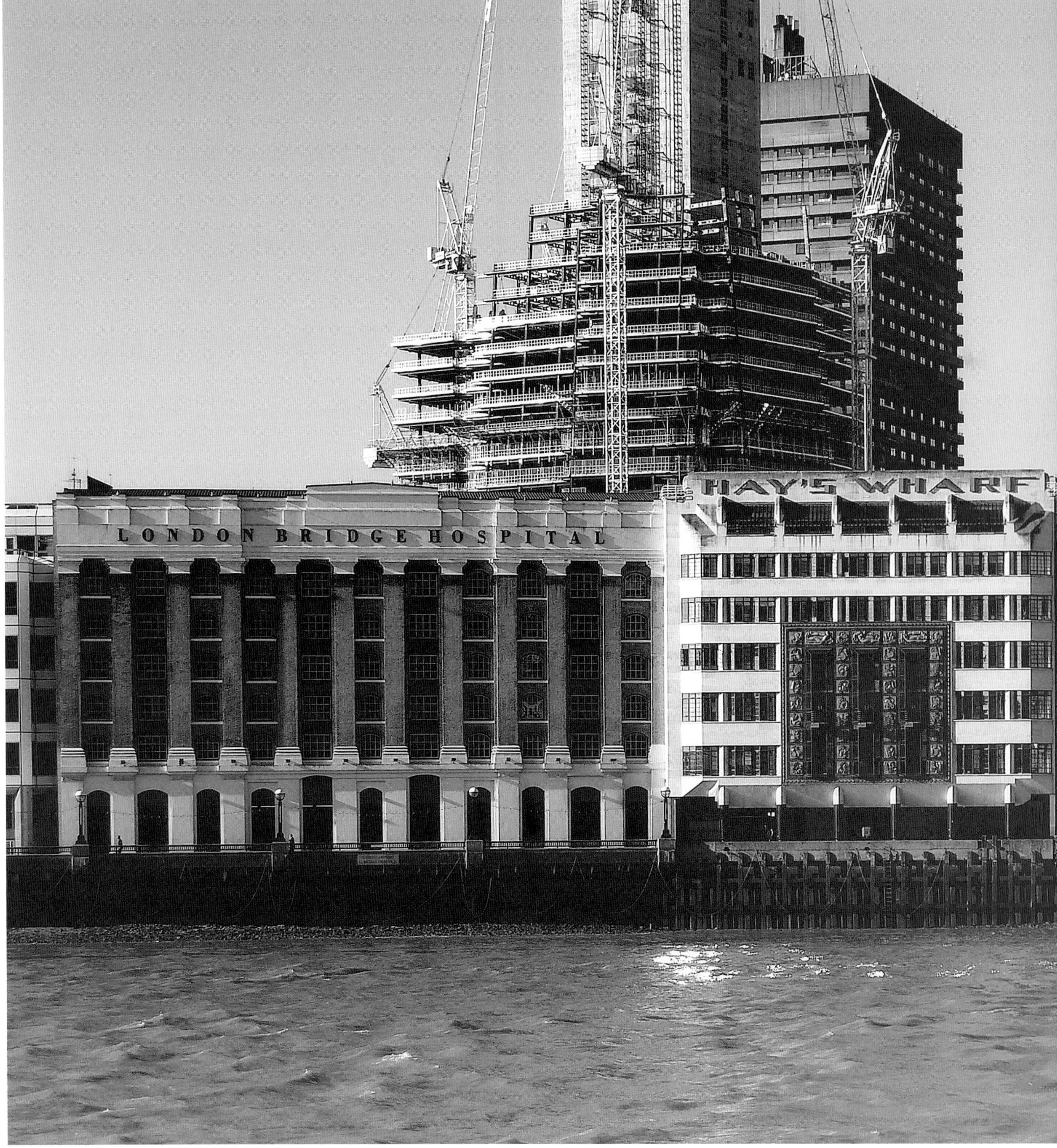
LONDON BRIDGE HOSPITAL
HAY'S WHARF

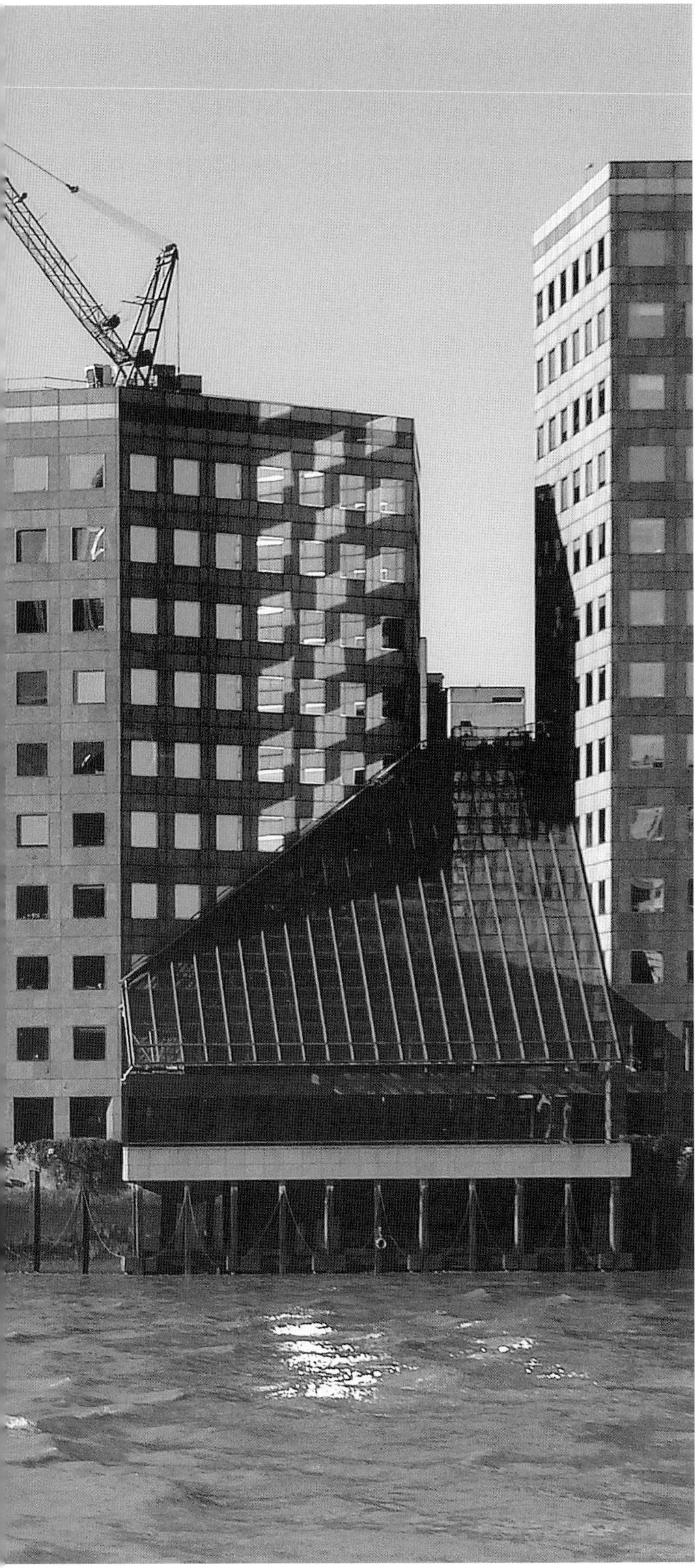

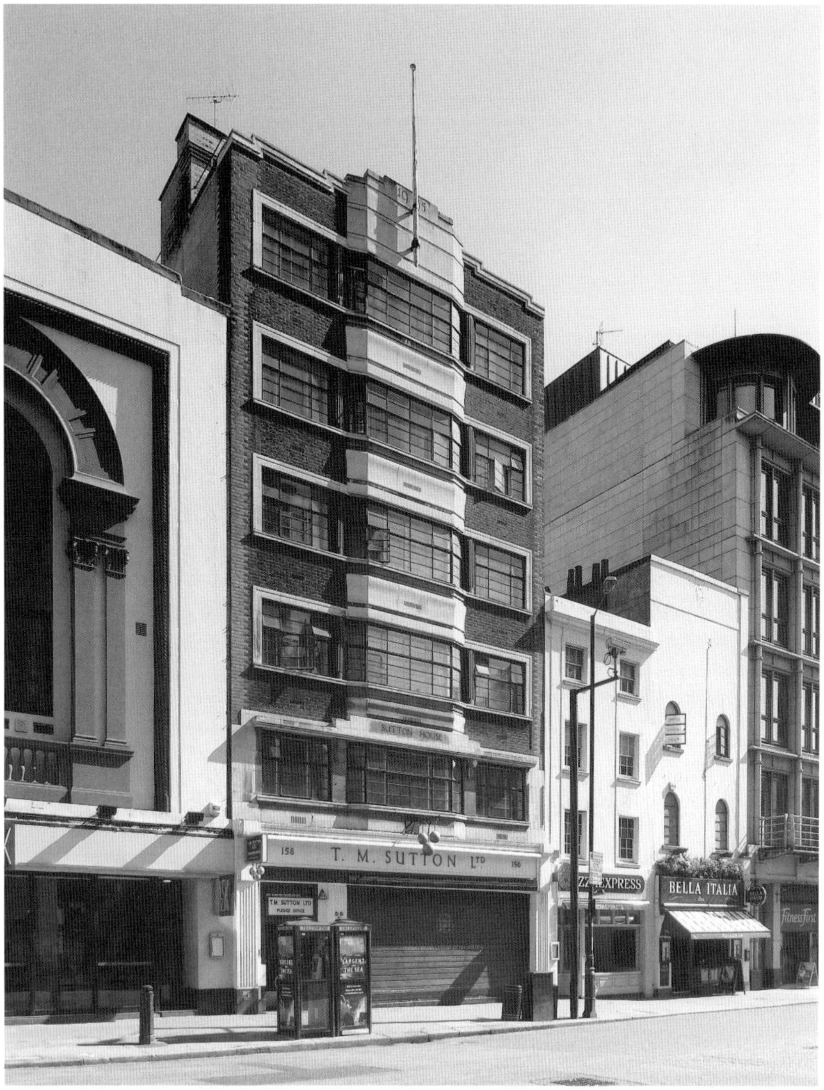
T. M. SUTTON Ltd
158
156
BELLA ITALIA

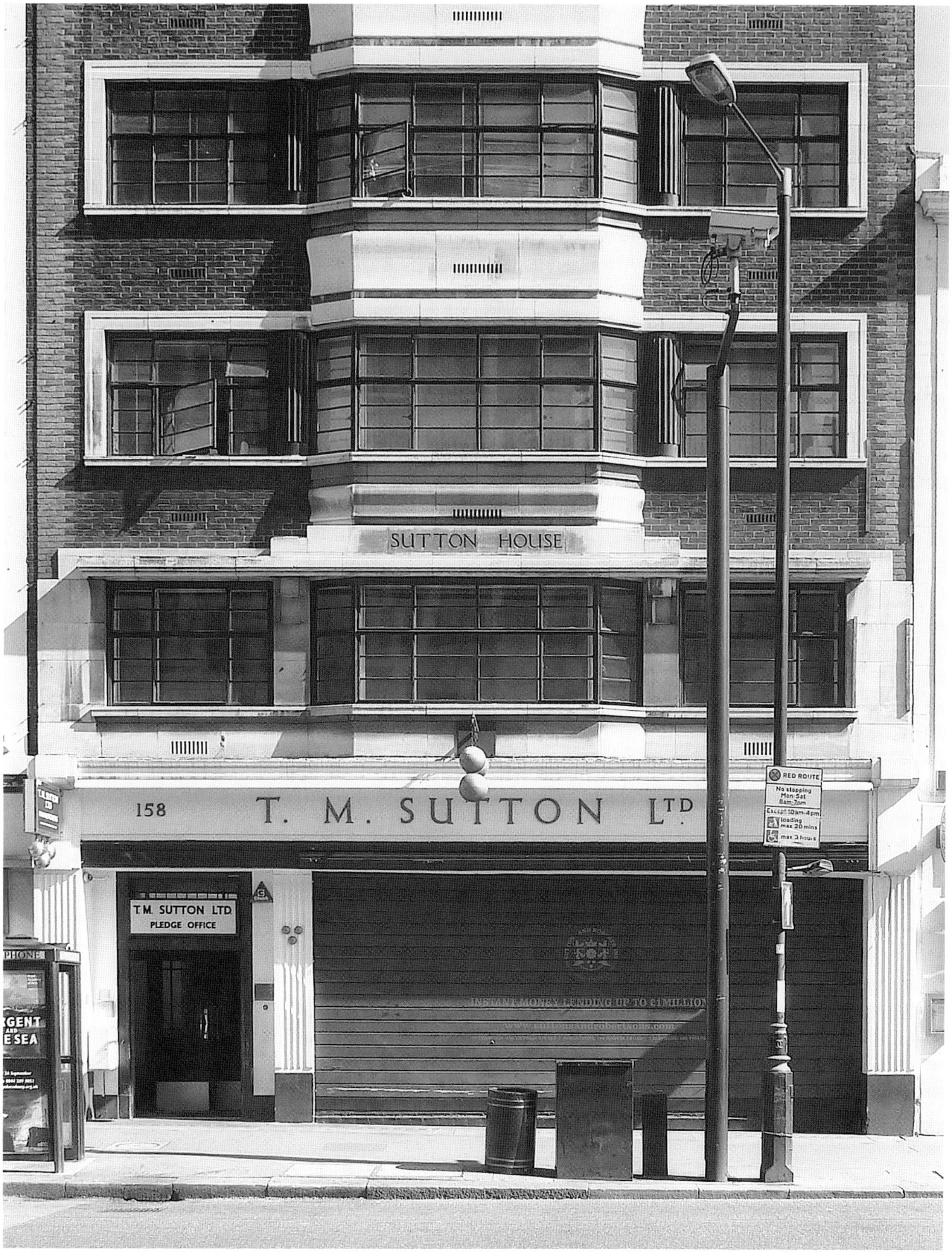
SUTTON HOUSE
158
T. M. SUTTON L^TD
T.M. SUTTON LTD.
PLEDGE OFFICE
RED ROUTE
No stopping
Mon-Sat
INSTANT MONEY LENDING UP TO £1MILLION

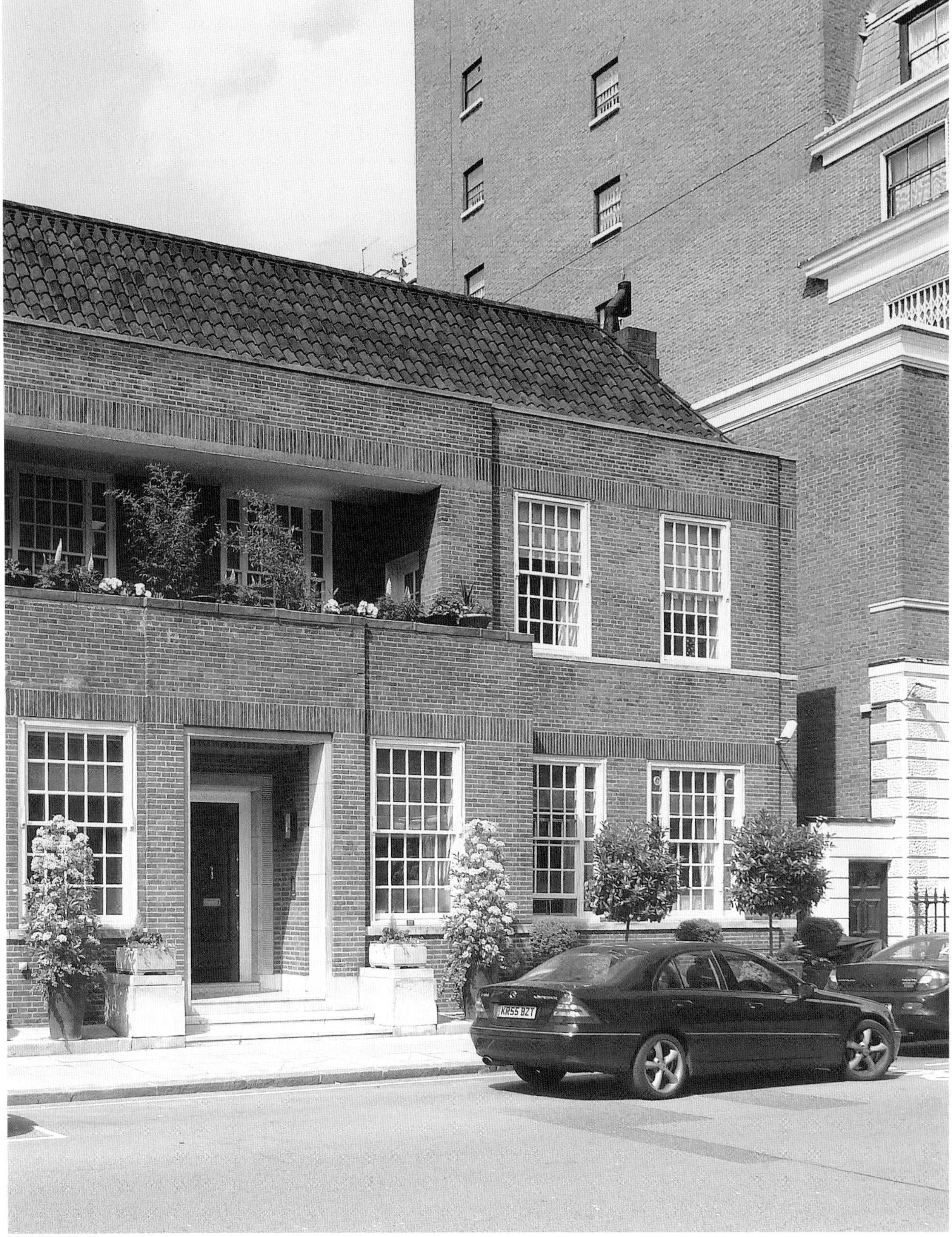
KR55 BZT

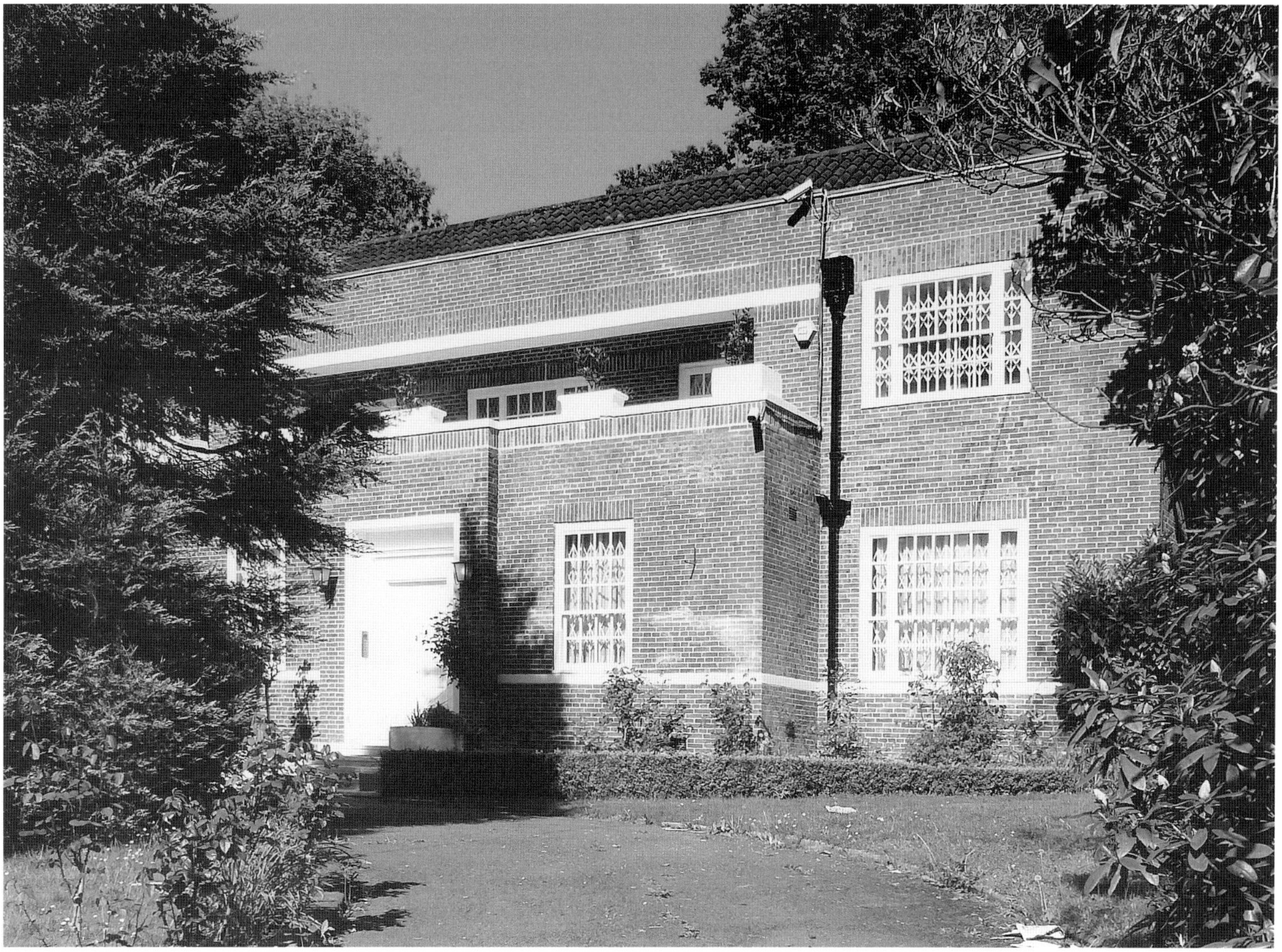

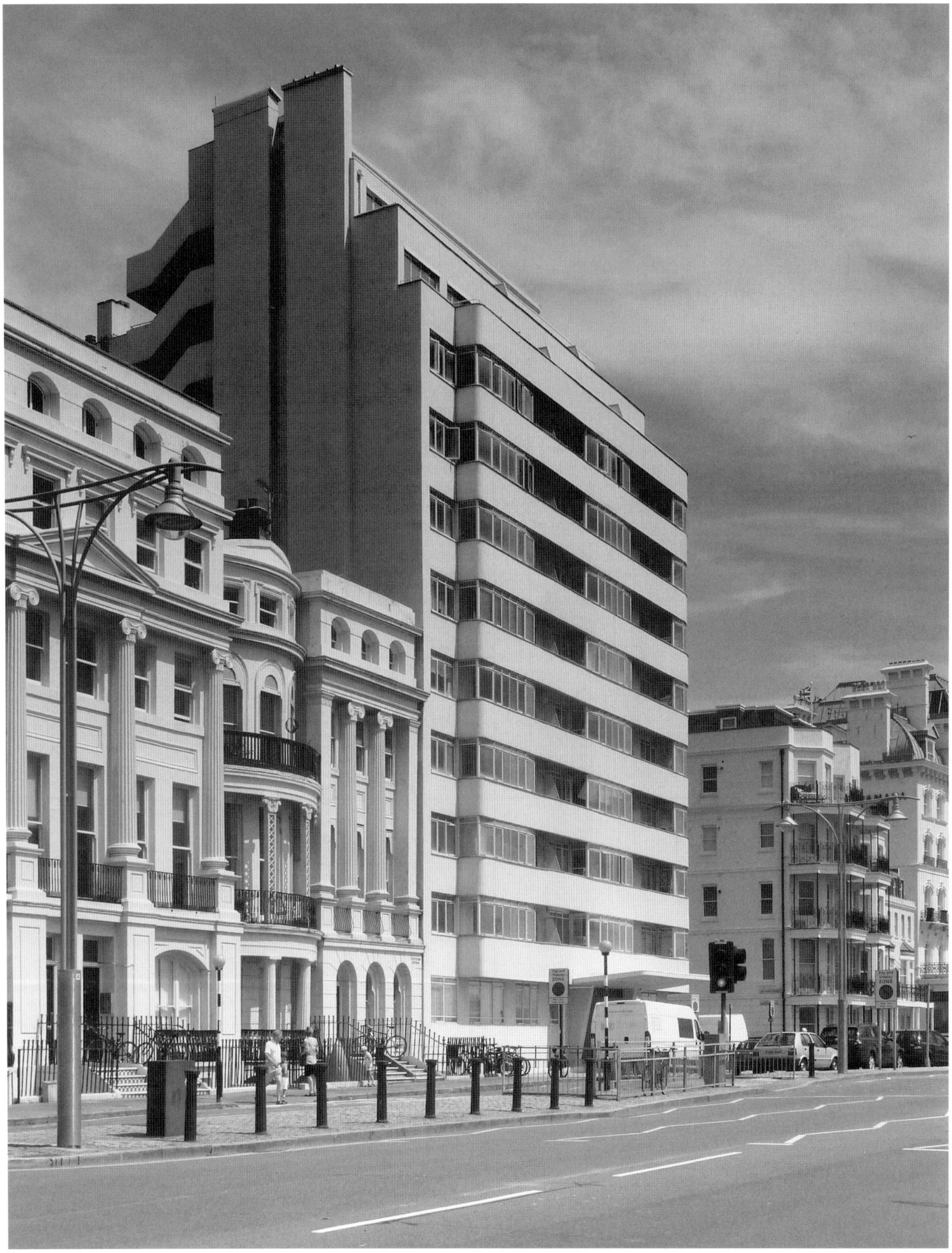

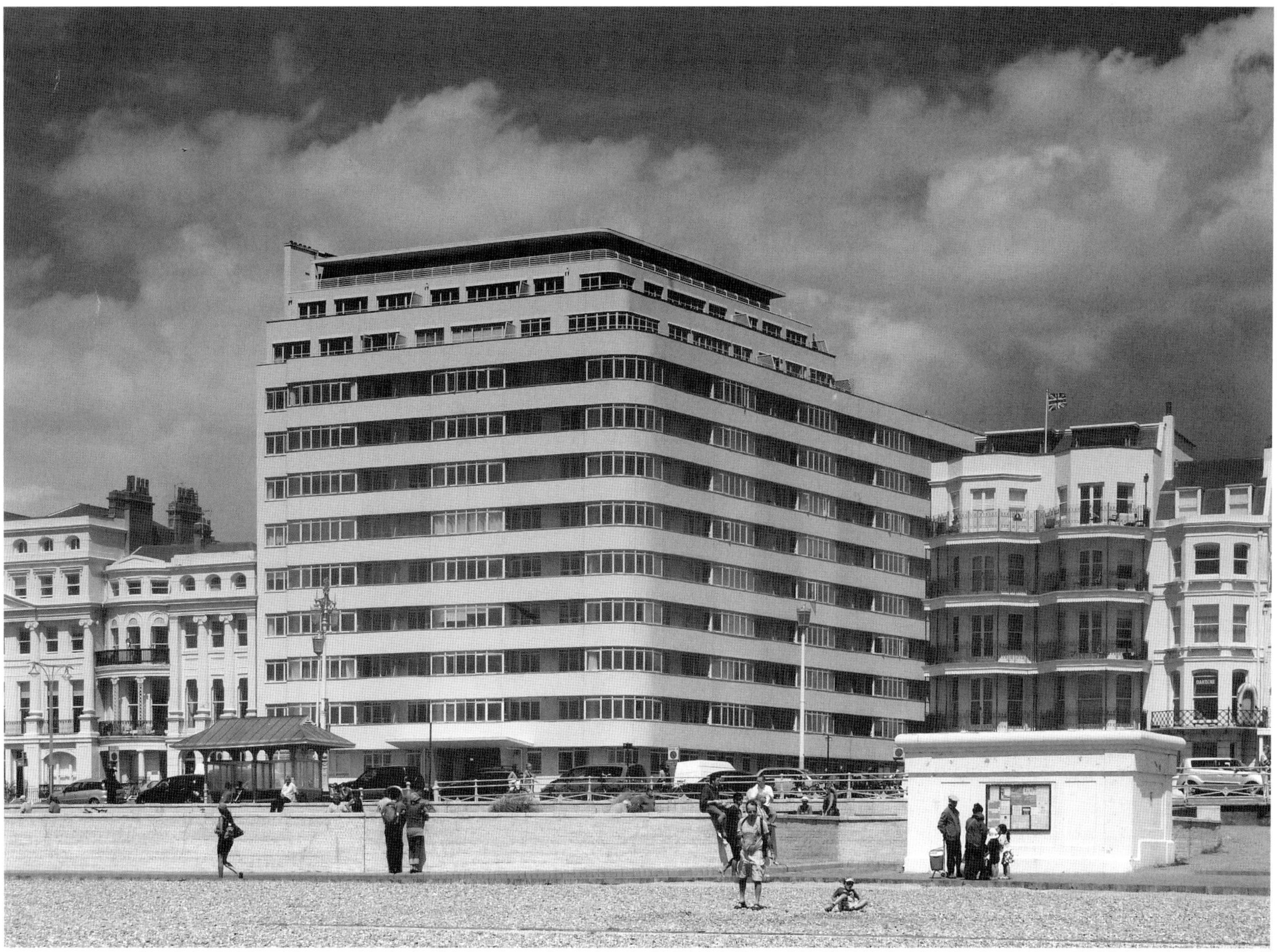

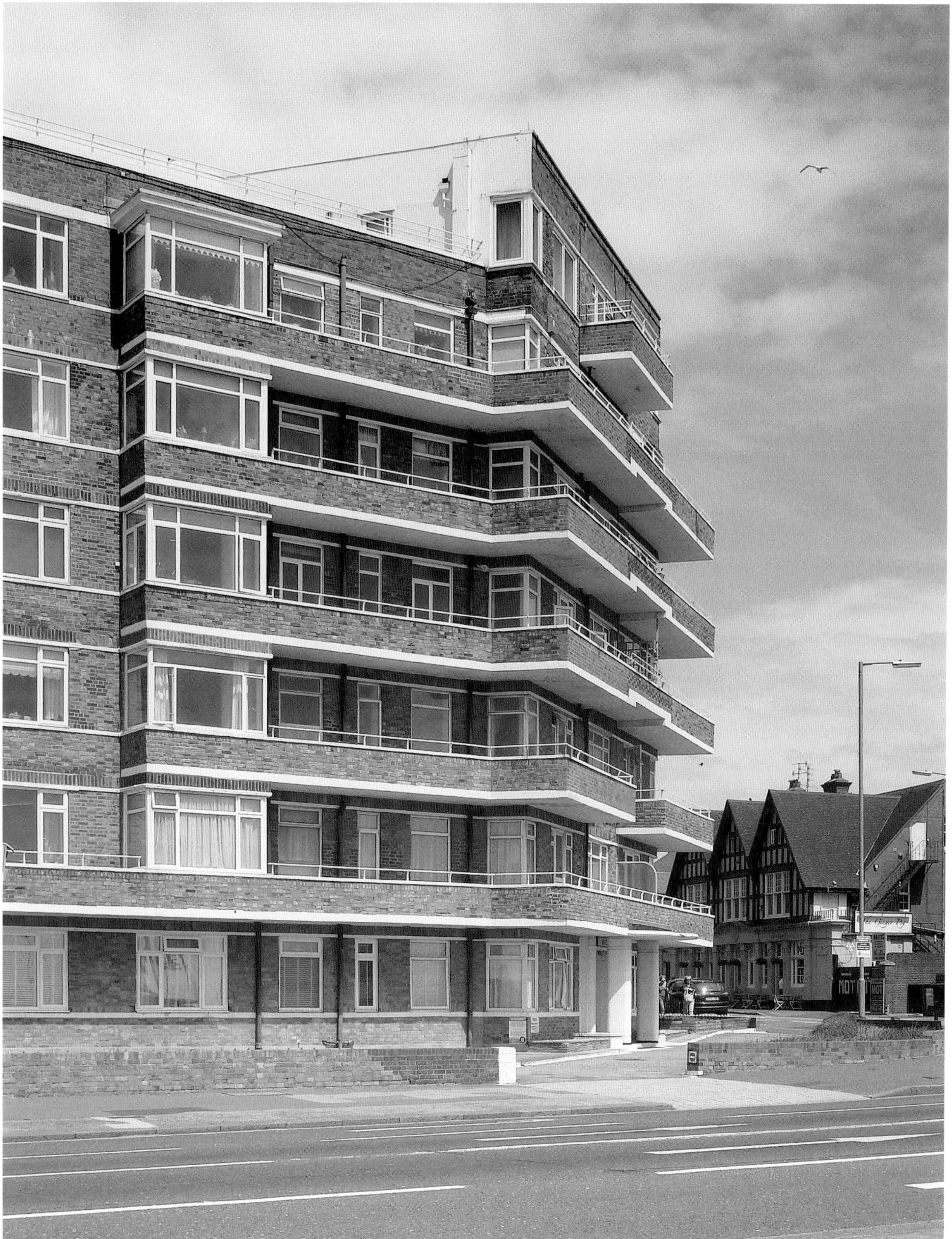

3

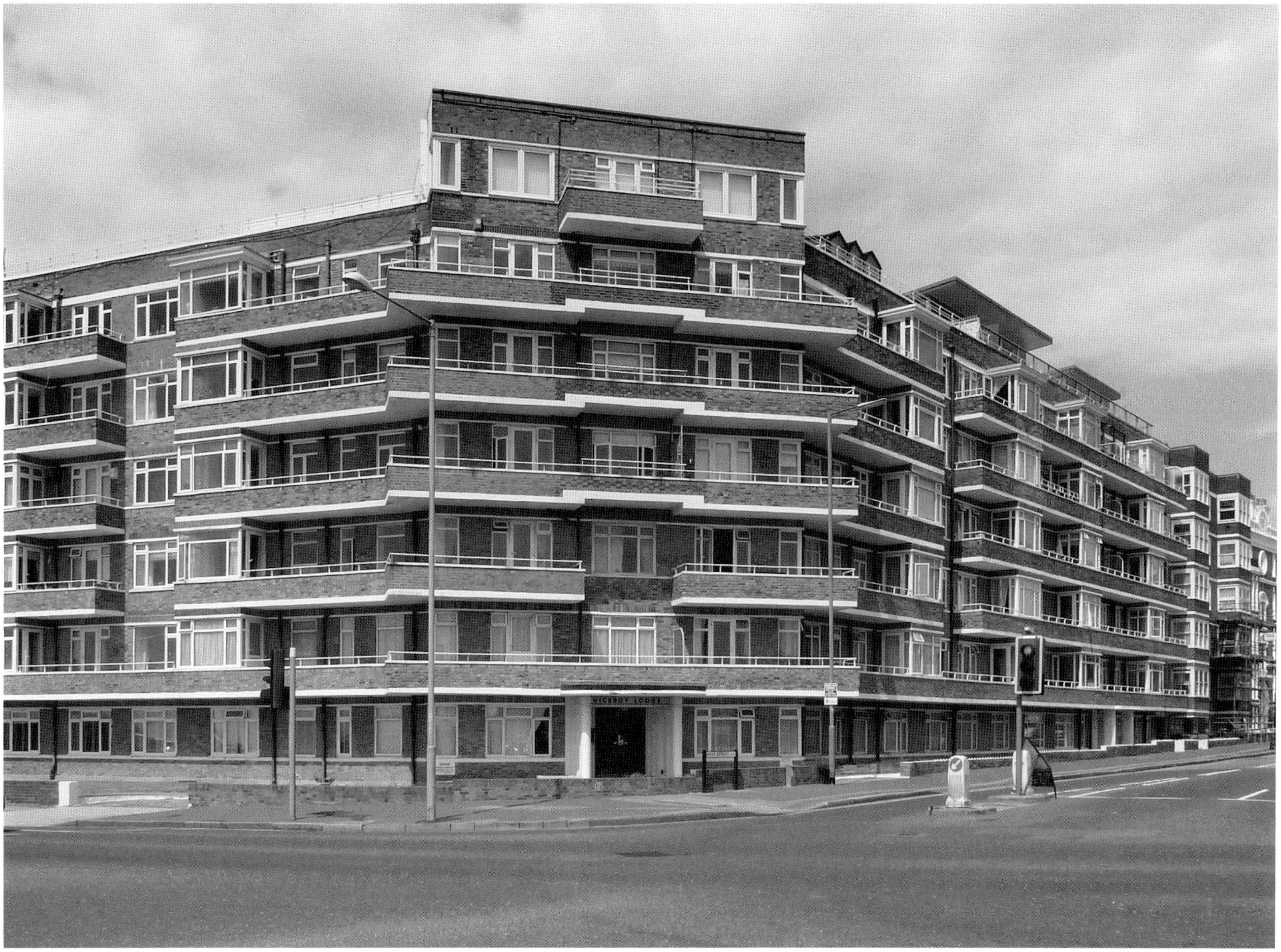

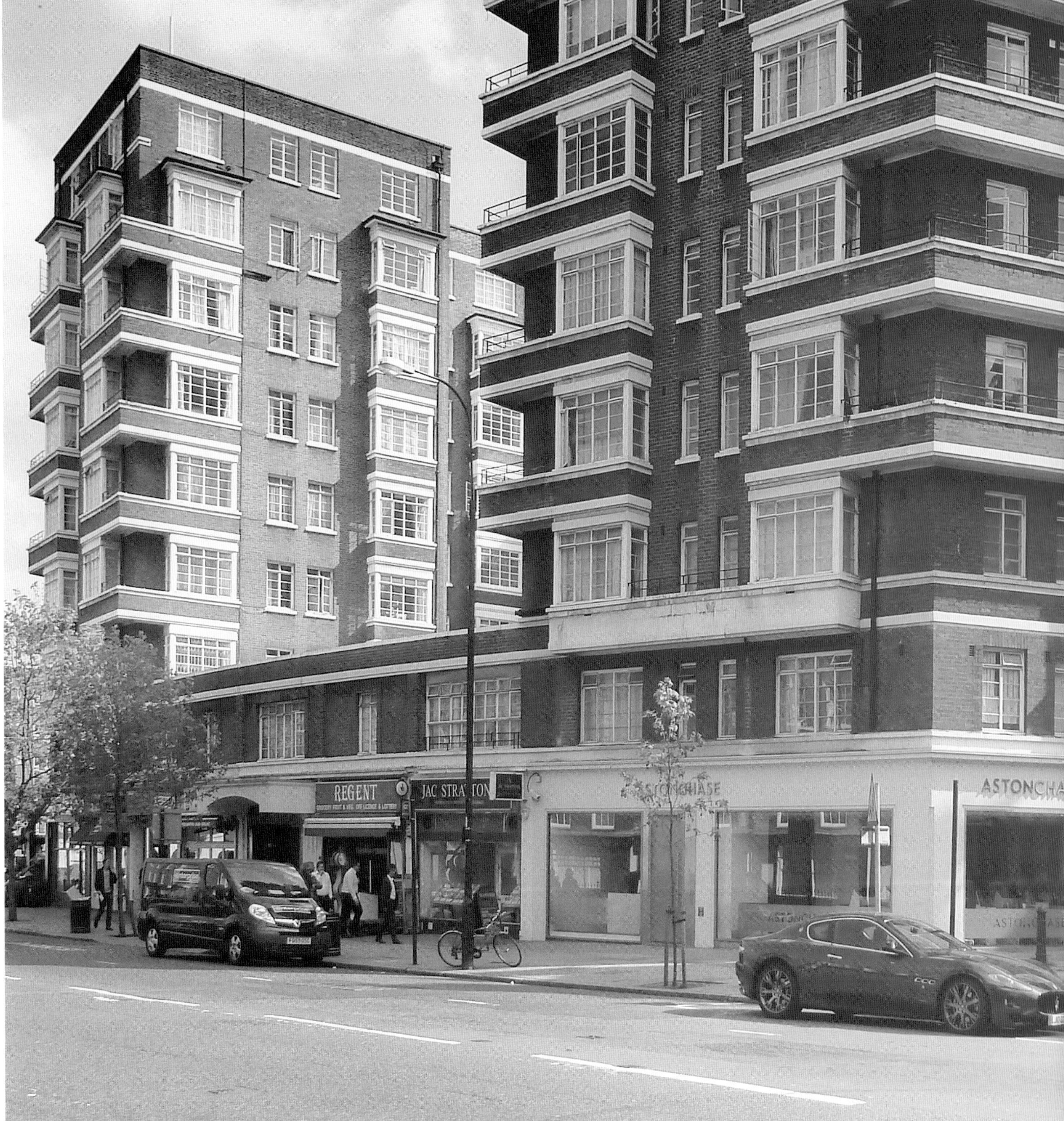
REGENT
ASTONCHASE

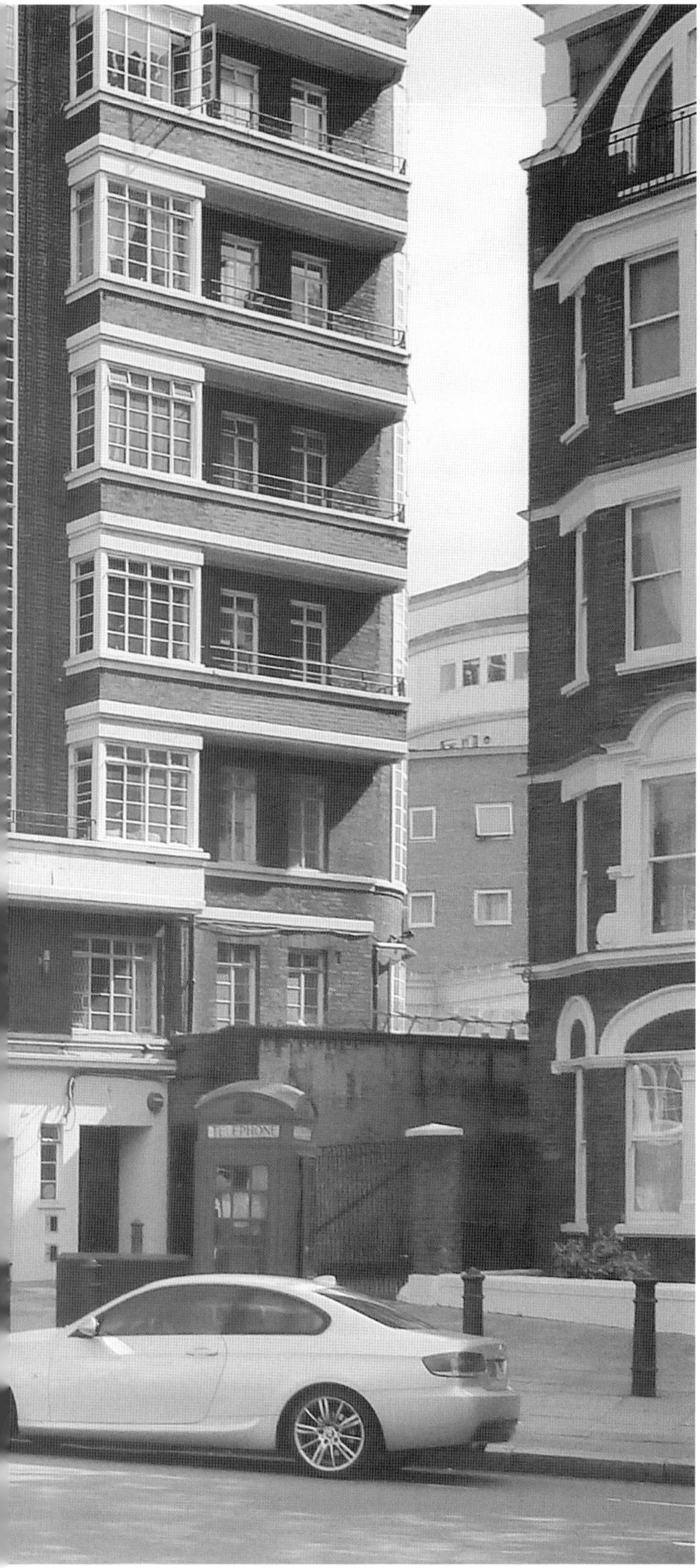

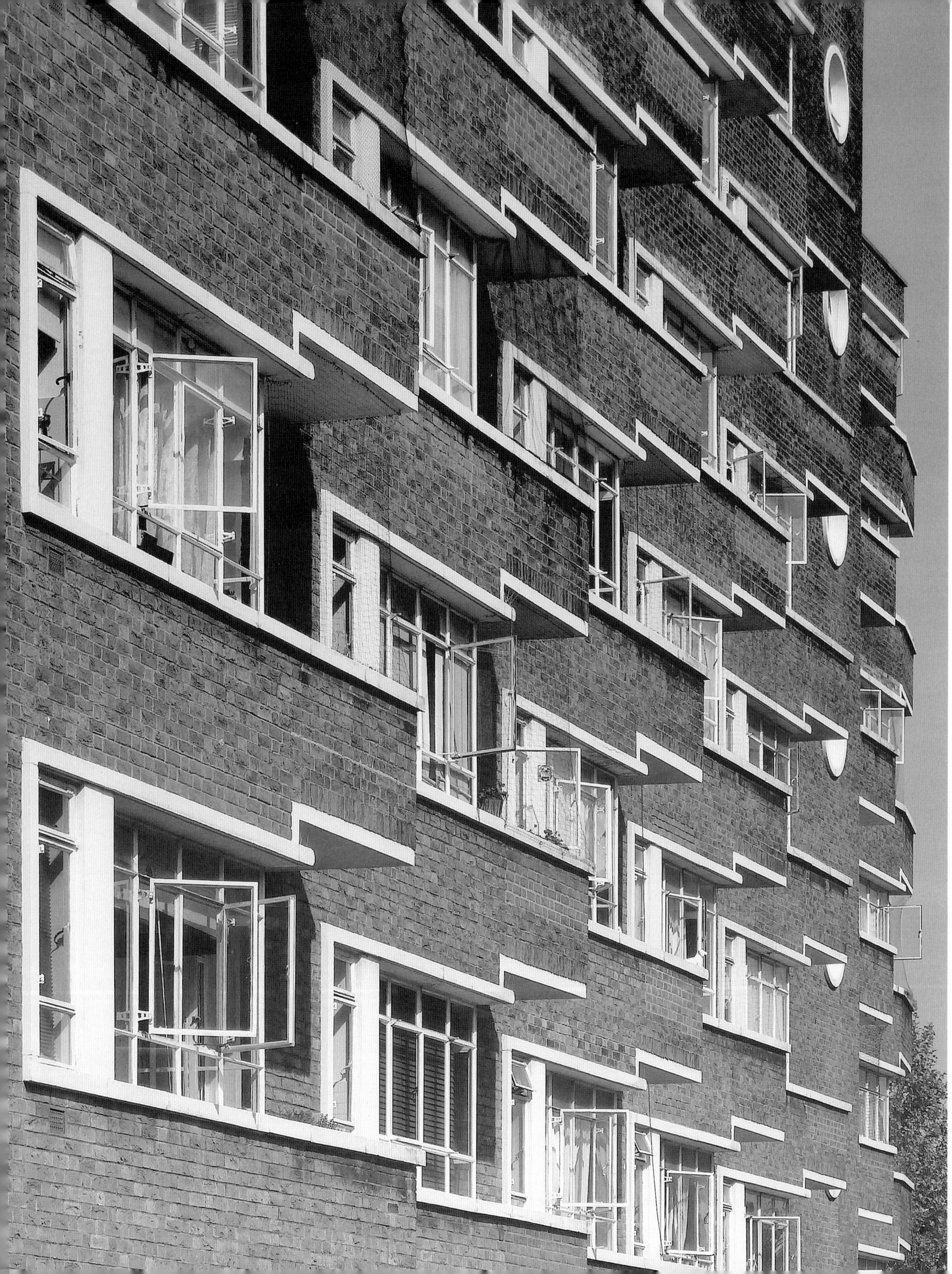

13

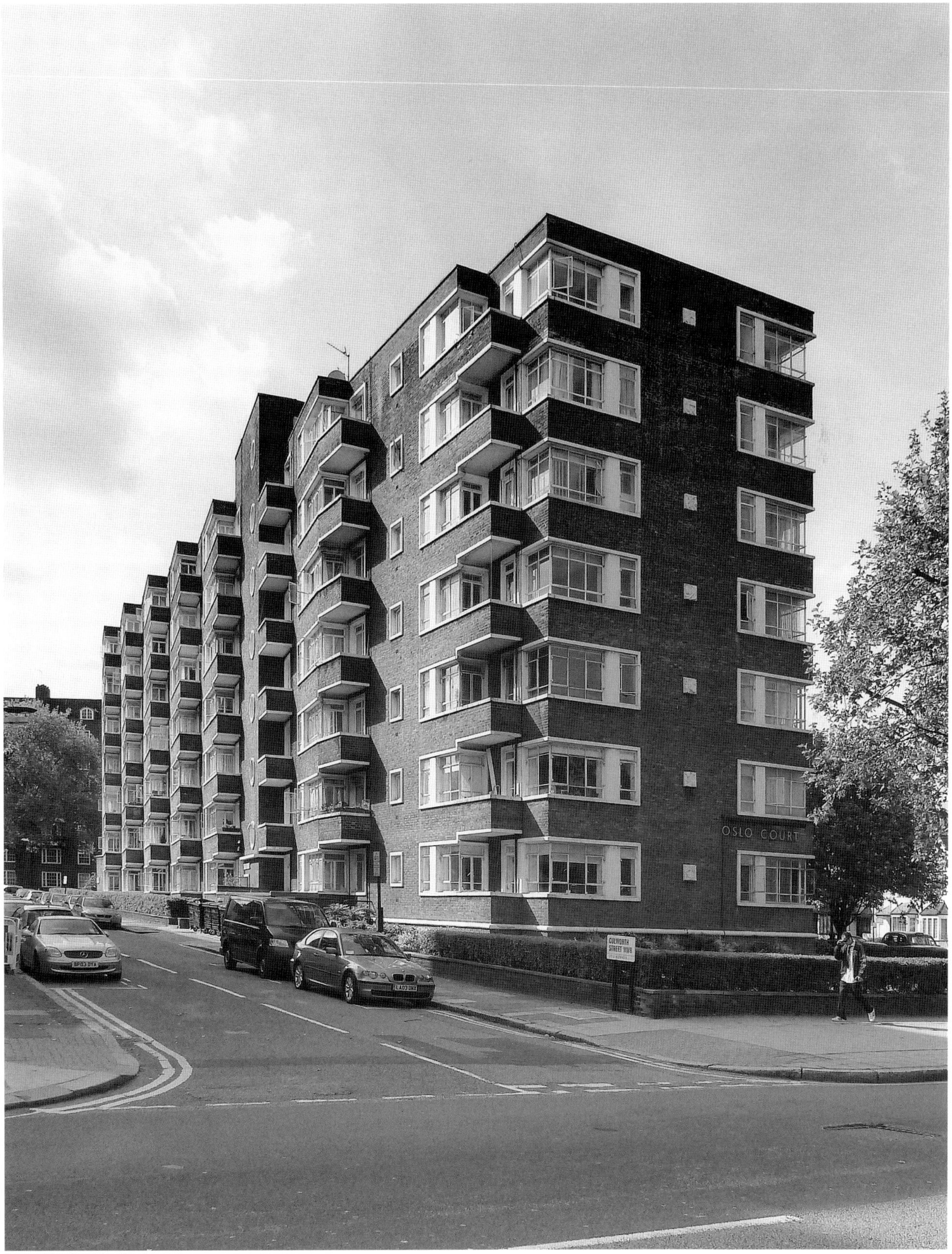
OSLO COURT

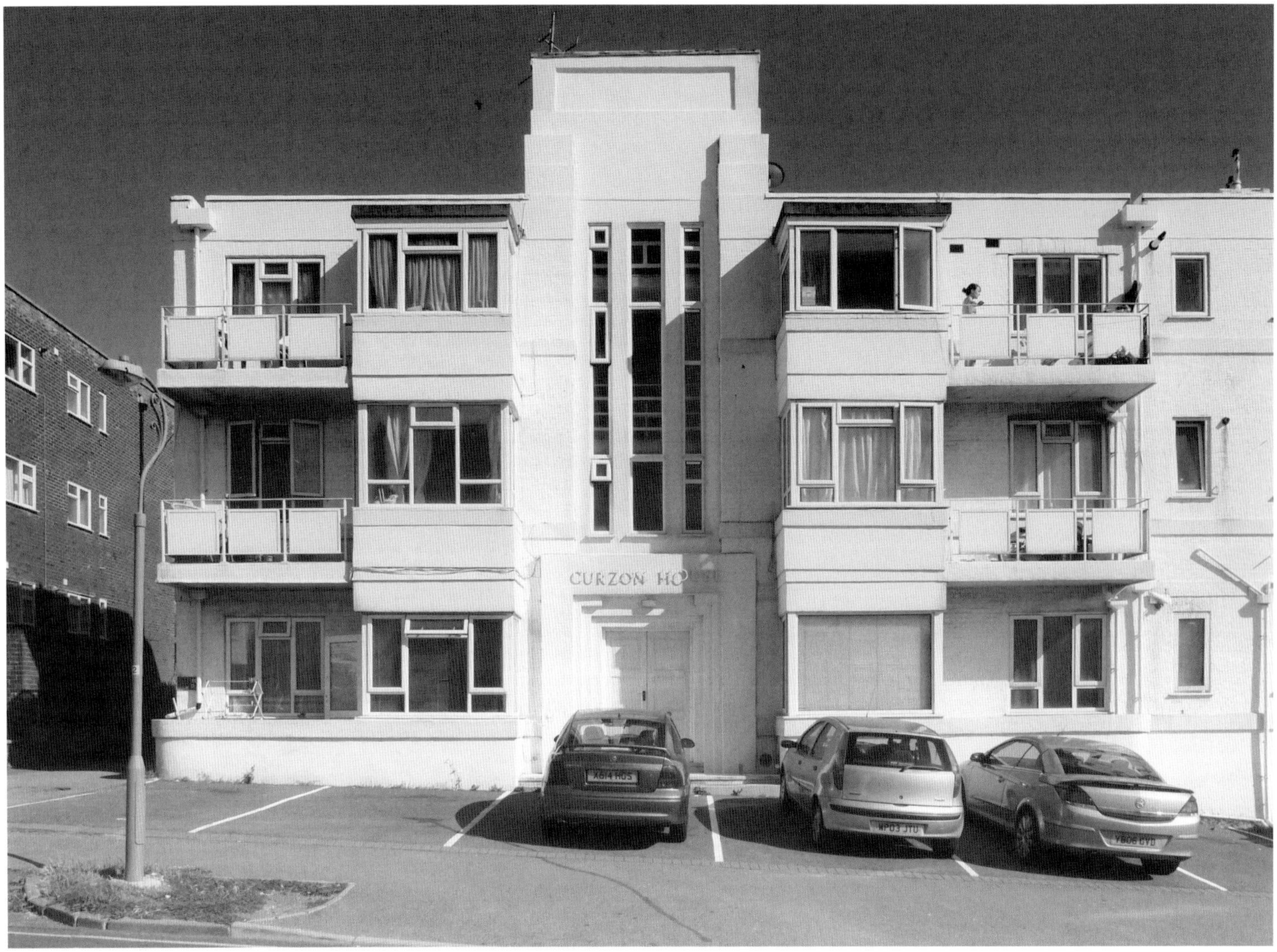

1

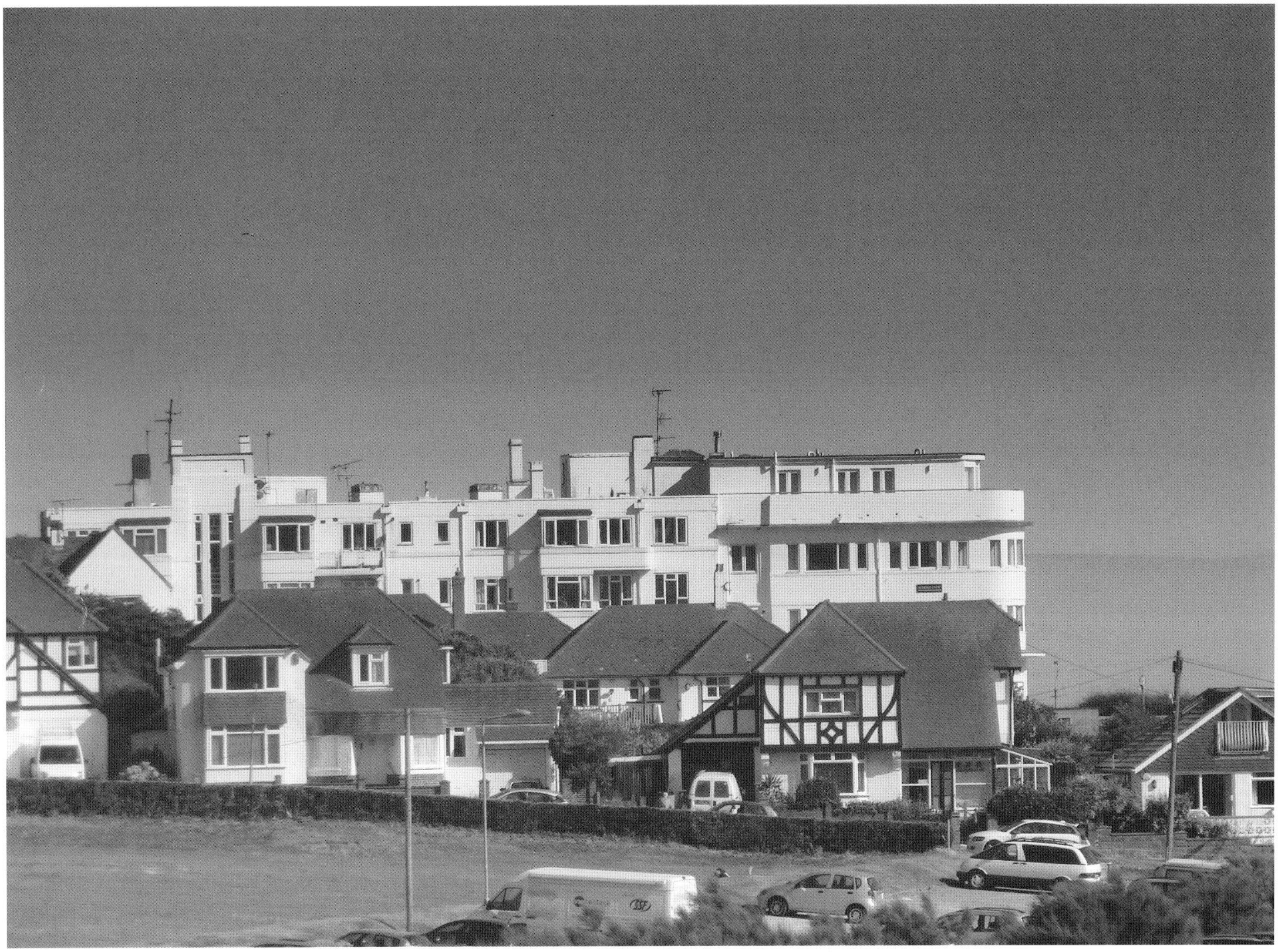

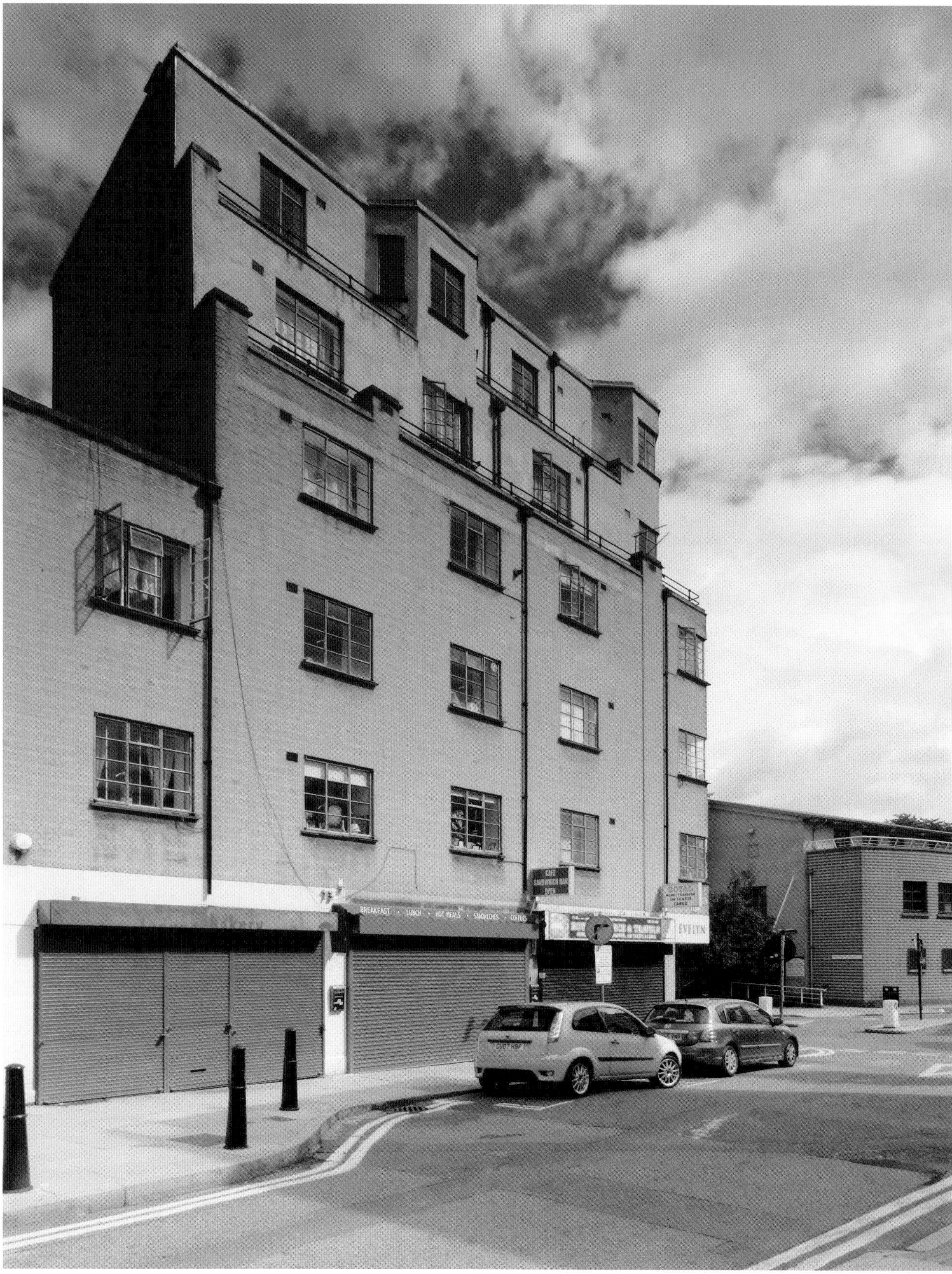
BREAKFAST • LUNCH • HOT MEALS • SANDWICHES • COFFEES
CAFE
SANDWICH BAR
OPEN
EVELYN

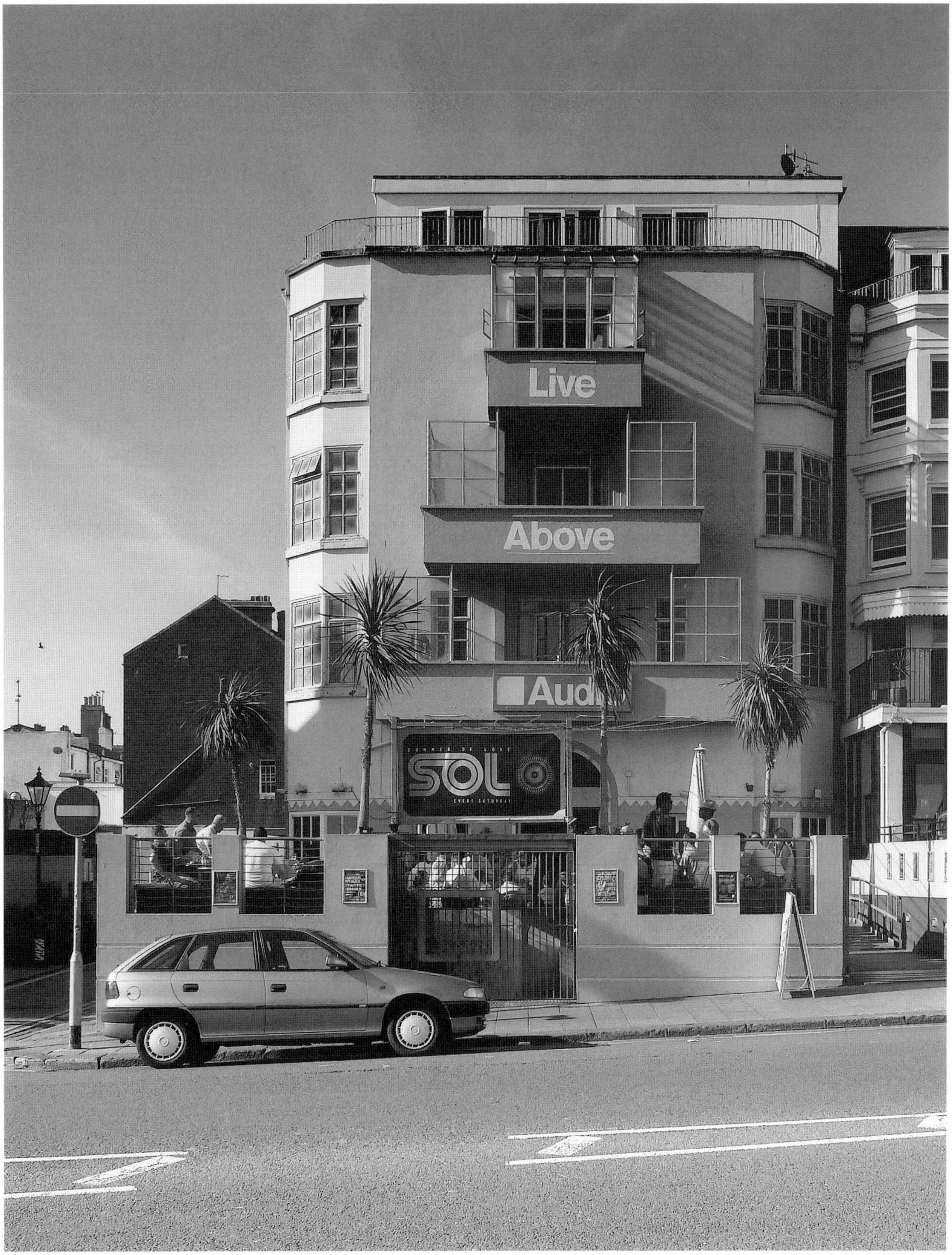
Live
Above
SOL

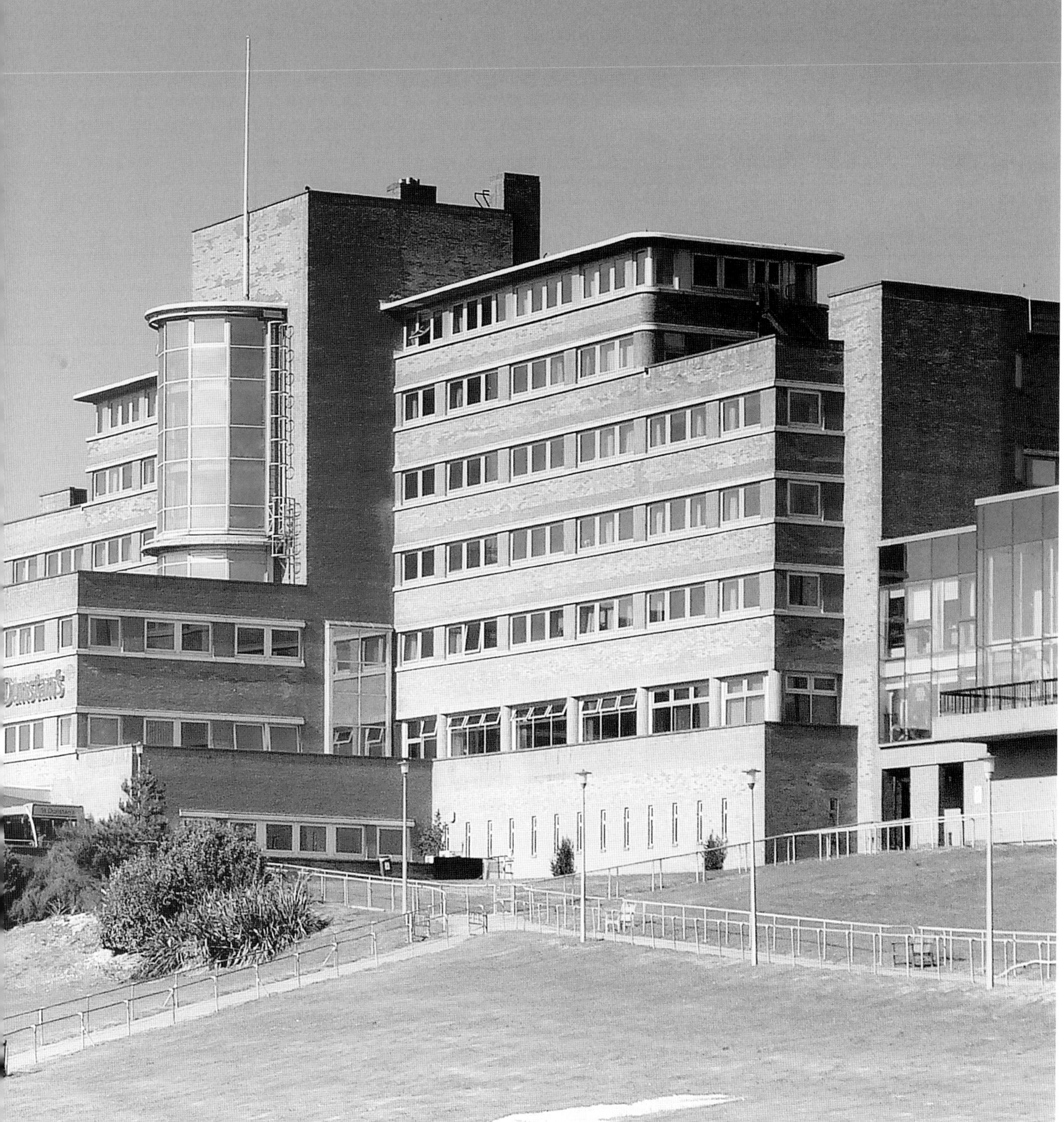

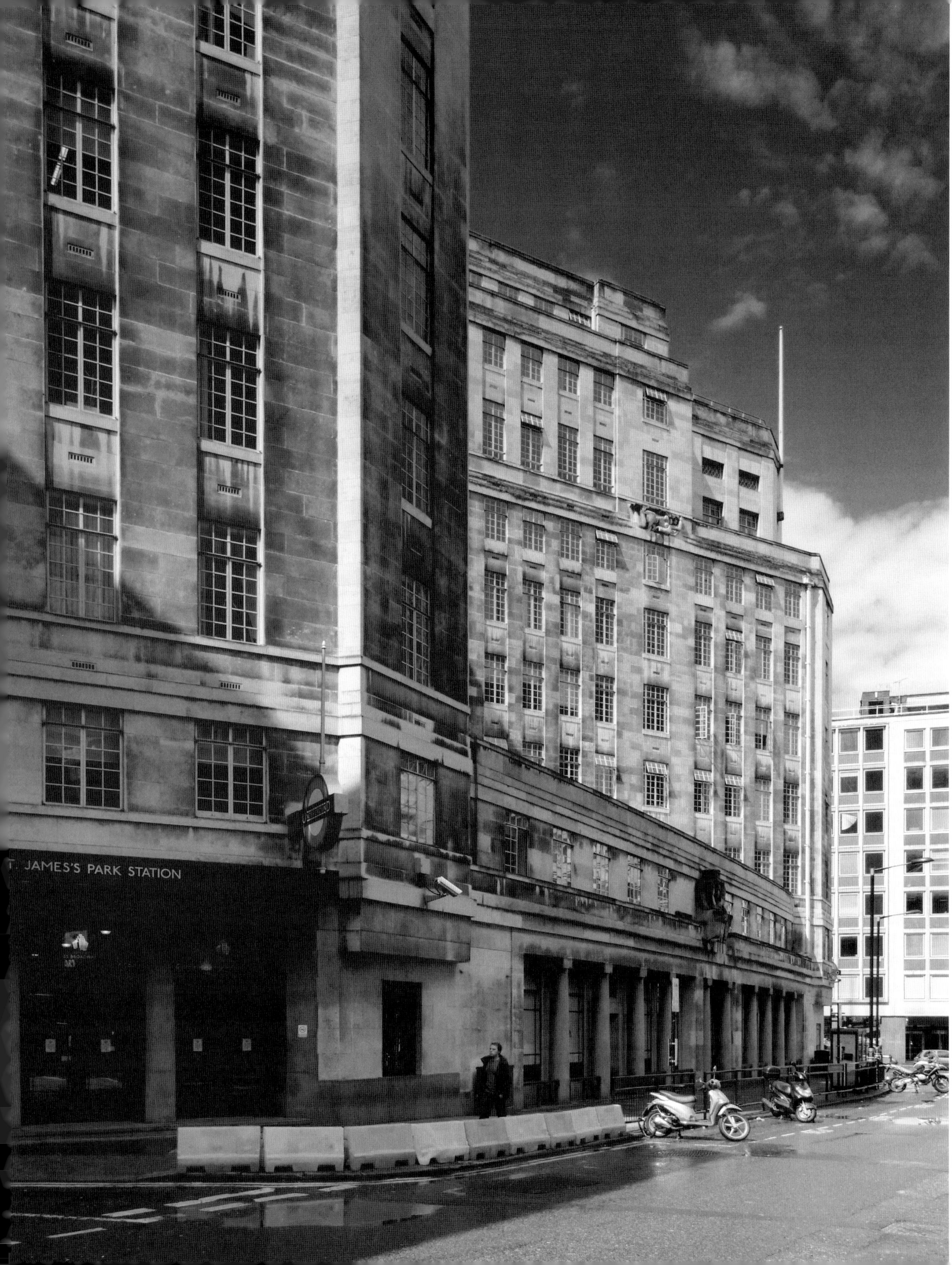
T. JAMES'S PARK STATION

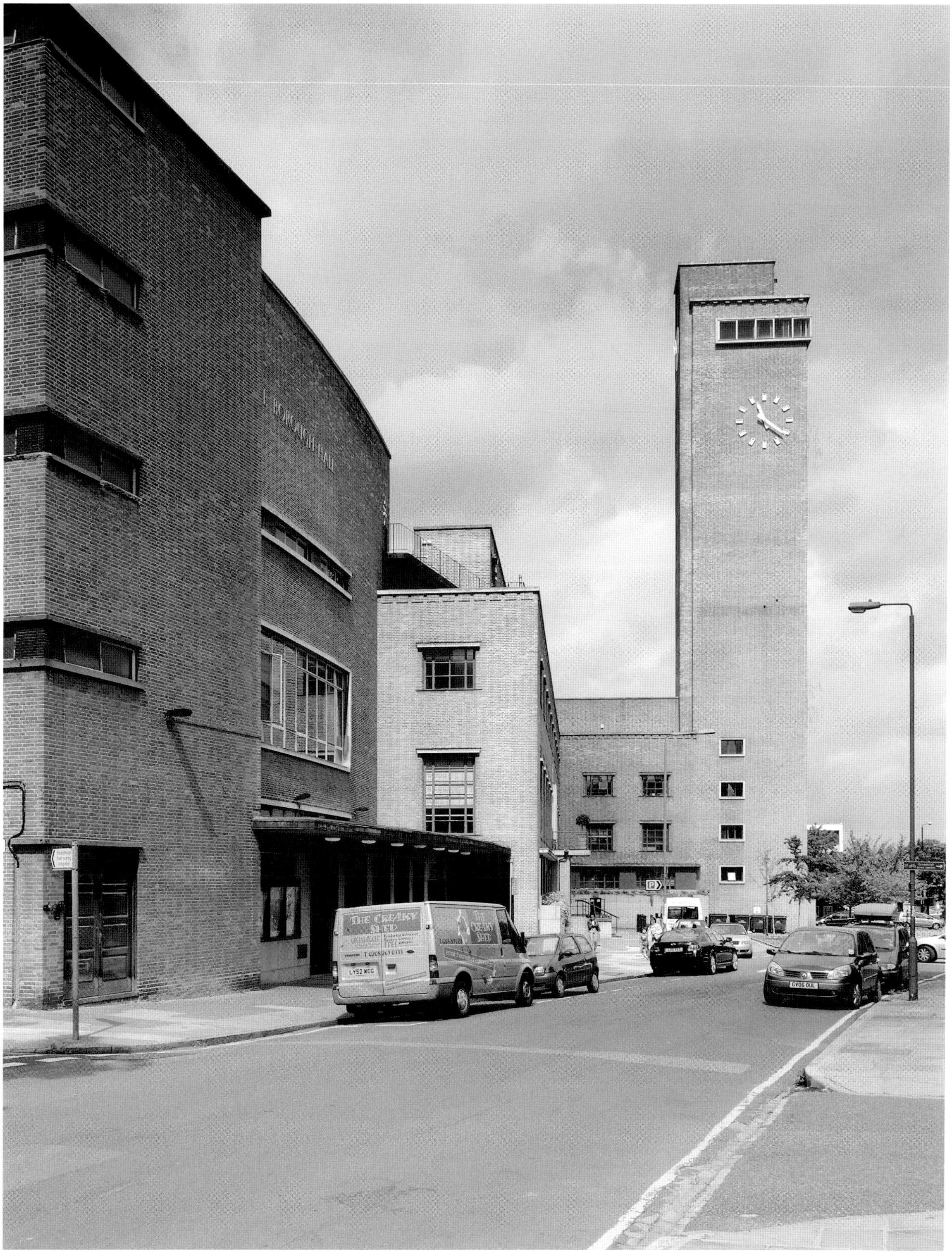
The Creaky Shed

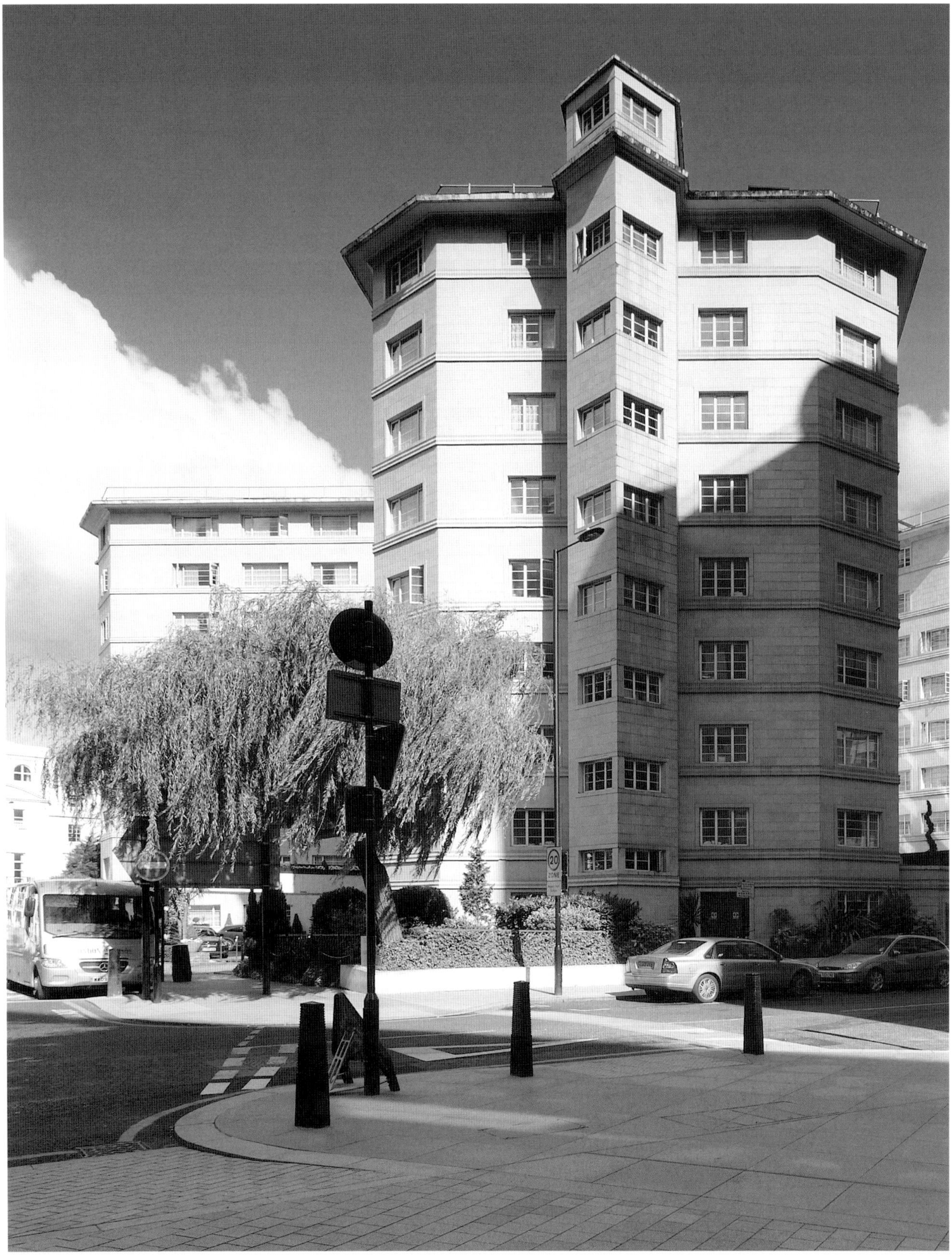
20
ZONE

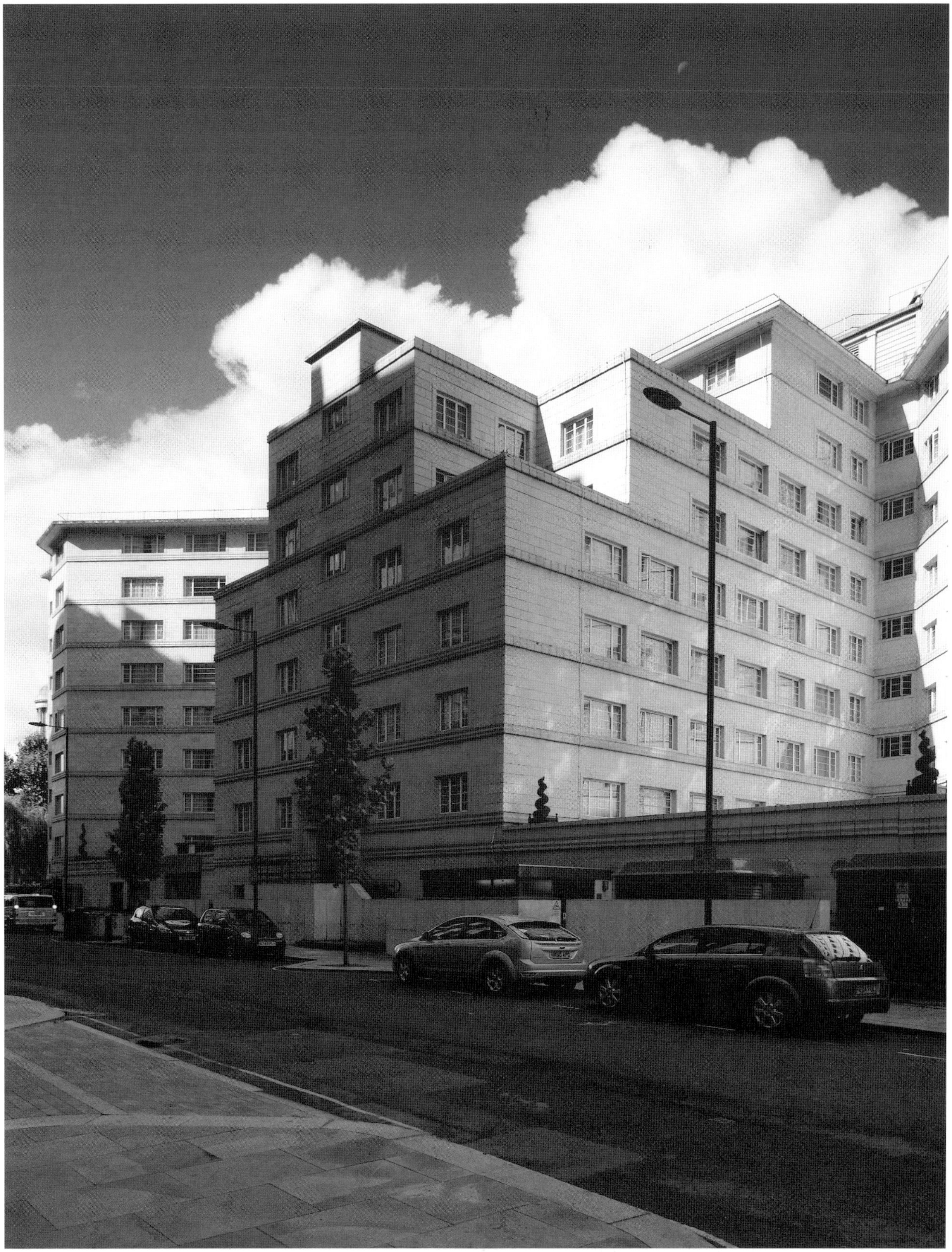

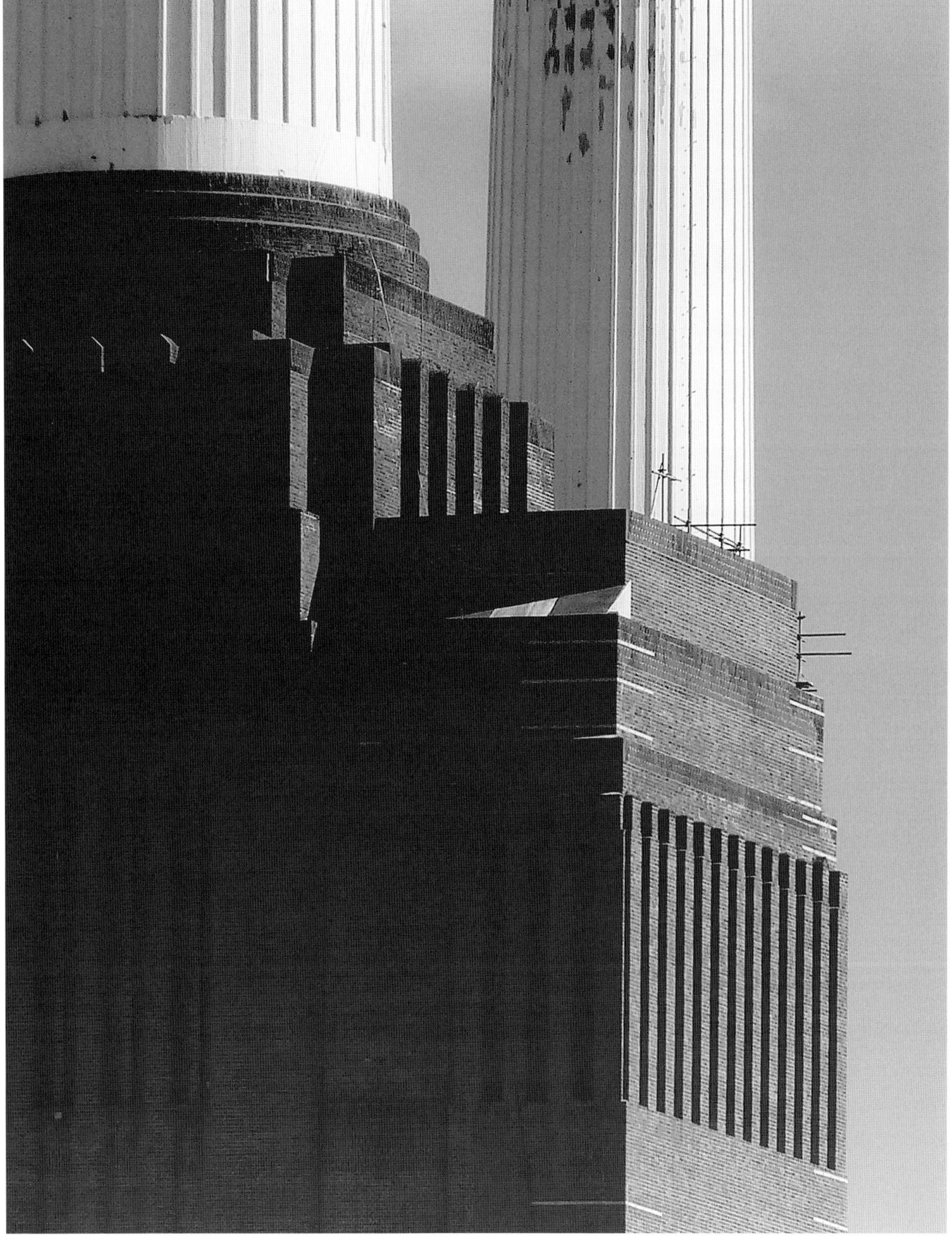

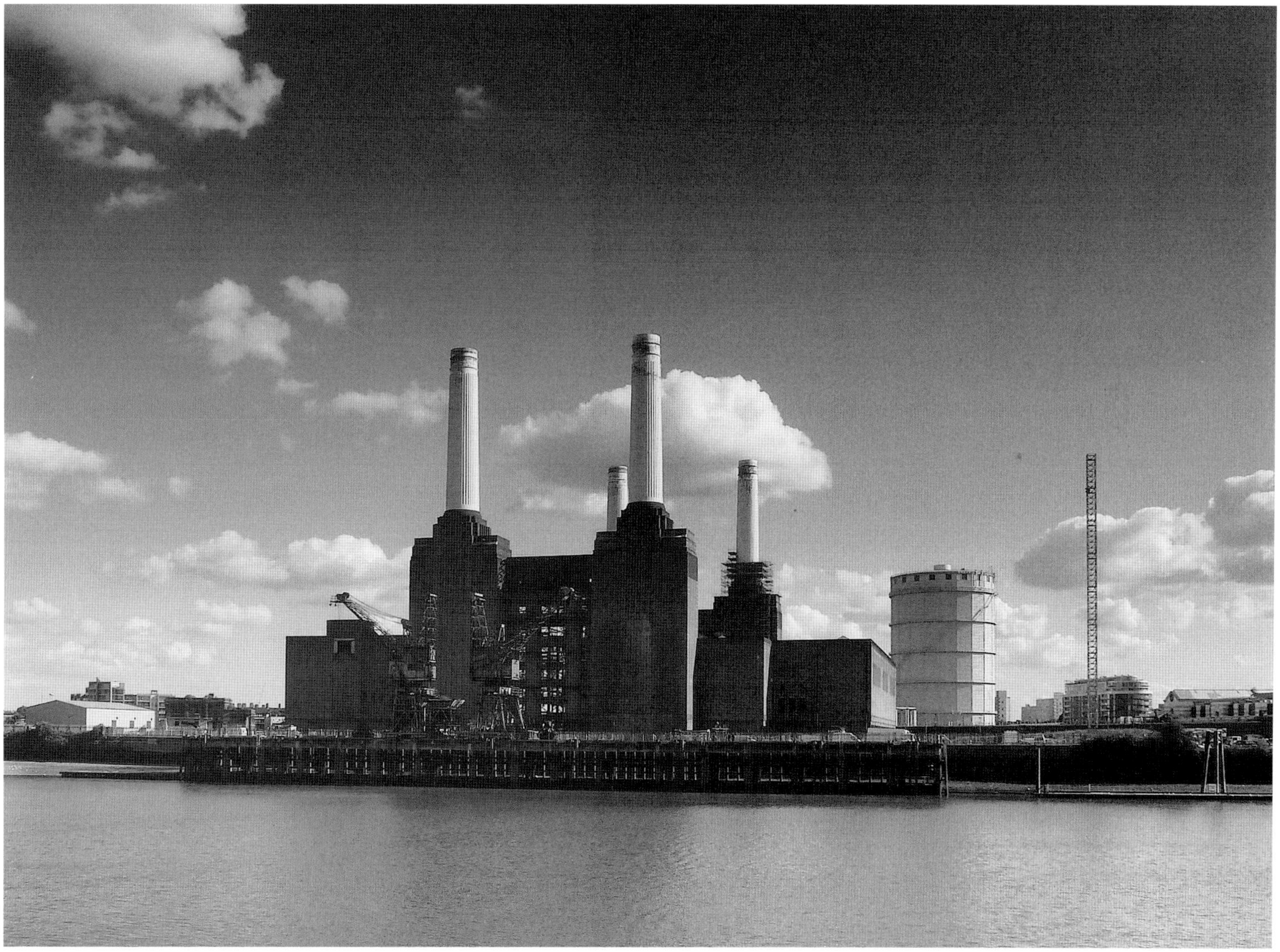

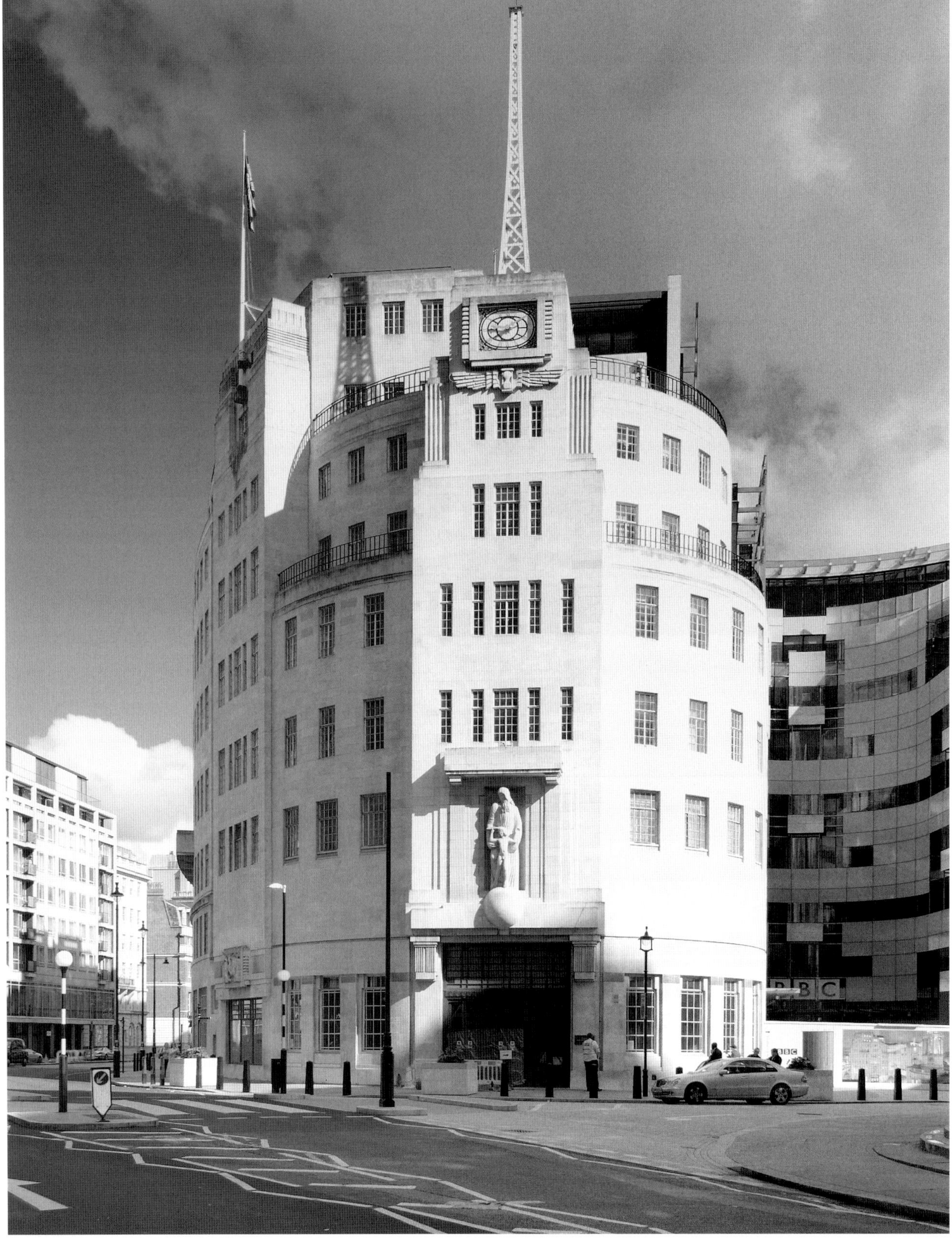
BBC

151

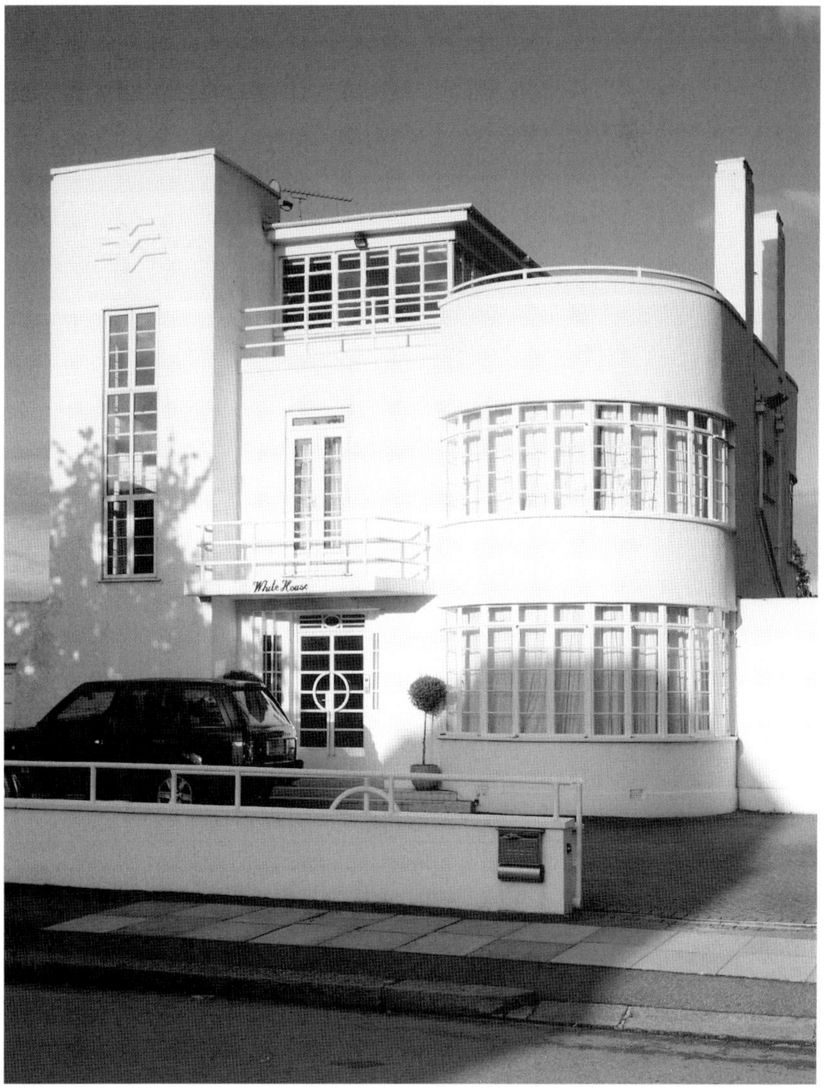

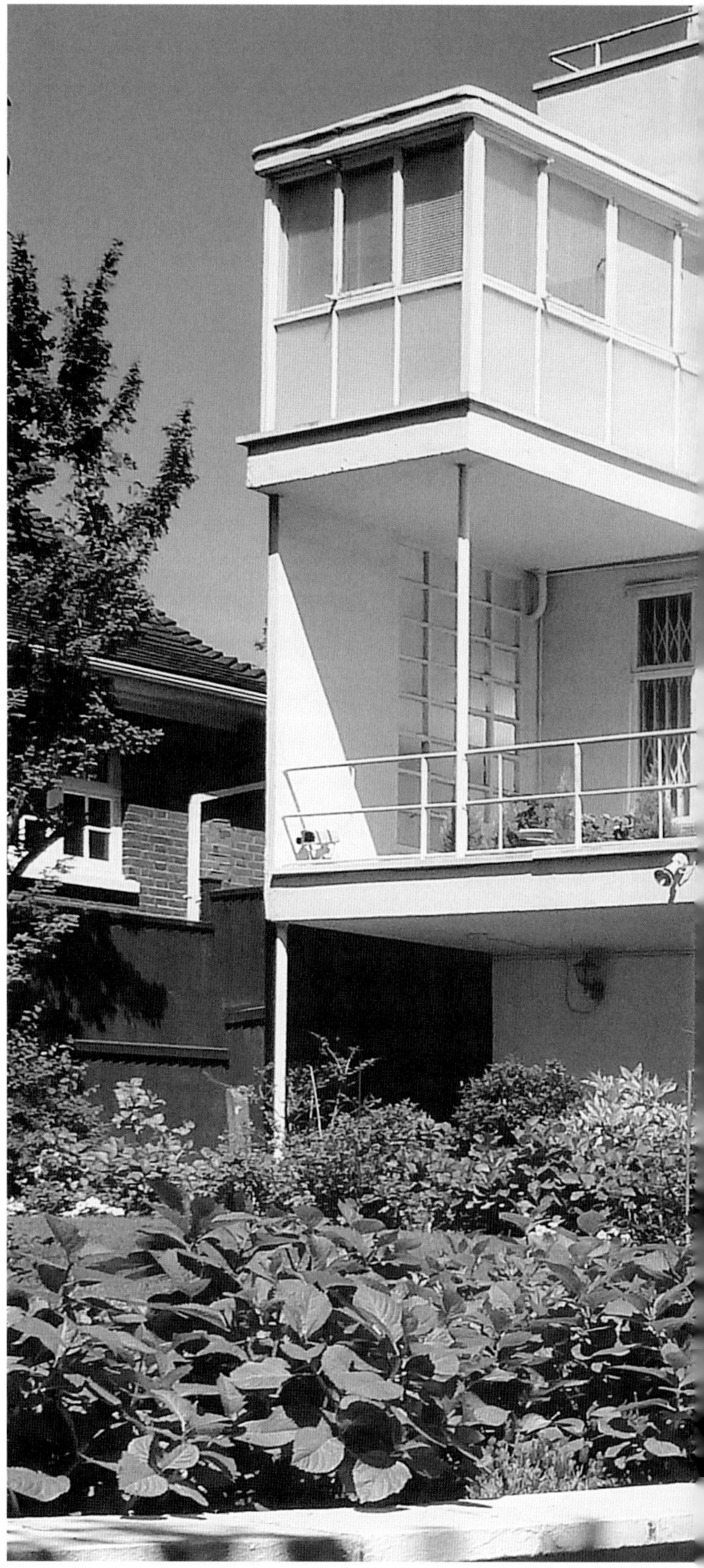

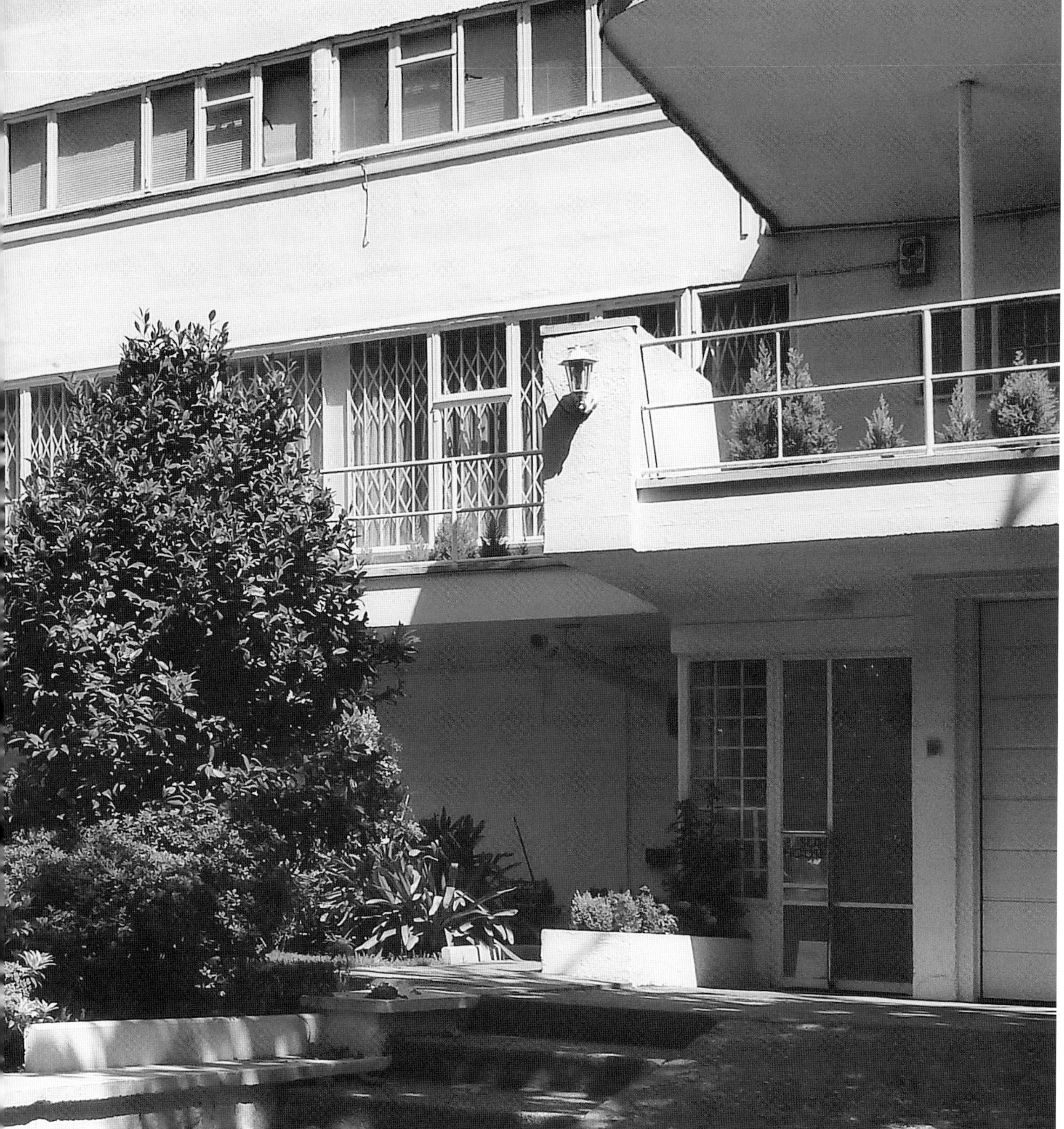

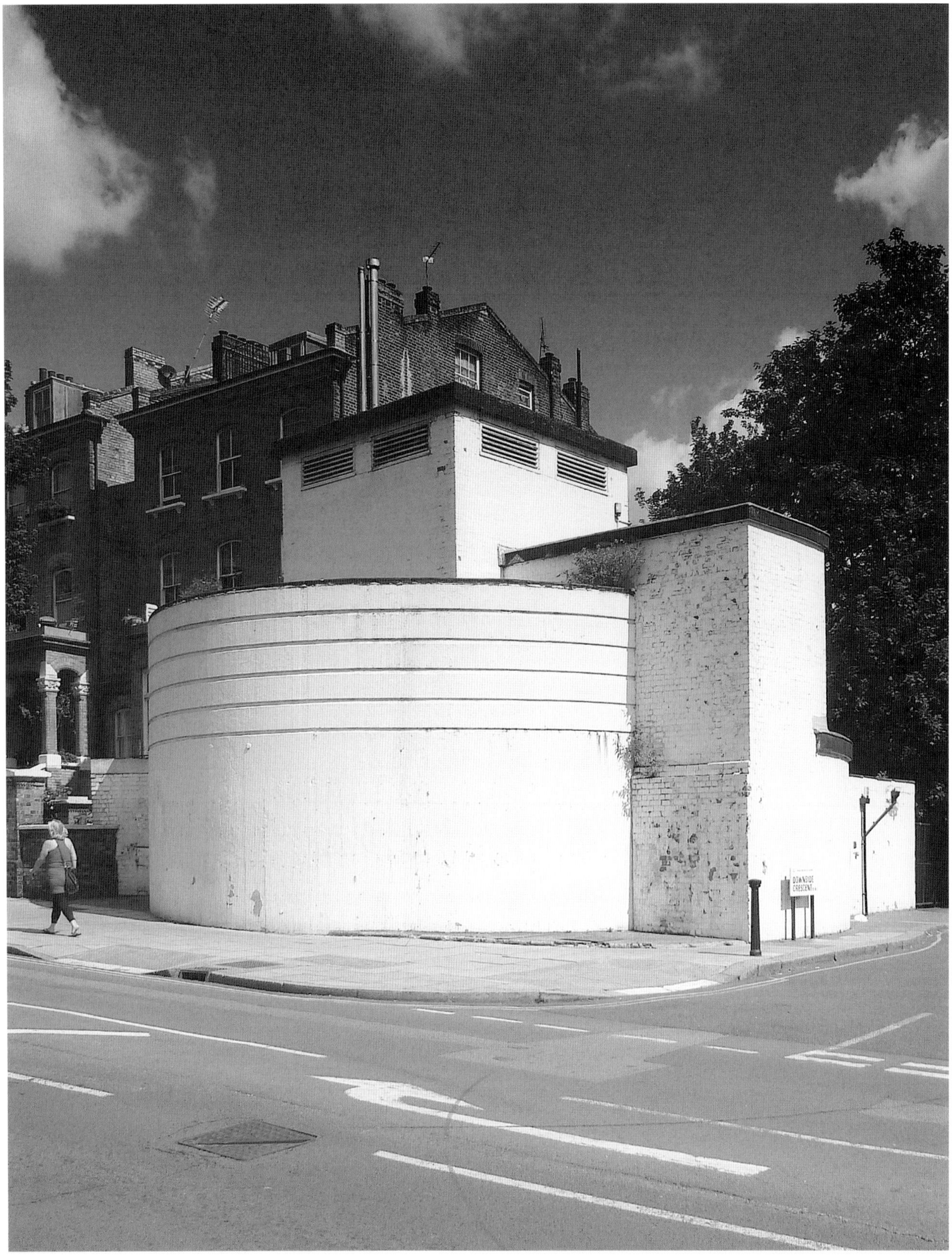
DOWNSIDE
CRESCENT

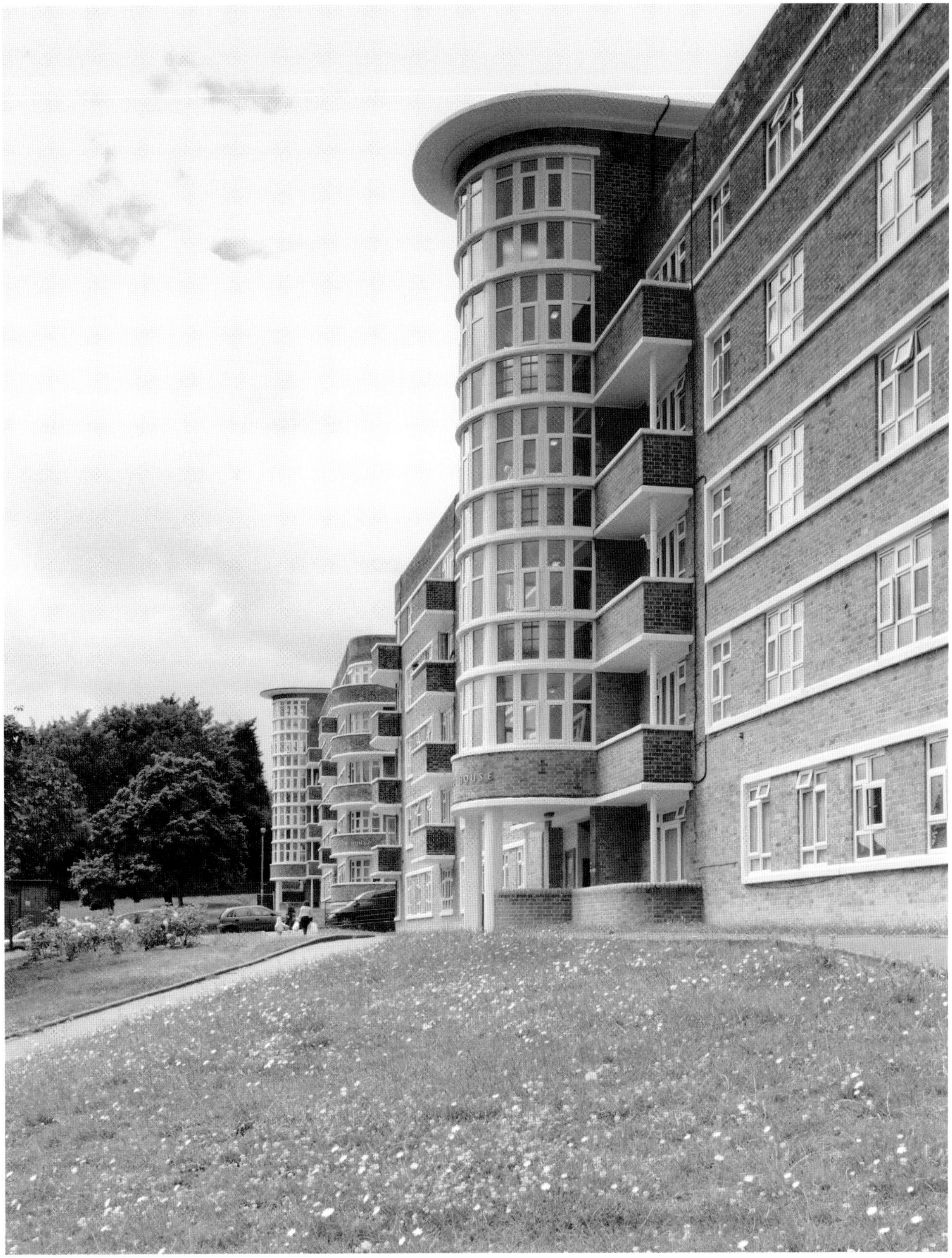

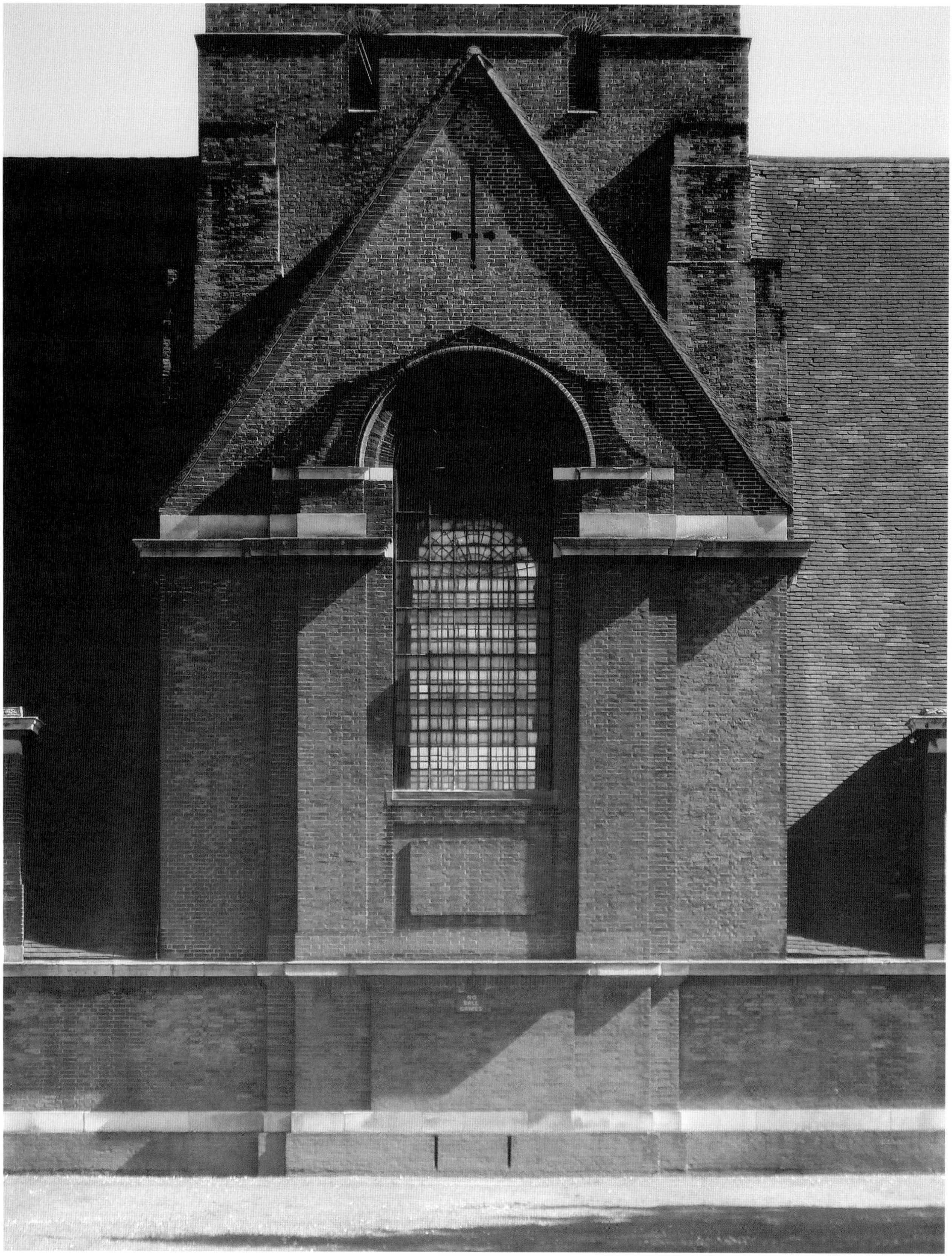

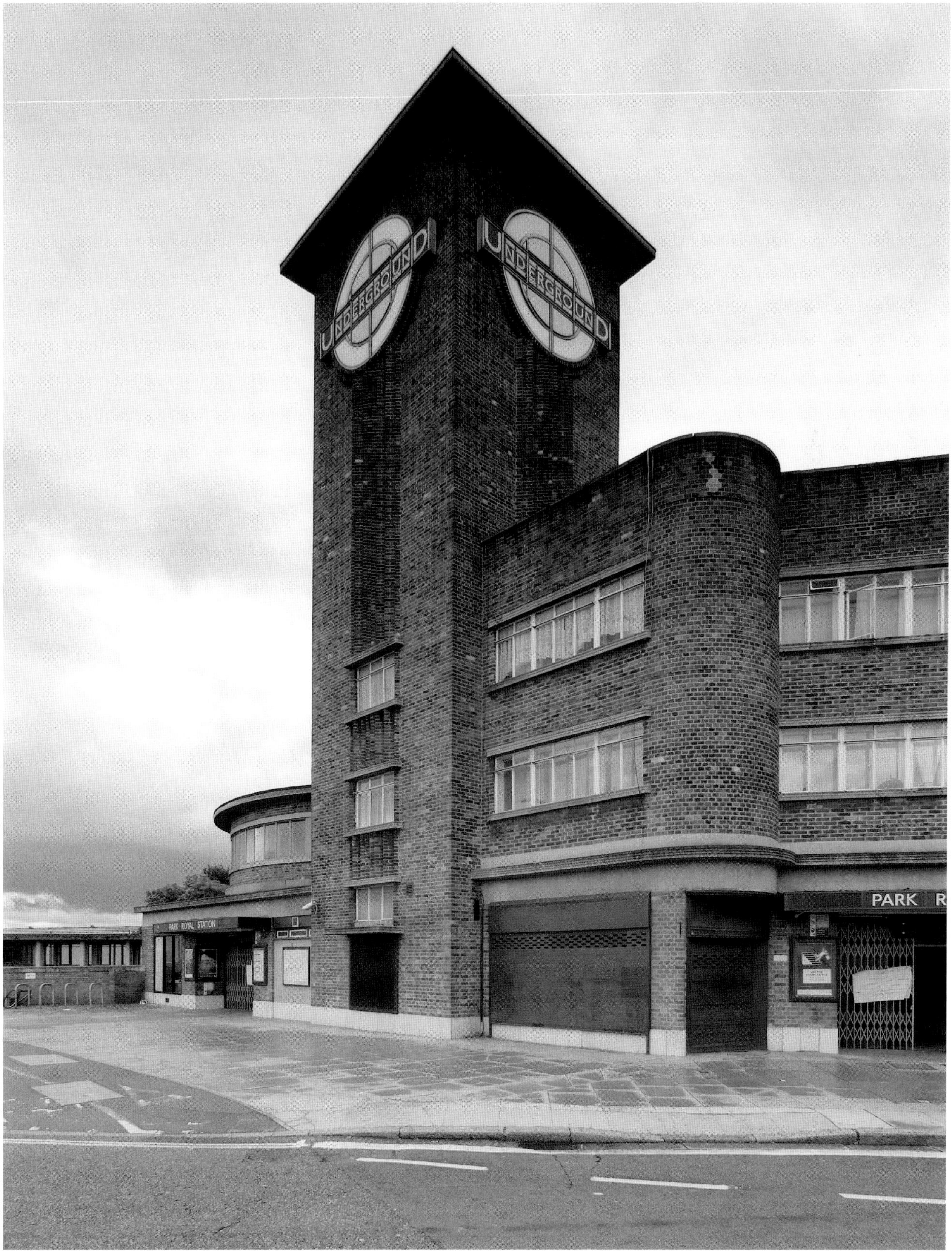
UNDERGROUND
UNDERGROUND
PARK ROYAL STATION
PARK R

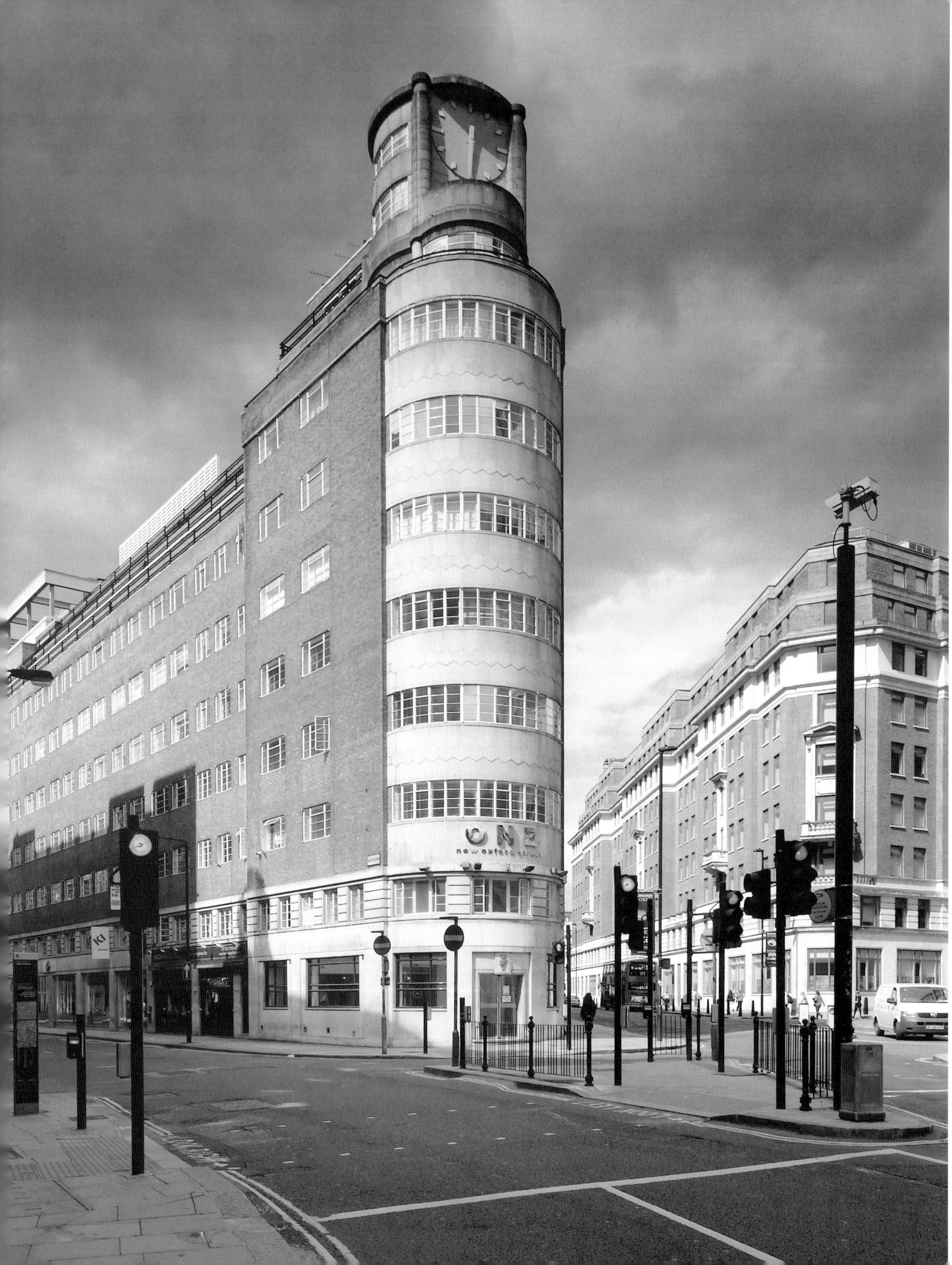
ONE
new oxford street

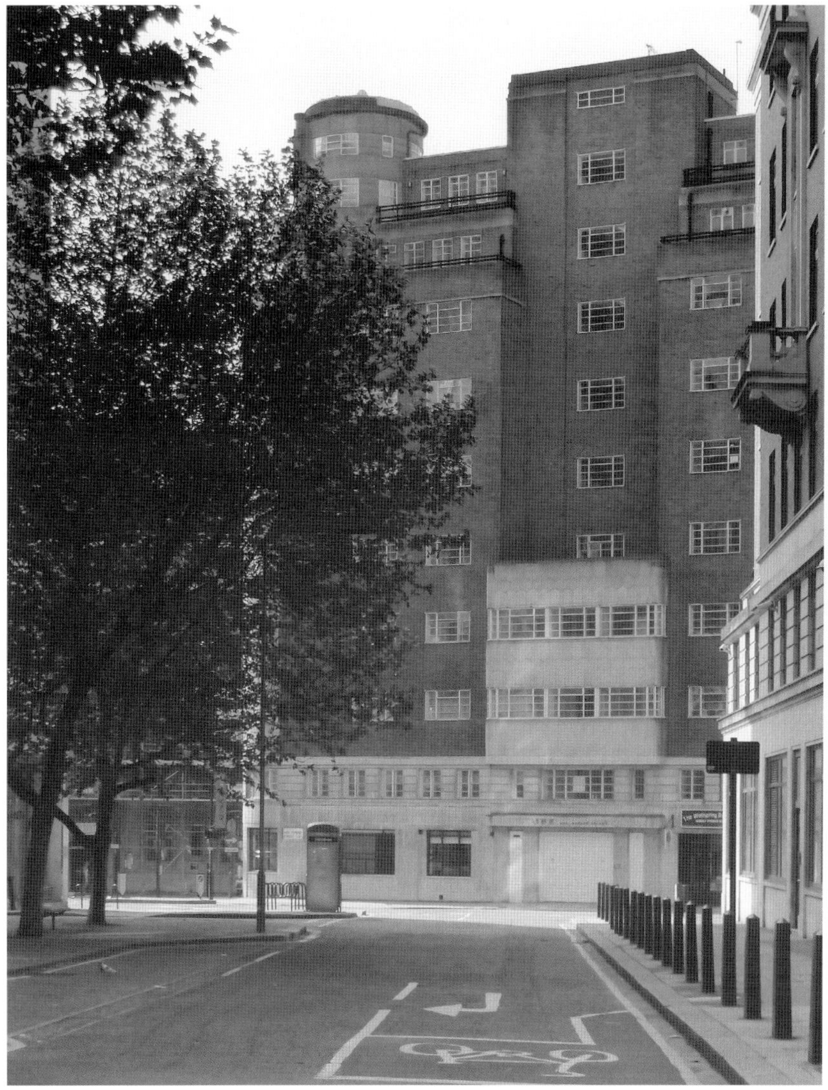

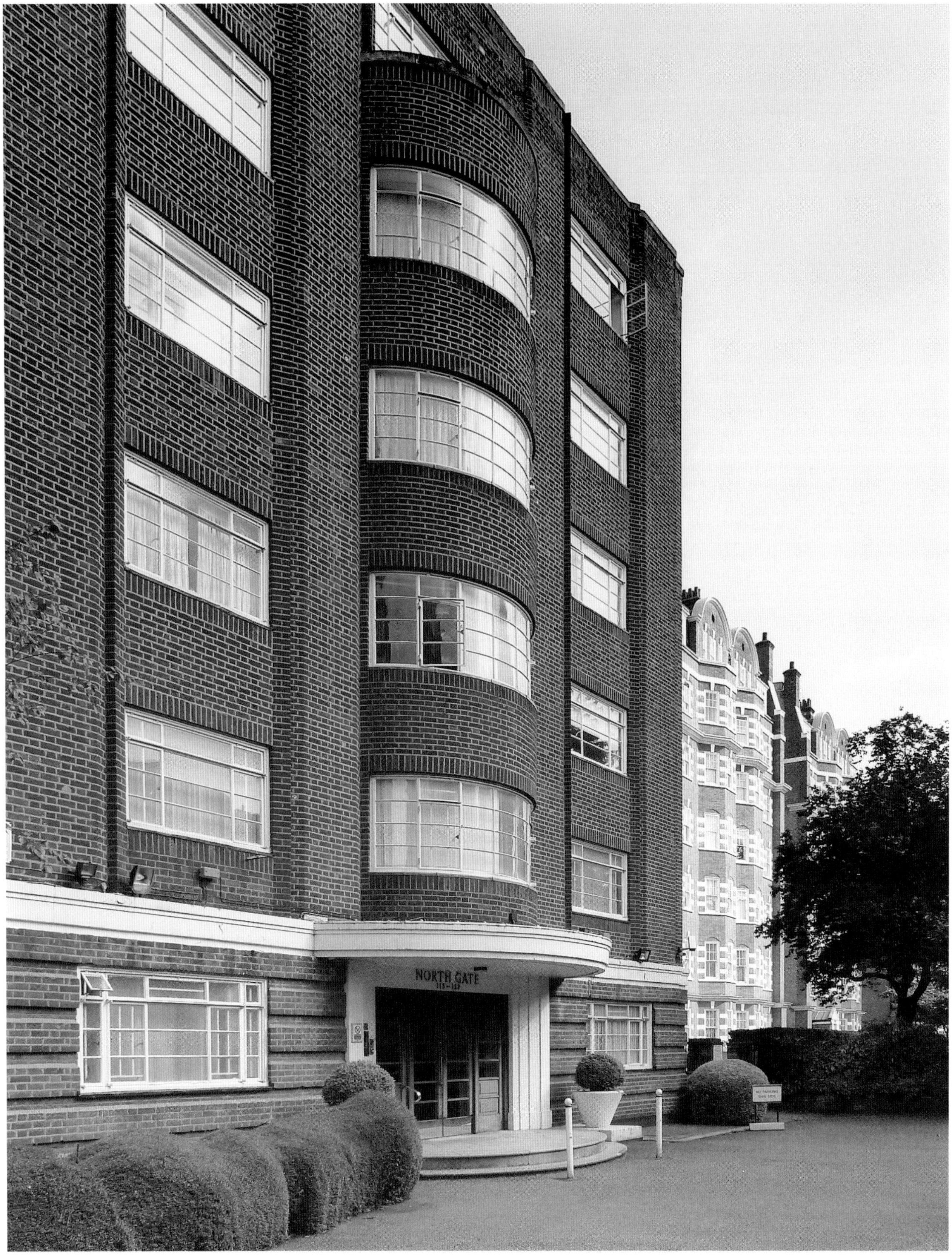

166

7

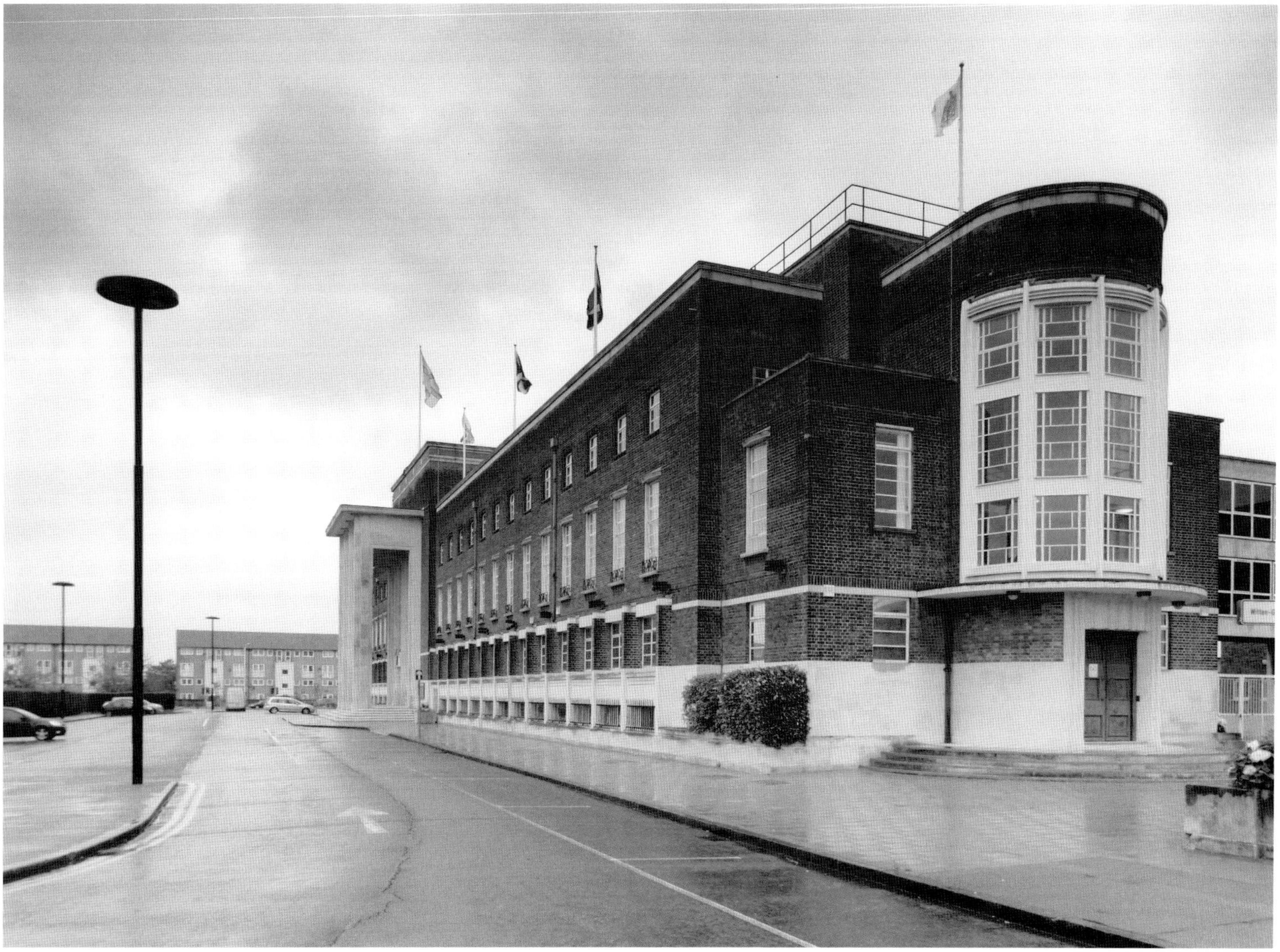

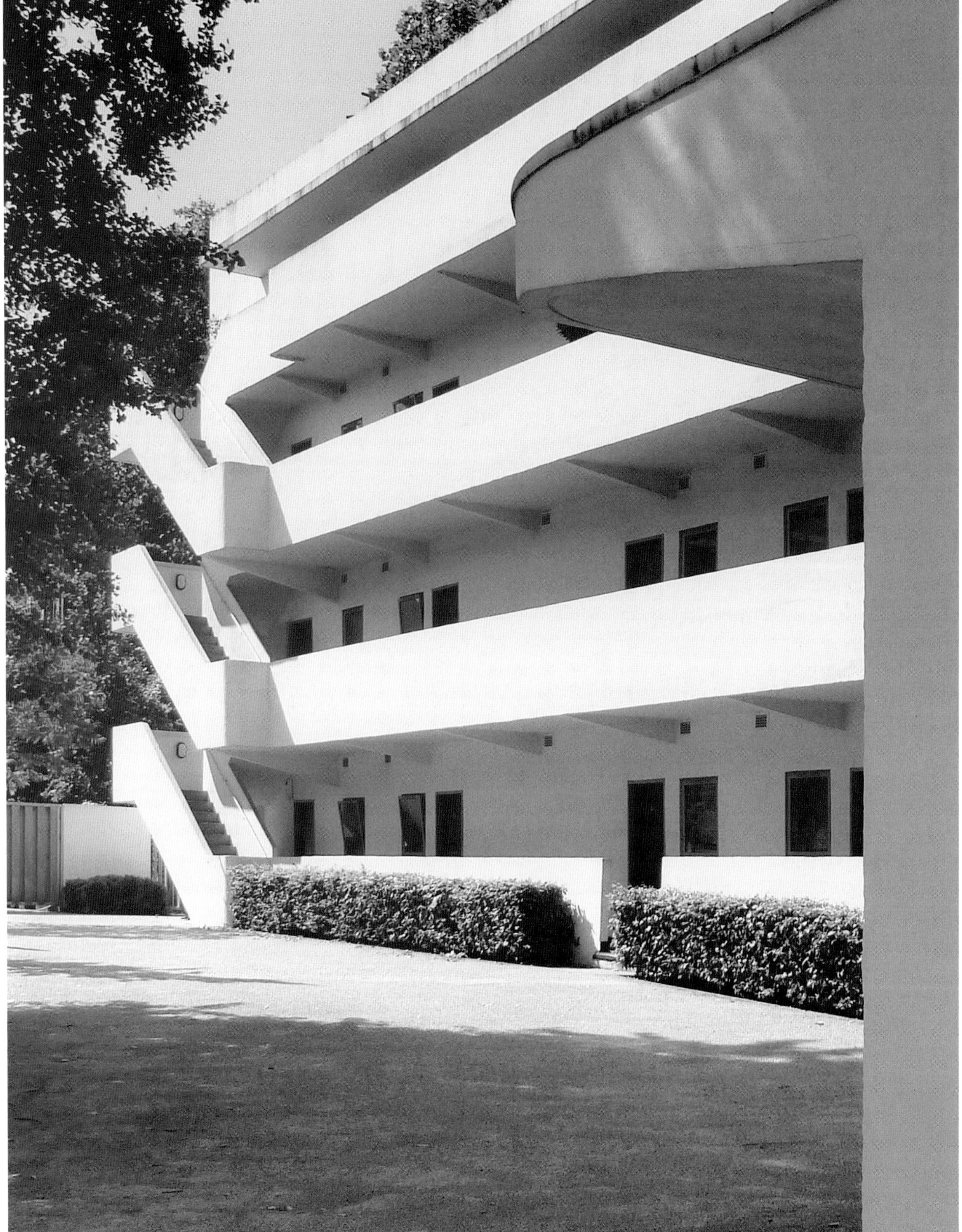

173

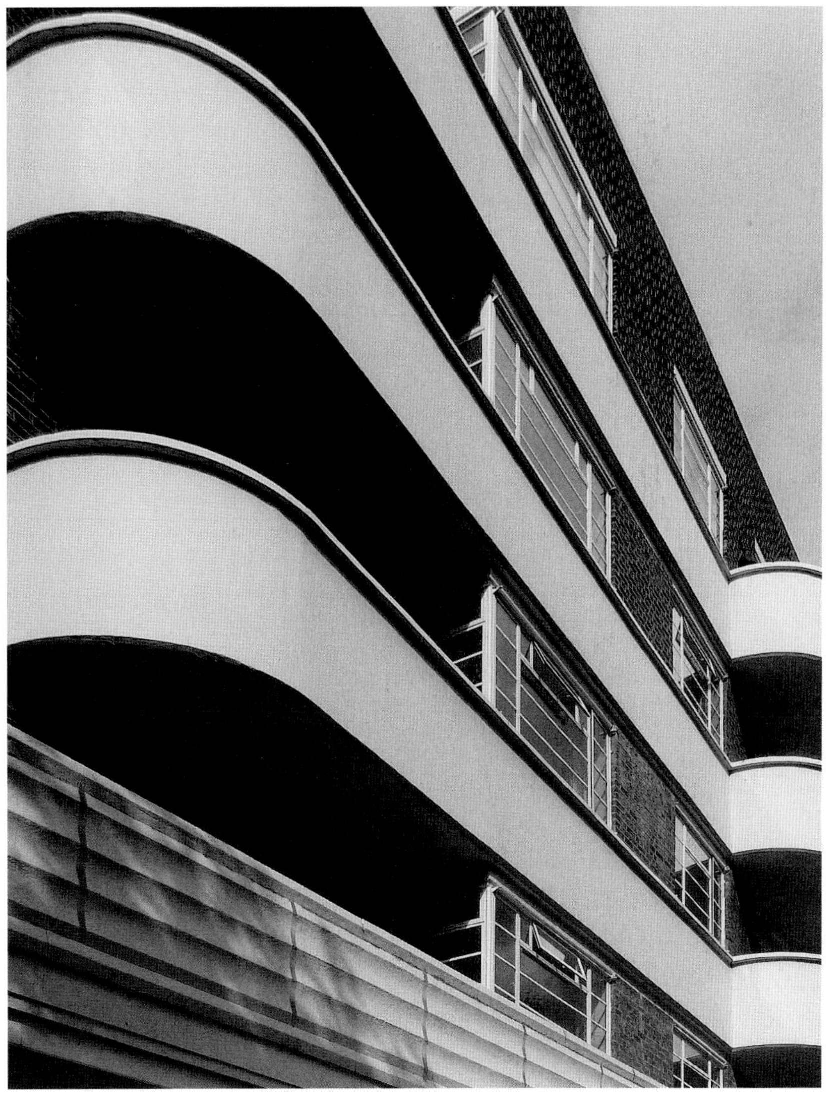

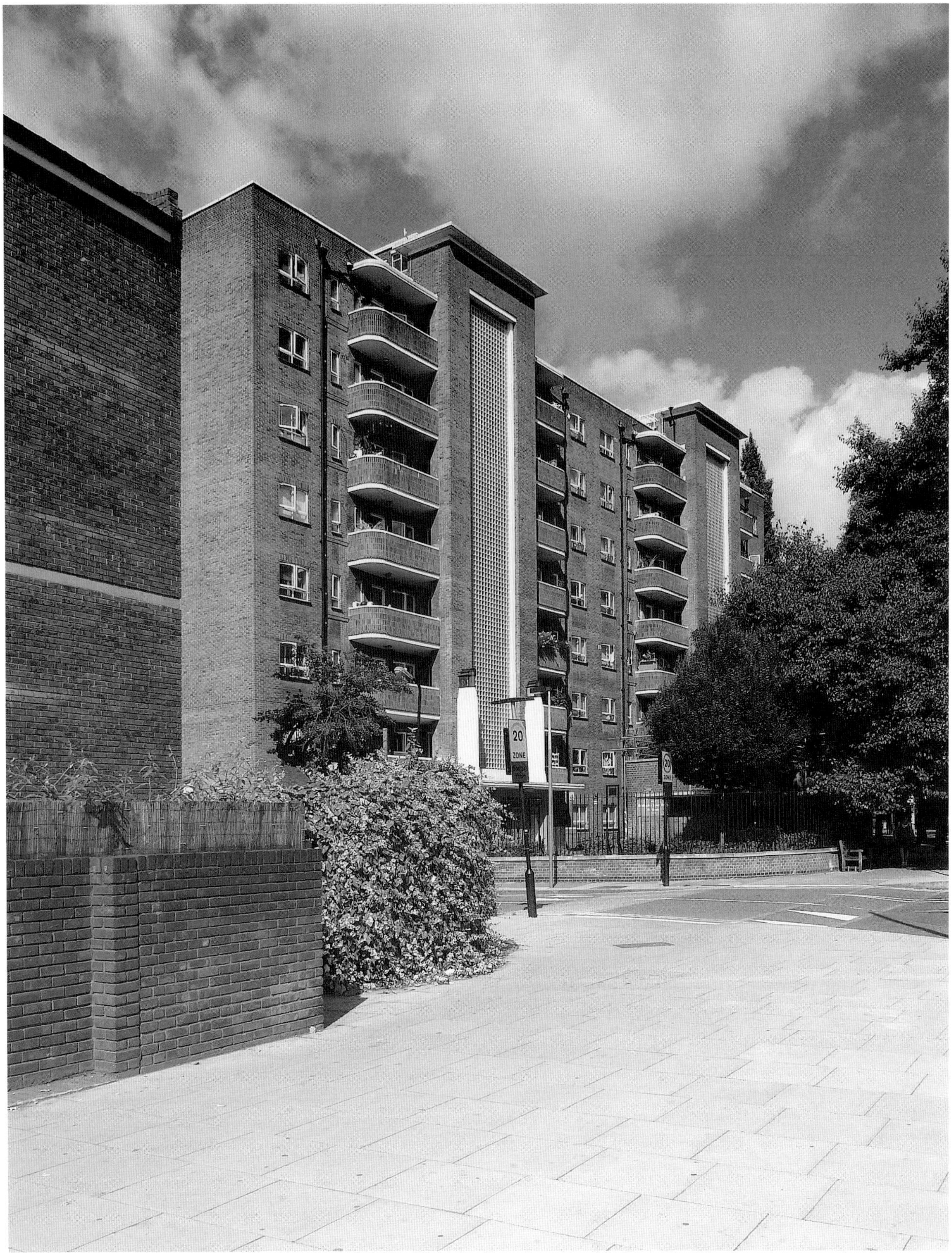
20
ZONE

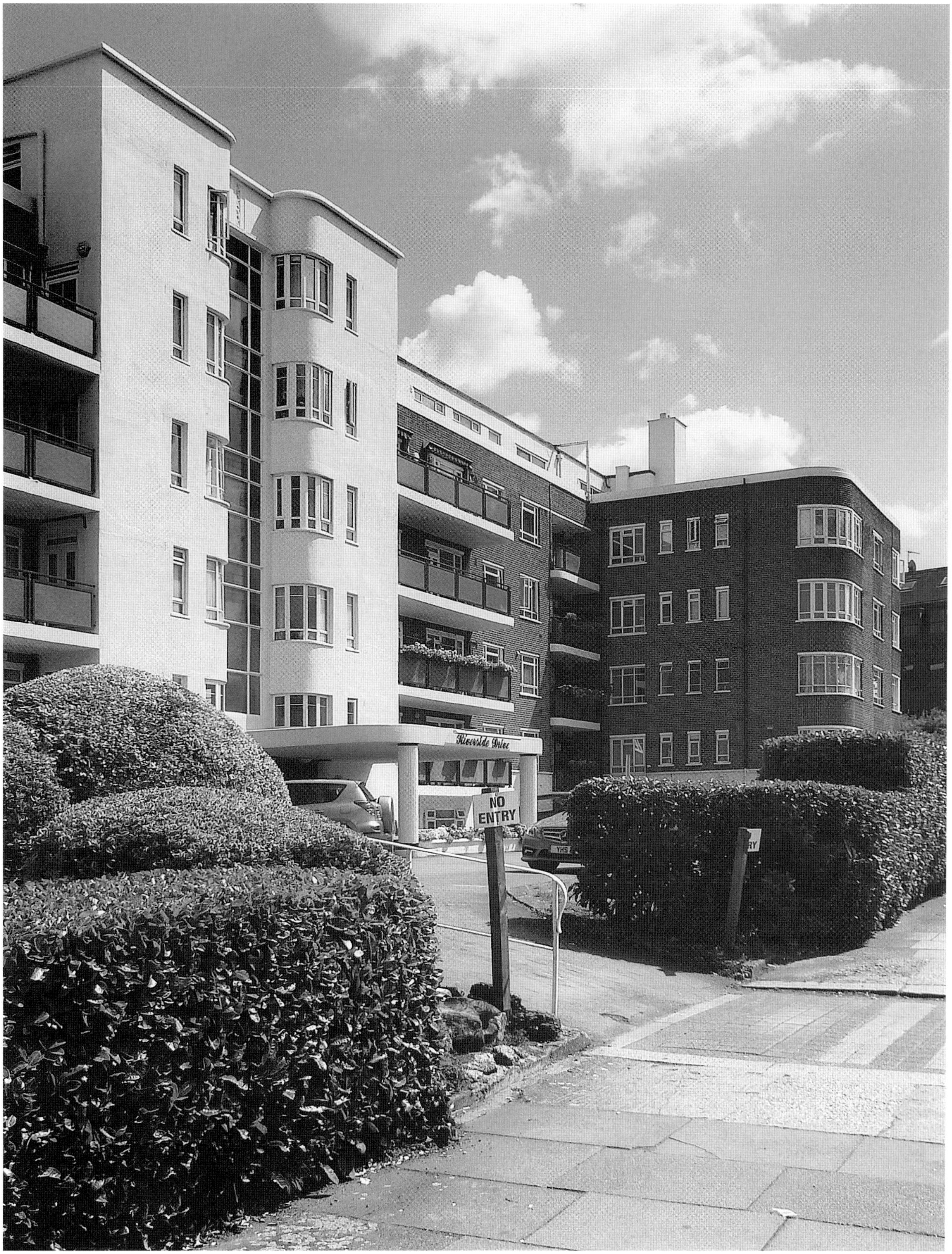
NO
ENTRY

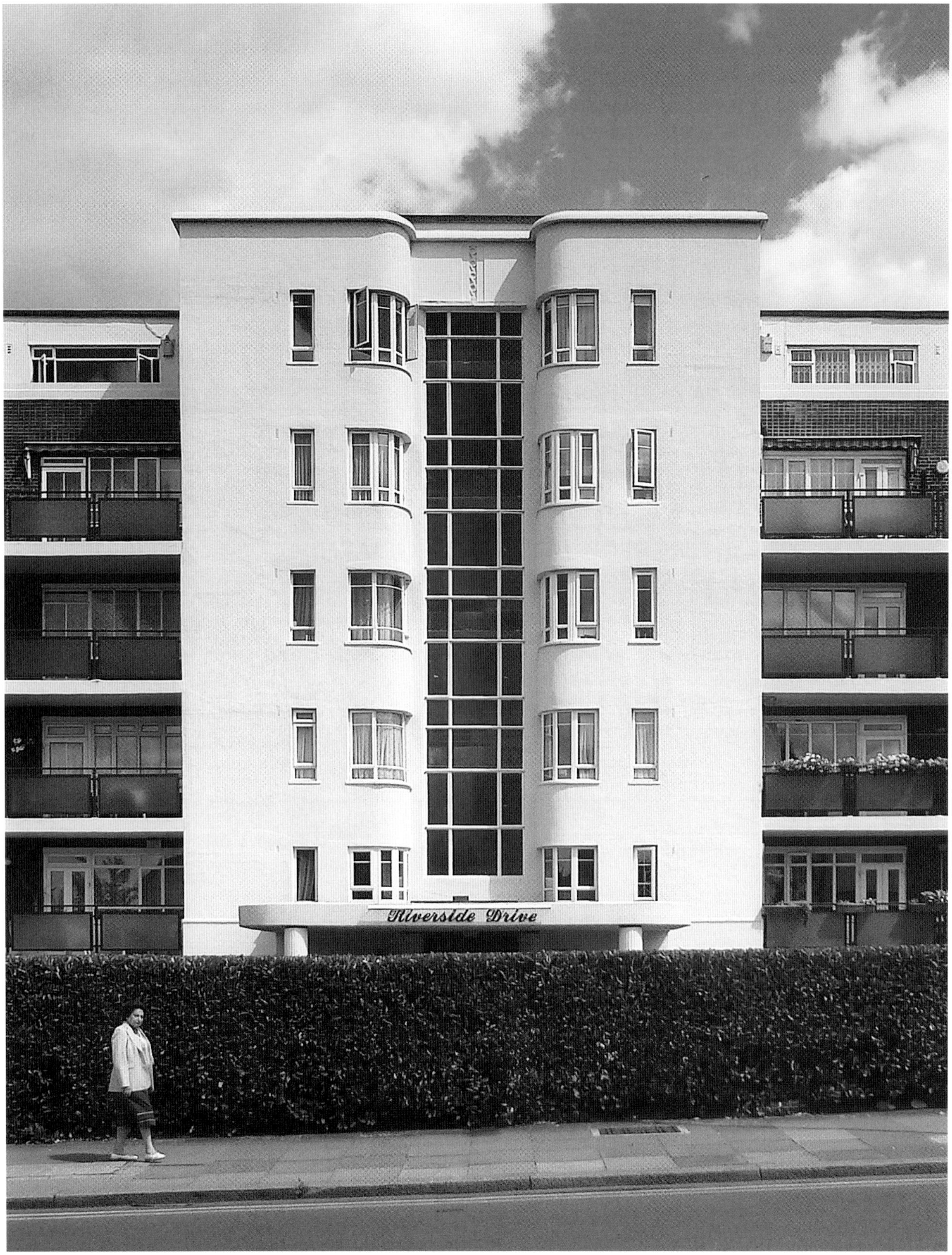
Riverside Drive

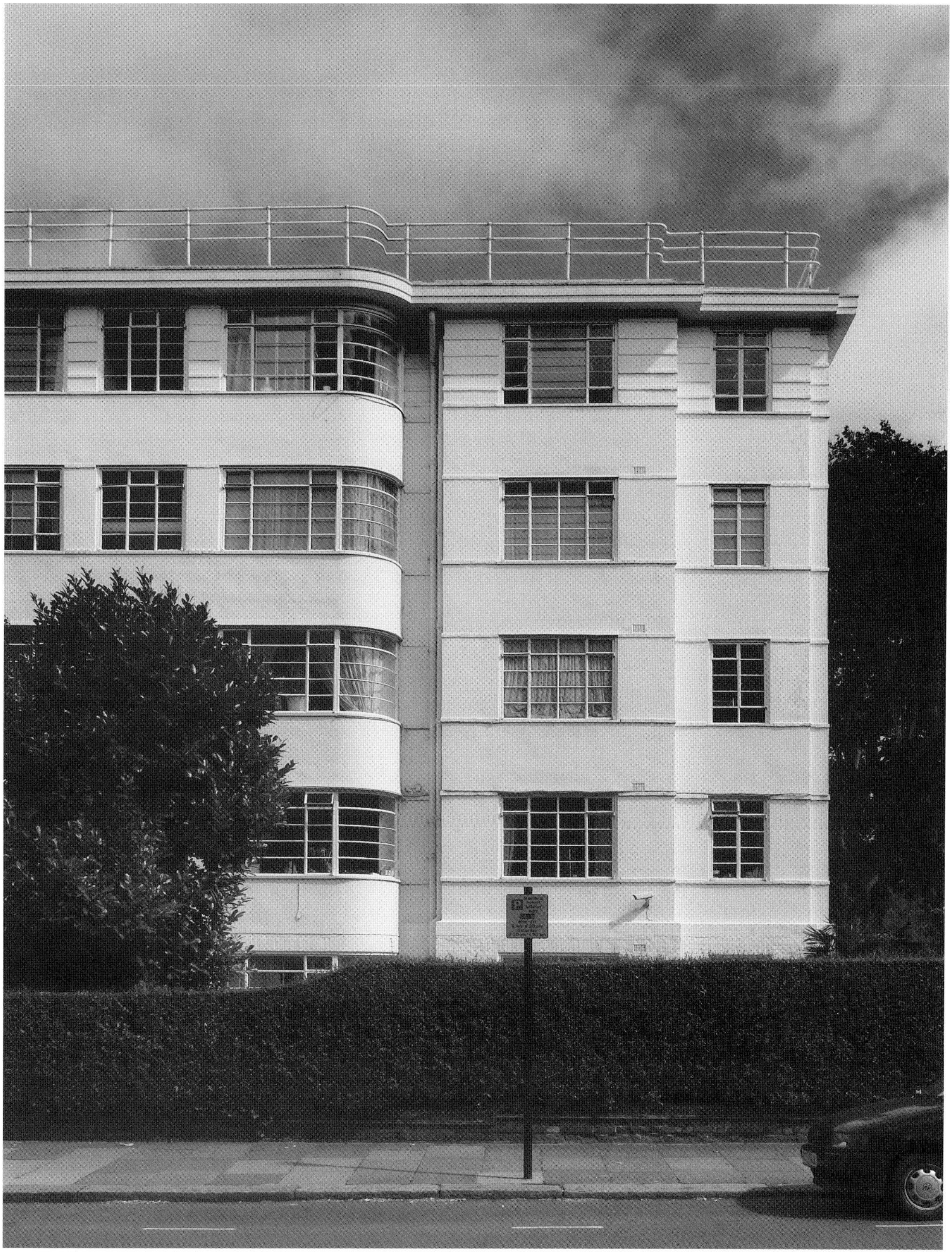

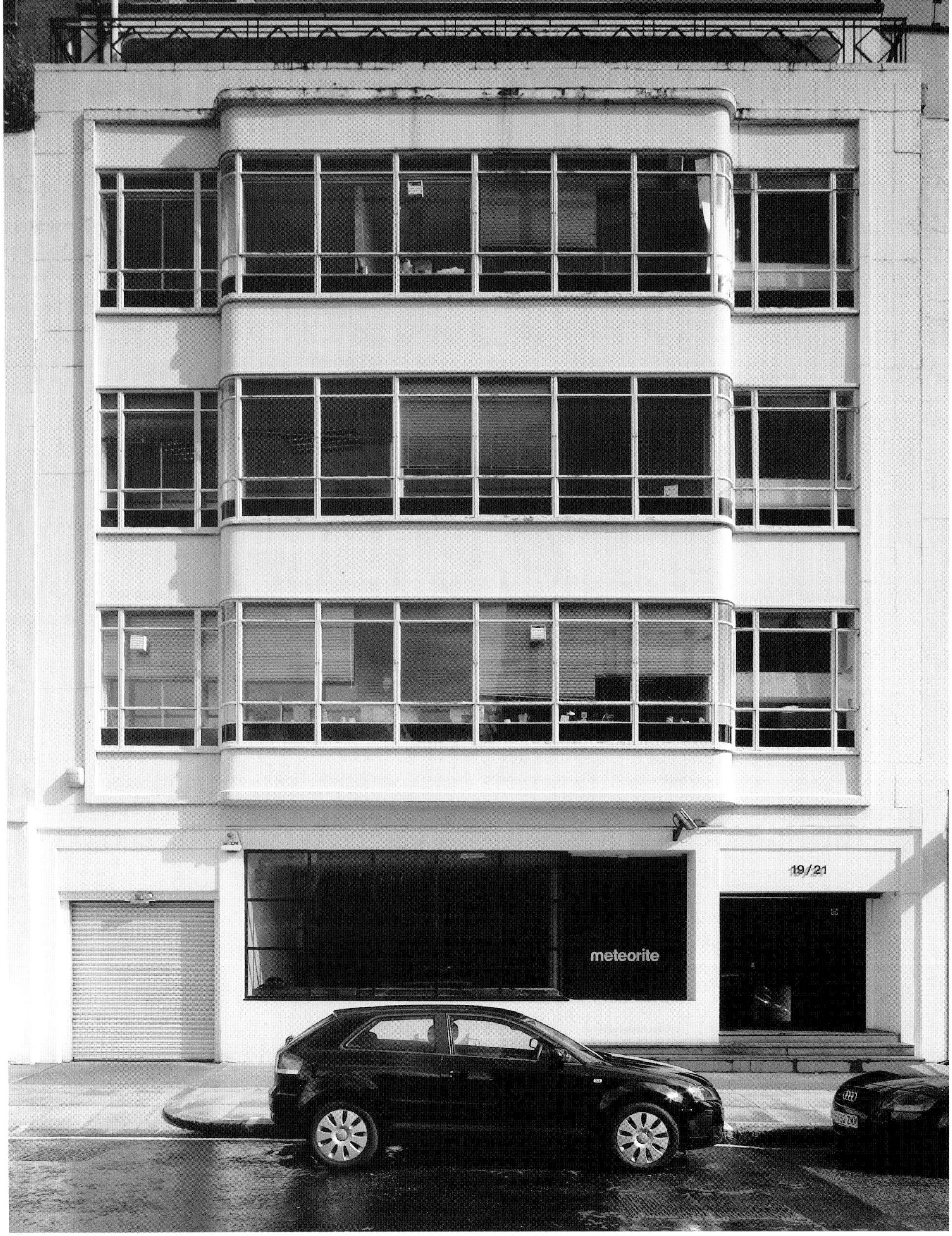
19/21
meteorite

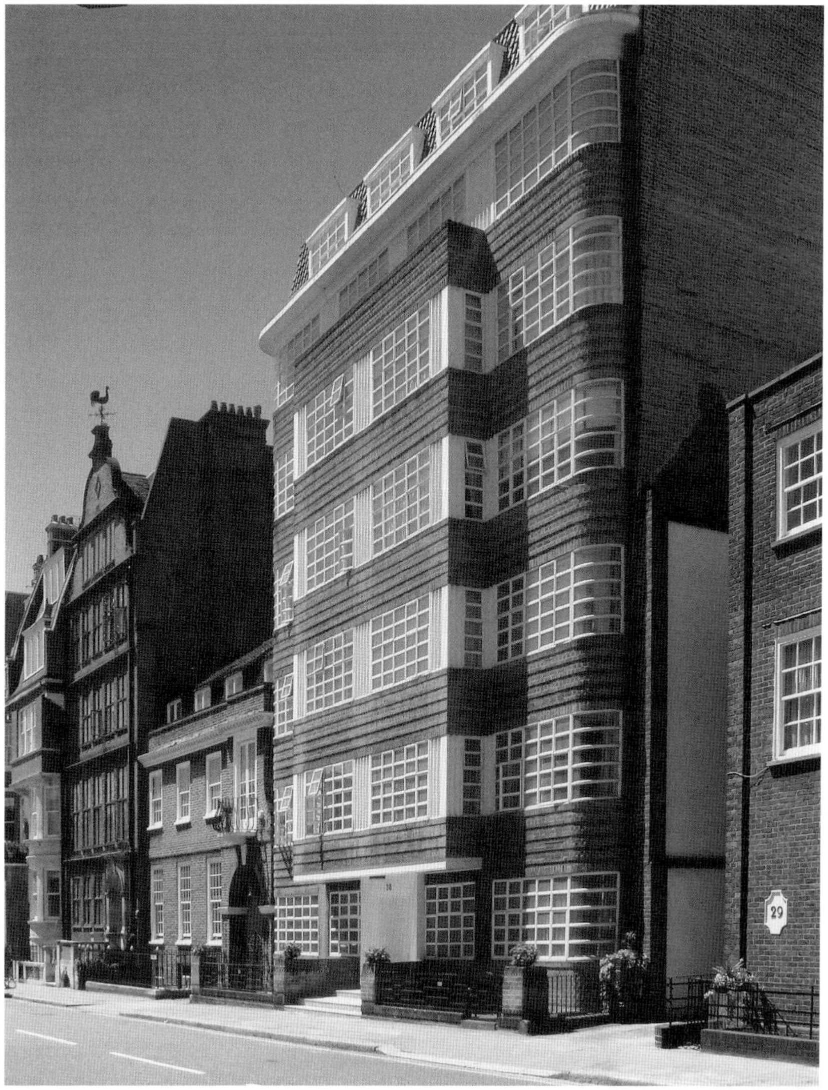
29

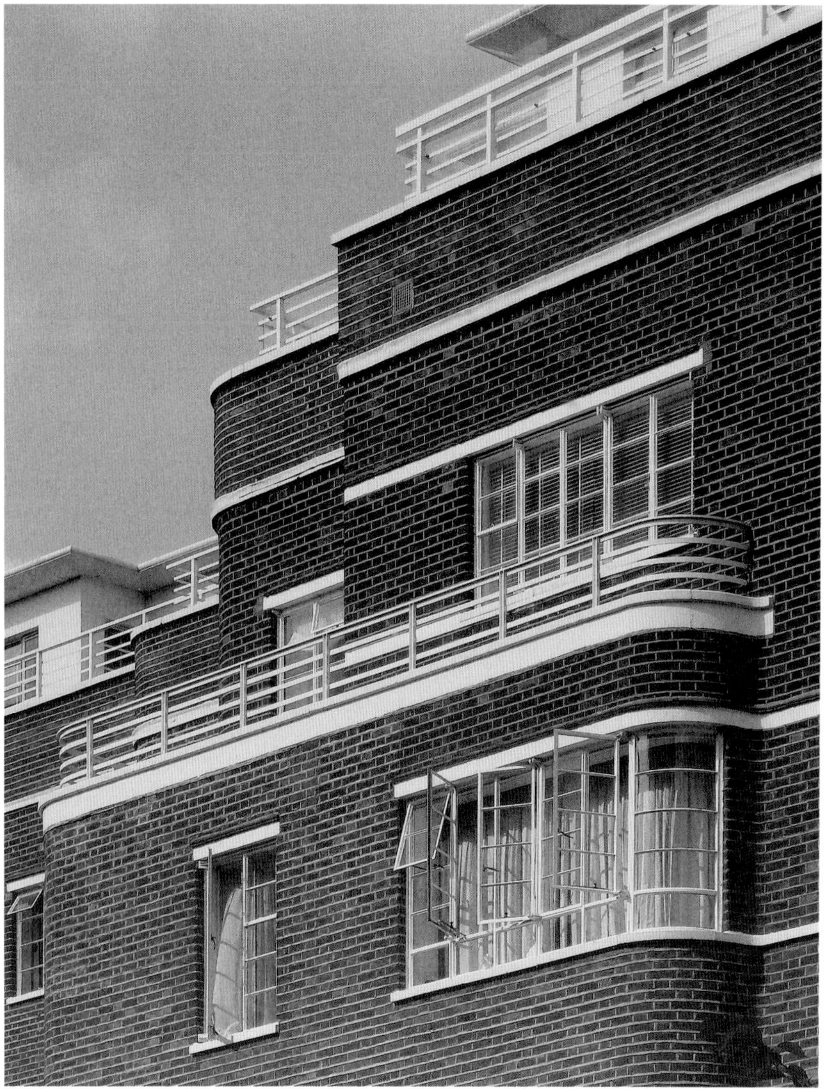

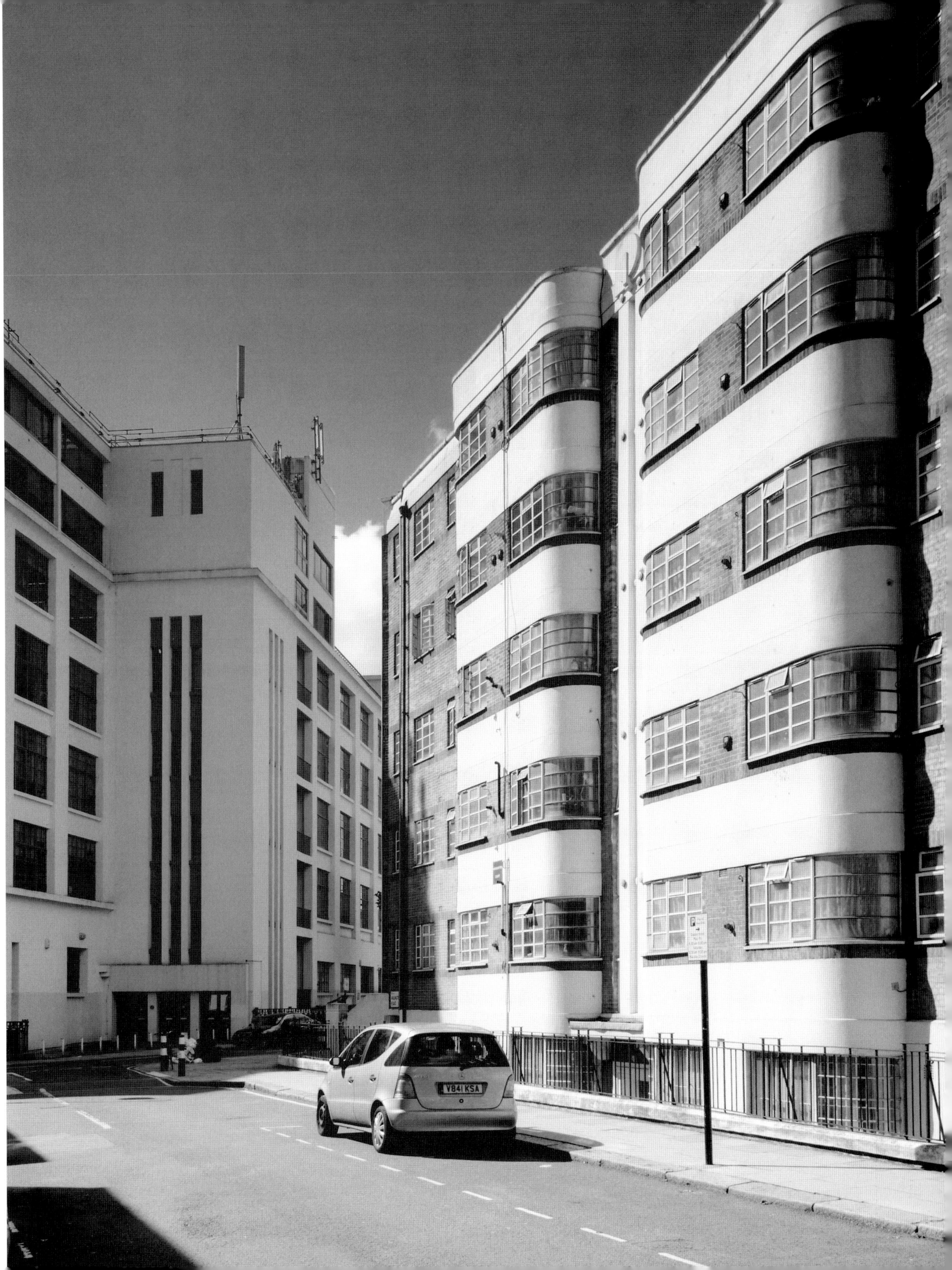
V841 KSA

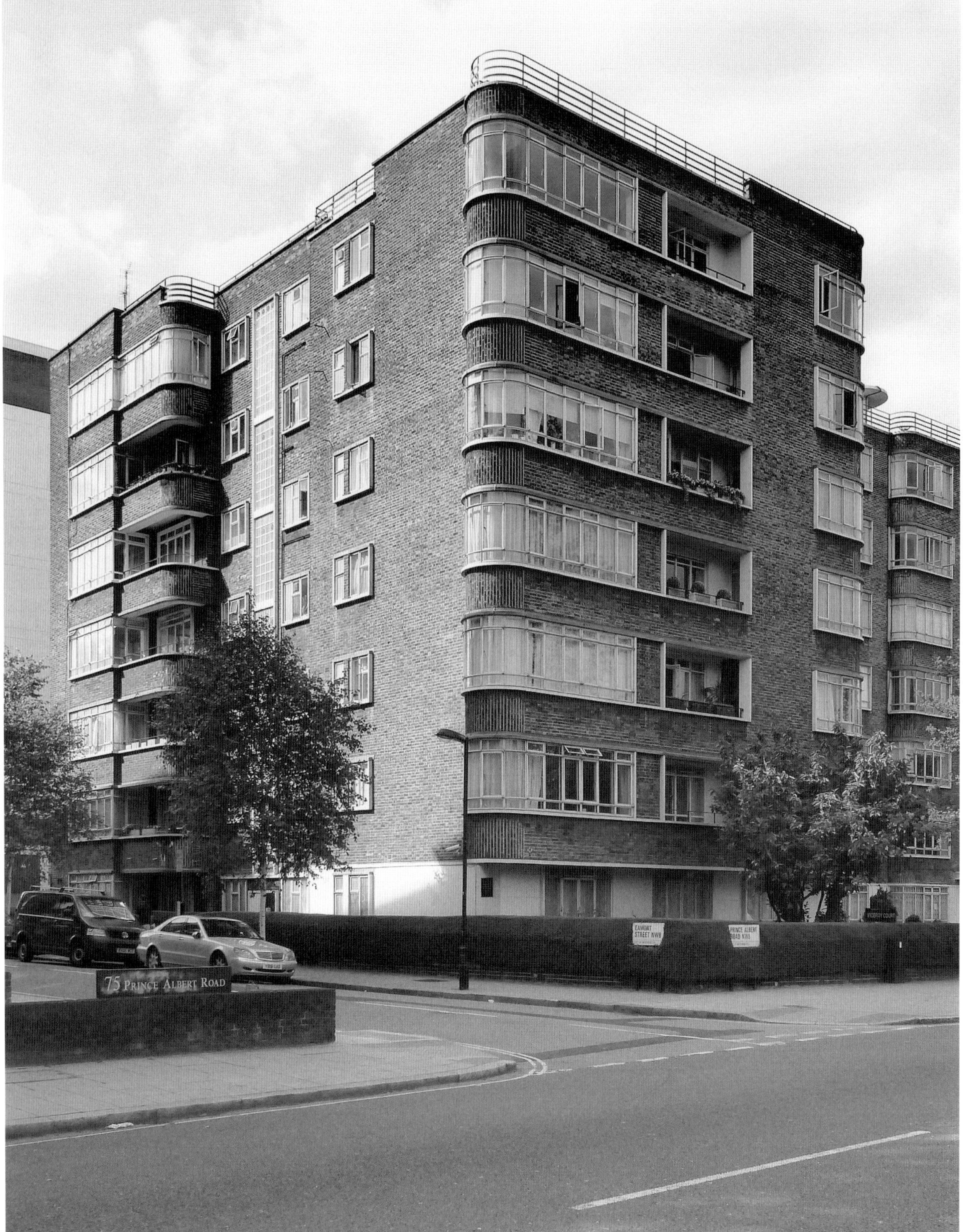
75 Prince Albert Road

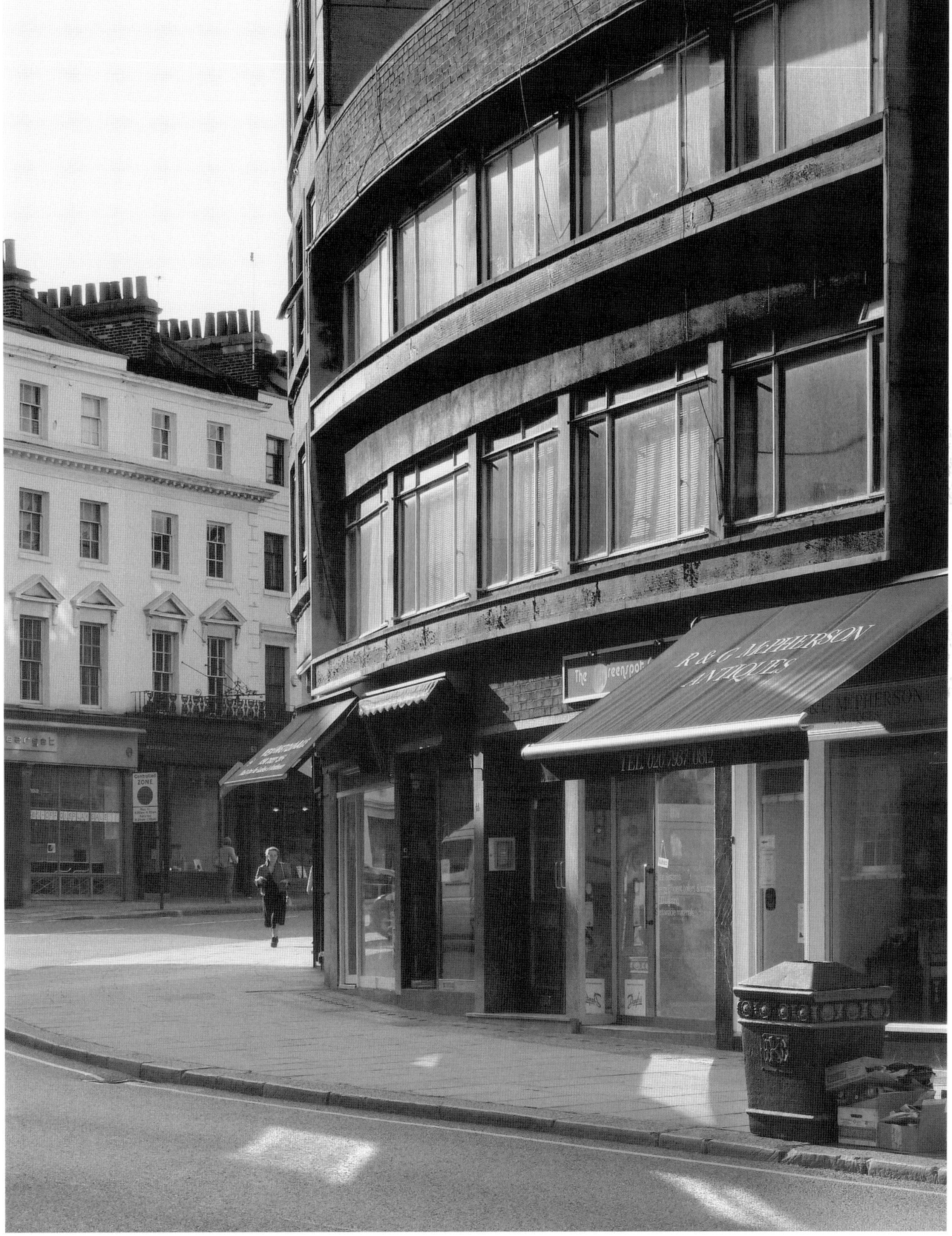
R & G McPHERSON
ANTIQUES
TEL. 020 7937 0812

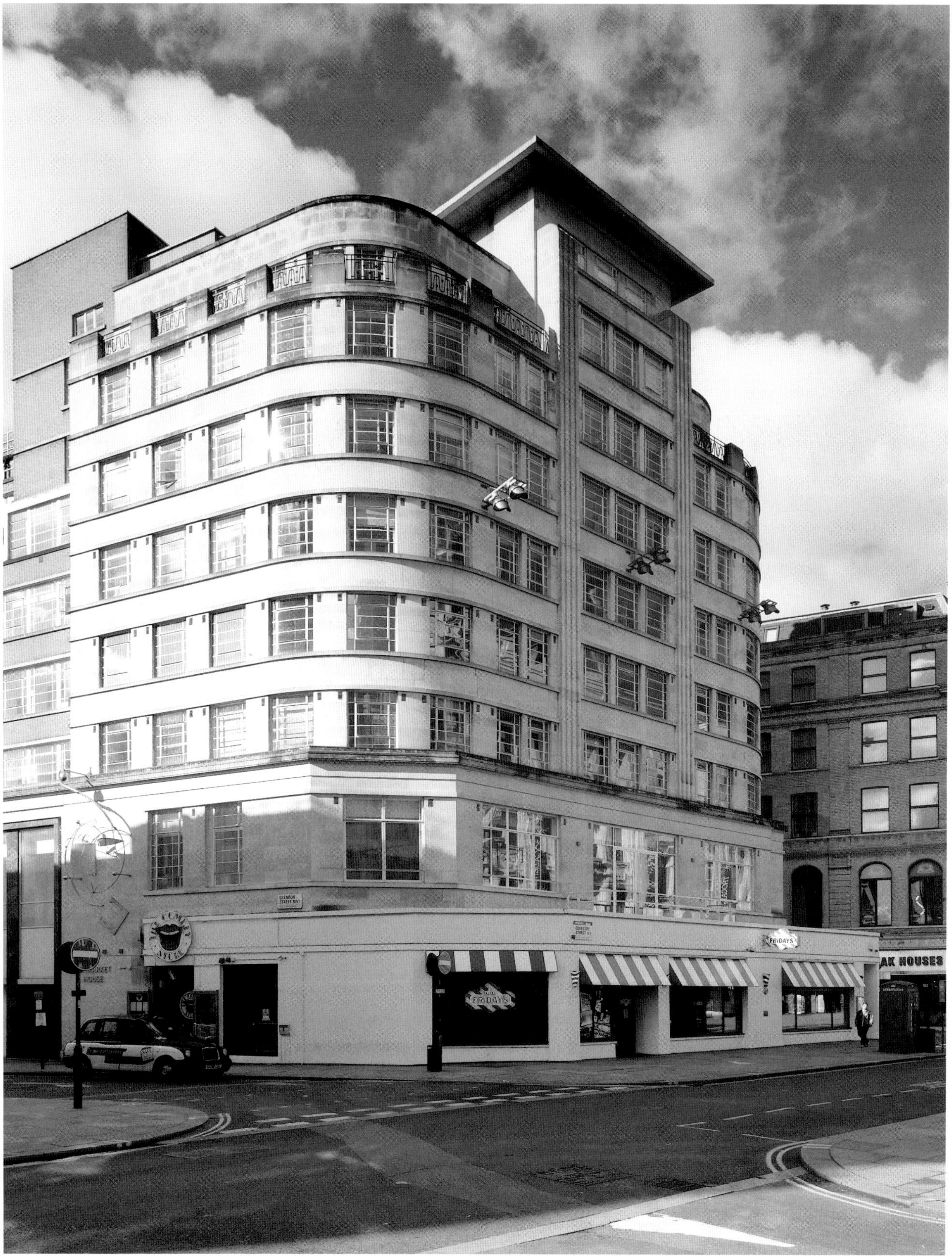

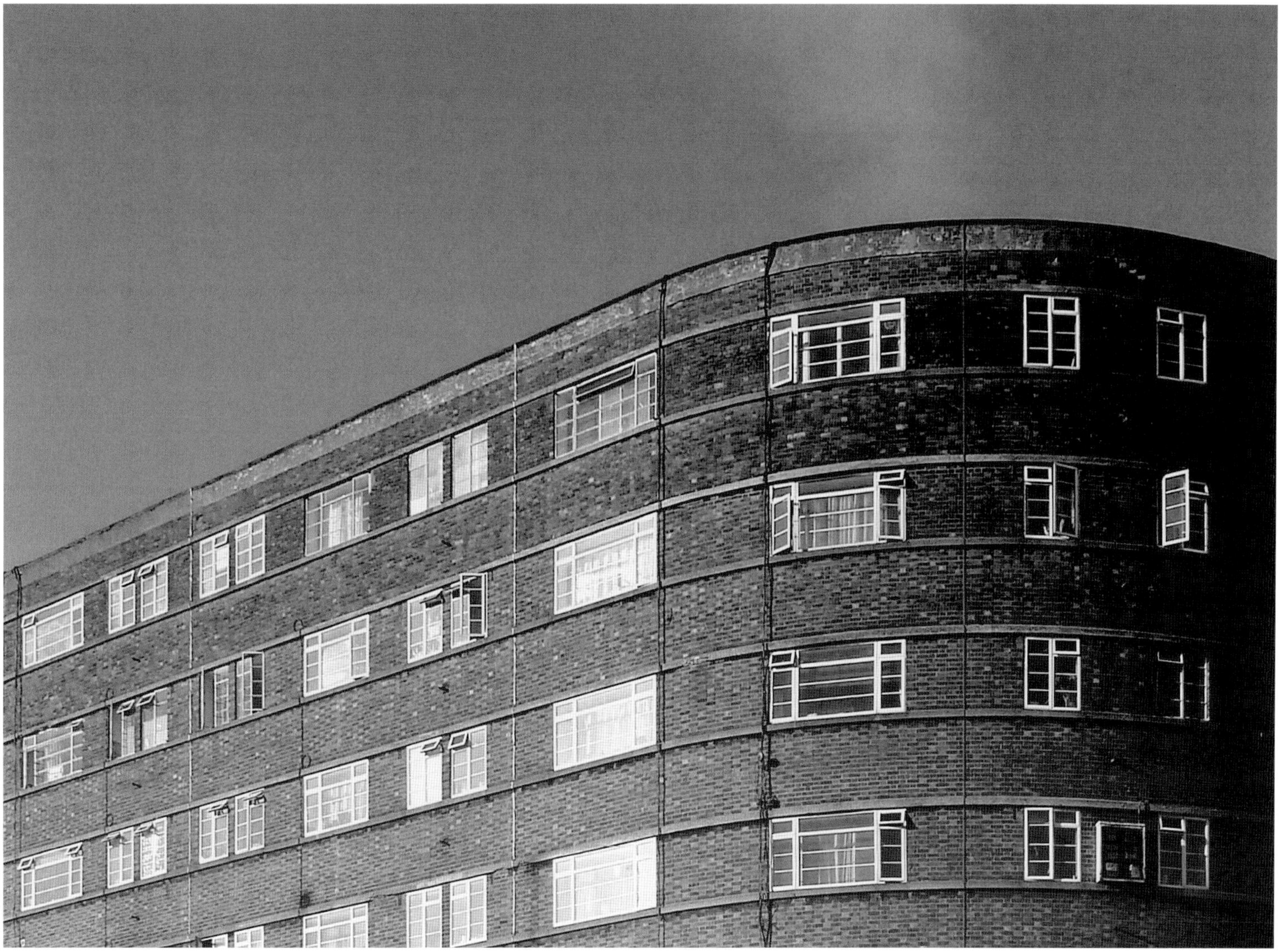

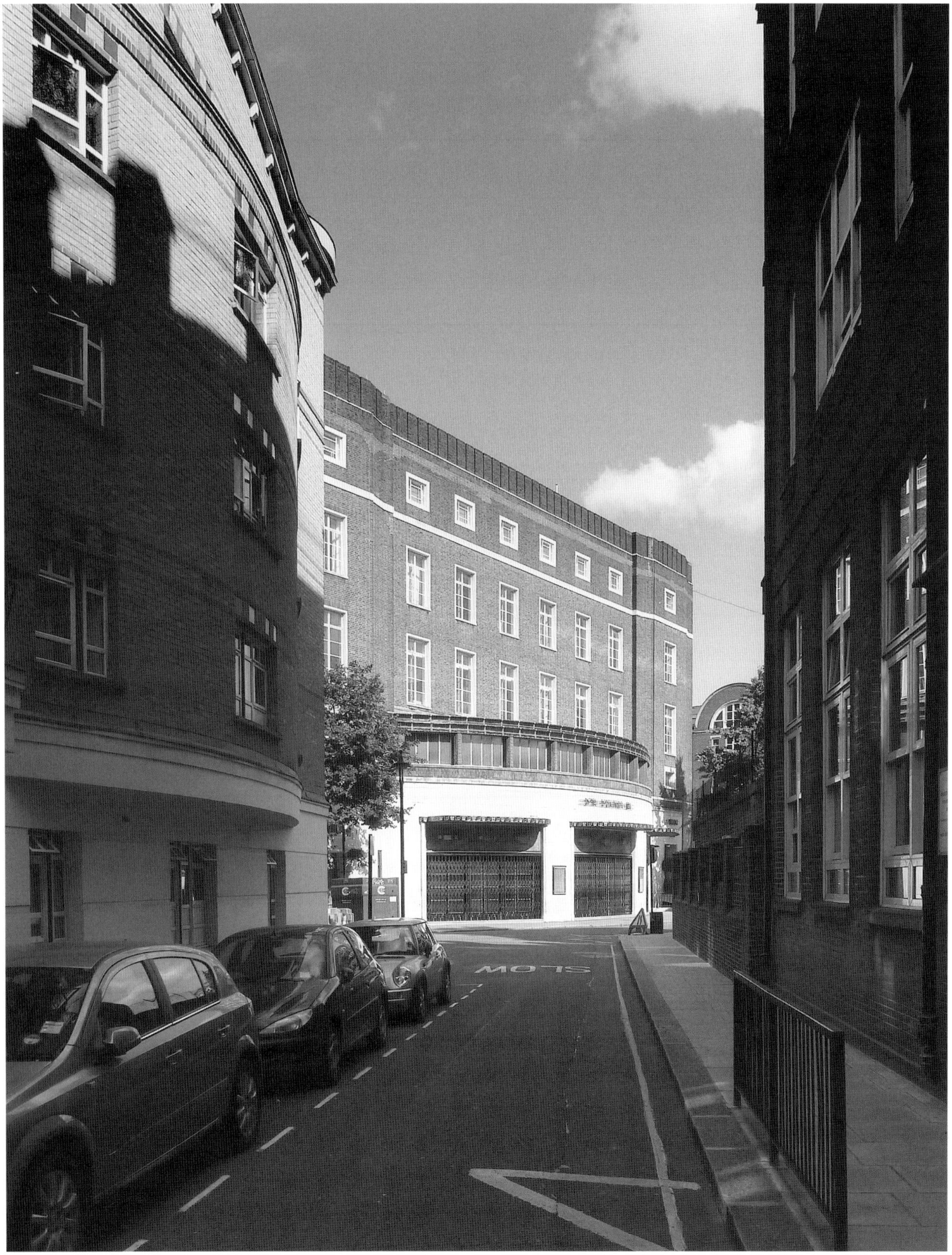
SLOW

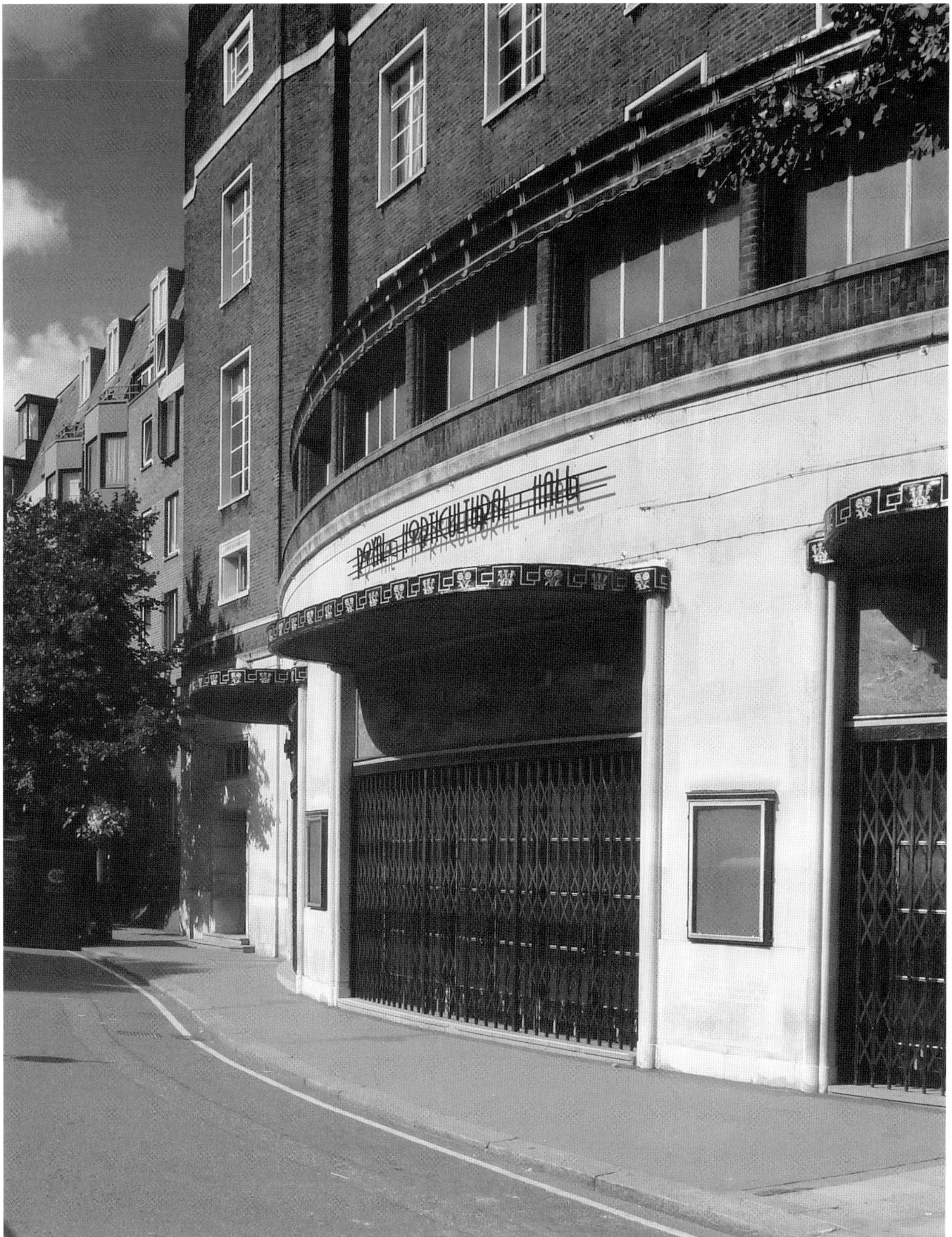
ROYAL HORTICULTURAL HALL

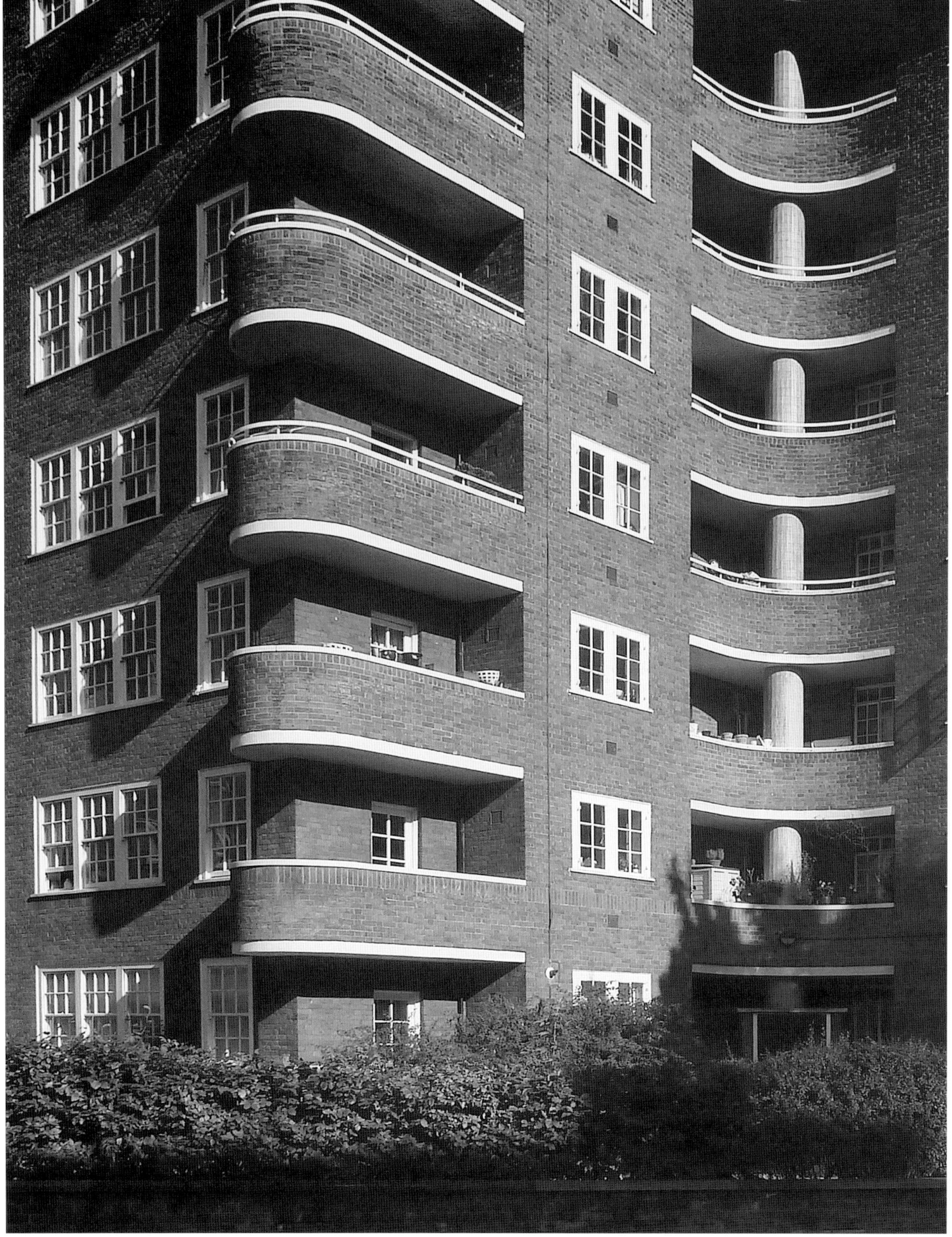

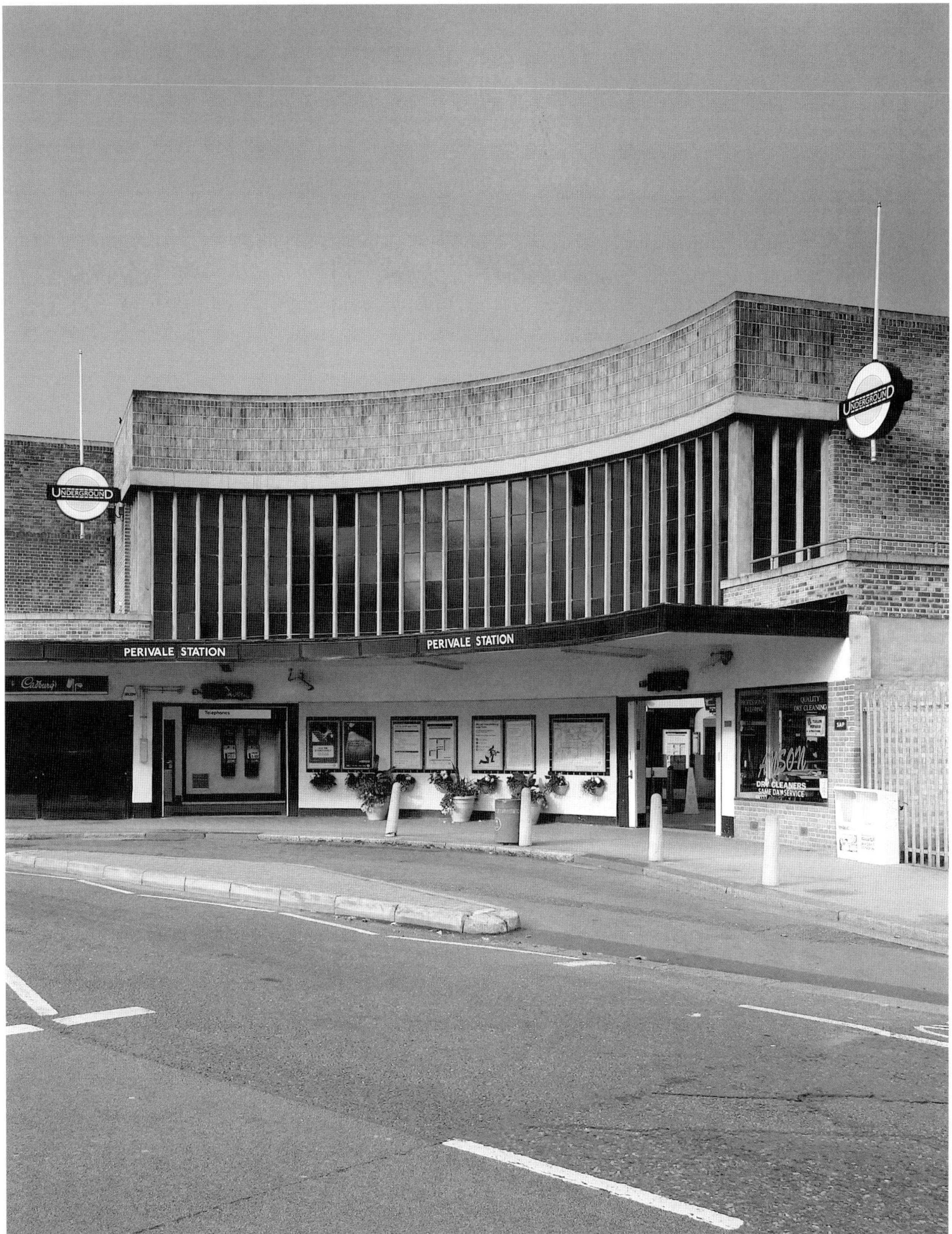
UNDERGROUND
UNDERGROUND
PERIVALE STATION
PERIVALE STATION
Telephones
DRY CLEANERS

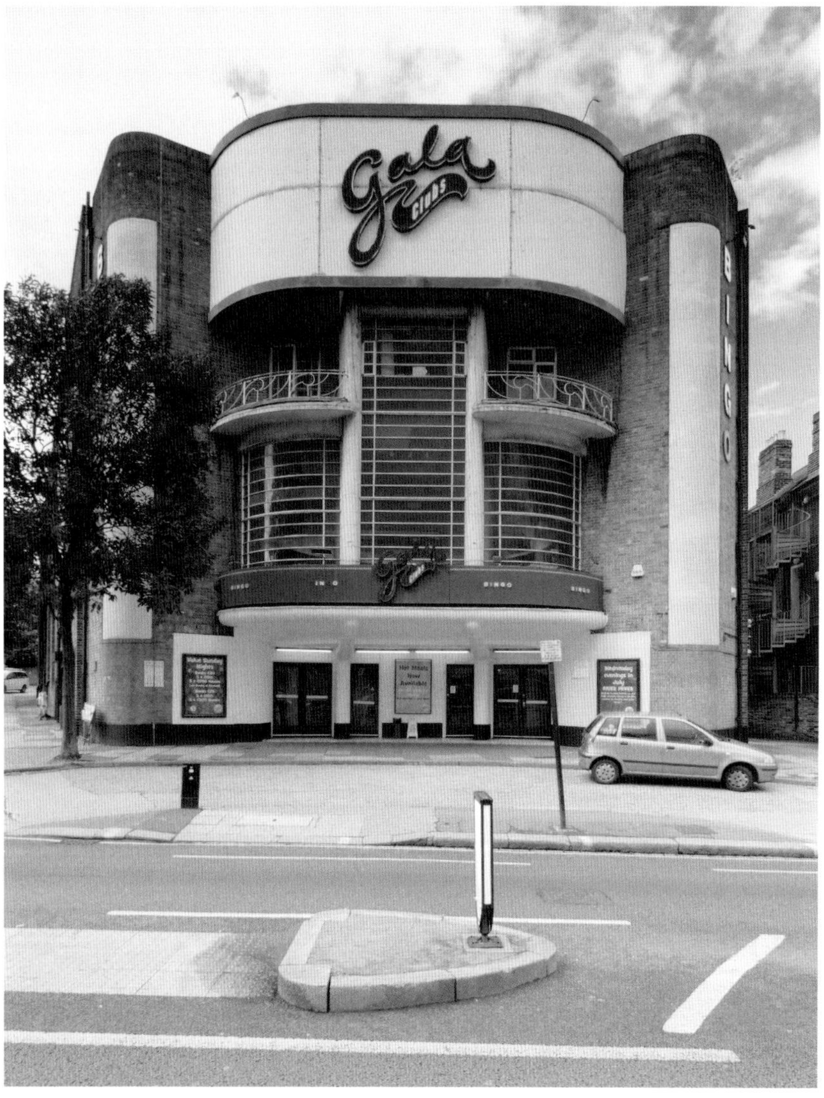
Gala
BINGO

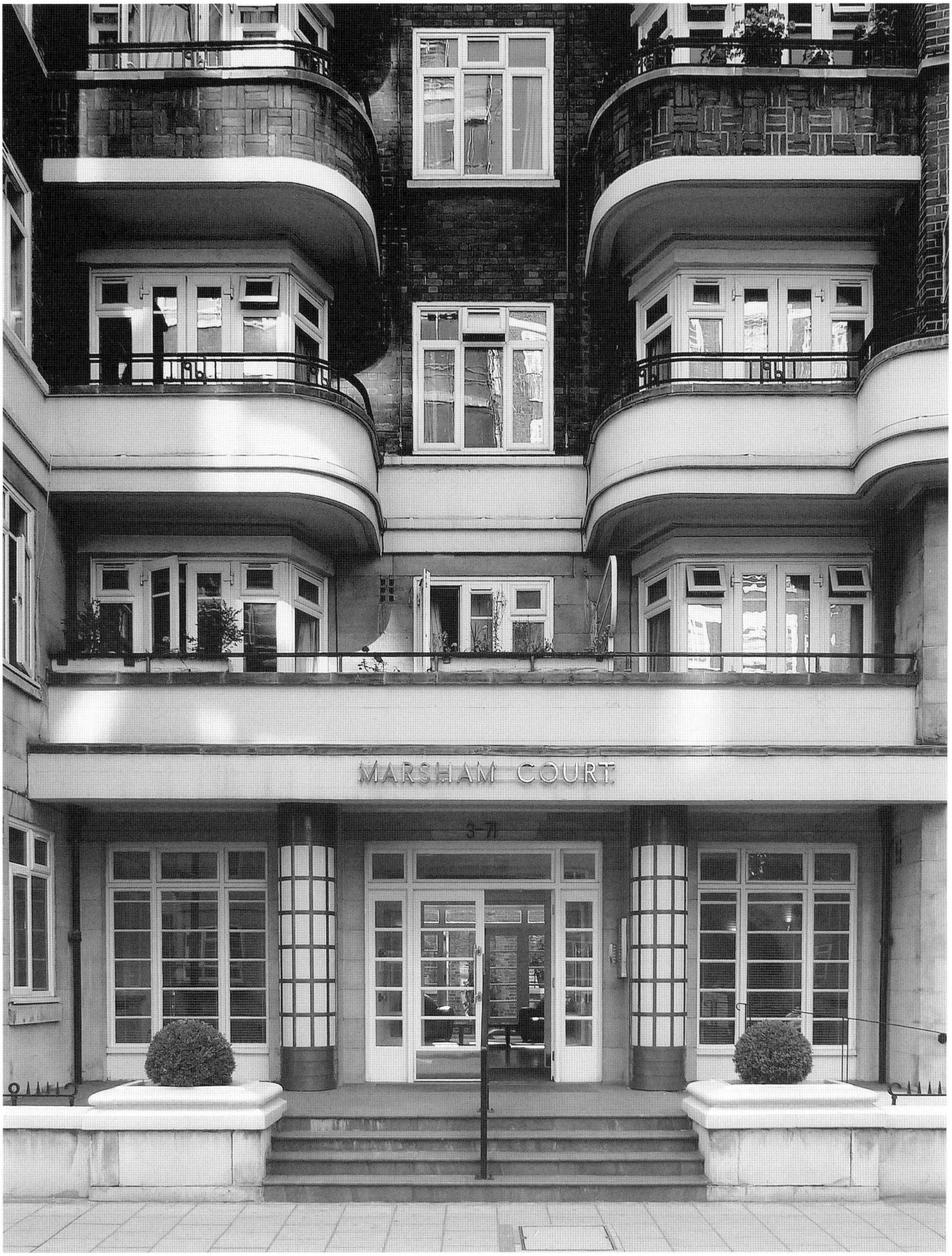
MARSHAM COURT
3–71

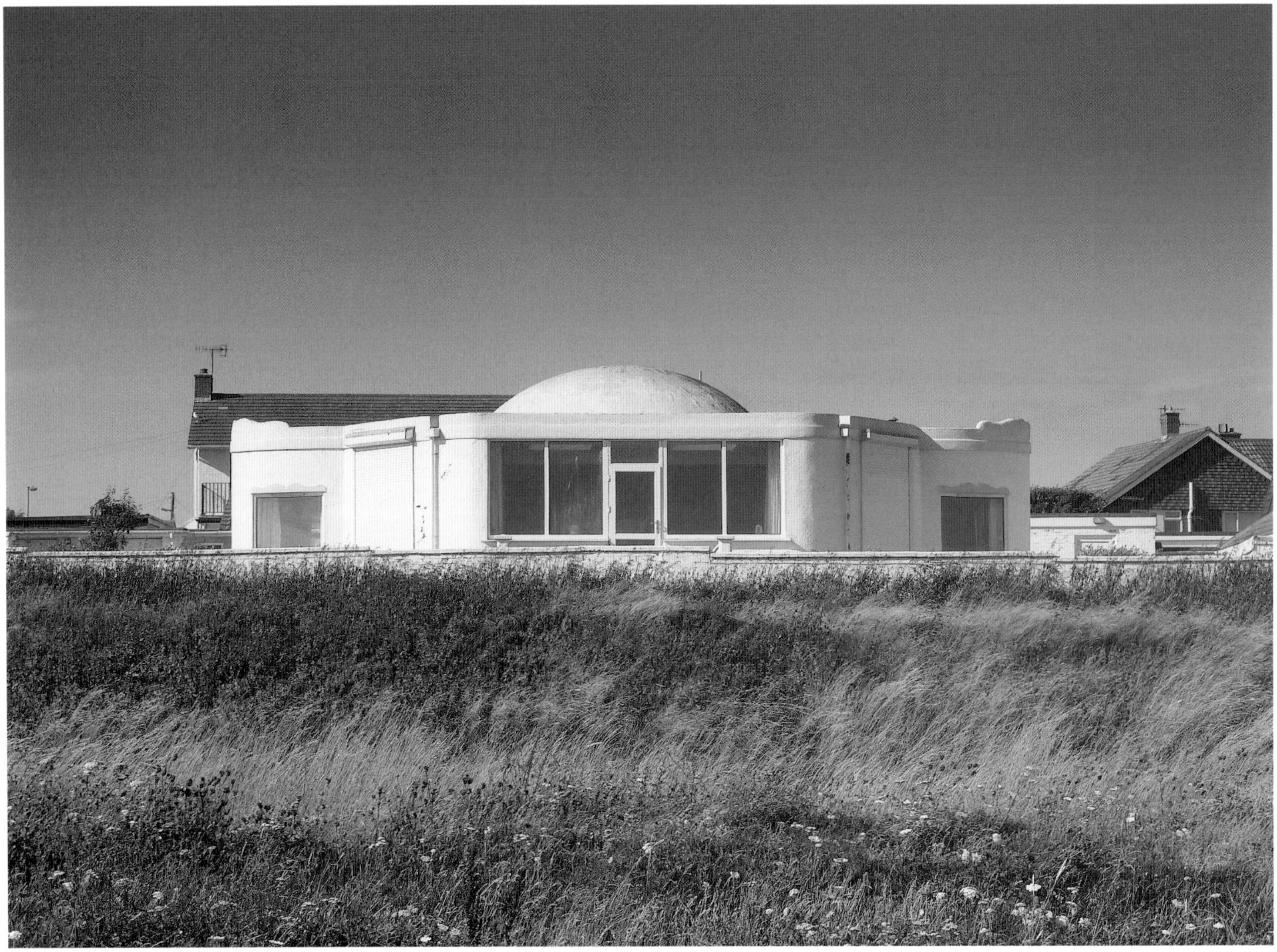

21

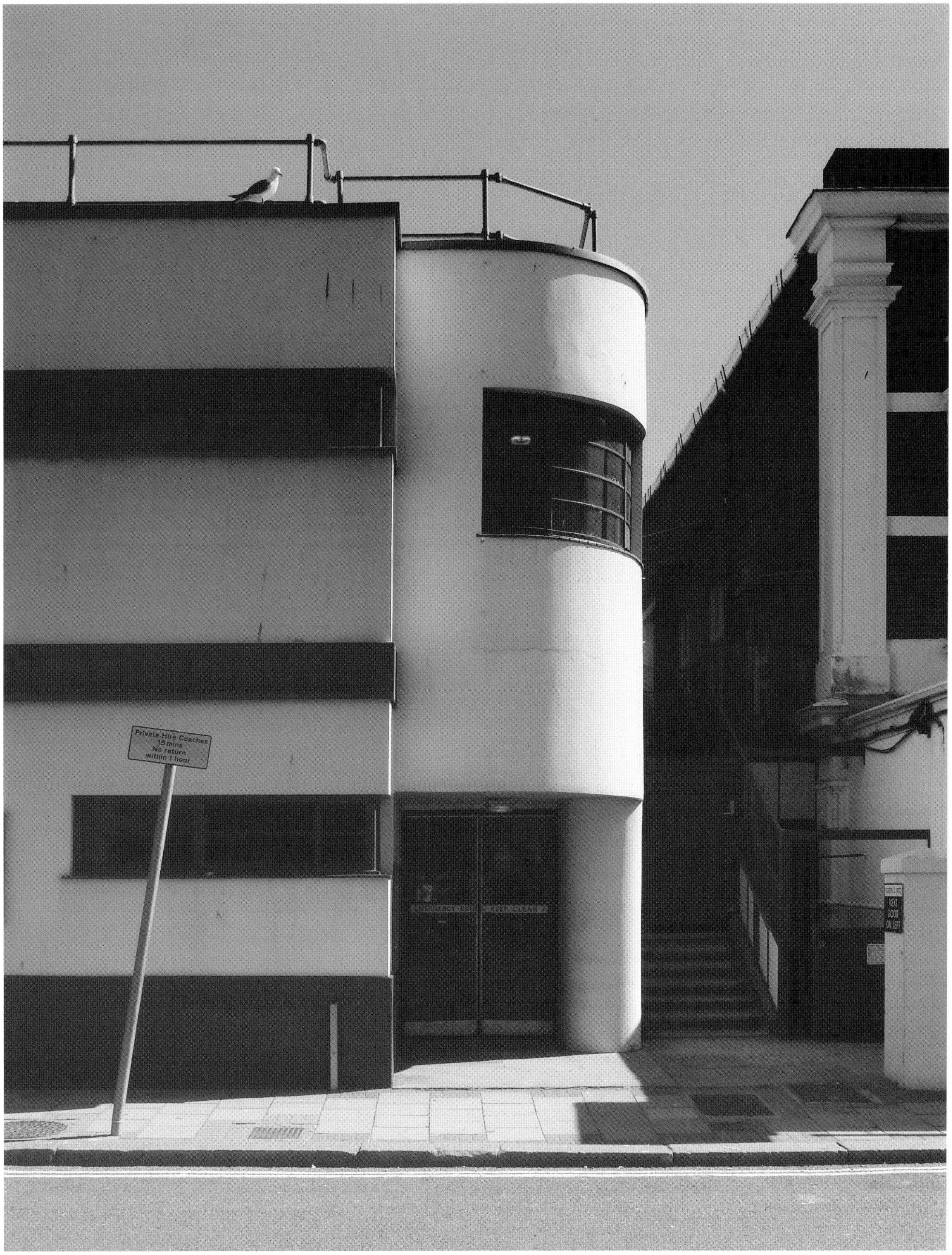
Private Hire Coaches
15 mins
No return
within 1 hour
KEEP CLEAR
NEXT
DOOR
ON LEFT

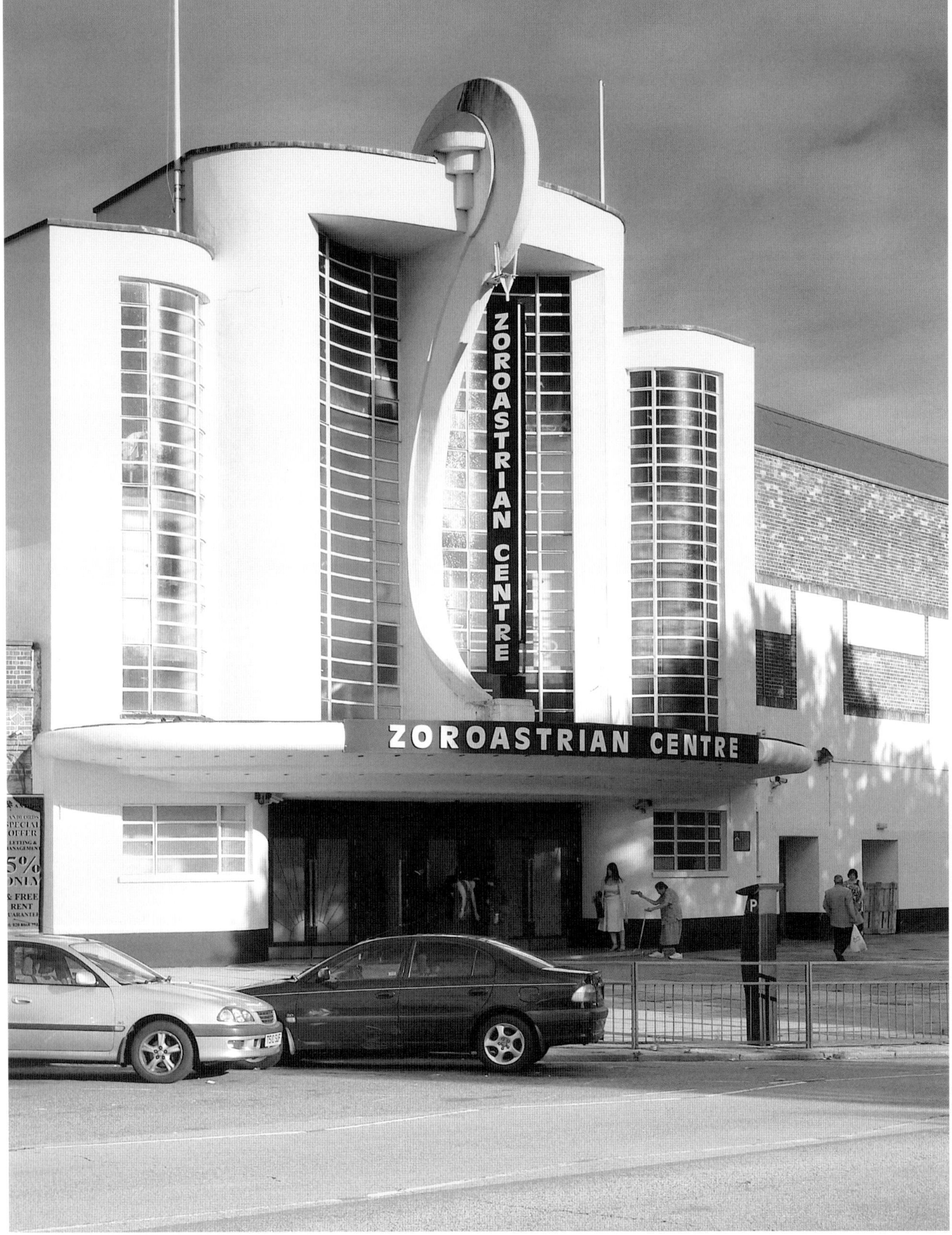
ZOROASTRIAN CENTRE
ZOROASTRIAN CENTRE

222

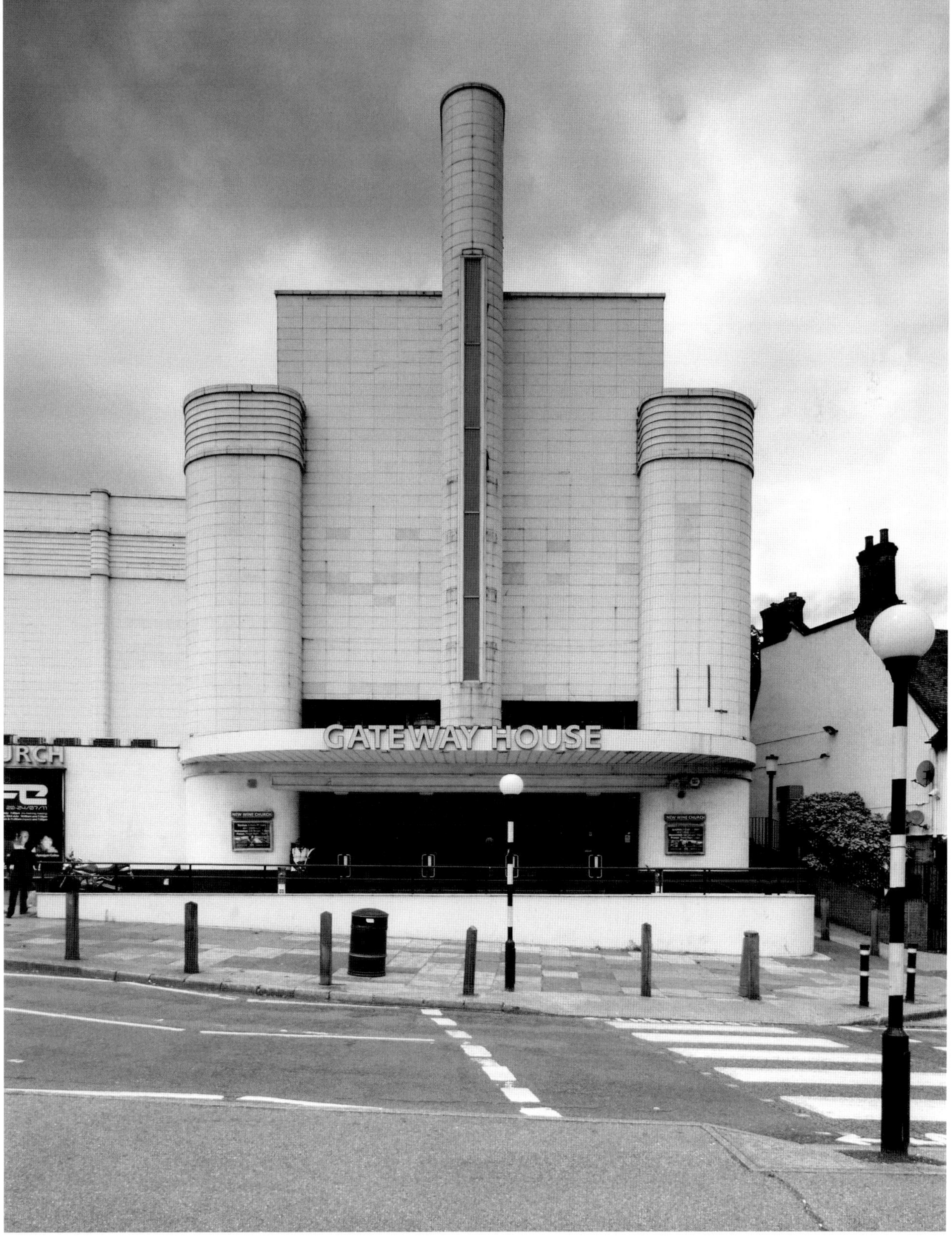

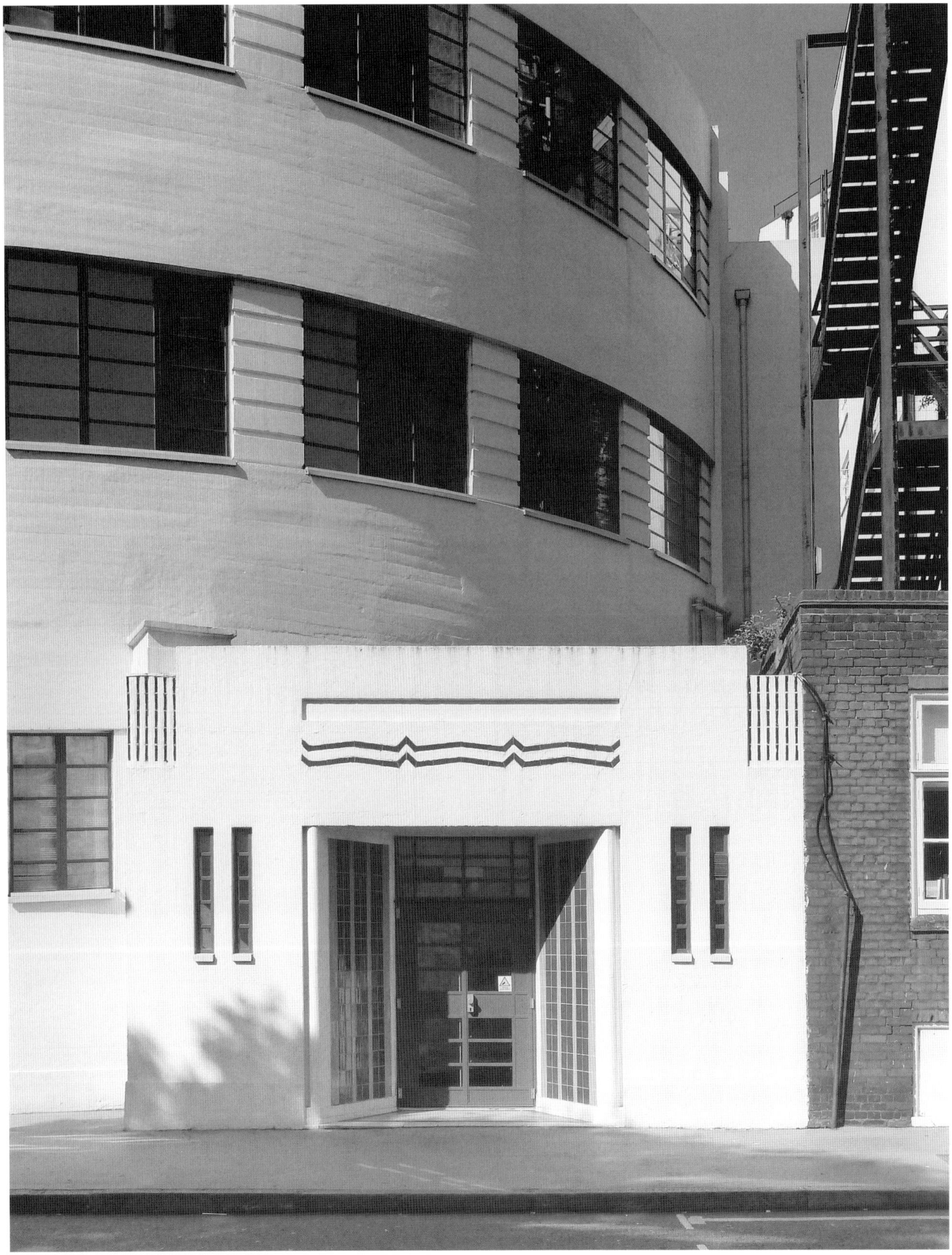

224

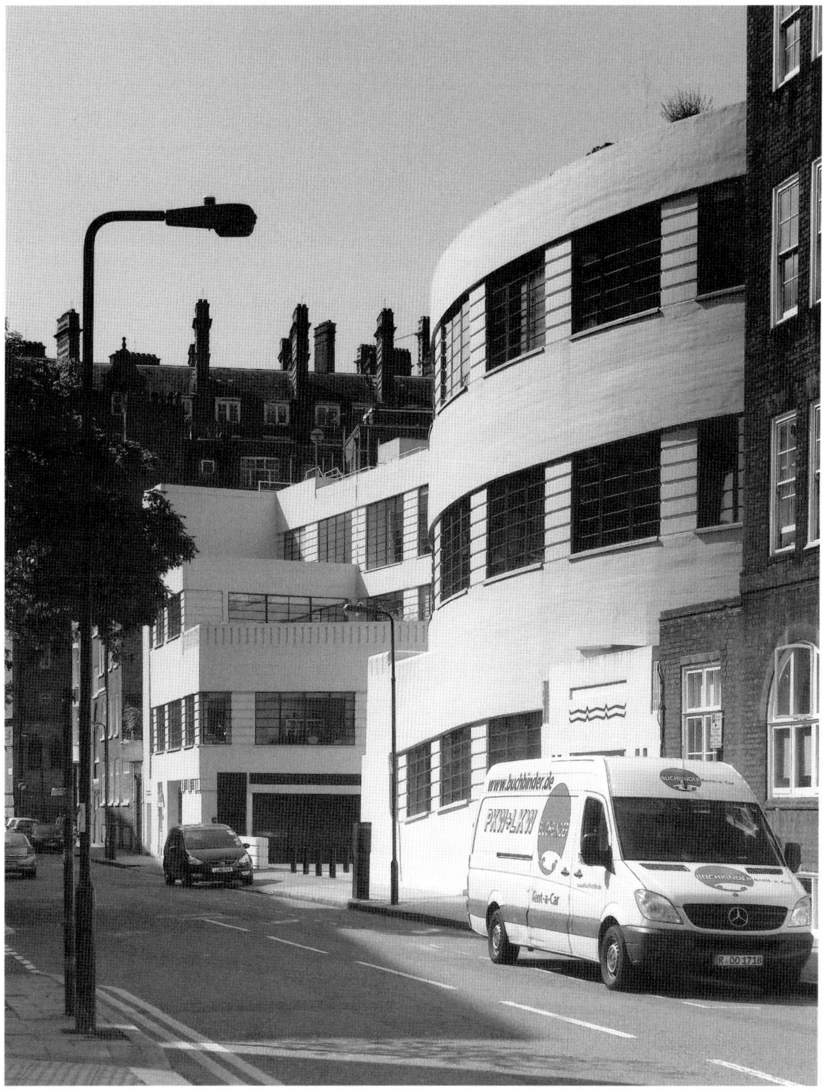
www.buchbinder.de
Rent-a-Car

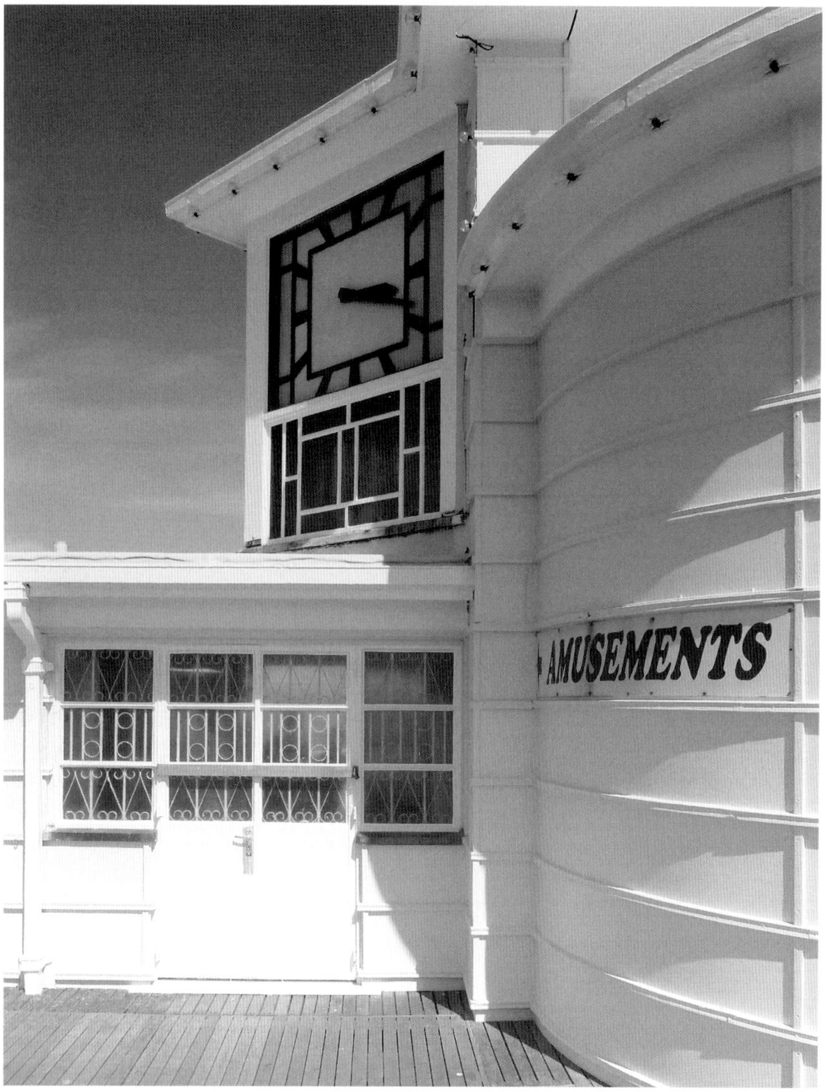
AMUSEMENTS

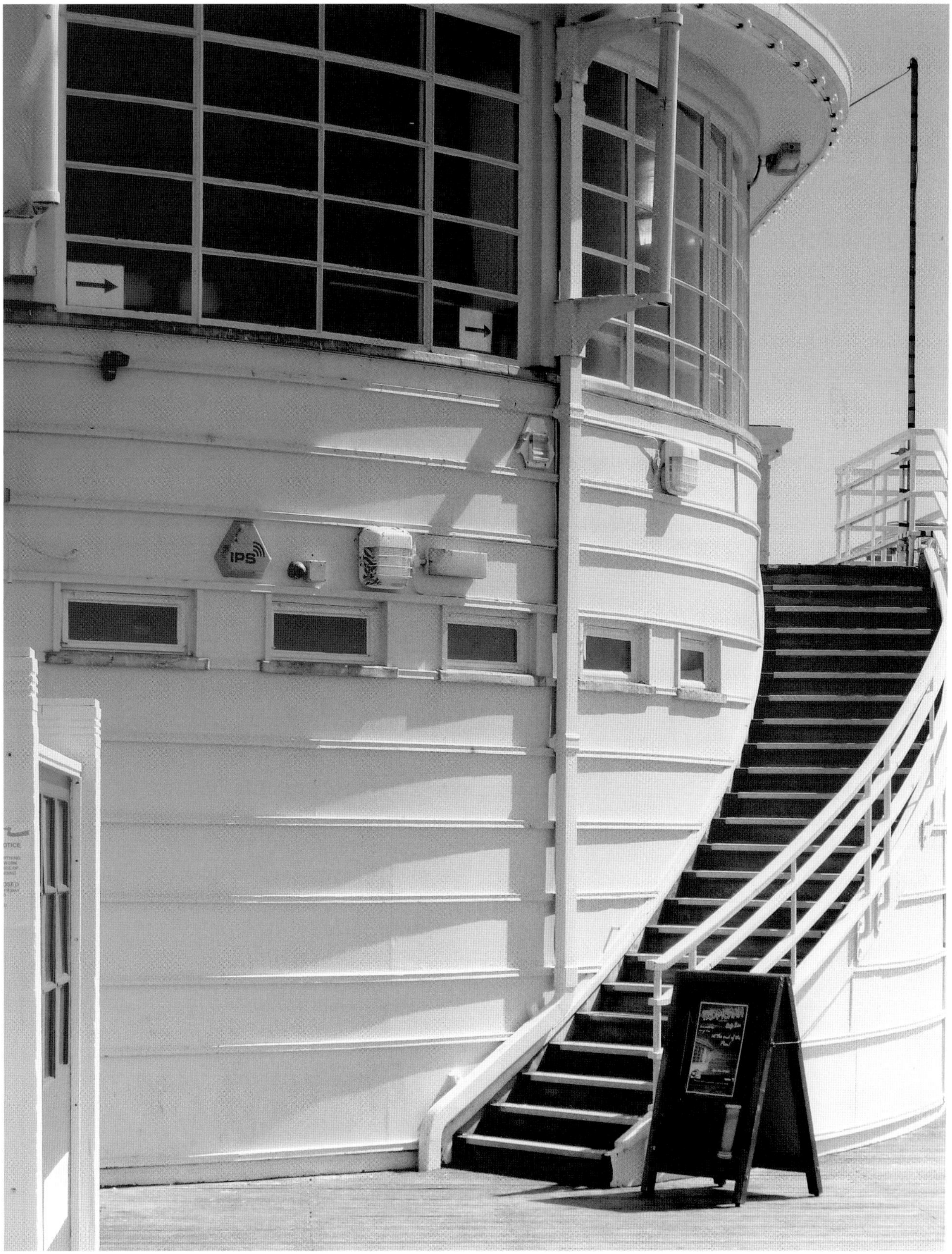
IPS

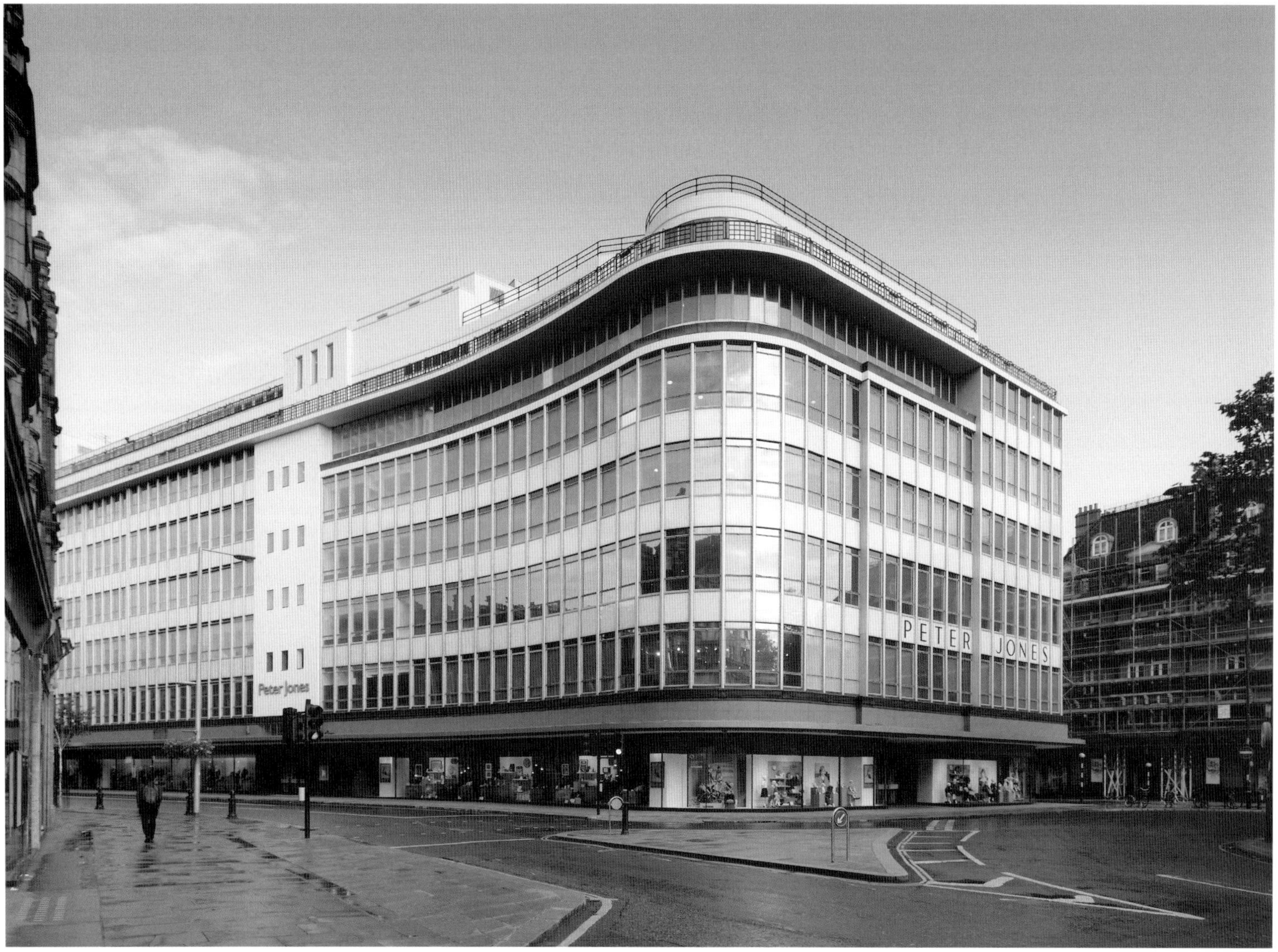
Peter Jones
PETER JONES

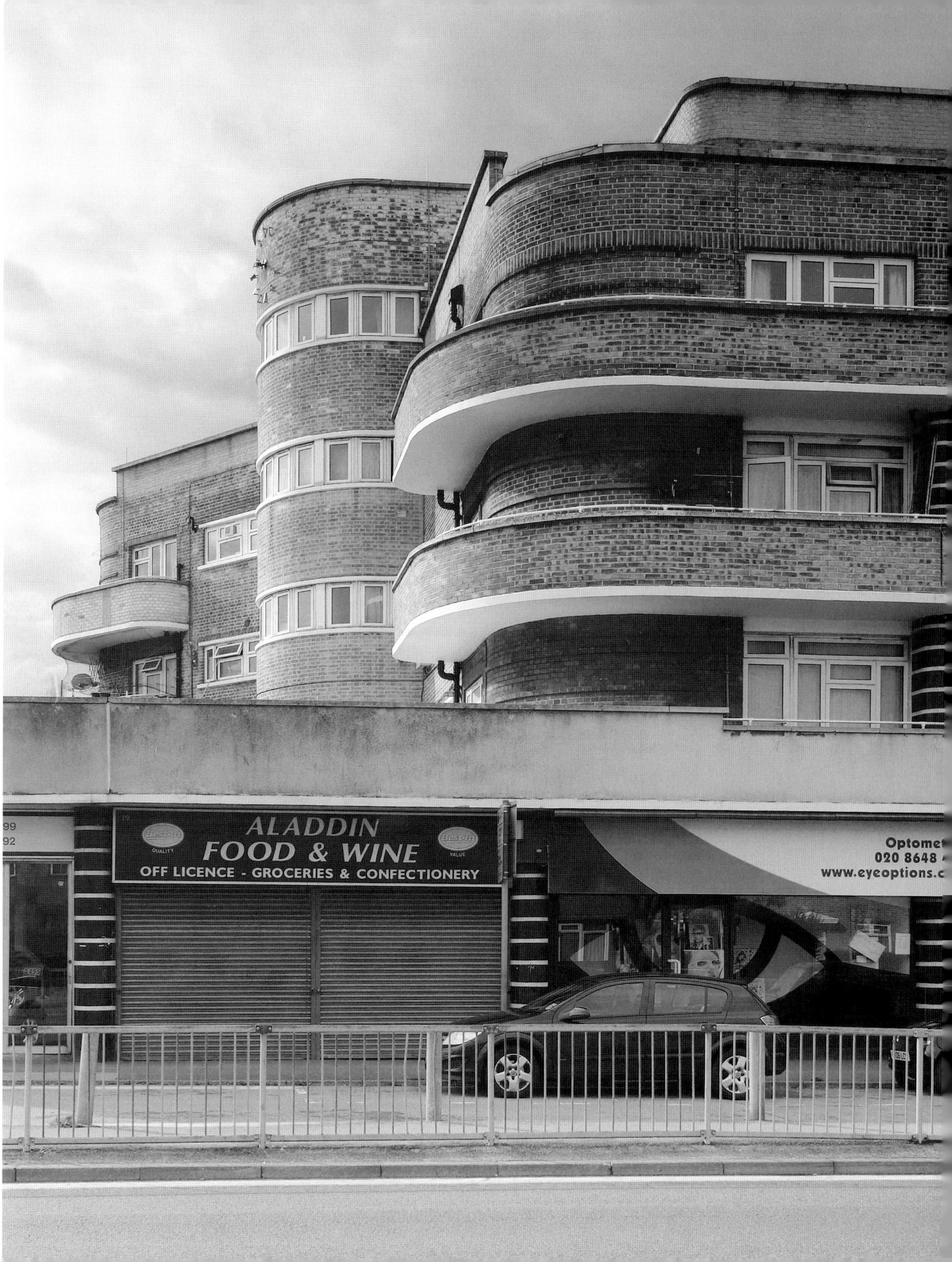
ALADDIN
FOOD & WINE
OFF LICENCE - GROCERIES & CONFECTIONERY

227

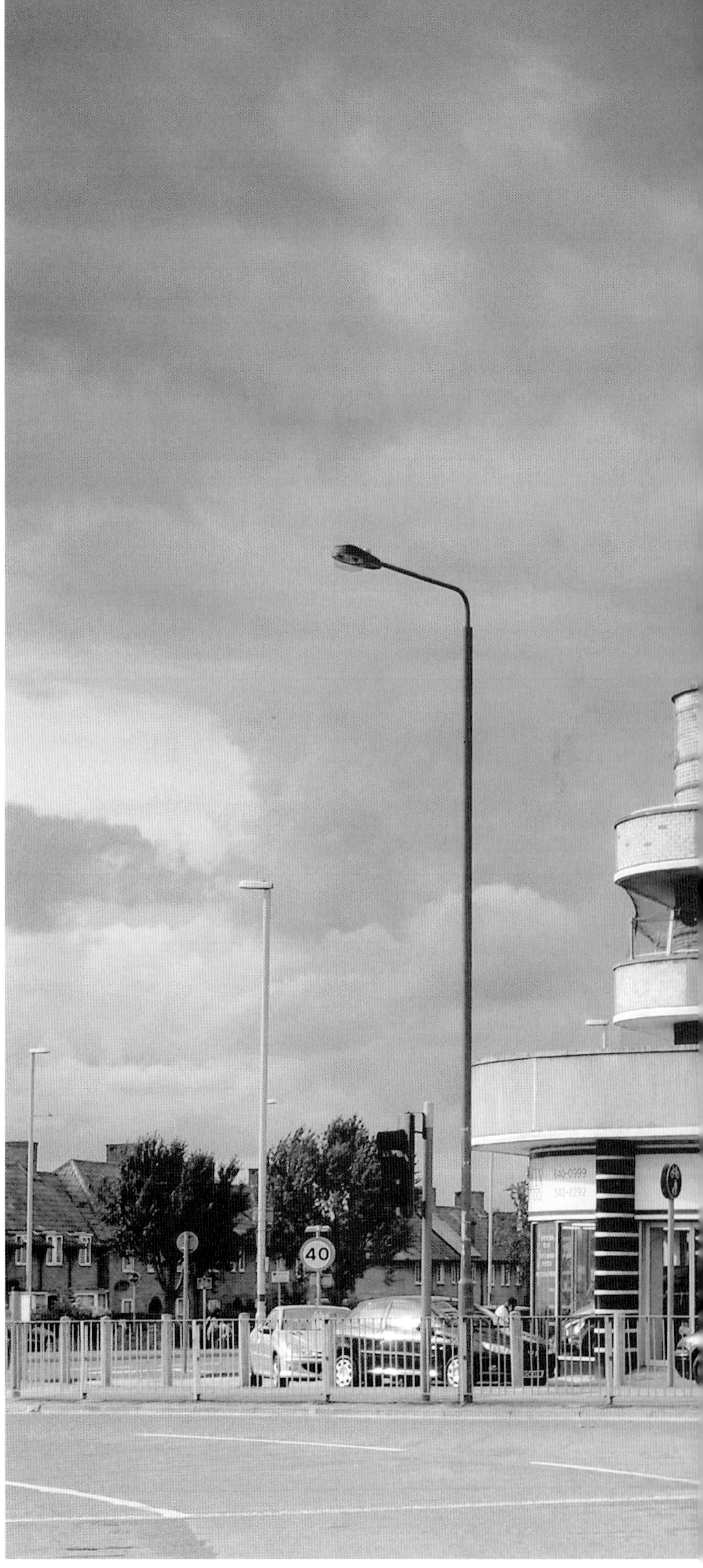

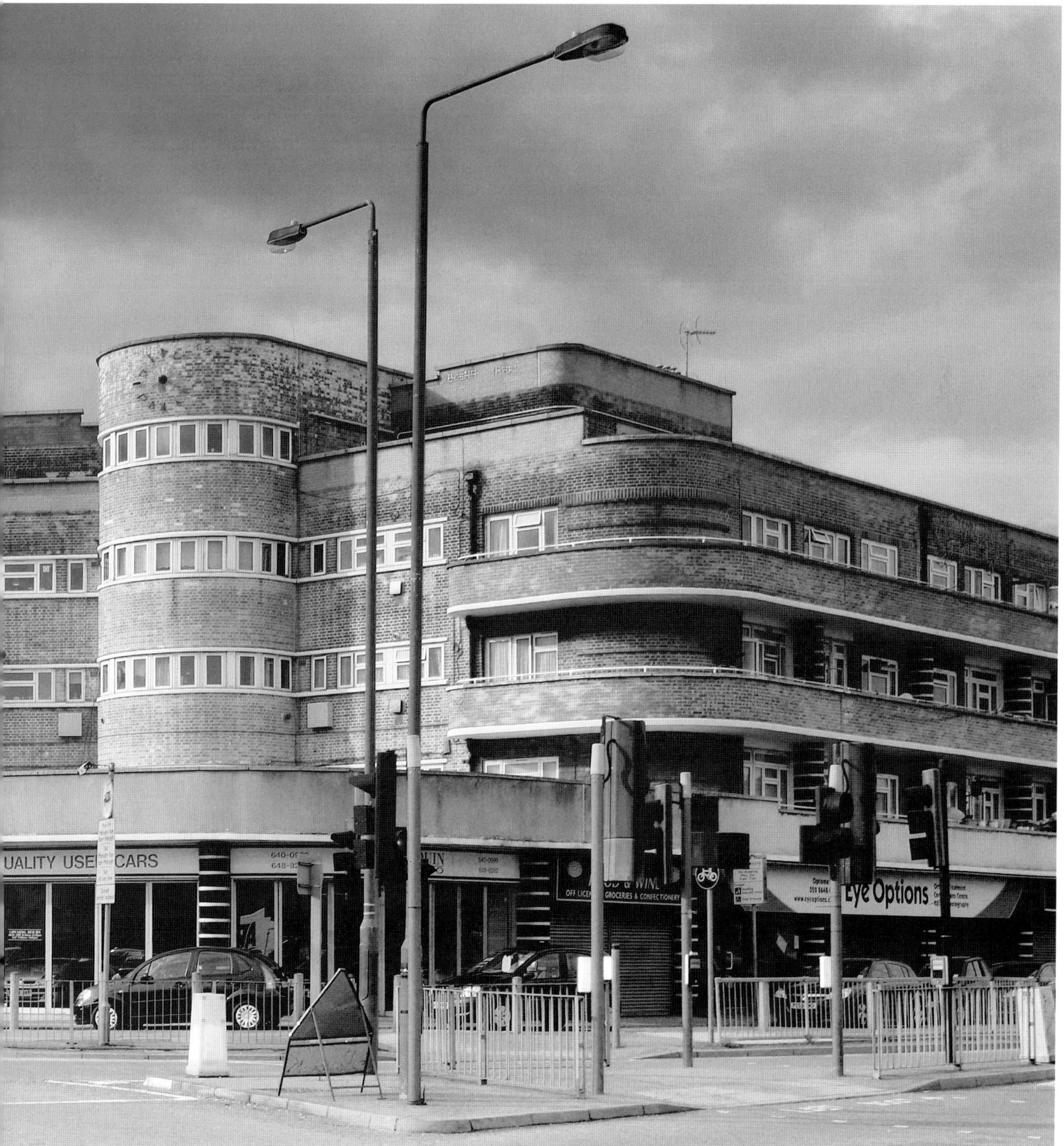
GROCERIES & CONFECTIONERY
Eye Options

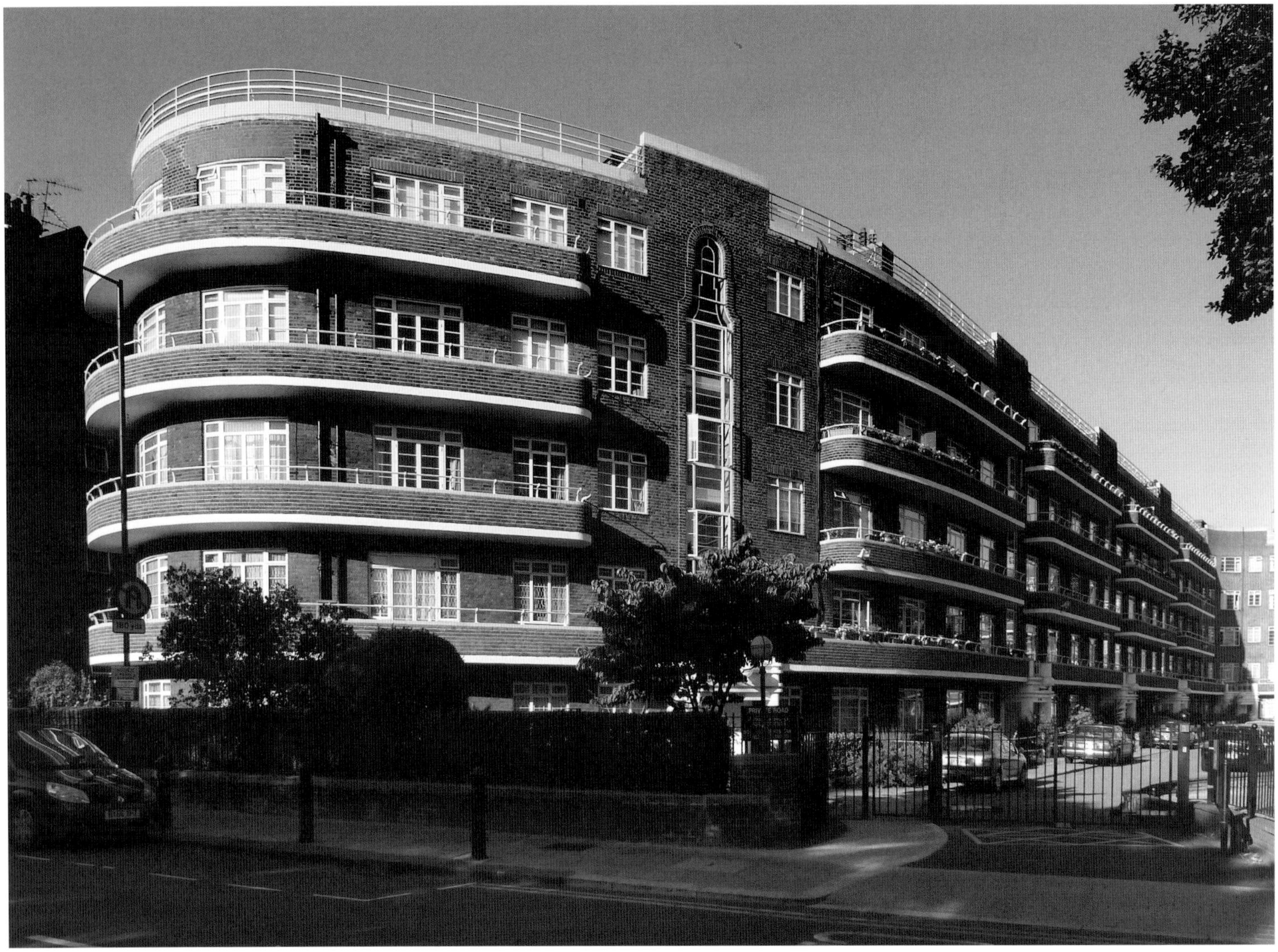

22

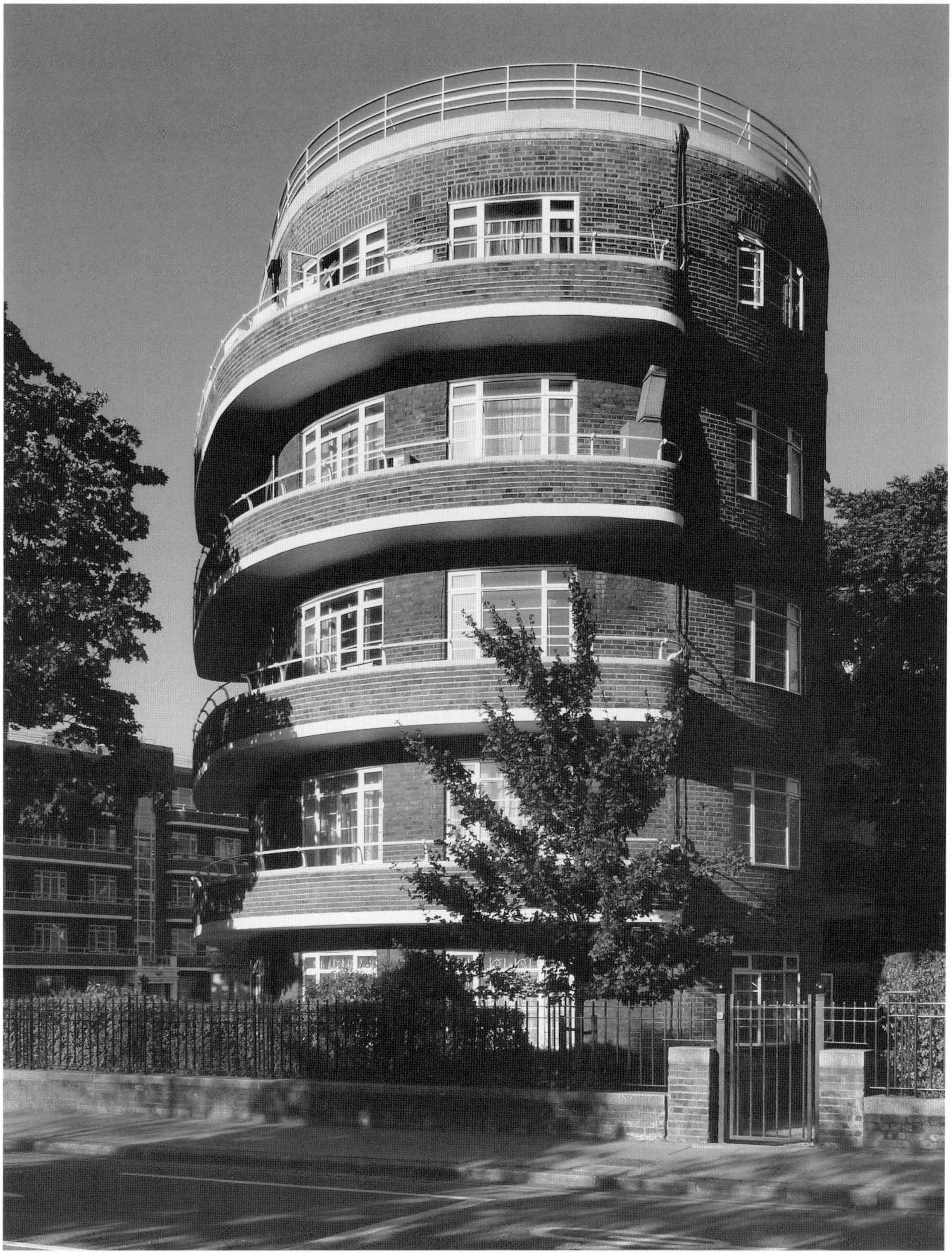

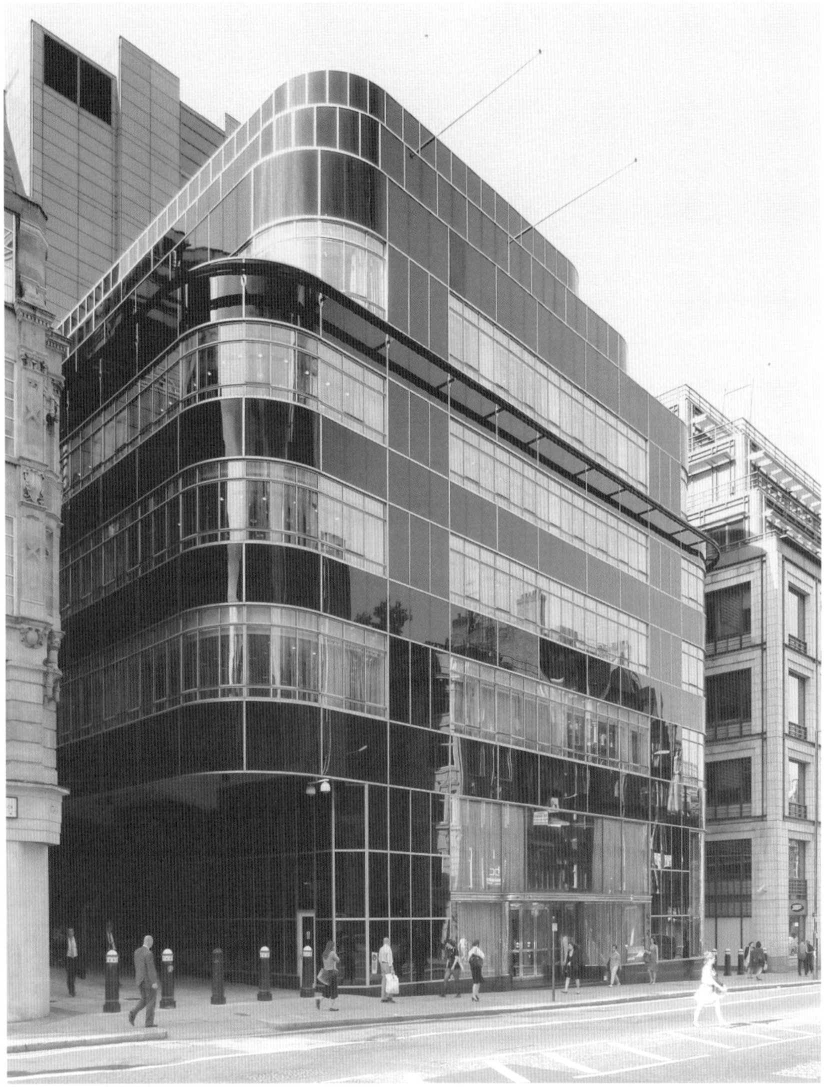

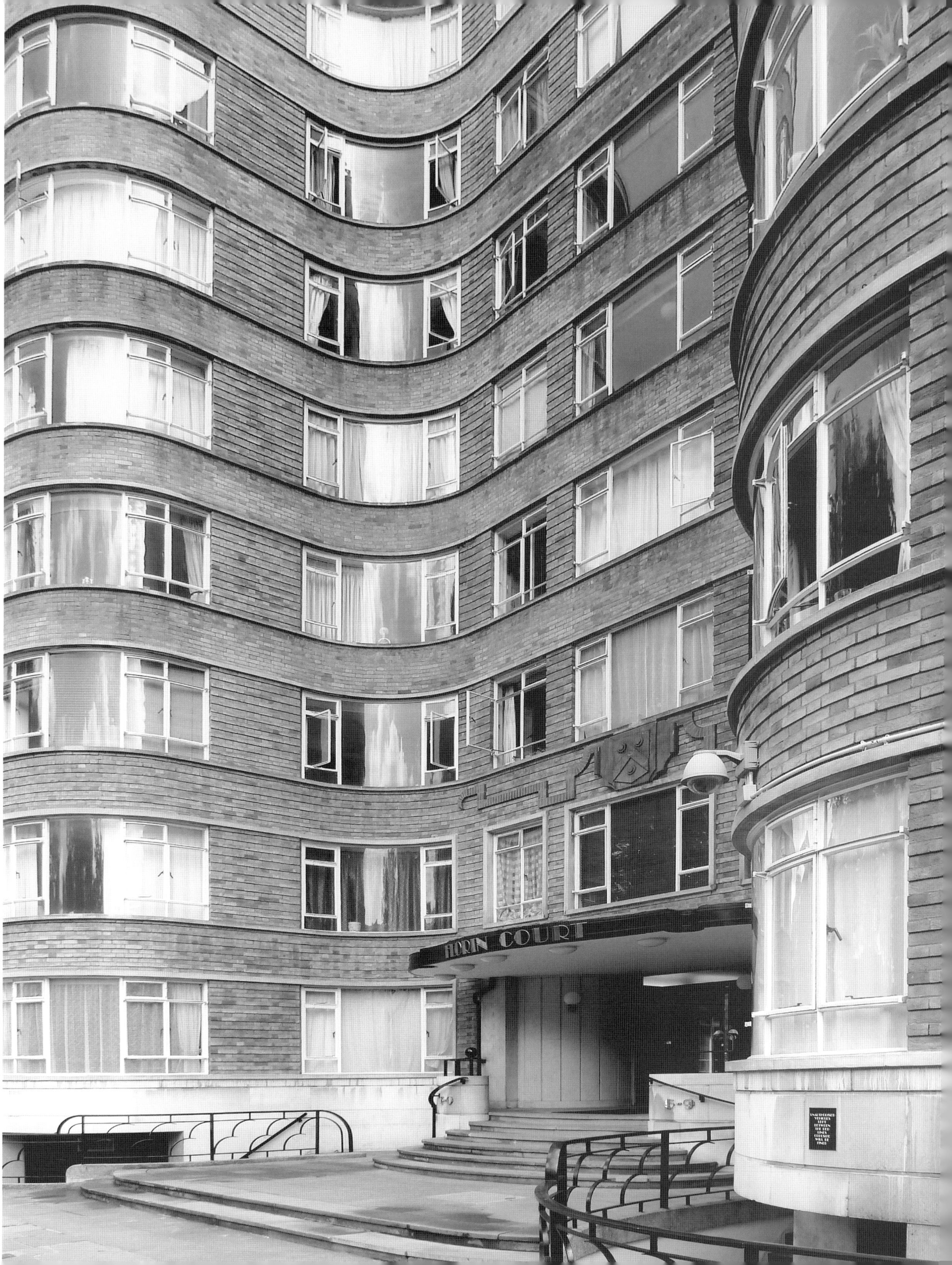
FLORIN COURT

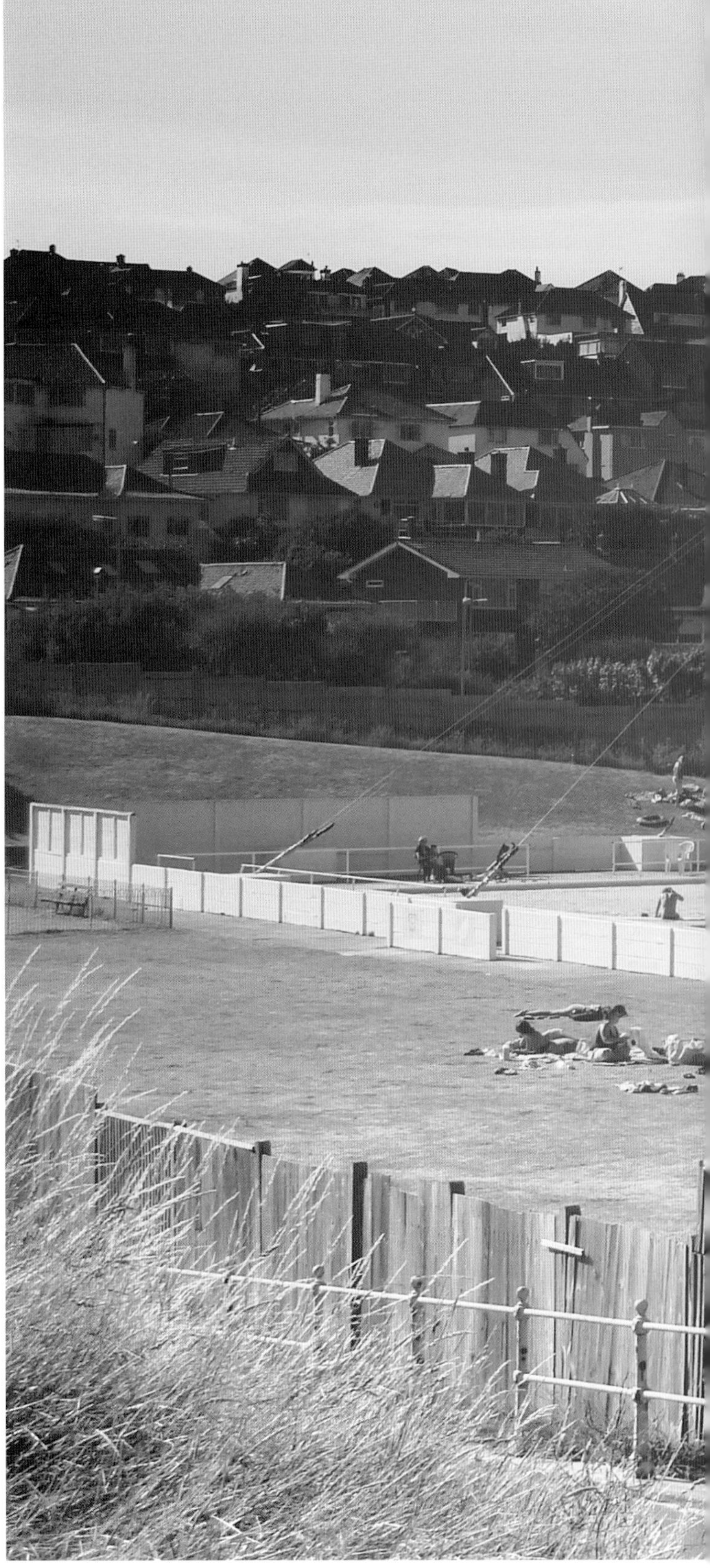

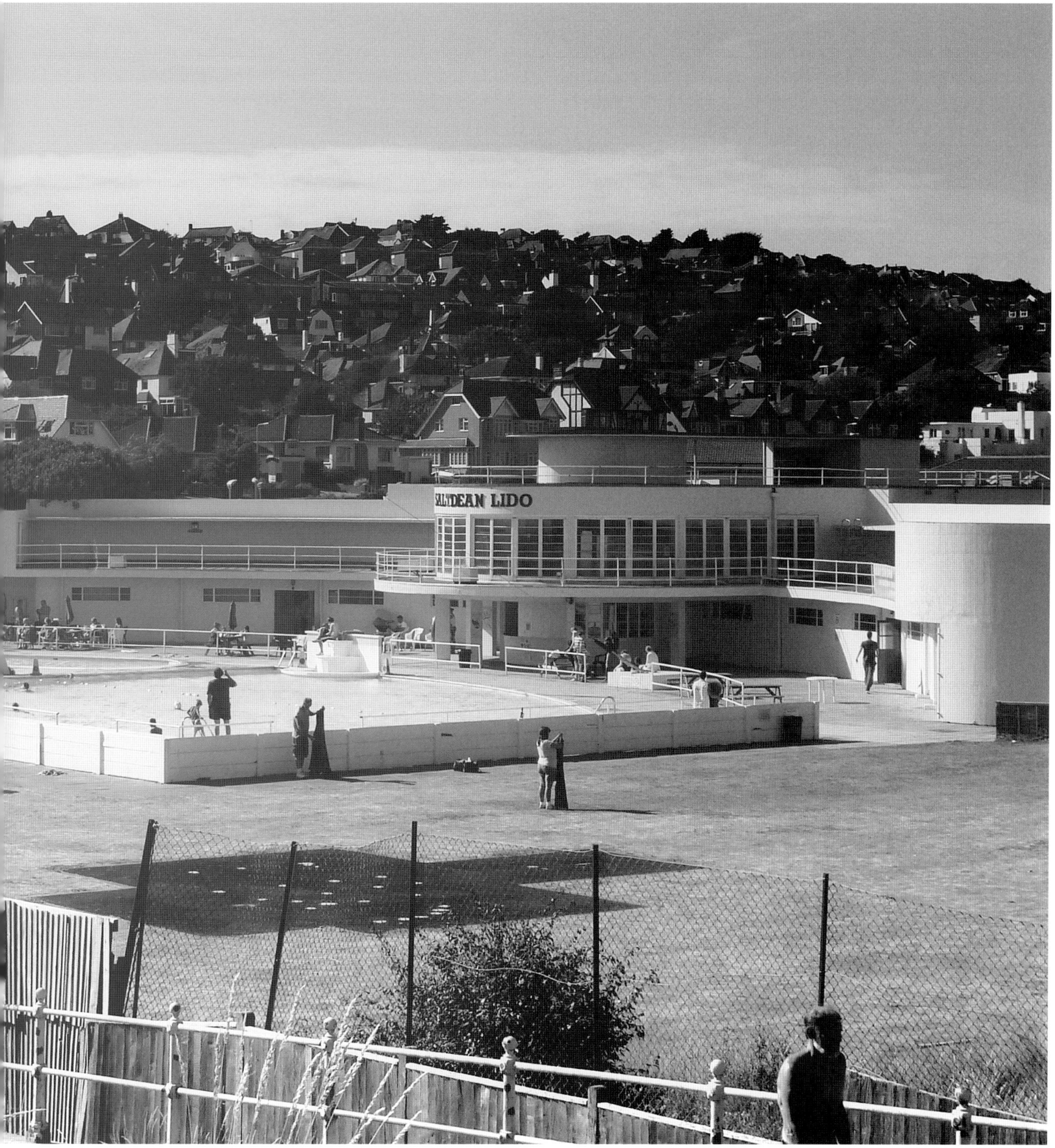
SALTDEAN LIDO

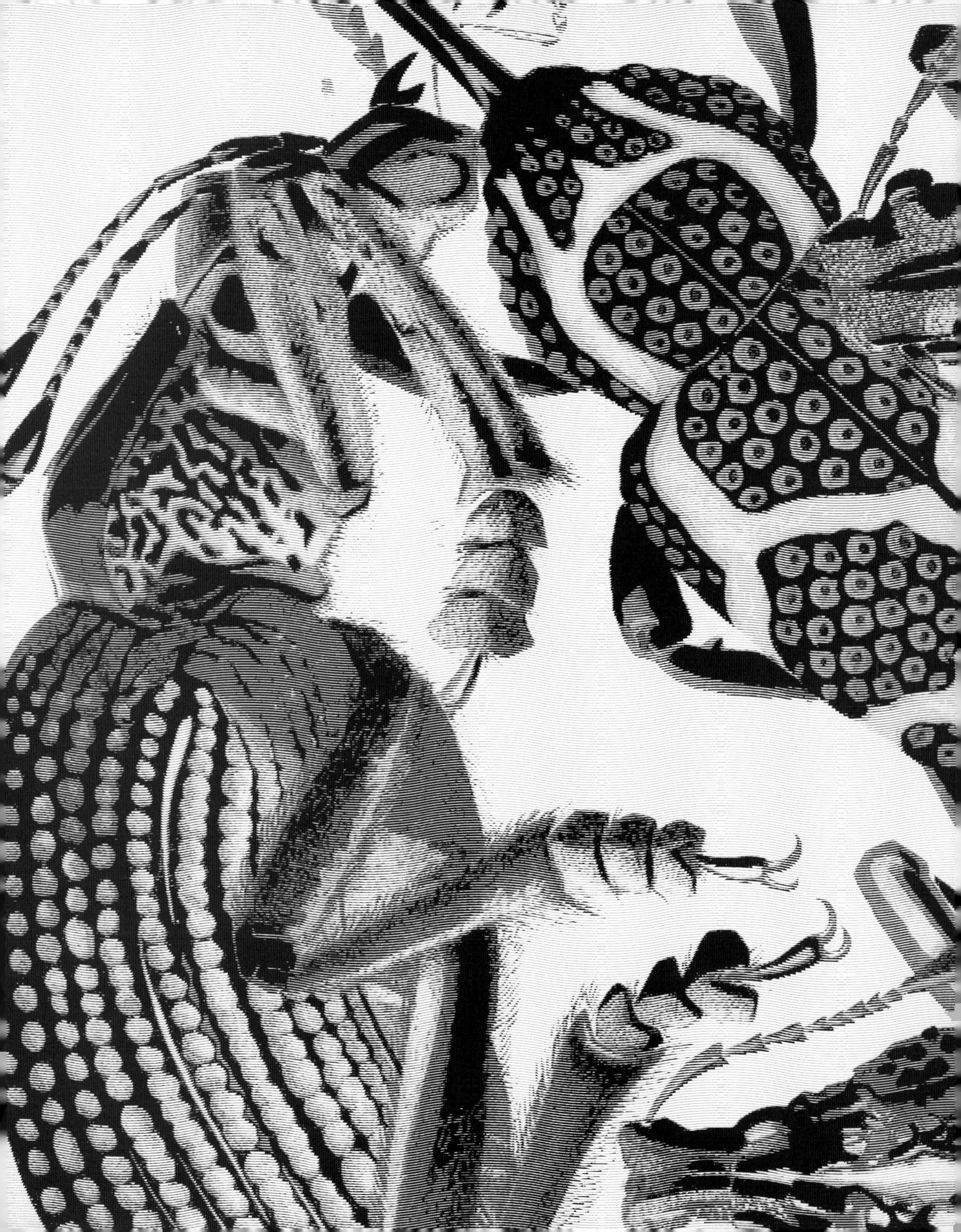

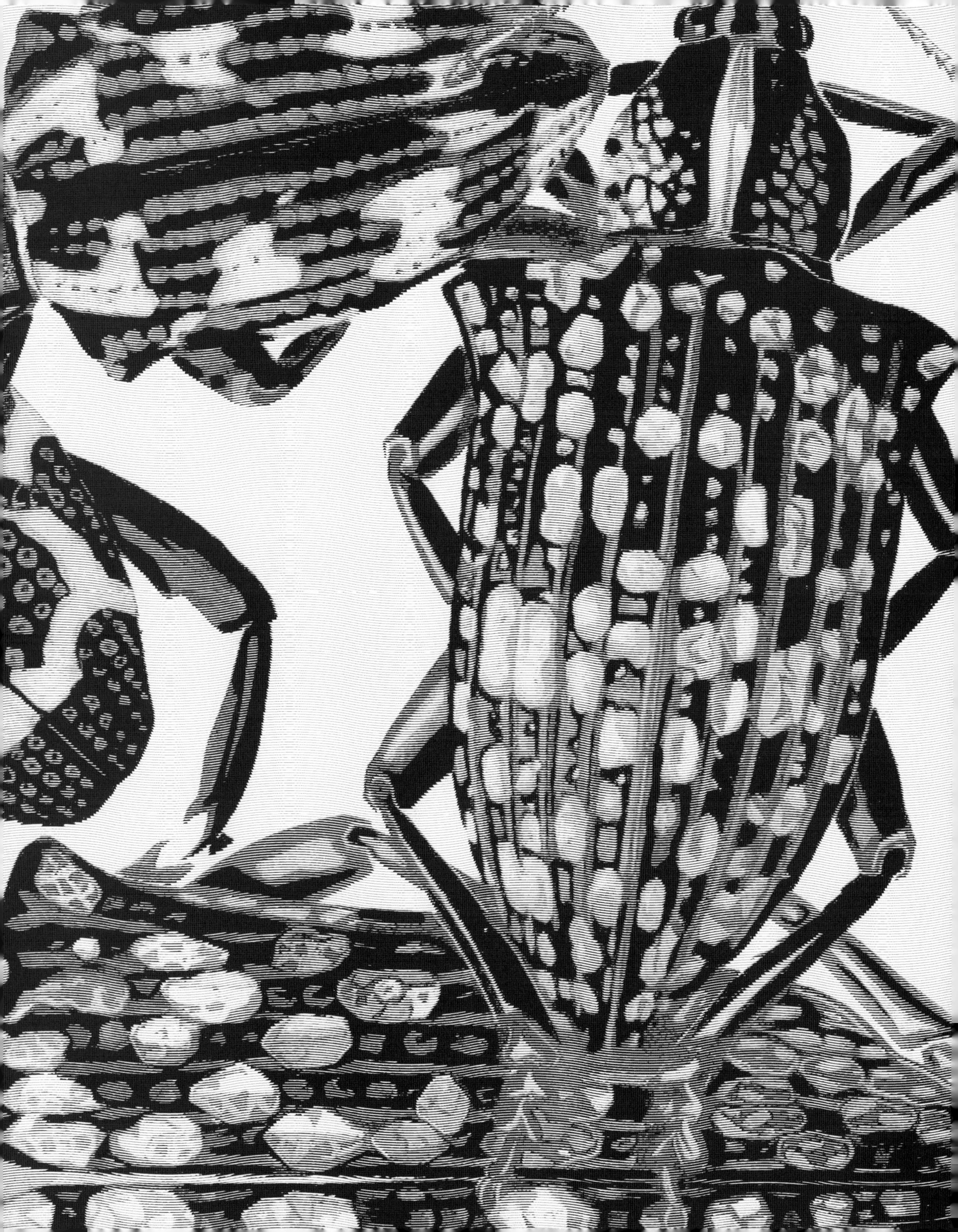

CATALOGUE KATALOG

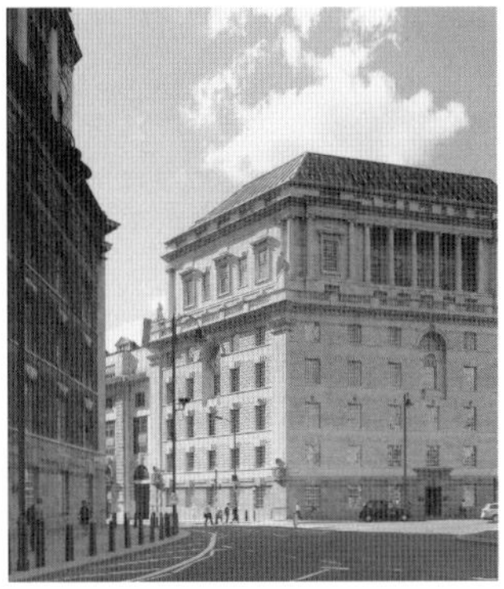

1

Imperial Chemical House (Nobel House), 1927–29
Millbank, Millbank, Westminster, London (K)
Frank Baines

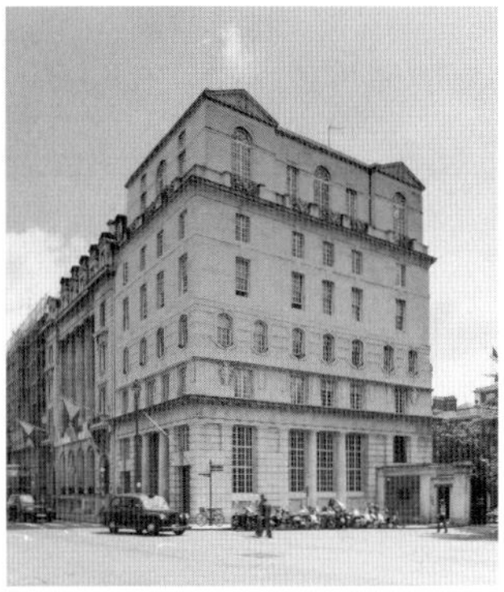

2

Bank and Flats Pall Mall, 1929
Pall Mall, St James's, Westminster, London (K)
Edwin Lutyens / Jenkins / William Henry Romaine-Walker

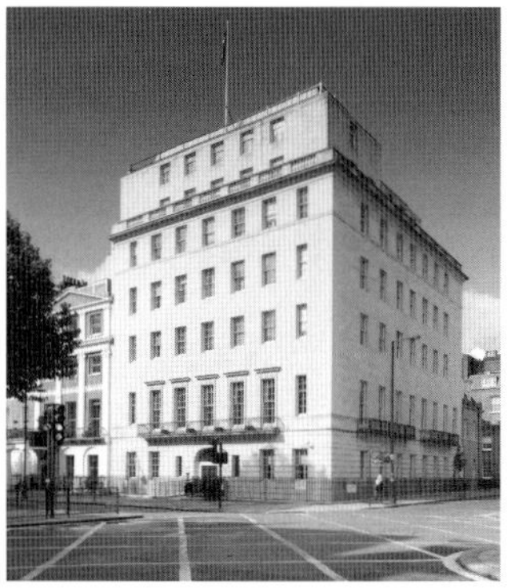

3

Flats 23 Portland Place, 1936
Portland Place, Fitzrovia, Westminster, London (J)
Newberry & Fowler

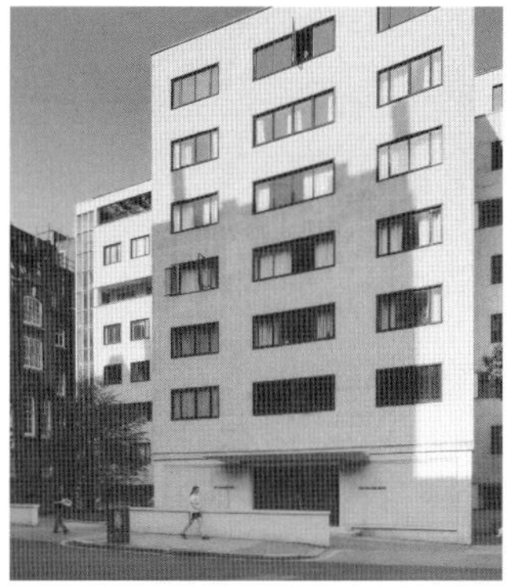

4

Flats Palace Gate, 1938
Palace Gate, Kensington, London (J)
Wells Coates

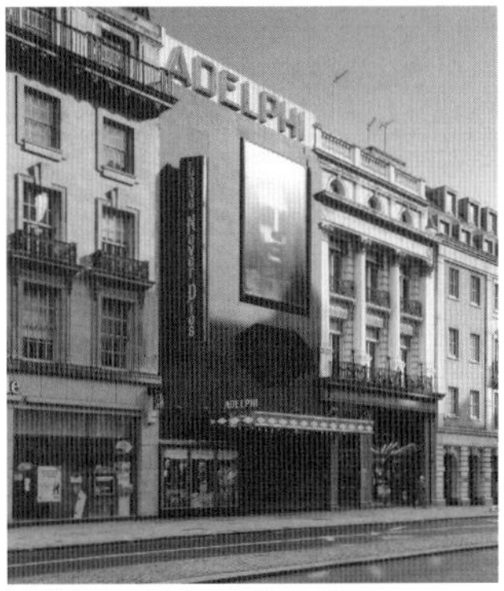

9

Adelphi Theatre, 1930
Strand, Covent Garden, Westminster, London (K)
Ernst Schaufelberg

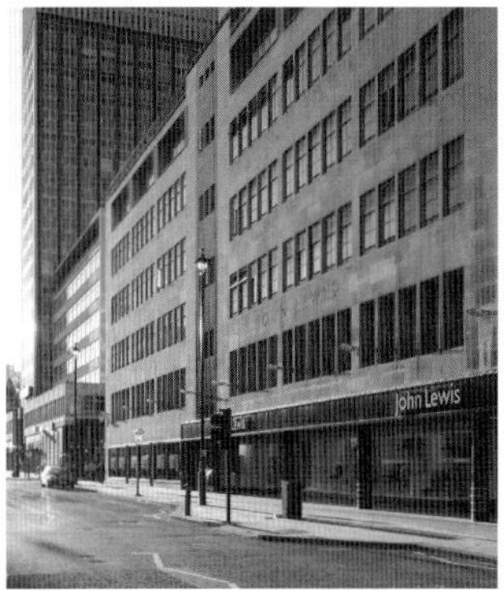

10

John Lewis Department Store, 1939
Oxford Street, Marylebone, Westminster, London (J)
Slater Moberly & Uren / Franz Singer

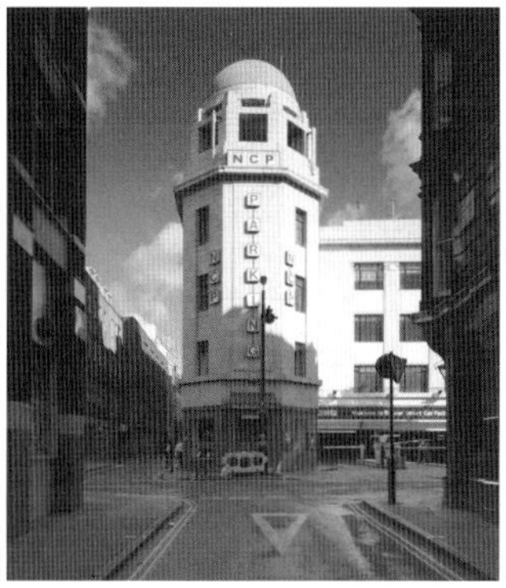

11

Lex Garage, 1928–29
Brewer Street, Soho, Westminster, London (K)
John James Joass / Robert Sharp

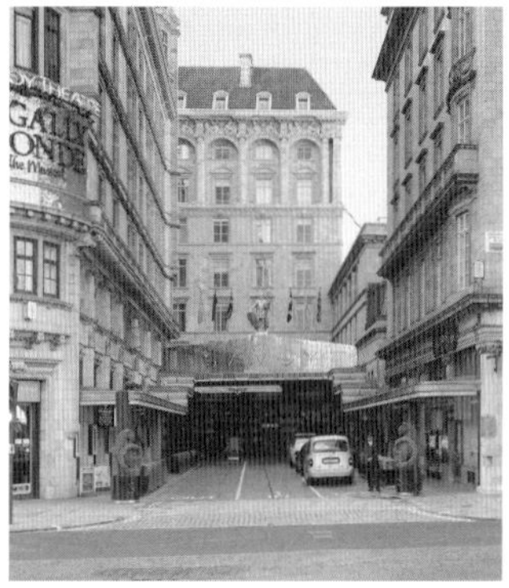

12

Savoy Hotel, Strand Entrance, 1929–30
Strand, Covent Garden, Westminster, London (K)
Easton & Robertson

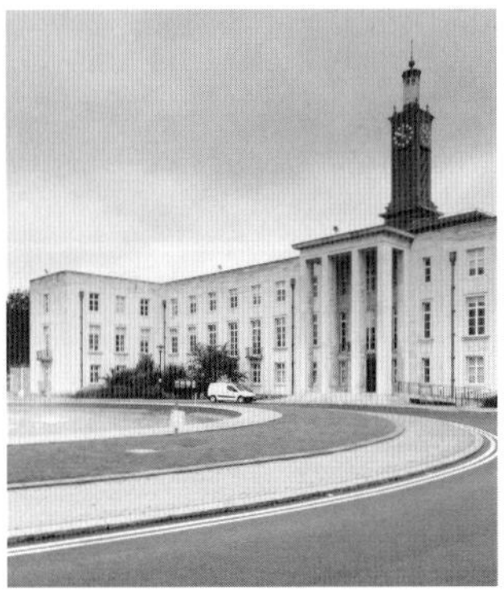

17

Walthamstow Town Hall, 1937–42
Forest Road, Waltham Forest, London
Philip Dalton Hepworth

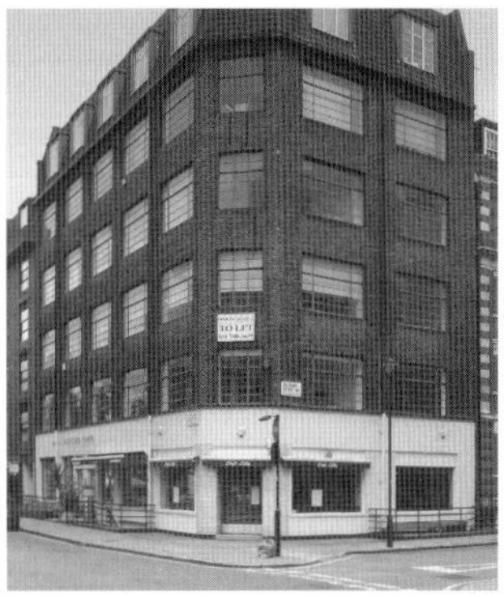

18

Bolsover House
Bolsover Street, Fitzrovia, Westminster, London (J)

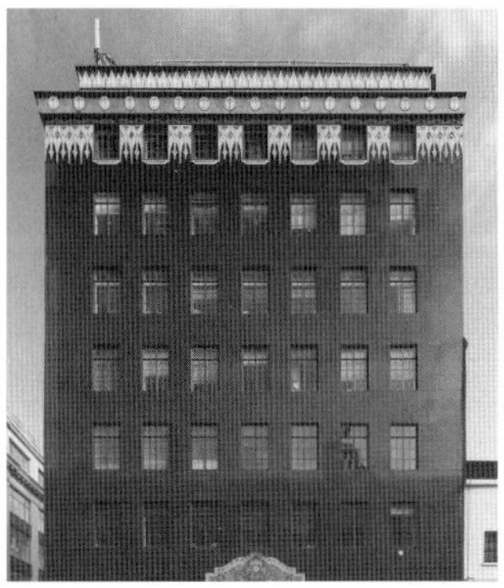

19

Ideal House (Palladium House), 1928
Great Marlborough Street / Argyll Street, Soho, Westminster, London (J)
Raymond Hood / Gordon Jeeves

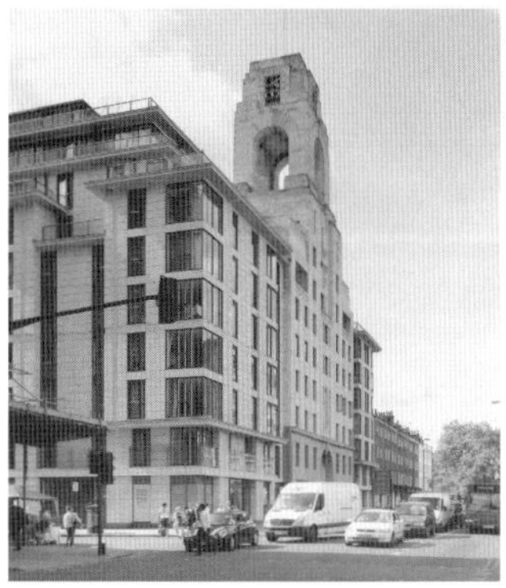

20

Abbey House, 1932?
Baker Street, Marylebone, Westminster, London (F)

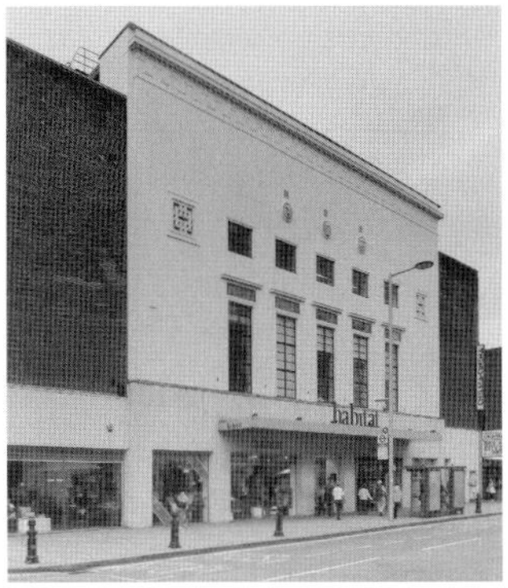

5

Picture Playhouse Chelsea *(Habitat Store Chelsea)*, 1913
King's Road, Chelsea, London (N)
Felix Joubert

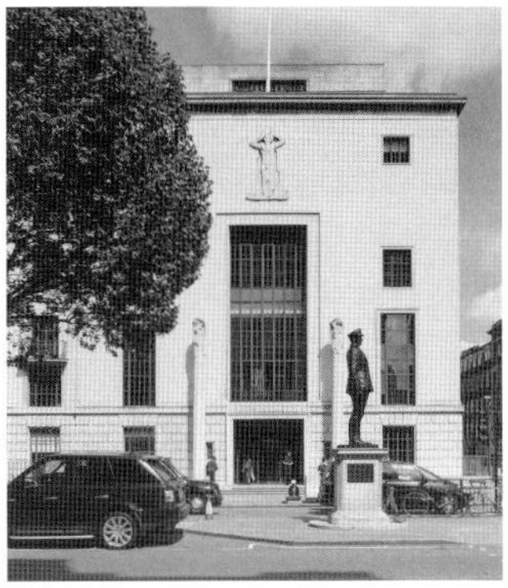

6

Royal Institute of British Architects, 1932–34
Portland Place, Fitzrovia, Westminster, London (J)
George Grey Wornum / James Woodford

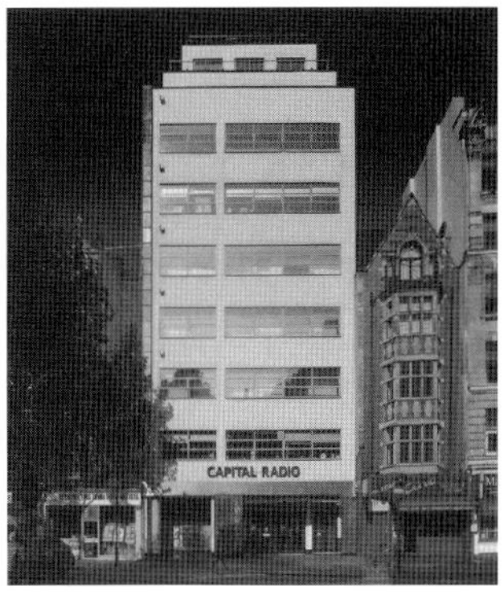

7

Capital Radio Building, 1953–54
Charing Cross Road / Leicester Square, Soho, Westminster, London (K)

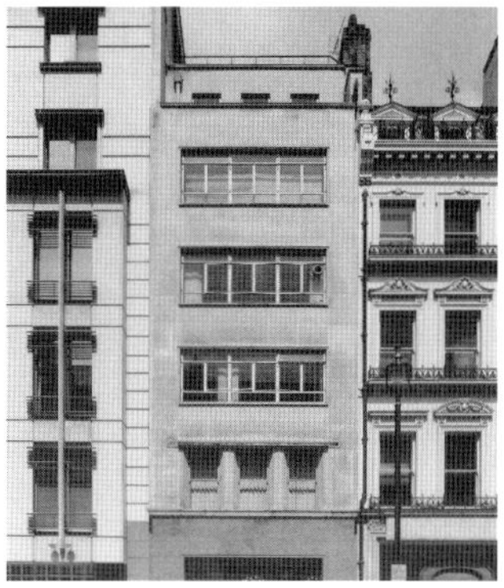

8

Flats Pall Mall
Pall Mall, St James's, Westminster, London (K)

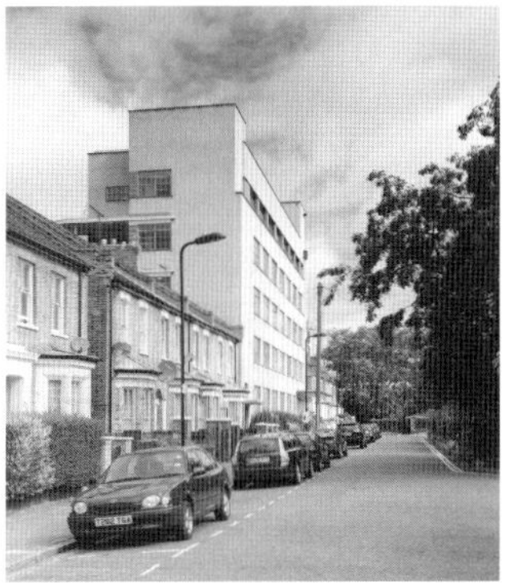

13

German Hospital, East Wing *(Flats Former German Hospital)*, 1935–36
Fassett Square, Hackney, London (H)
Thomas Tait

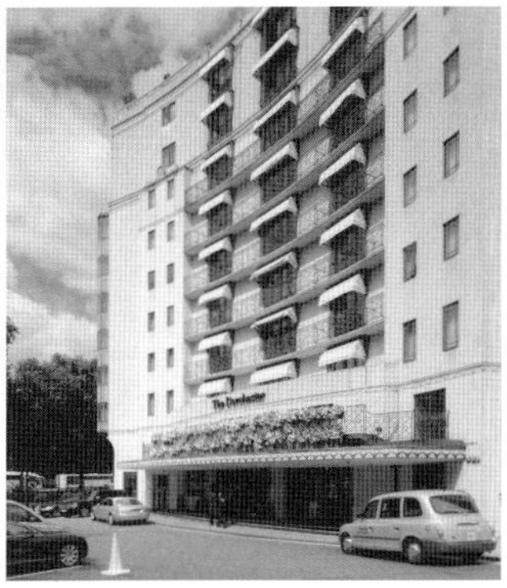

14

Dorchester Hotel, 1929–30
Park Lane, Mayfair, Westminster, London (J)
Owen Williams / William Curtis Green

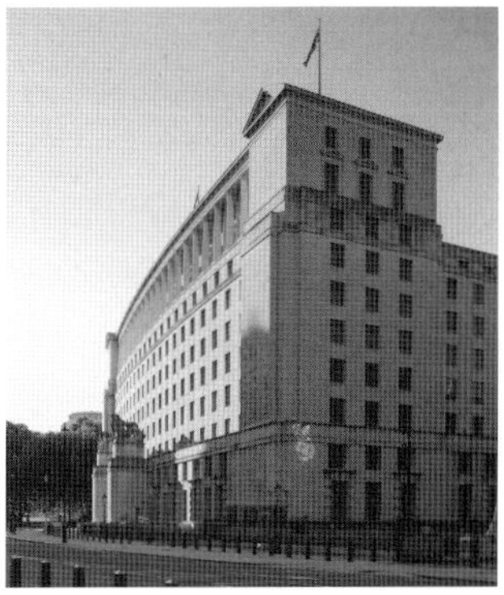

15

Ministry of Defence, 1939–59
Richmond Terrace, Whitehall, Westminster, London (K)
Vincent Harris

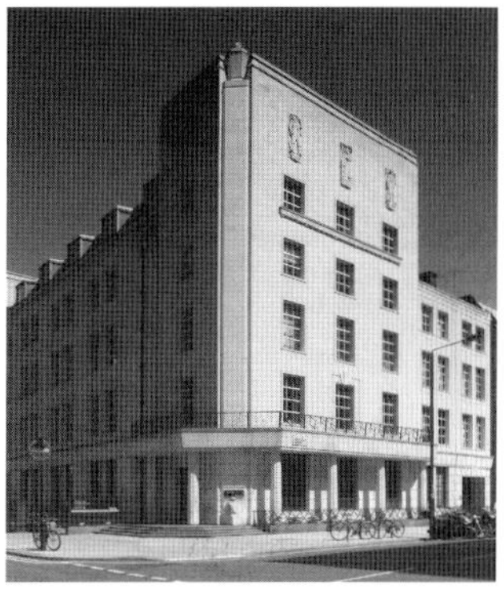

16

Bentham House, 1954–58
Endsleigh Street, Bloomsbury, Camden, London (G)
H. & H. Martin Lidbetter

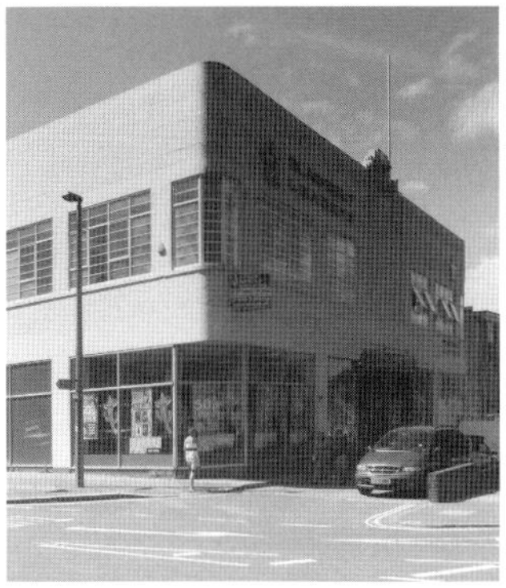

21

Blockbuster Store Worthing
Stoke Abbott Road / Chapel Road, Worthing, Sussex

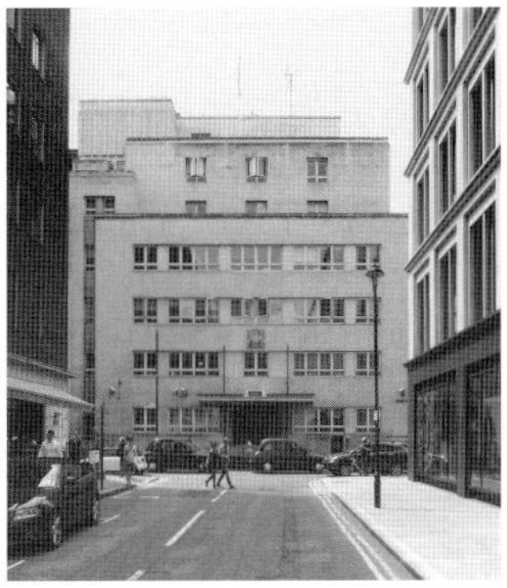

22

West End Central Police Station, 1938–39
Savile Row, Mayfair, Westminster, London (J)
Burnet Tait & Lorne

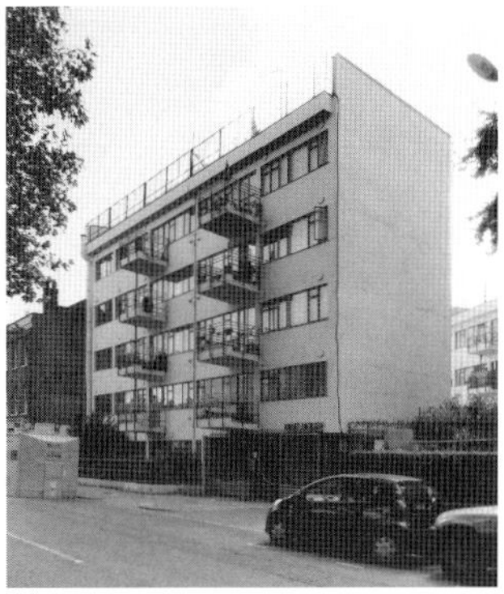

23

Kent House, 1936
Ferdinand Street, Chalk Farm, Camden, London (F)
Connell Ward & Lucas

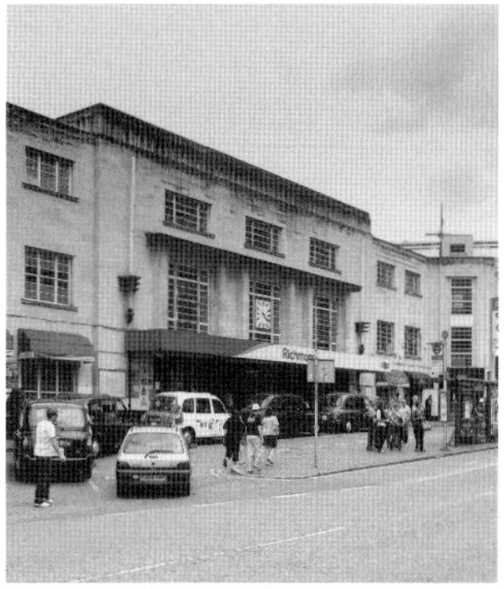

24

Richmond Railway Station, 1936–37
Kew Road, Richmond, Greater London
J.R. Scott

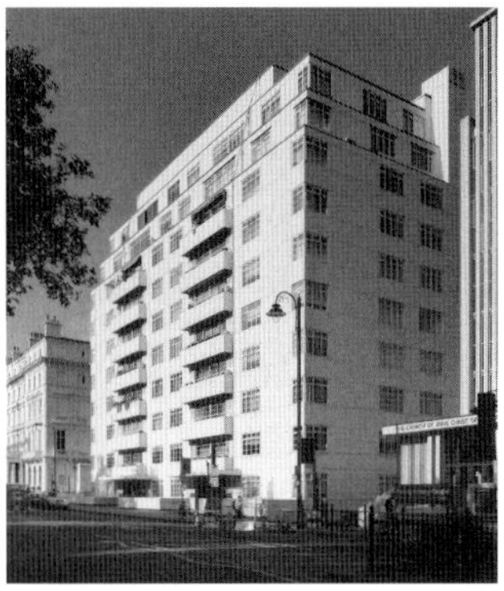

25

Flats Princes Gate, c. 1935
Exhibition Road / Watts Way, Kensington, London (J)
Adie Button & Partners

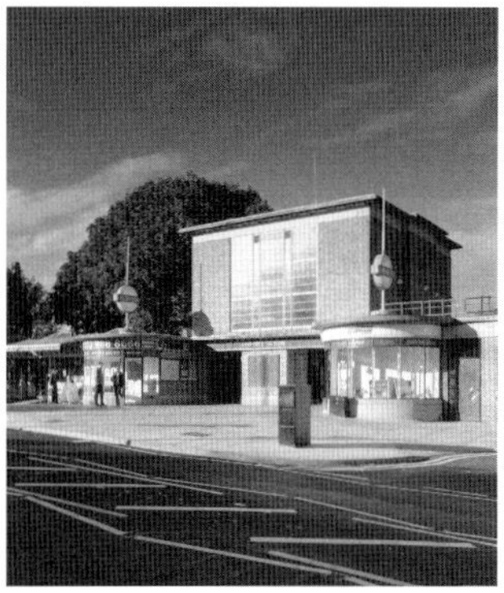

26

Eastcote Underground Station, 1938–39
Field End Road, Hillingdon, Greater London
Adams Holden & Pearson

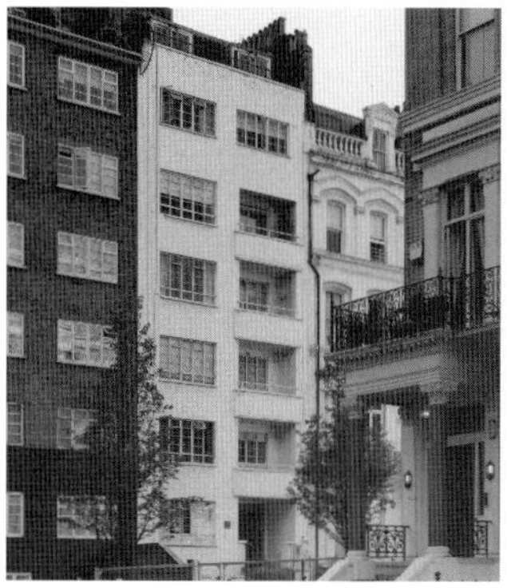

27

Flats Vicarage Gate
Vicarage Gate, Kensington, London (I)

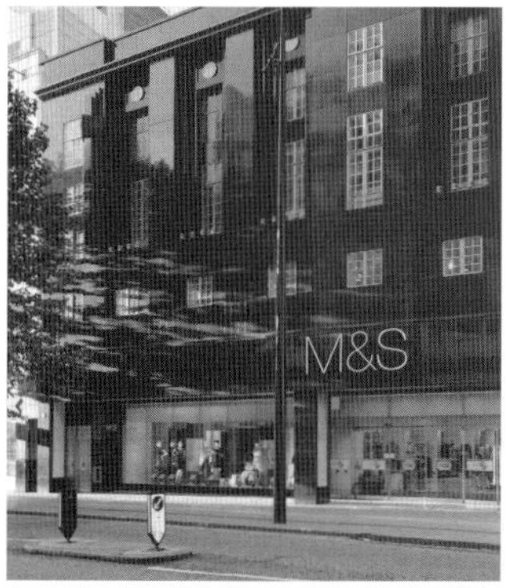

28

The Pantheon (*Marks & Spencer Oxford Street*), 1937–38
Oxford Street, Soho, Westminster, London (K)
Robert Lutyens

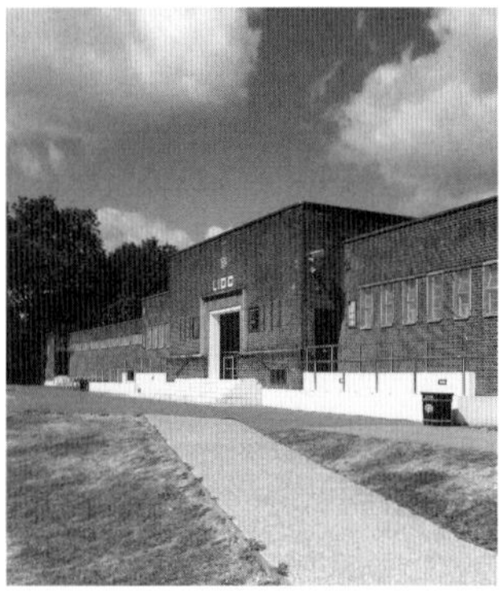

33

Parliament Hill Lido, c. 1938
Parliament Hill Fields, Gospel Oak, Camden, London (B)
Harry Rowbotham / T.L. Smithson

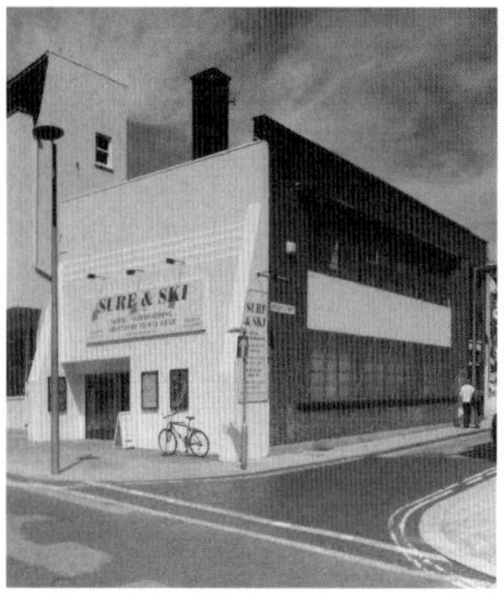

34

Surf & Ski Store Brighton
Regent Street / Church Street, Brighton, Sussex

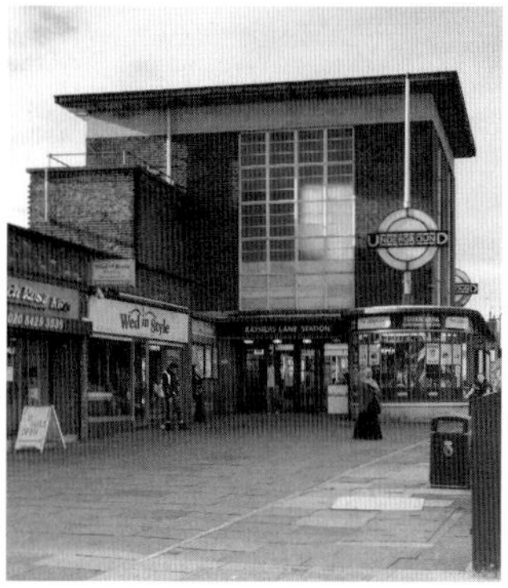

35

Rayners Lane Underground Station, 1938
Alexandra Avenue, Harrow, Greater London
Charles Holden / Reginald Harold Uren

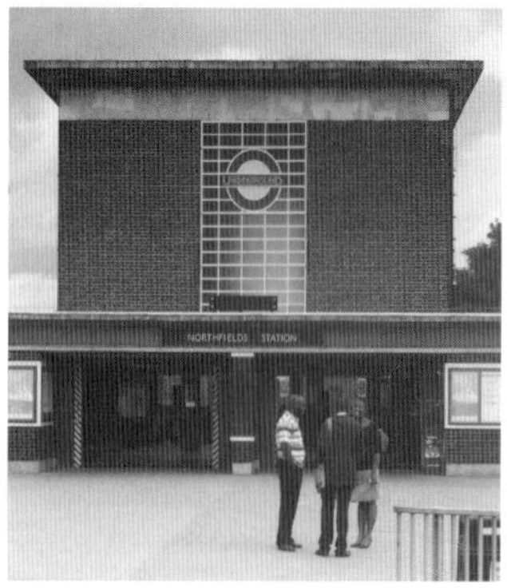

36

Northfields Underground Station, 1932–33
Northfield Avenue, Ealing, London
Charles Holden / Stanley A. Heaps

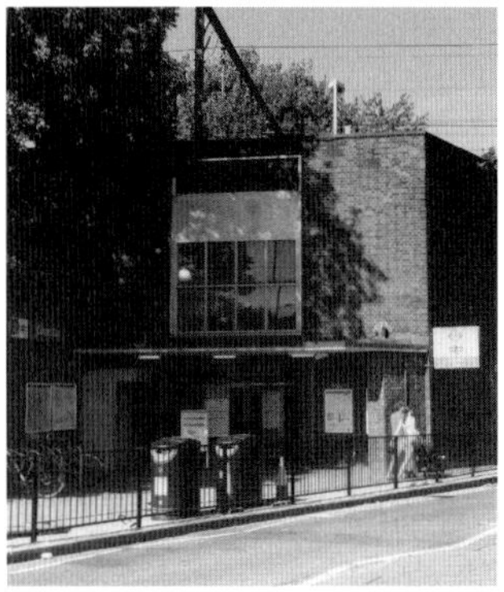

41

Gospel Oak Railway Station
Gorden House Road, Gospel Oak, Camden, London (F)

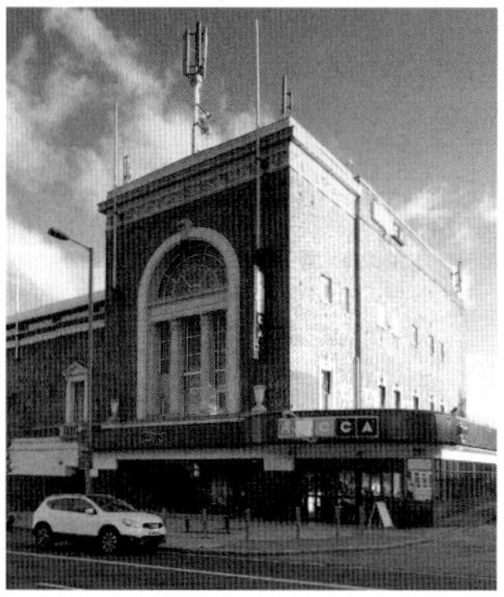

42

Savoy Cinema Burnt Oak, 1936
Burnt Oak Broadway, Edgware, Greater London
George Coles

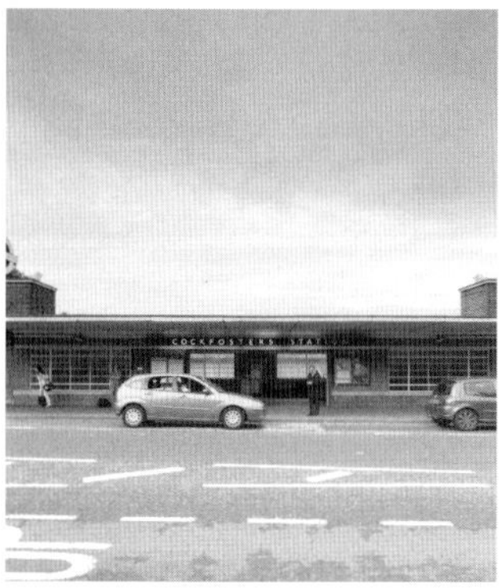

43

Cockfosters Underground Station, 1932–33
Cockfosters Road, Enfield, Greater London
Charles Holden

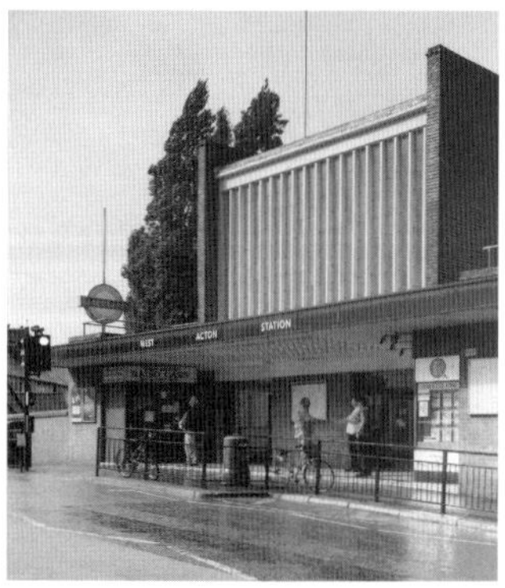

44

West Acton Underground Station, 1938–40
Prince's Gardens, Ealing, London
Brian Lewis

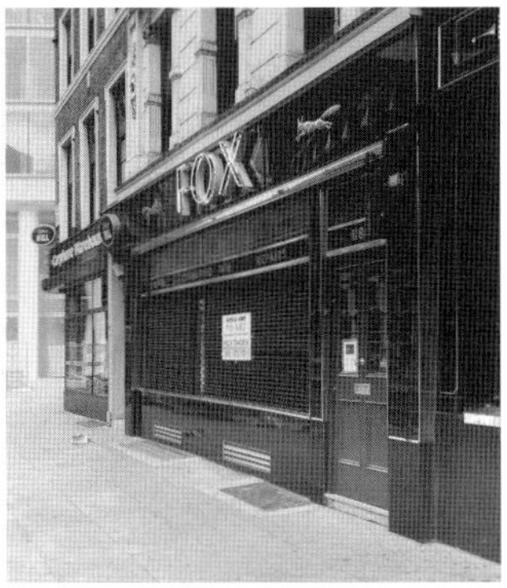

29

Fox Umbrellas Shop, 1937
London Wall / Moorgate,
City of London, London (L)
Pollard

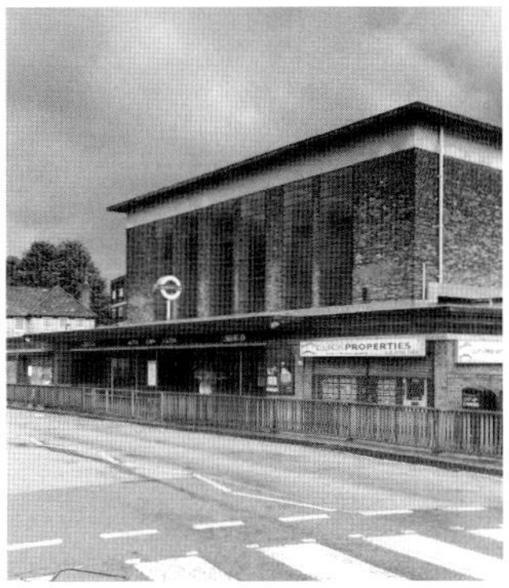

30

Acton Town Underground Station, 1932–33
Gunnersbury Lane, Ealing, London
Charles Holden

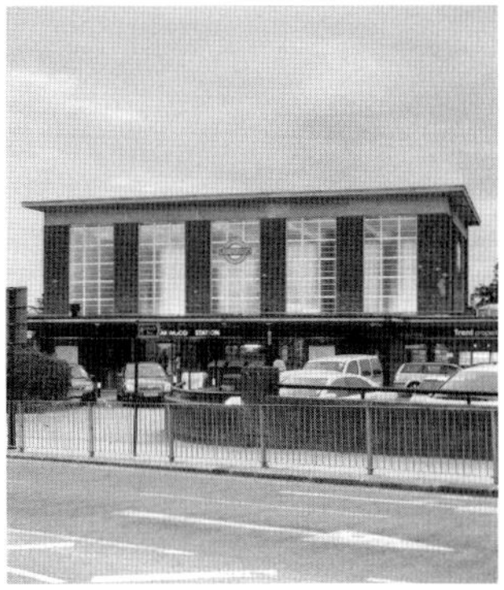

31

Oakwood Underground Station, 1932–33
Bramely Road, Enfield, London
Charles Holden / C.H. James

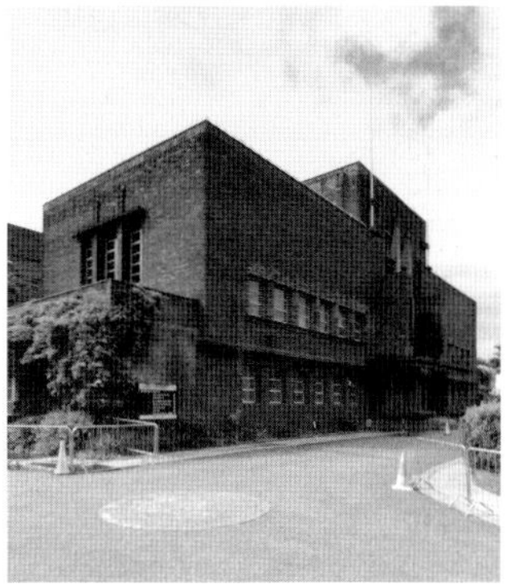

32

Royal Masonic Hospital, 1930–34
Ravenscourt Park, Hammersmith, London
Burnet Tait & Lorne

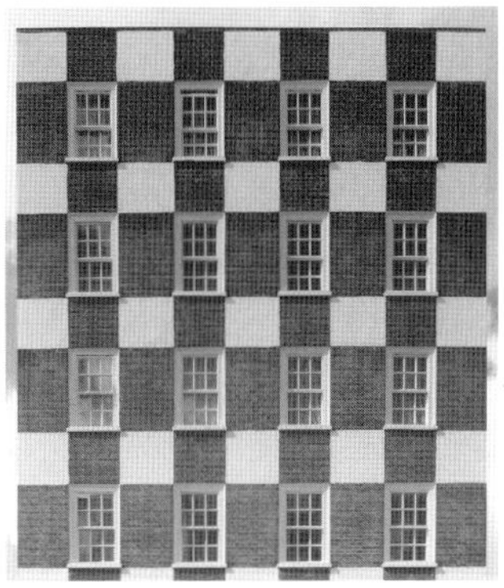

37

Grosvenor Estate, 1928–30
Page Street / Vincent Street, Pimlico,
Westminster, London (K)
Edwin Lutyens

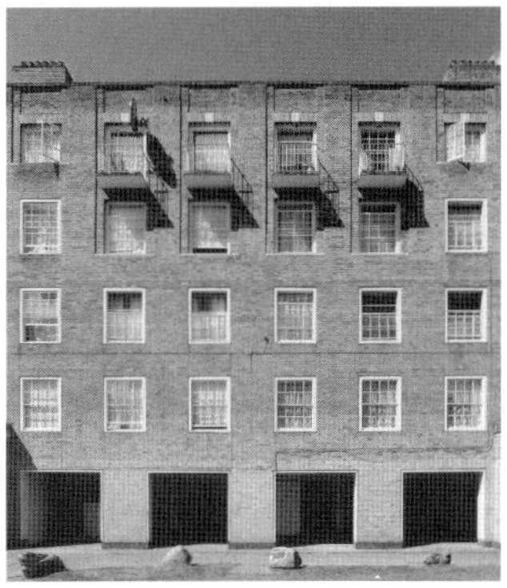

38

Barnfield and Woodfield, 1948–50
Parkhill Road, Hampstead,
Camden, London (F)
Farquarson & McMorran

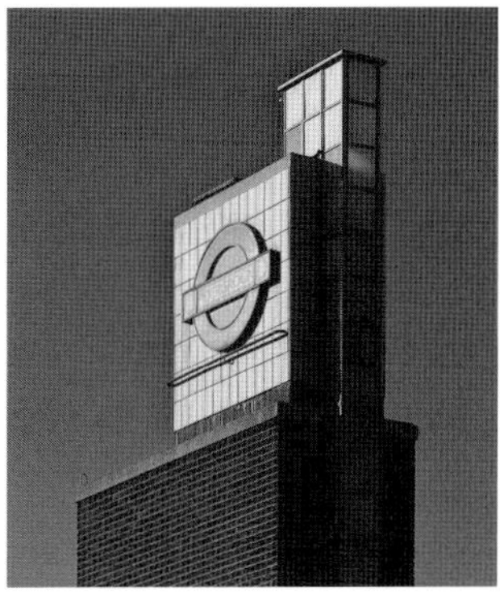

39

Boston Manor Underground Station, 1934
Boston Manor Road, Brentford, Greater London
Charles Holden

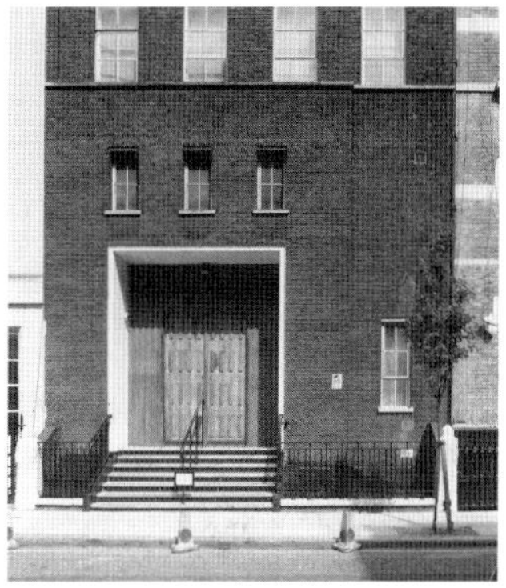

40

Central Synagogue, 1956–58
Hallam Street, Fitzrovia,
Westminster, London (J)
Edmund Wilford

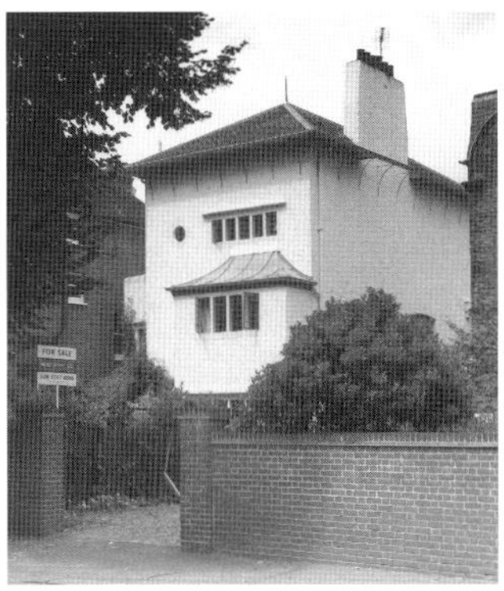

45

House 14 South Parade, 1889–94
South Parade, Hounslow, London
C.F.A. Voysey

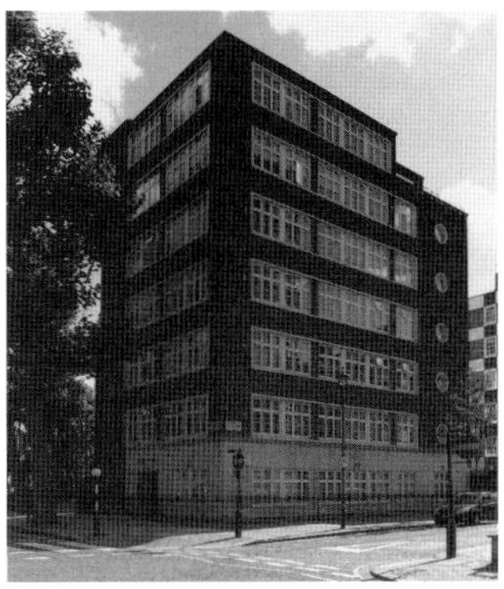

46

Hepburn House
Marsham Street / Vincent Street, Millbank,
Westminster, London (K)

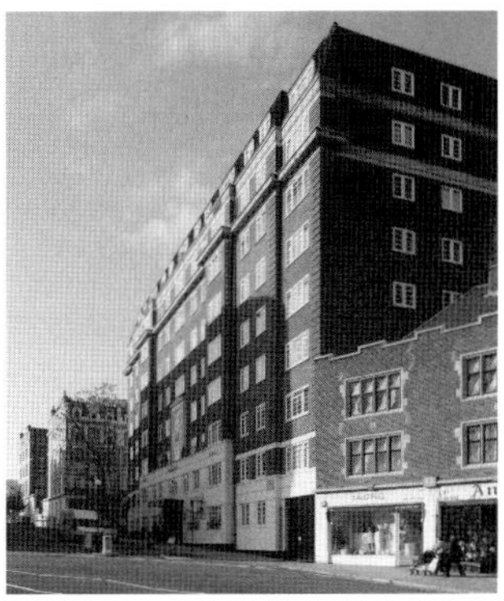

47

Vicarage Court, 1934?
Vicarage Gate, Kensington, London (I)

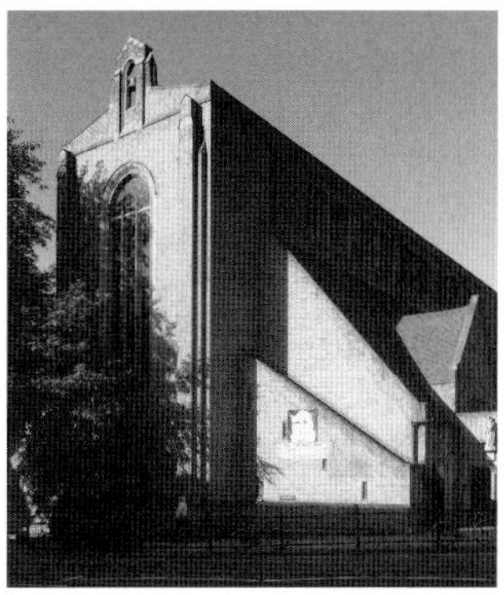

48

Church of Our Lady of Mount Carmel,
1954–59
Kensington Church Street,
Kensington, London (I)
Giles Gilbert Scott

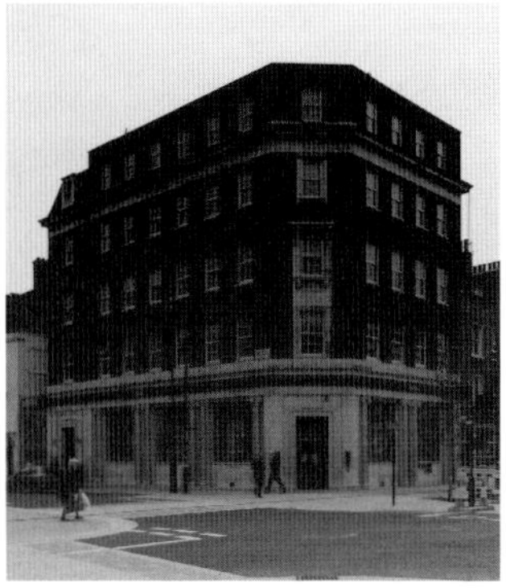

49

Ebury House
Ebury Street / Elizabeth Street, Belgravia, Westminster, London (J)

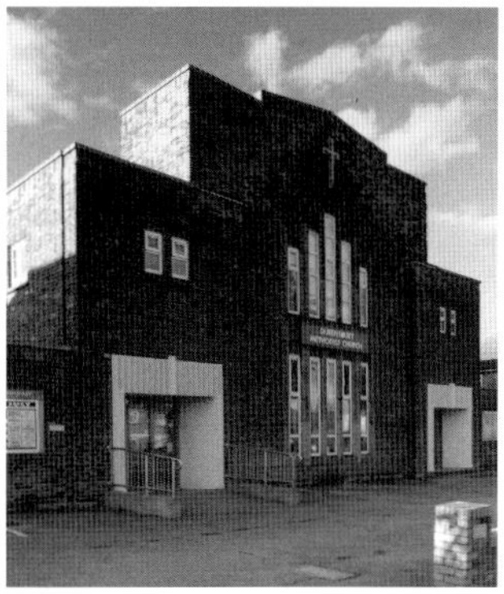

50

Queensbury Methodist Church, 1938?
Beverley Drive, Edgware, Greater London

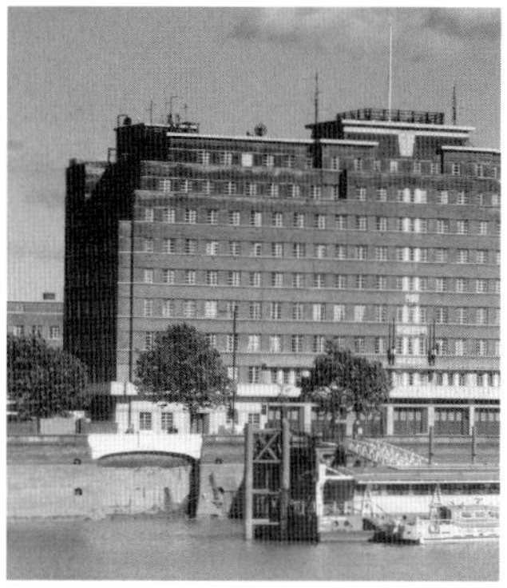

51

Fire Brigade Headquarters, 1937
Albert Embankment, Lambeth, London (K)
E.P. Wheeler

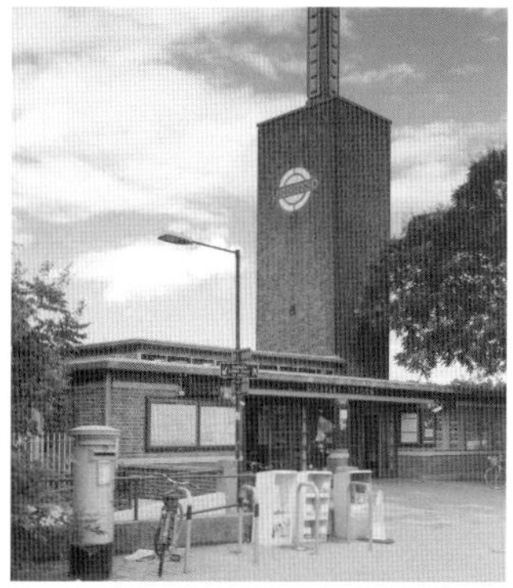

52

Osterley Underground Station, 1930–33
Great West Road, Isleworth, Greater London
Charles Holden / Stanley A. Heaps
Tower, 1935–36
Day Welch & Lander

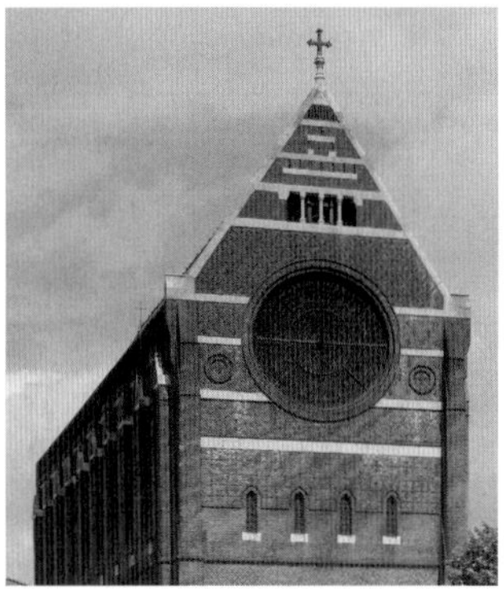

57

St Bartholomew, 1872–74, 1895–1910
Ann Street, Brighton, Sussex
Edmund Scott / Henry Wilson

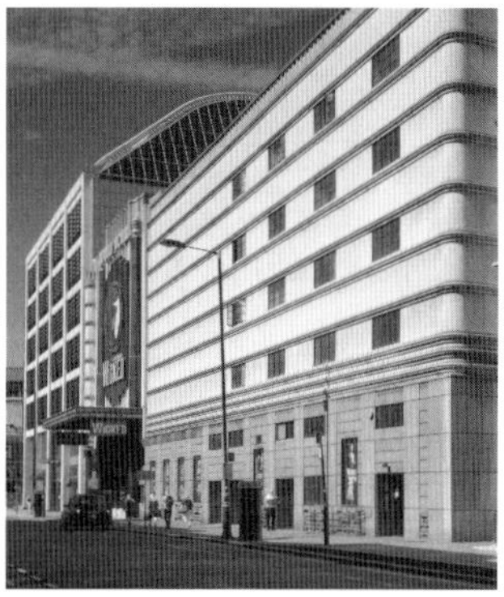

58

Apollo Victoria Theatre, 1928–30
Wilton Road, Pimlico, Westminster, London (J)
E. Wamsley Lewis

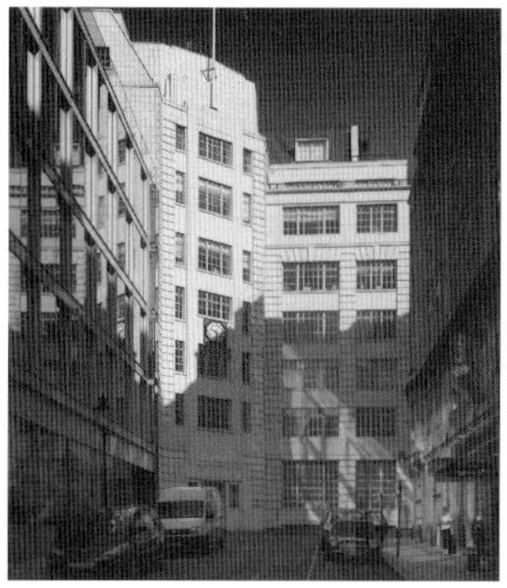

59

Strand Palace Hotel Extension, 1928–30
Exeter Street, Covent Garden, Westminster, London (K)
F.J. Wills

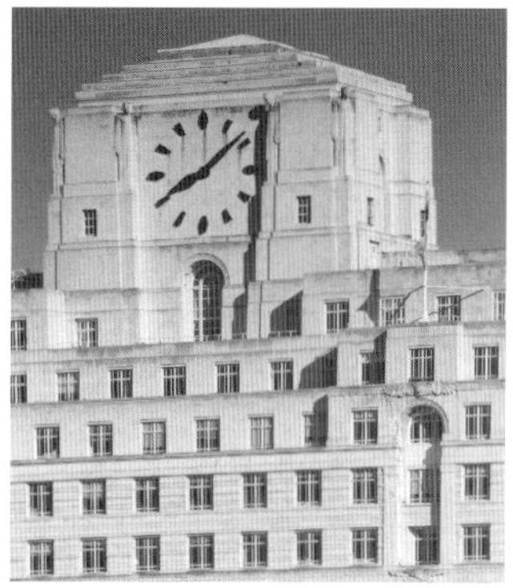

60

Shell-Mex House, 1931
Strand / Victoria Embankment, City of London, London (K)
Messrs Joseph

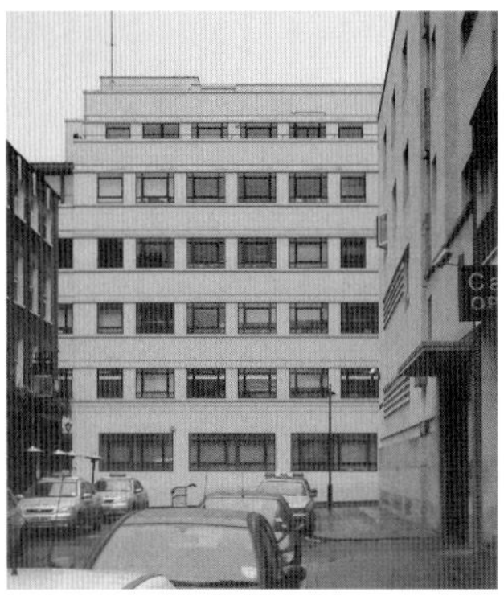

65

Offices Savile Row, 1937–38
Savile Row, Mayfair, Westminster, London (J)
Gordon Jeeves

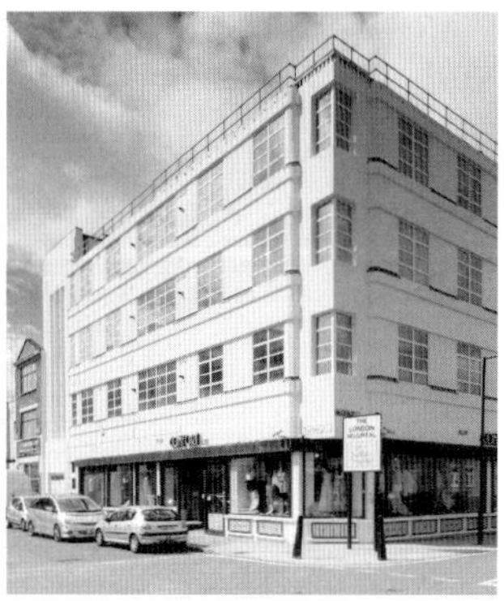

66

Levy Factory and Showroom, 1932
Turner Street / Nelson Street, Tower Hamlets, London (L)
H. Victor Kerr

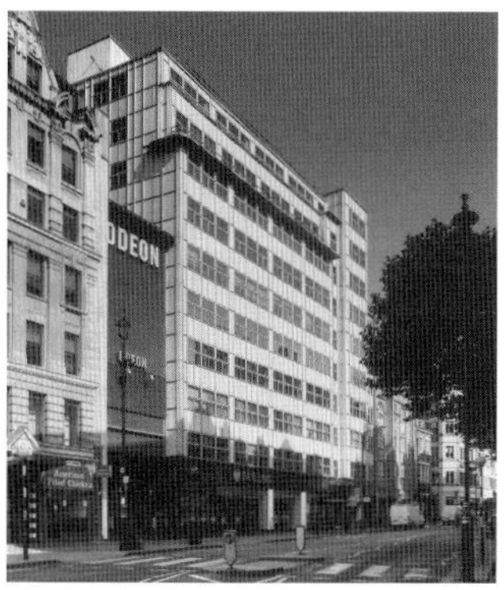

67

Alhambra House, 1938
Charing Cross Road, Soho, Westminster, London (K)
Andrew Mather / Harry Weedon

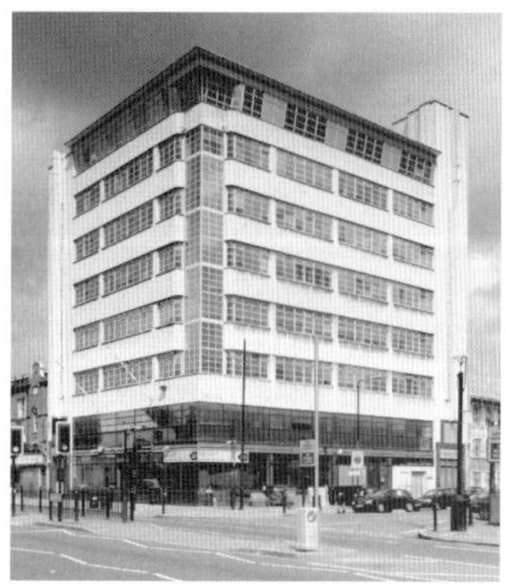

68

Cheviot House, 1937
Commercial Road, Tower Hamlets, London (L)
G.G. Wimbourne

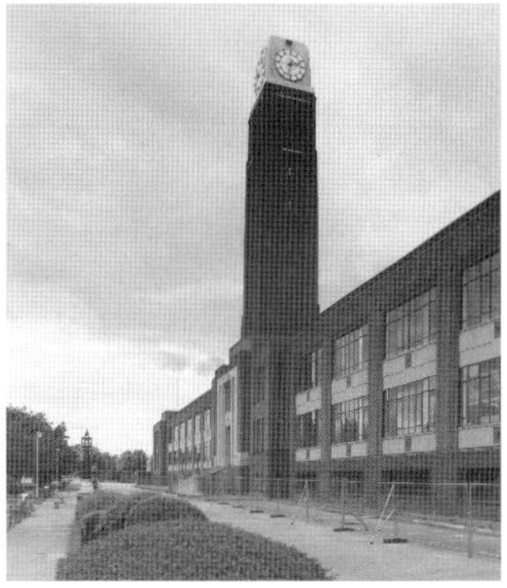

53

Gillette Factory, 1936–37
Syon Lane, Isleworth, Greater London
Banister Fletcher

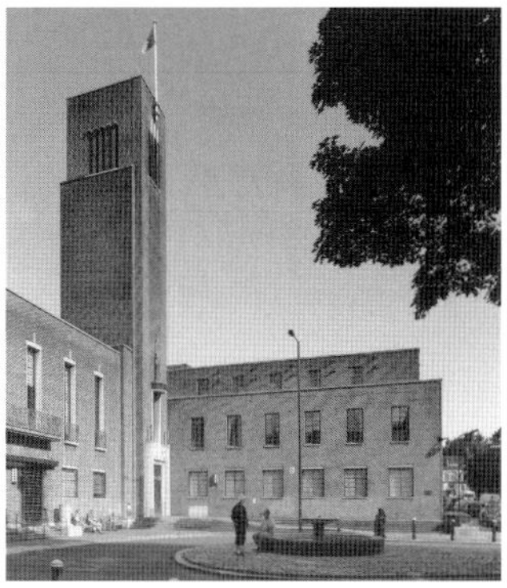

54

Hornsey Town Hall, 1933–35
The Broadway, Haringey, London (C)
Reginald Harold Uren

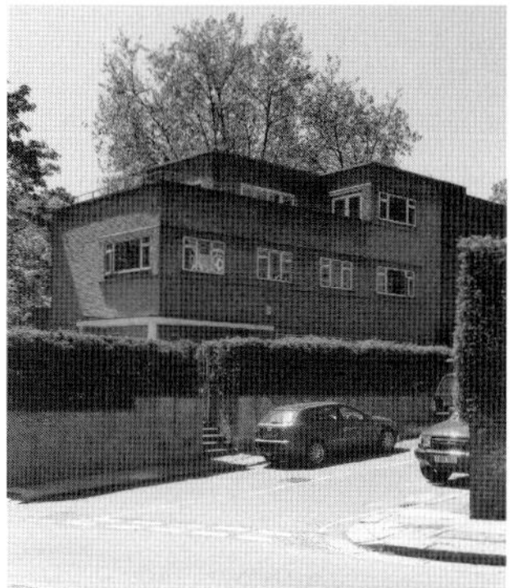

55

Semi-detached Houses Frognal Close, 1937
Frognal Close, Frognal, Camden, London (F)
Ernst Ludwig Freud

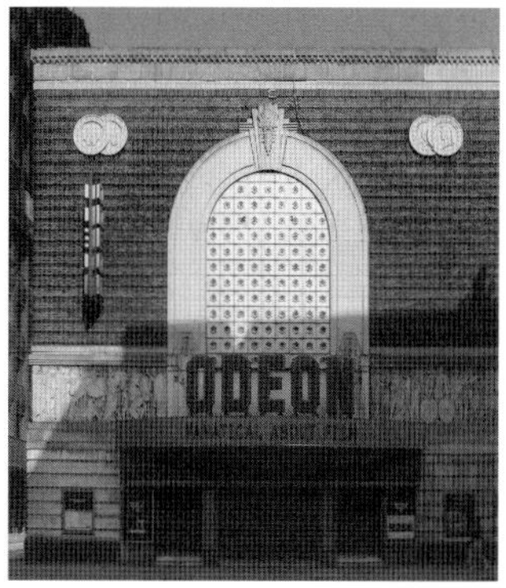

56

Saville Theatre (Odeon Cinema Shaftesbury Avenue), 1931
Shaftesbury Avenue, Soho, Westminster, London (K)
T.P. Bennett & Son / Bertie Crewe

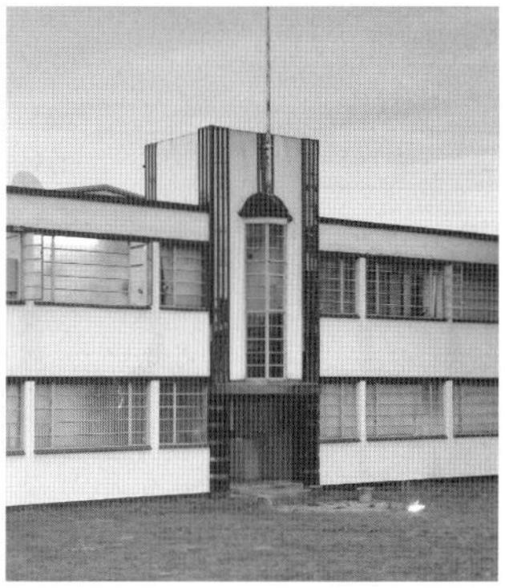

61

Ripaults Factory, 1936
Southbury Road, Enfield, Greater London
A.H. Durnford

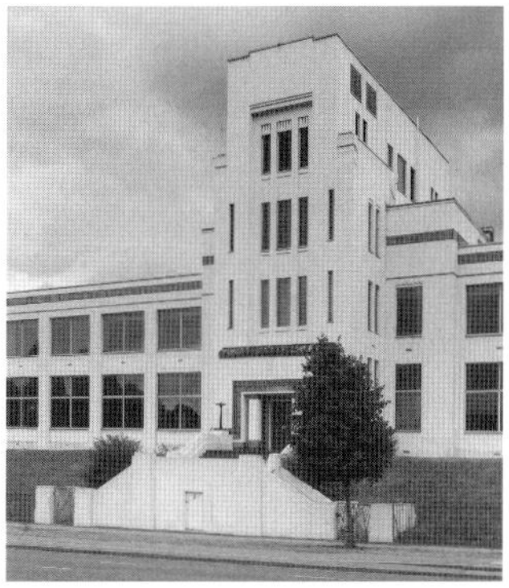

62

Pyrene Factory, 1930
Great West Road, Brentford, Greater London
Wallis Gilbert & Partners

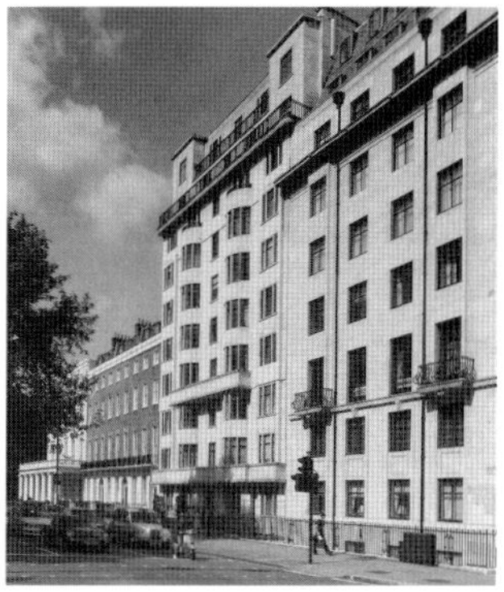

63

Flats 88 Portland Place
Portland Place, Fitzrovia, Westminster, London (J)

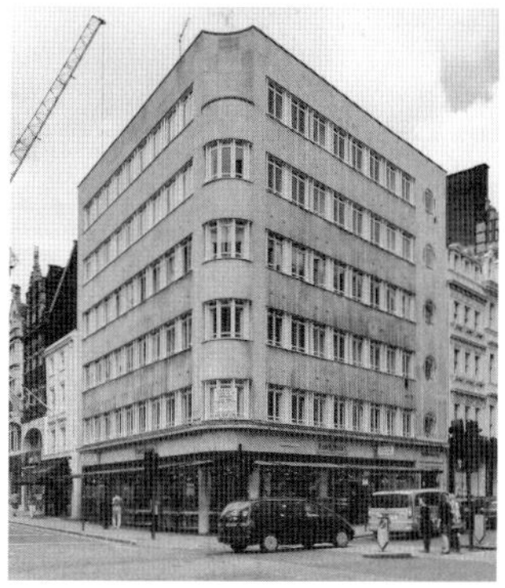

64

Offices New Bond Street, 1939
New Bond Street, Mayfair, Westminster, London (J)
Wimperis Simpson & Guthrie

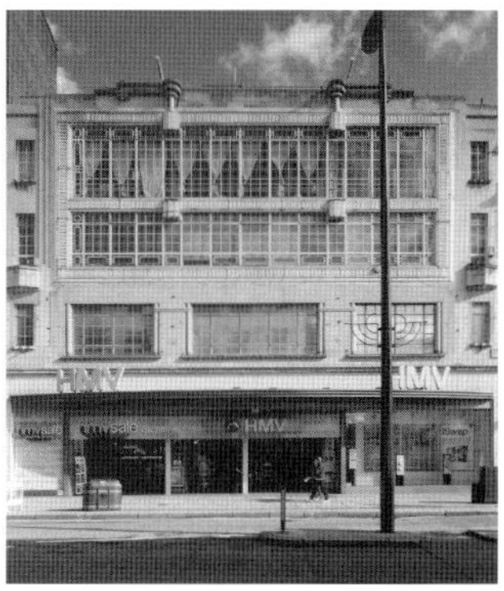

69

HMV Store Oxford Street, 1931
Oxford Street, Soho, Westminster, London (K)
Elcock & Sutcliffe

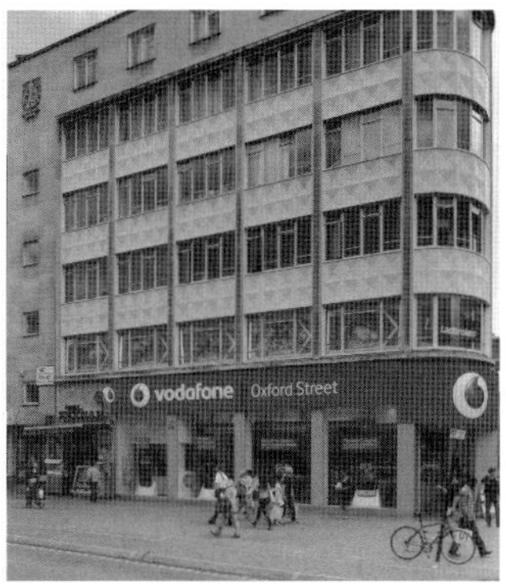

70

Barratt House
Oxford Street, Marylebone, Westminster, London (J)

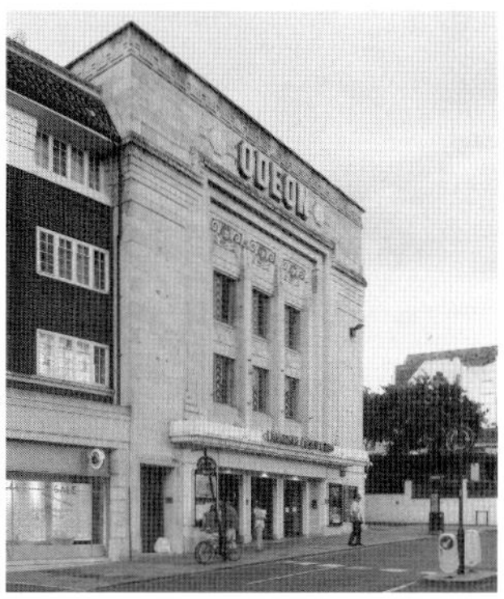

71

Odeon Cinema Richmond, 1929?
Petersham Road / Bridge Street, Richmond, Greater London
Julian Leathart / W.F. Grange

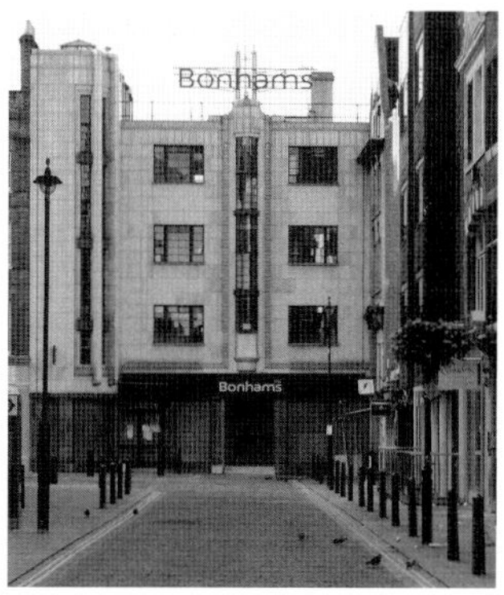

72

Bonhams Storehouse (*Phillips Storehouse*), 1938
Blenheim Street / Woodstock Street, Mayfair, Westminster, London (J)
Fuller Hall & Foulsham

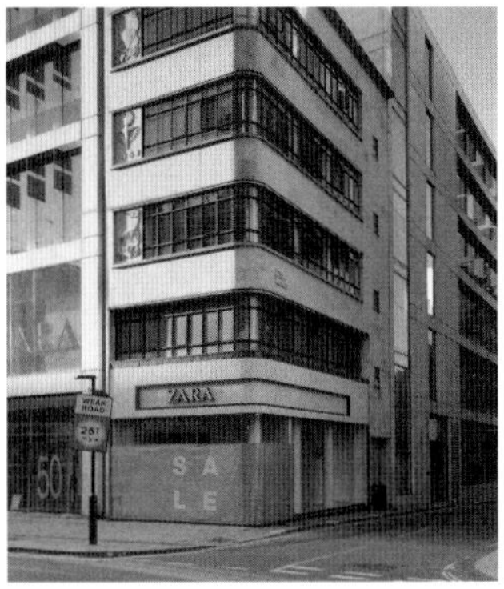

73

ZARA Store Oxford Street, 1959–62
Oxford Street / Hills Place, Soho, Westminster, London (J)
Ronald Ward & Partners

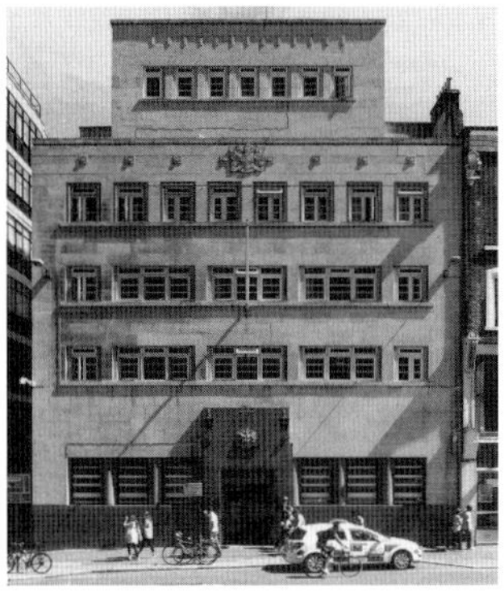

74

Bishopsgate Police Station
Bishopsgate, City of London, London (L)
Vine & Vine

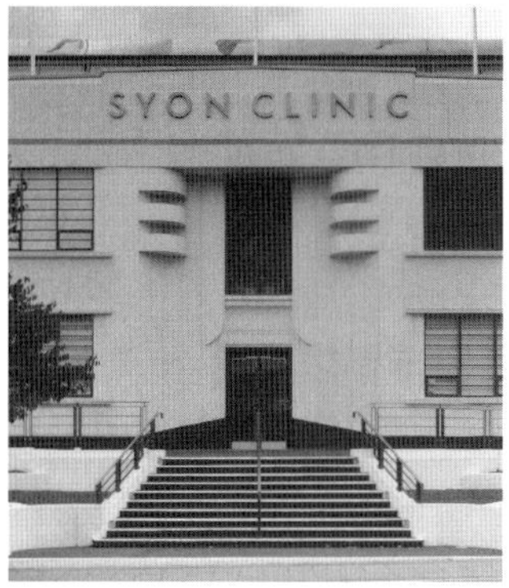

75

Coty Factory (Syon Clinic), 1932
Great West Road, Brentford, Greater London
Wallis Gilbert & Partners

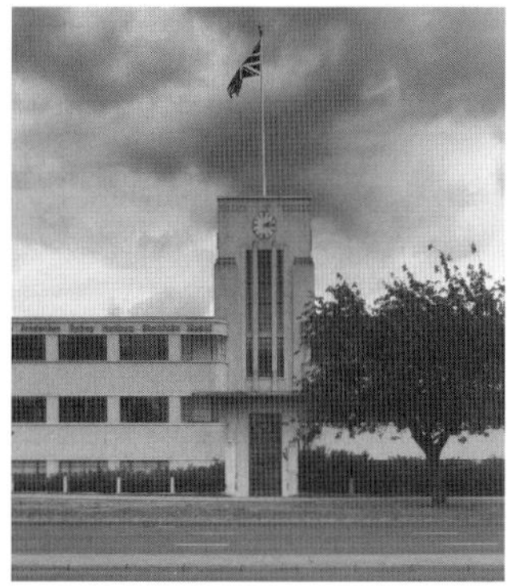

76

Currys Factory and Offices (*JCDecaux Offices*), 1935
Great West Road, Isleworth, Greater London
F.E. Simpkins

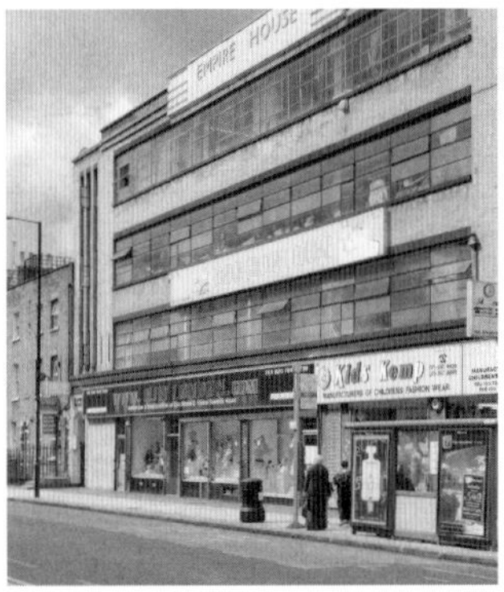

81

Empire House, 1934
New Road, Tower Hamlets, London (L)
H. Victor Kerr

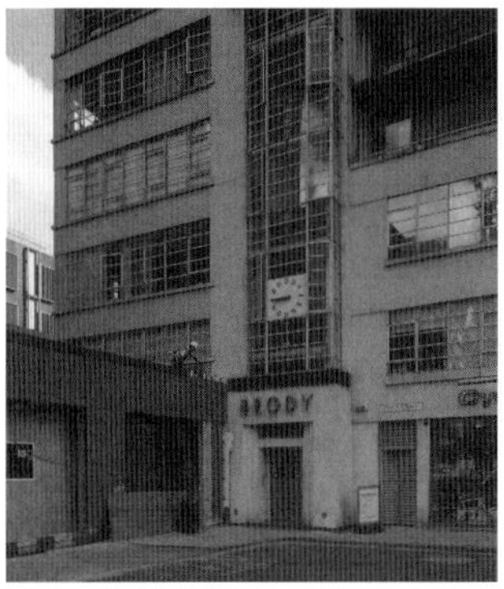

82

Brody House, 1938
Strype Street, Tower Hamlets, London (L)

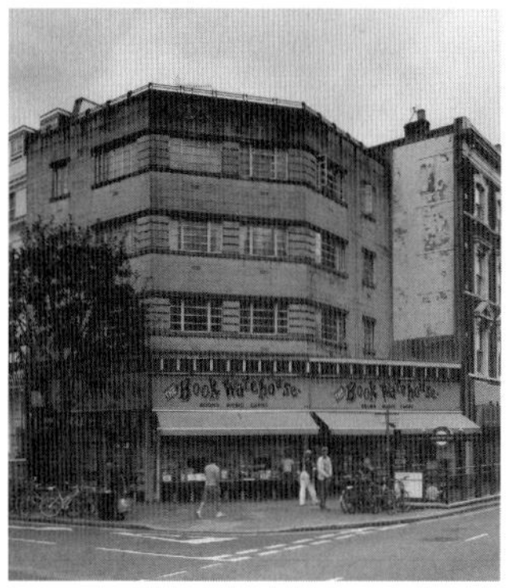

83

Flats Pembridge Gardens
Pembridge Gardens / Notting Hill Gardens, Kensington, London (I)

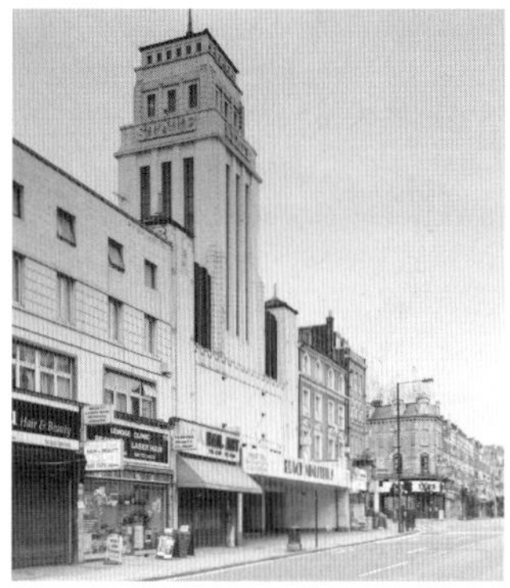

84

Gaumont 'State' Cinema Kilburn, 1937
Kilburn High Road, Kilburn, Camden, London (E)
George Coles

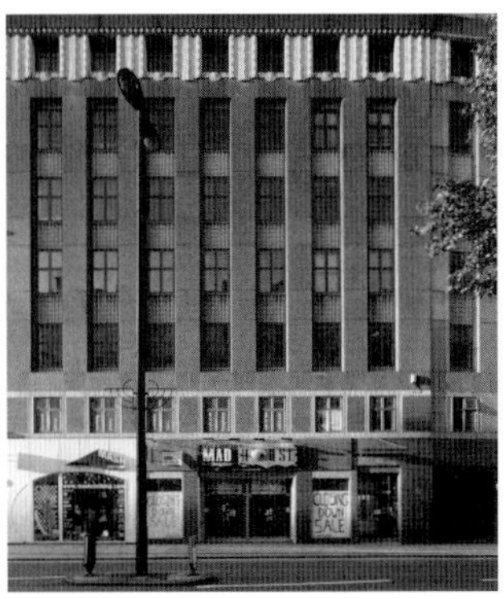

89

Offices Oxford Street, 1929–30, 1952
Oxford Street / Dean Street, Soho, Westminster, London (K)
Gordon Jeeves / H.A. Welch

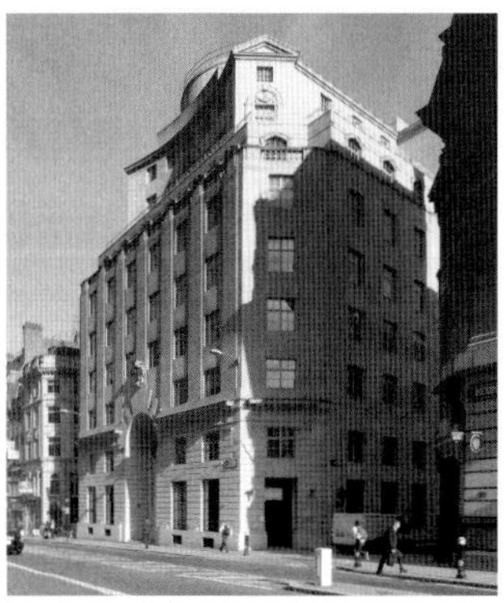

90

Reuters and Press Association Headquarters, 1934–38
Fleet Street, City of London, London (K)
Edwin Lutyens / Smee & Houchin

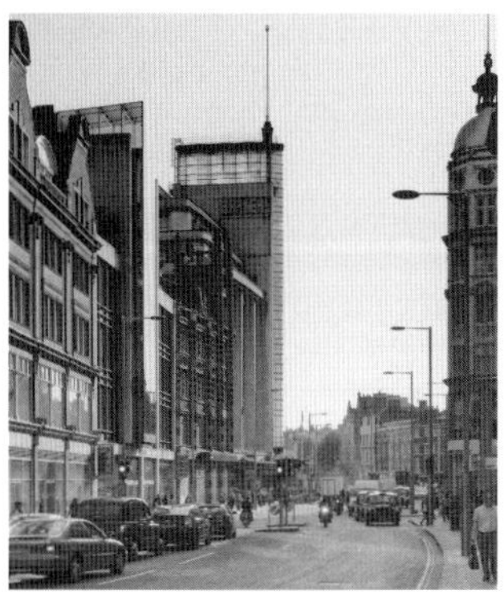

91

Barkers Department Store, 1937–38
Kensington High Street, Kensington, London (I)
Bernard George

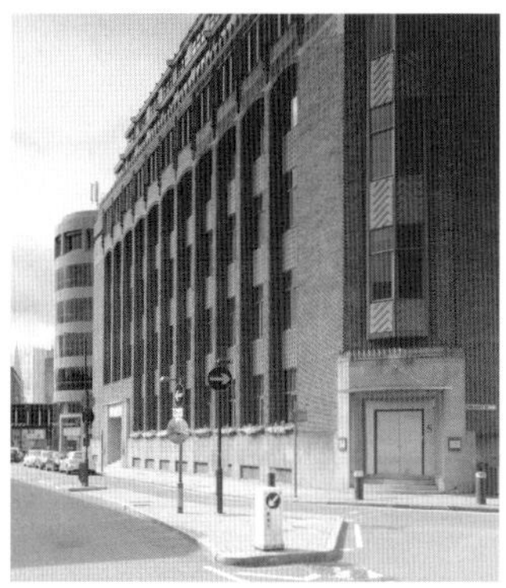

92

Offices One Prescot Street, 1930–33
Prescot Street, Tower Hamlets, London (L)
L.G. Ekins

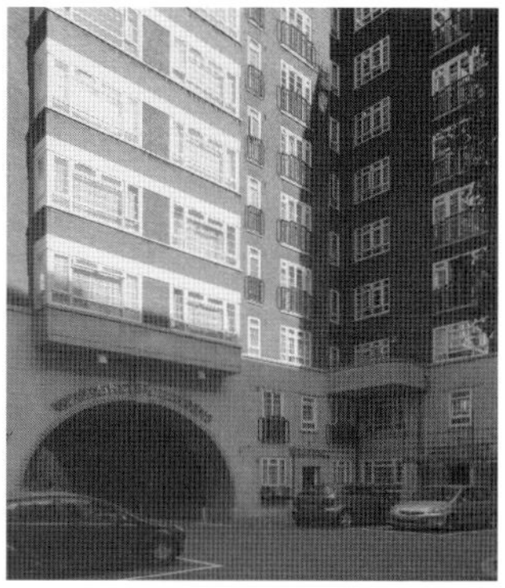

77

Westminster Gardens, 1935–36
Marsham Street, Millbank, Westminster, London (K)
T.P. Bennett & Son

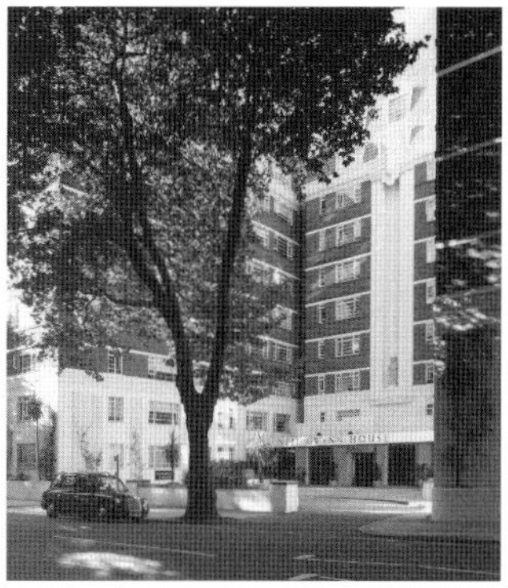

78

Nell Gwynn House, 1930s
Sloane Avenue, Kensington, London (J)

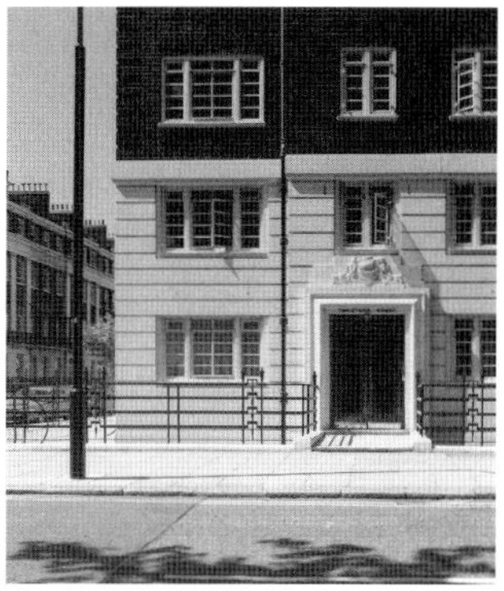

79

Tavistock Court
Tavistock Square, Bloomsbury, Camden, London (G)

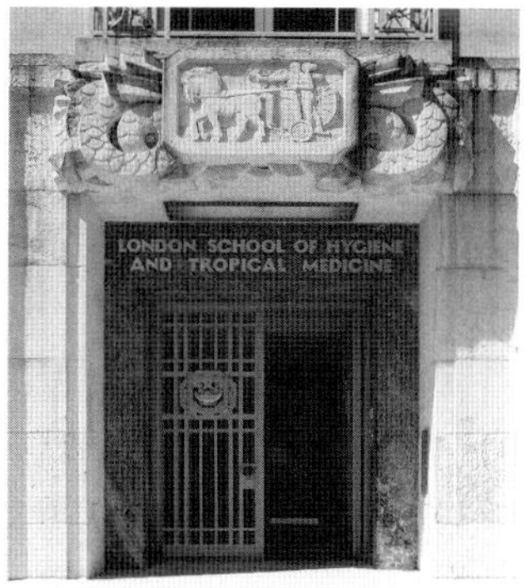

80

School of Hygiene and Tropical Medicine, 1926–28
Keppel Street, Bloomsbury, Camden, London (K)
P. Morley Horder / Verner O. Rees

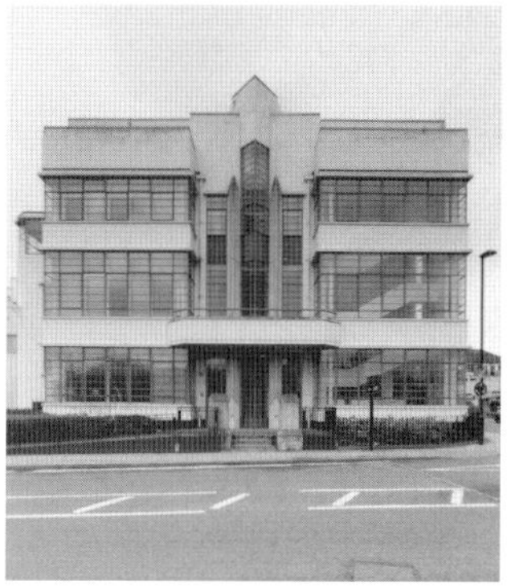

85

Hoover Factory Canteen, 1938
Western Avenue, Greenford, Greater London
Wallis Gilbert & Partners

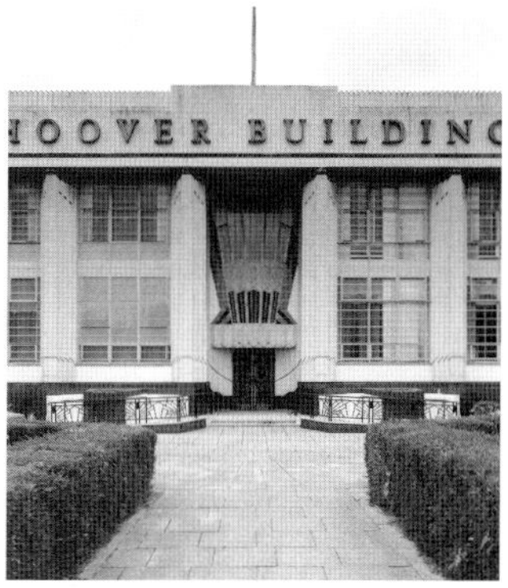

86

Hoover Factory (*Tesco Supermarket Western Avenue*), 1932–35
Western Avenue, Greenford, Greater London
Wallis Gilbert & Partners

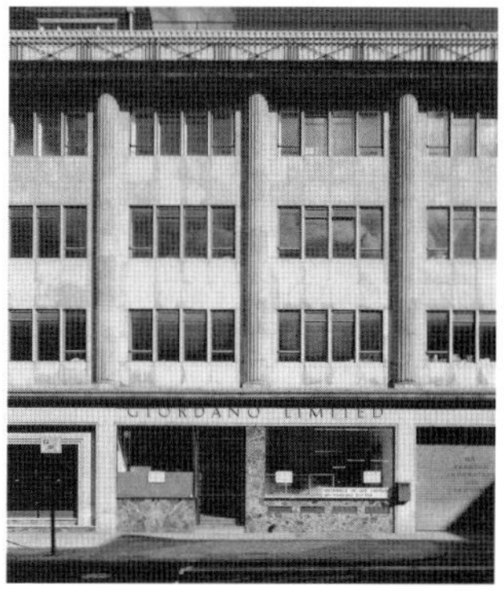

87

Giordano Limited
Windmill Street, Fitzrovia, Camden, London (K)

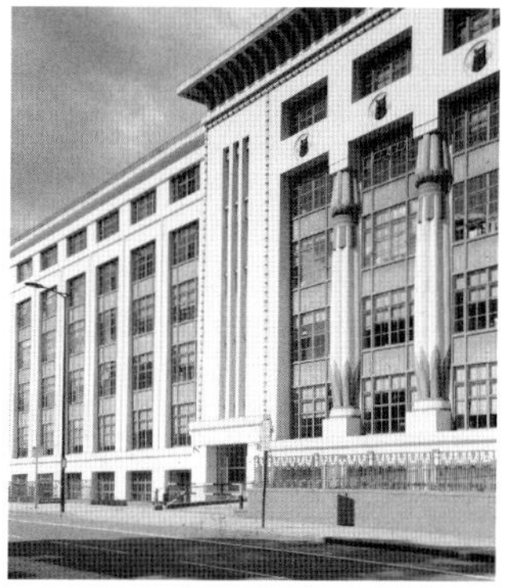

88

Carreras Cigarette Factory, 1926
Hampstead Road, Camden Town, Camden, London (F)
Marcus Evelyn Collins / O.H. Collins / Arthur George Porri

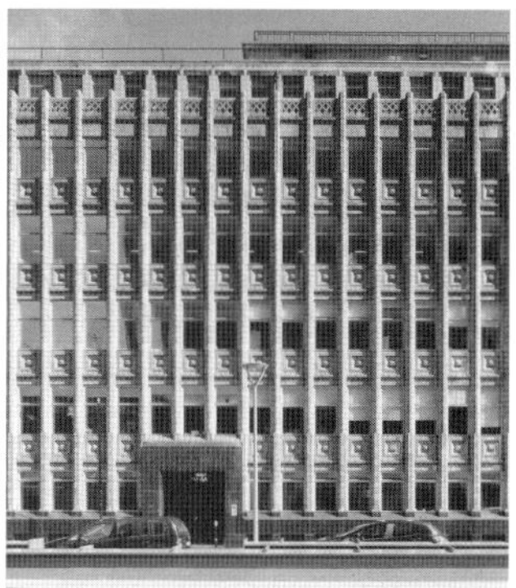

93

Holland House, 1914–16
Bury Street, City of London, London (L)
Hendrik Petrus Berlage

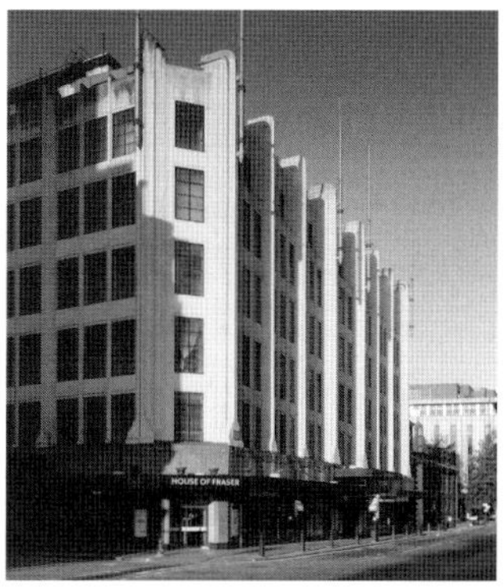

94

House of Fraser Department Store (DH Evans Department Store), 1935–37
Oxford Street, Marylebone, Westminster, London (J)
Louis Blanc

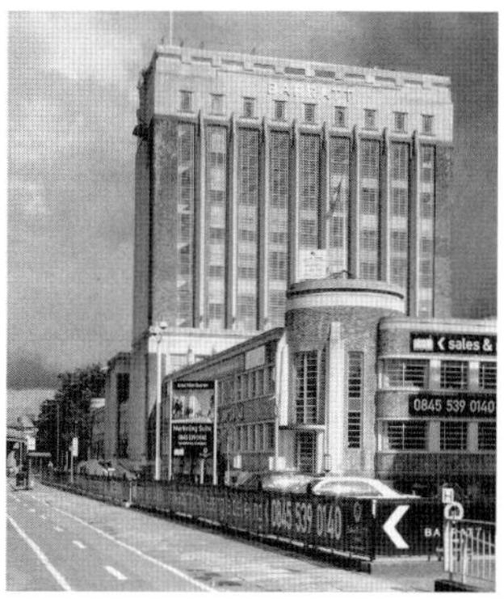

95

Simmonds Aerocessories Factory (Beechams Factory, *Barrat Flats*), 1938–42
Great West Road, Brentford, Greater London
Wallis Gilbert & Partners

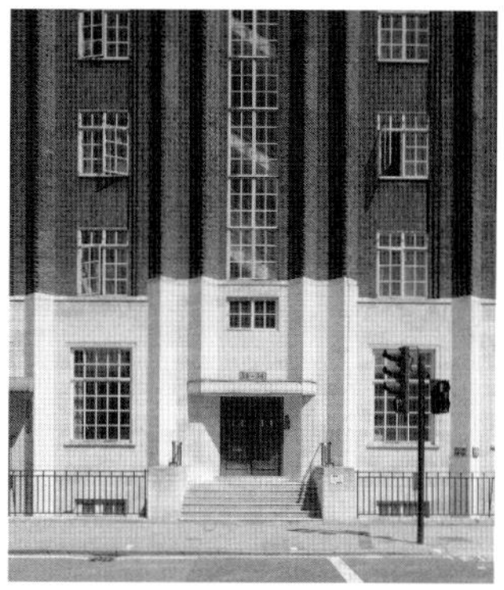

96

Warwickshire House
Gower Street, Bloomsbury, Camden, London (K)

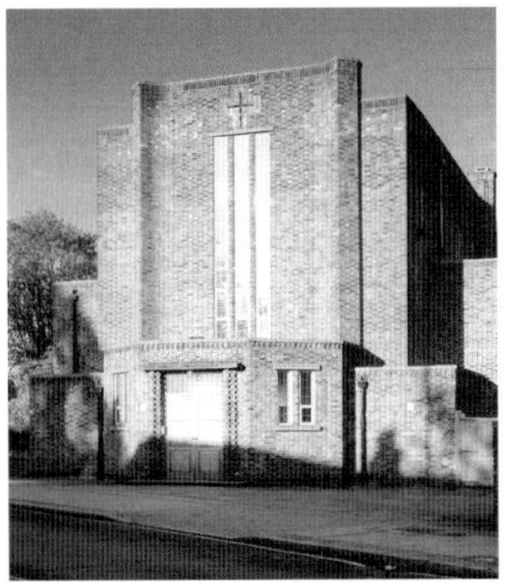

97

Hendon Methodist Church, 1937
The Burroughs, Barnet, London (A)
Day Welch & Lander

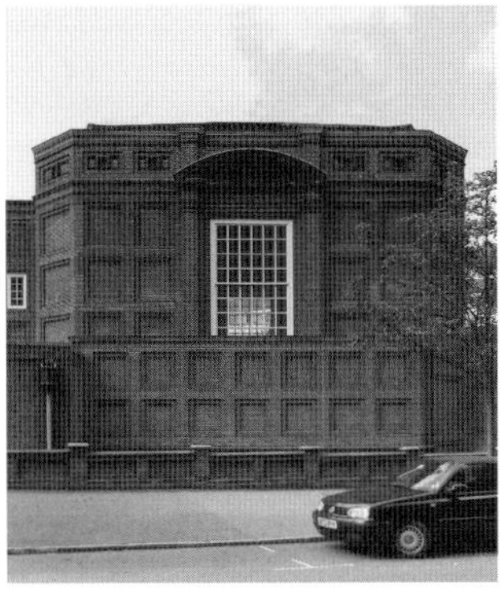

98

Richmond First Church of Christ Scientist, 1939–53
Sheen Road / Paradise Road, Richmond, Greater London
Braxton Sinclair & Barton

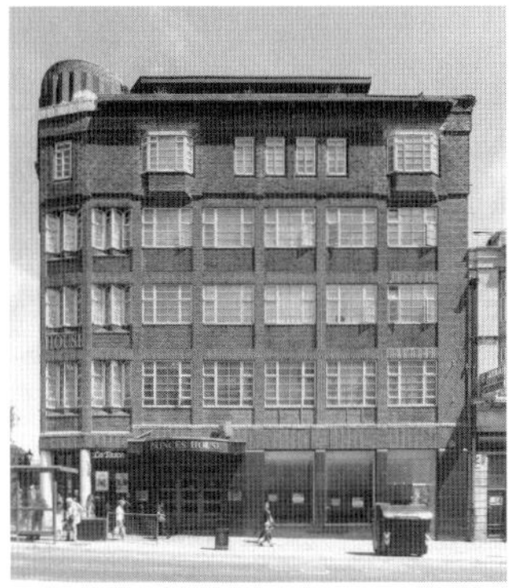

99

Princes House, 1935–36
North Street, Brighton, Sussex
Harry Stuart Goodhart-Rendel

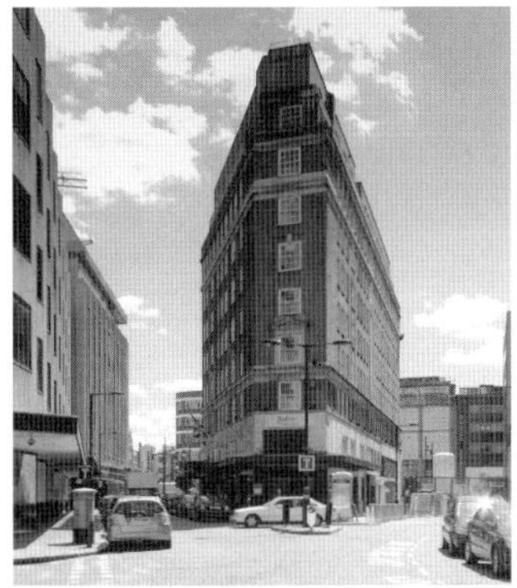

100

Radisson Edwardian Berkshire Hotel, 1935
Oxford Street, Marylebone, Westminster, London (J)
Gunton & Gunton

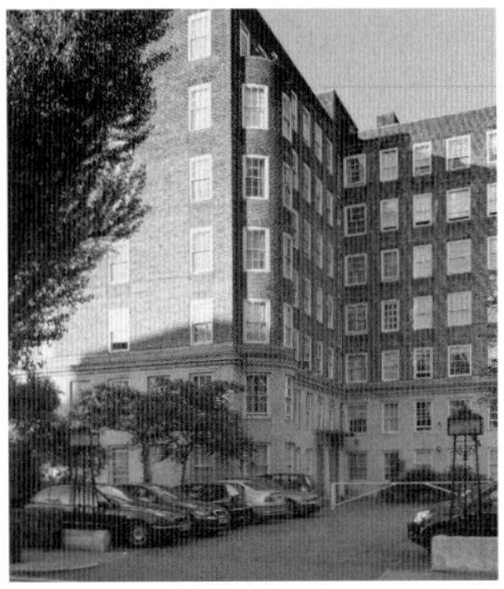

105

South Lodge
Circus Road, St John's Wood, Westminster, London (F)

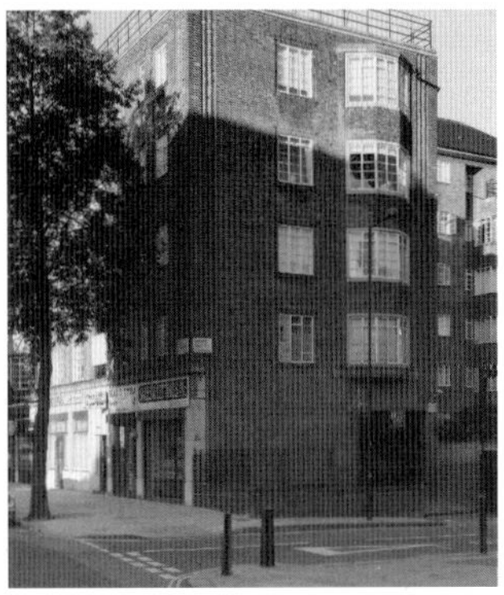

106

Hamilton Court, 1937
Maida Vale, Maida Vale, Westminster, London (F)
Beresford Marshall

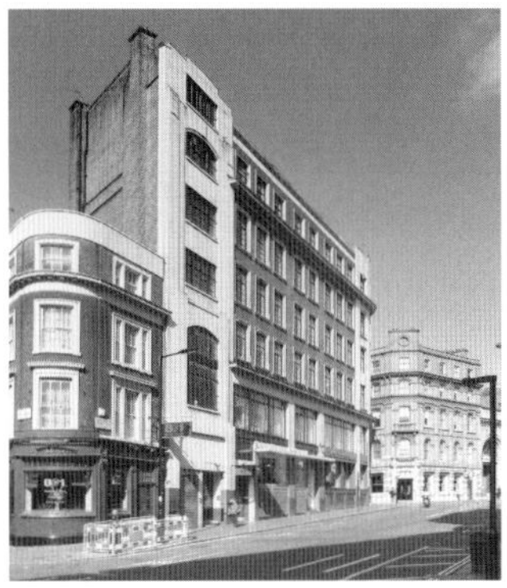

107

Offices Wellington Street
(G. Monro & Co. Offices), 1936
Wellington Street, Covent Garden, Westminster, London (K)
Epps & Powder

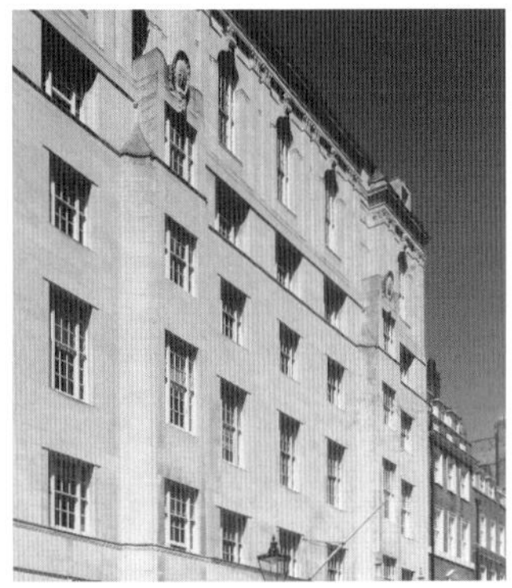

108

Flats Lincoln's Inn Fields, 1936–37
Lincoln's Inn Fields, Holborn, Camden, London (K)
Wimperis Simpson & Guthrie / William Curtis Green

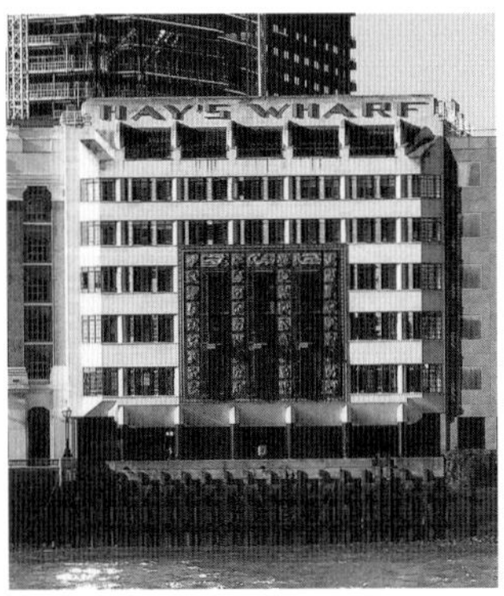

113

St Olaf House (Hay's Wharf), 1931
Tooley Street, Southwark, London (L)
Harry Stuart Goodhart-Rendel

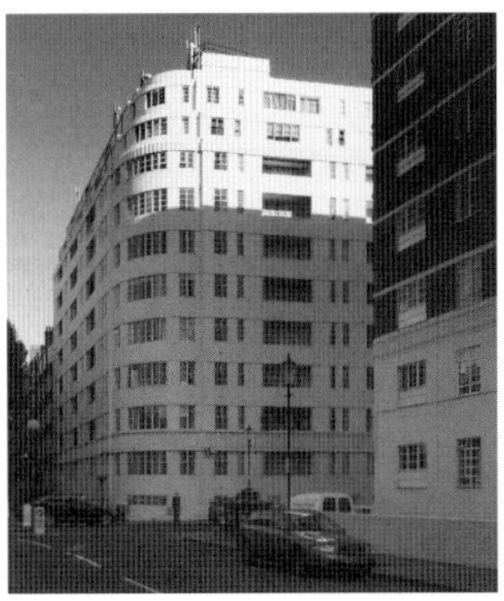

114

Sloane Avenue Mansions, 1930s
Sloane Avenue, Kensington, London (J)

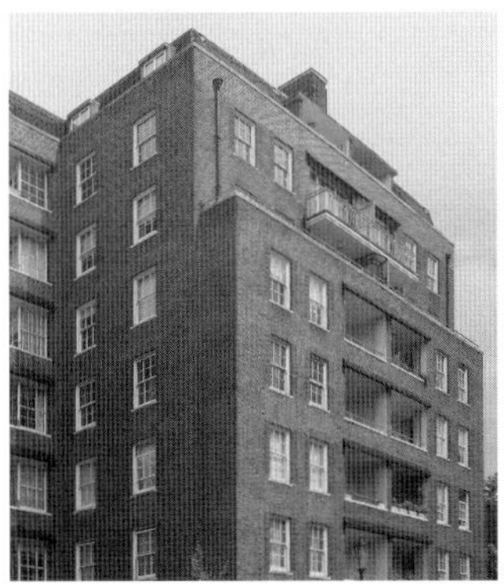

115

Chesil Court, 1930s
Chelsea Manor Street, Chelsea, London (N)

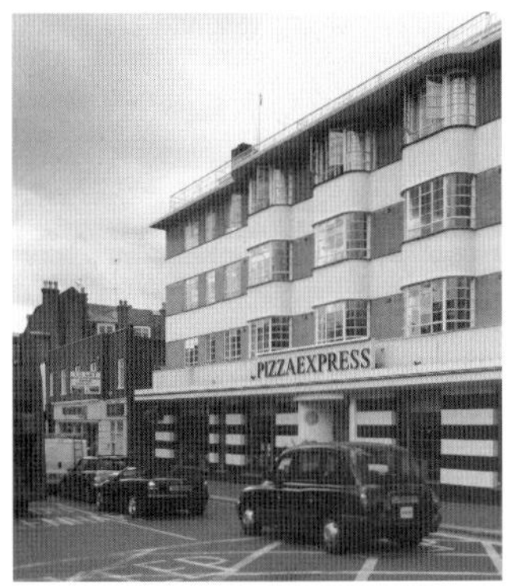

116

Lion House, 1930s
Red Lion Street, Richmond, Greater London

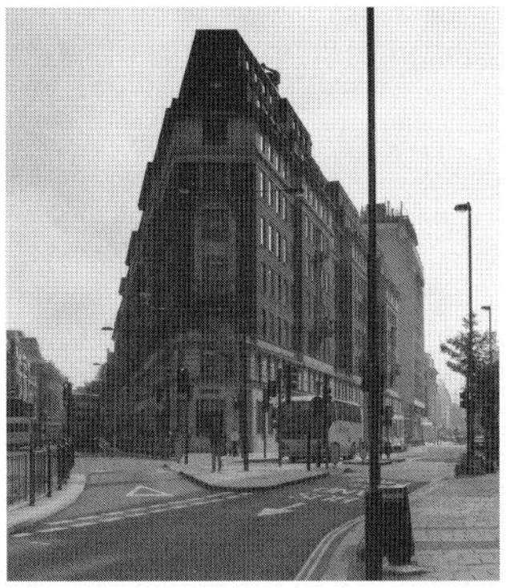

101

St George's Court, 1948–50
New Oxford Street / Bloomsbury Way, Holborn, Camden, London (K)
Lewis Solomon

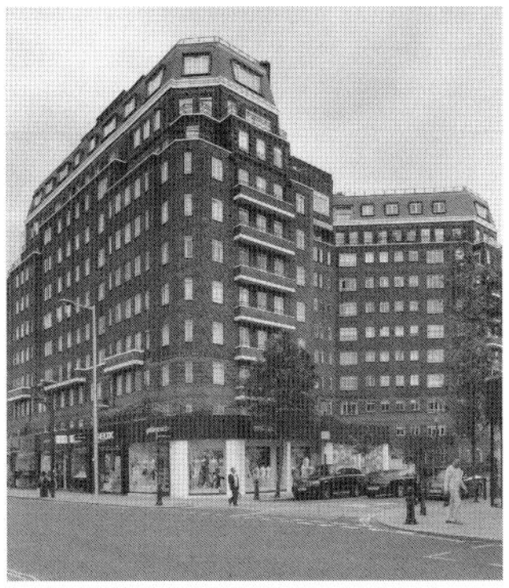

102

Whitelands House, 1937?
King's Road, Chelsea, London (J)

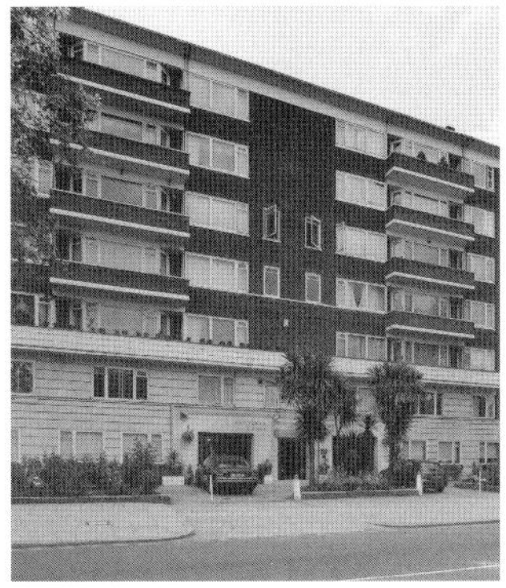

103

Bentinck Close
Prince Albert Road, St John's Wood, Westminster, London (F)

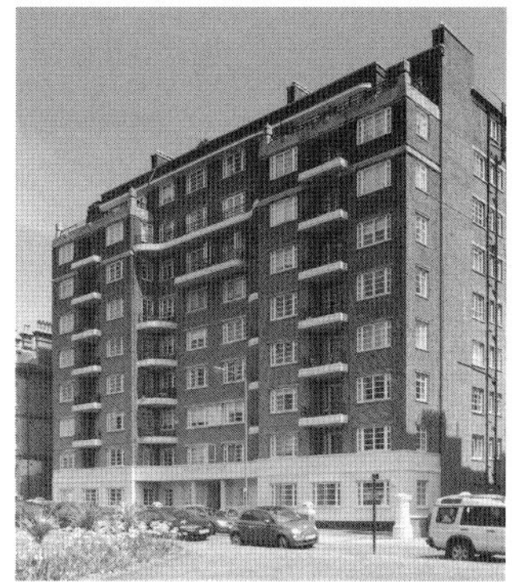

104

Flats Grand Avenue, 1935–38
Grand Avenue, Hove, Sussex
Murrell & Piggott

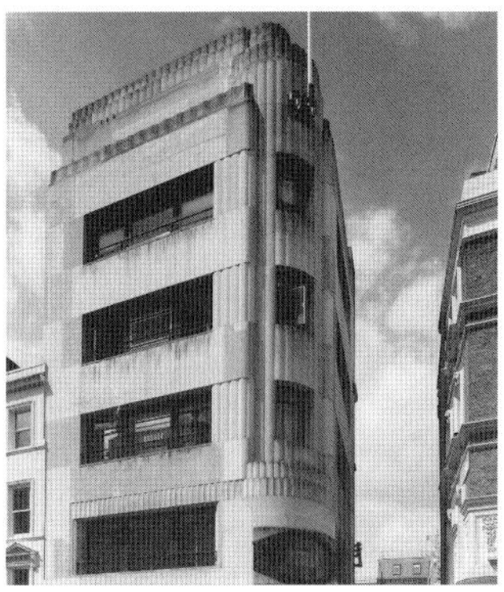

109

Bechstein Pianos' Showroom and Offices, 1929
Brook Street, Mayfair, Westminster, London (J)
Burnet Tait & Partners

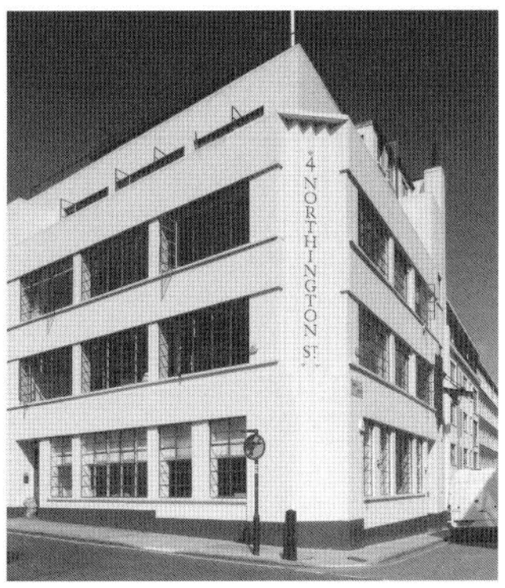

110

Offices Northington Street
Northington Street, Bloomsbury, Camden, London (K)

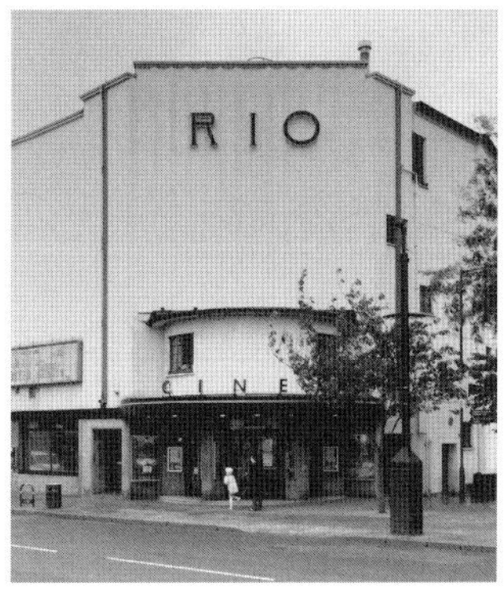

111

The Rio Cinema, 1937
Kingsland High Street, Hackney, London (H)
Frank Ernest Bromige

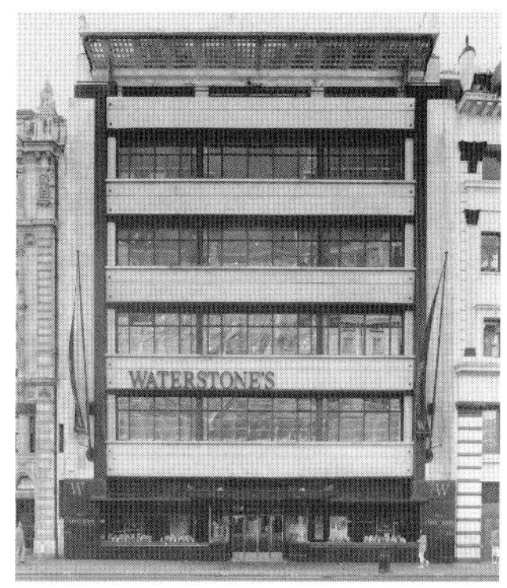

112

Simpson's Department Store (*Waterstone's Bookshop Piccadilly*), 1935
Piccadilly, Westminster, London (K)
Joseph Emberton

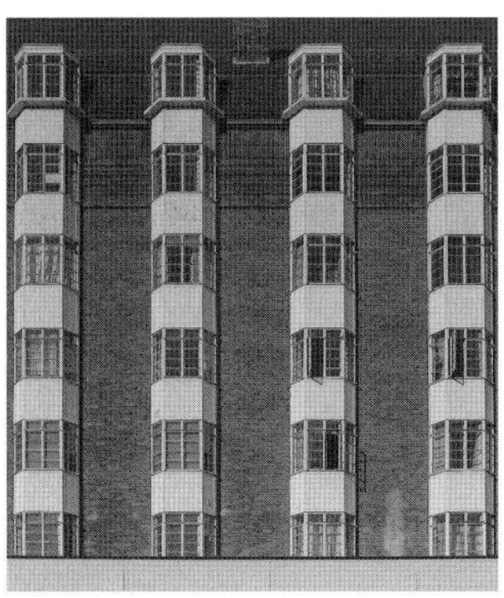

117

Latymer Court, 1934?
Hammersmith Road, Hammersmith, London (I)
Gordon Jeeves?

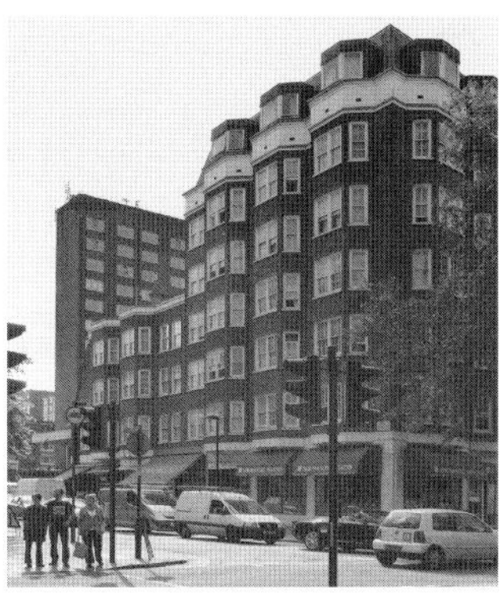

118

Flats Park Road
Park Road, St John's Wood, Westminster, London (F)

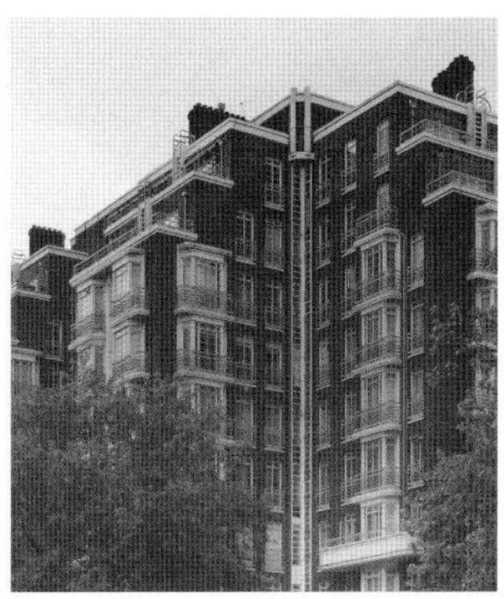

119

Dorset House, 1935
Marylebone Road, Marylebone, Camden, London (J)
T.P. Bennett & Son / Joseph Emberton

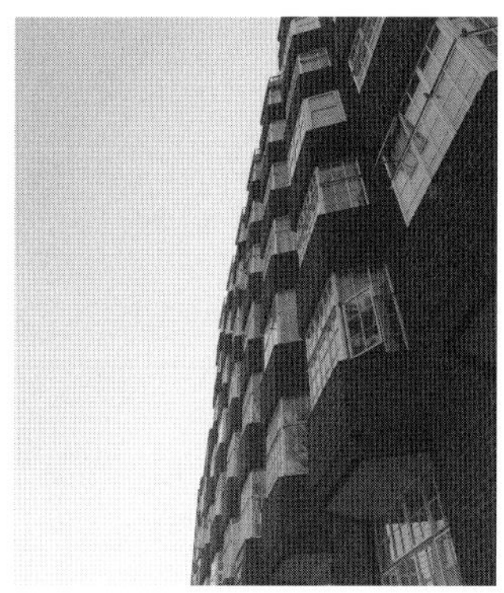

120

Russell Court
Woburn Place, Bloomsbury, Camden, London (G)

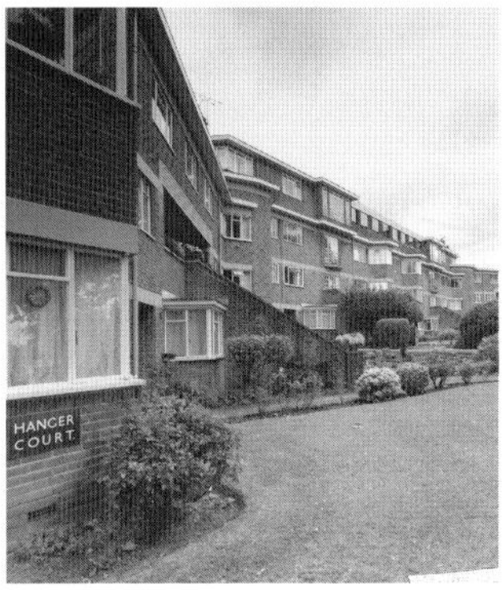

121

Hanger Court, 1935
Heathcroft / Corringway, Ealing, London
Day Welch & Lander

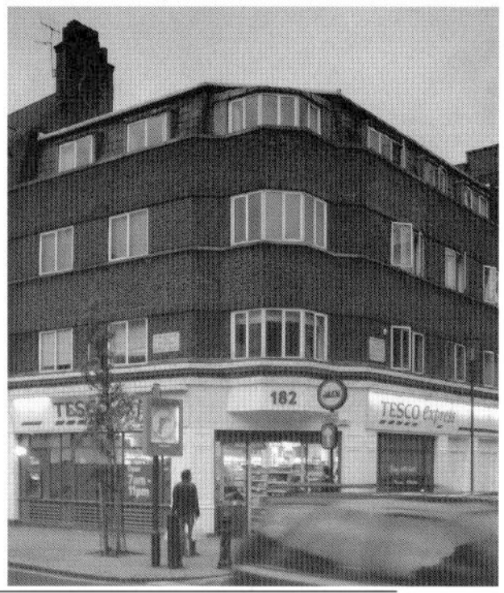

122

Flats Gilston Road
Fulham Road / Gilston Road, Chelsea, London (N)

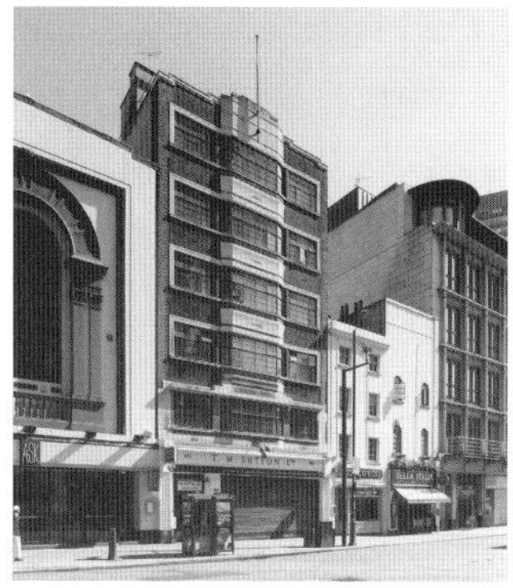

123

Sutton House, 1934–35
Victoria Street, Millbank, Westminster, London (J)
Reginald W. Lone

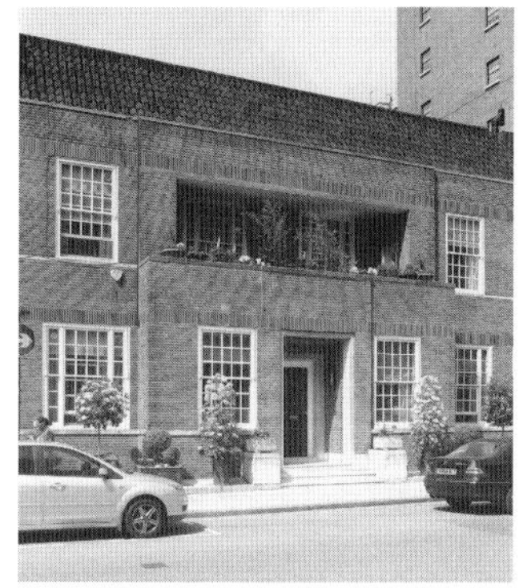

124

House 22 Weymouth Street, 1936
Weymouth Street, Marylebone, Westminster, London (J)
Giles Gilbert Scott

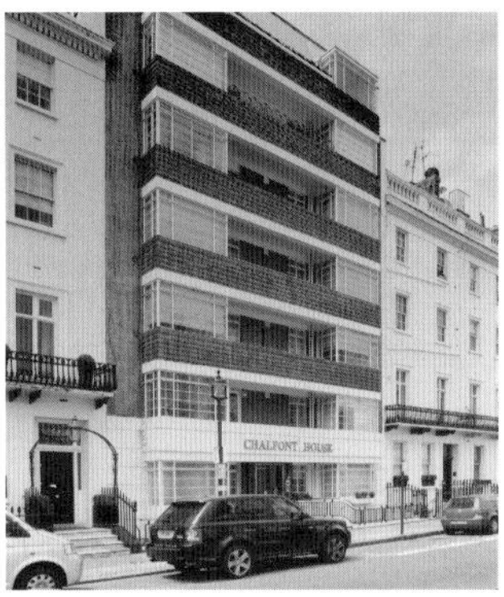

129

Chalfont House
Chesham Street, Belgravia, Westminster, London (J)

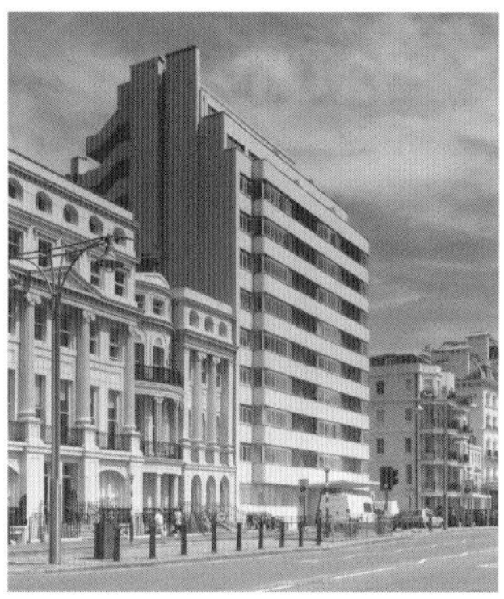

130

Embassy Court, 1934–35
King's Road, Brighton, Sussex
Wells Coates

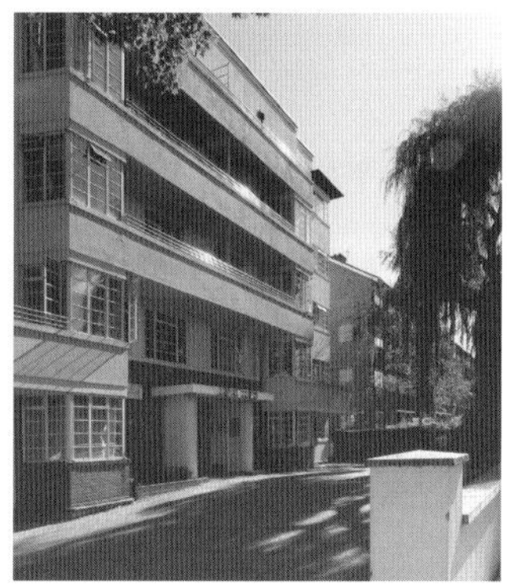

131

Hylda Court
St Alban's Road, Kentish Town, Camden, London (B)

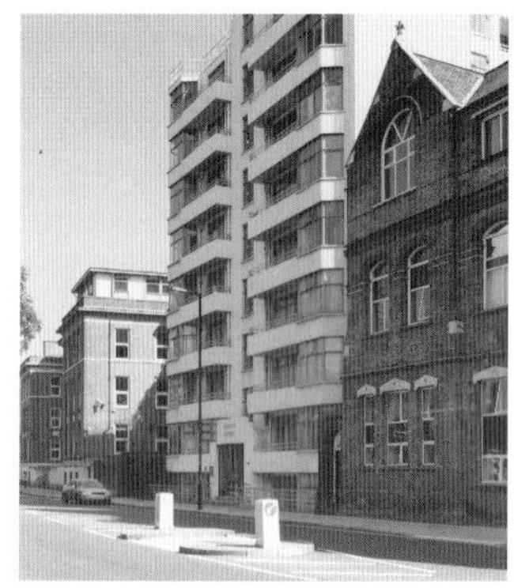

132

Trinity Court
Gray's Inn Road, Bloomsbury, Camden, London (G)

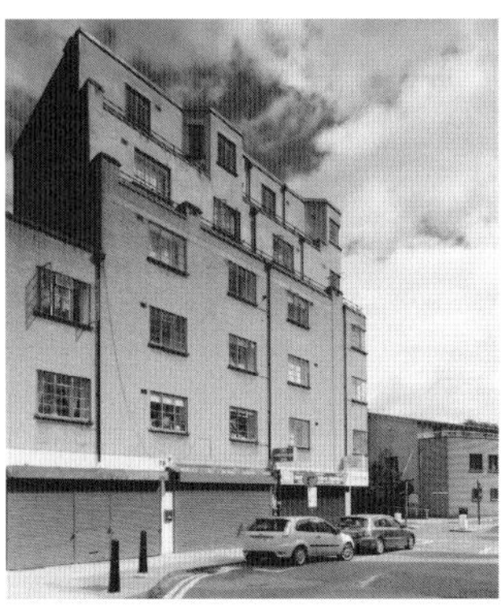

137

Evelyn House, 1936
Greatorex Street, Tower Hamlets, London (L)
Edgar Tanner

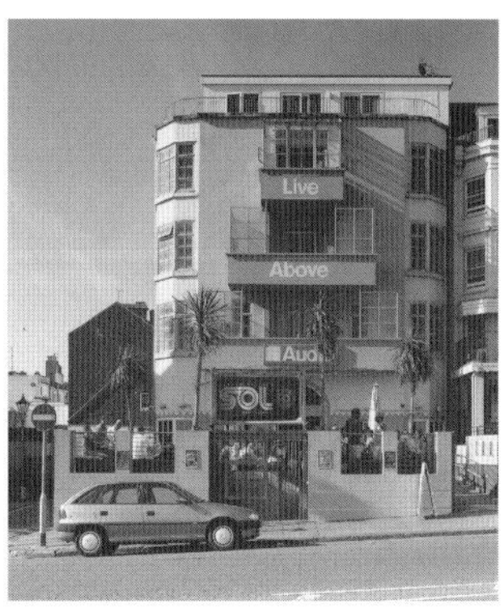

138

Flats Broad Street
Broad Street, Brighton, Sussex

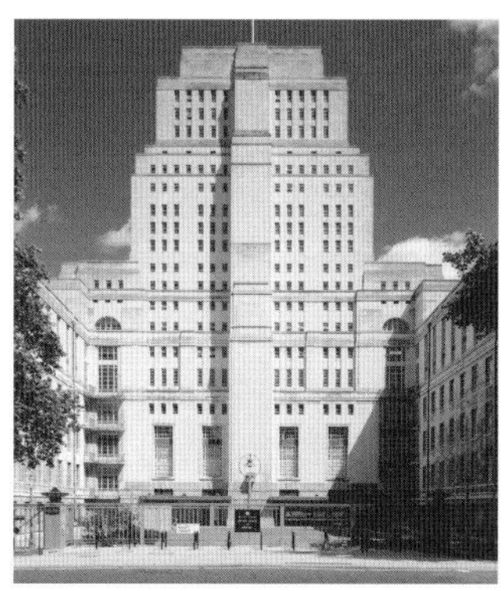

139

Senate House, University of London, started 1932
Malet Street / Montague Place, Bloomsbury, Camden, London (K)
Charles Holden

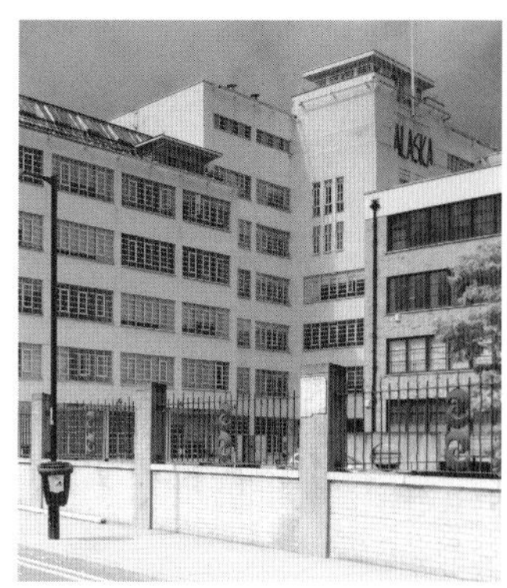

140

Alaska Factory (Martin's), 1932–34
Grange Road, Southwark, London (L)
Wallis Gilbert & Partners

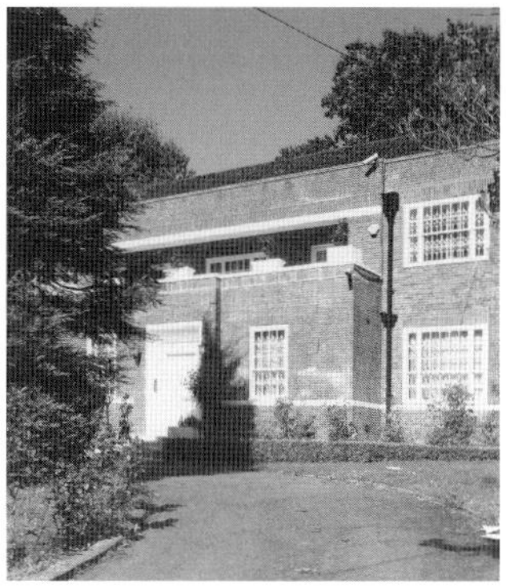

125

Spaniards Mount, 1936
Winnington Road, Hampstead Garden Suburb, Barnet, London (B)
Adrian Scott

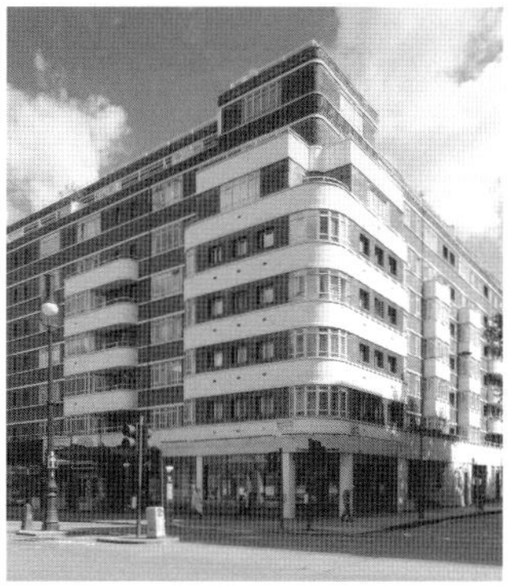

126

Paramount Court, 1930s?
Tottenham Court Road / University Street, Holborn, Camden, London (G)

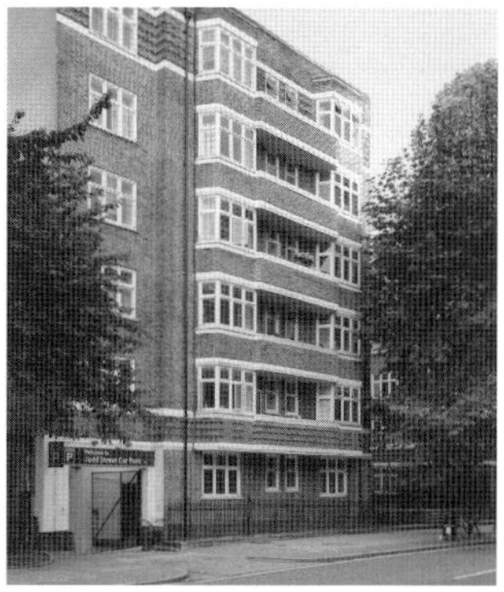

127

Clare Court
Judd Street, Holborn, Camden, London (G)

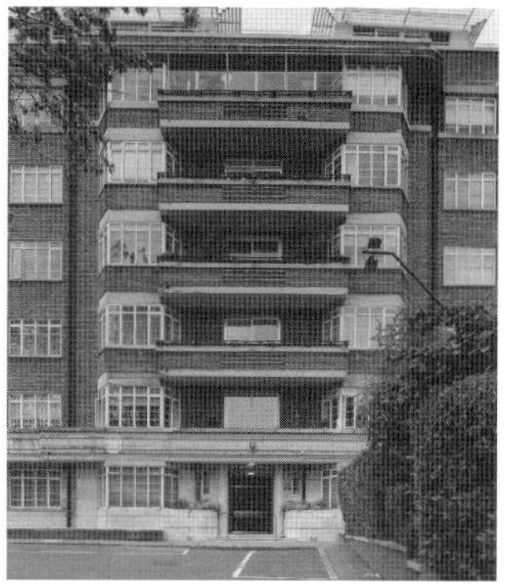

128

St James's Close
St James's Terrace, St John's Wood, Westminster, London (F)

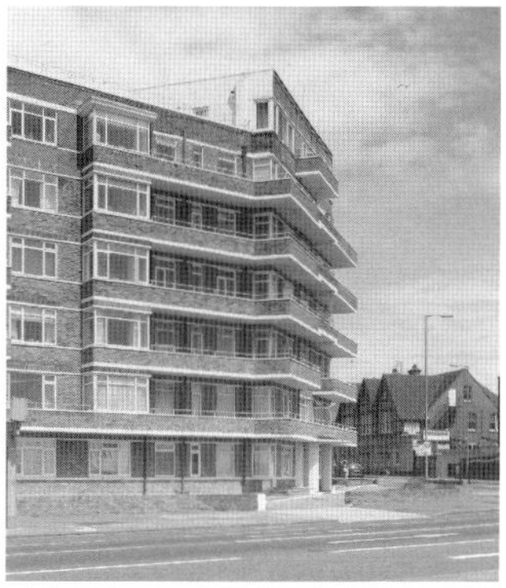

133

Viceroy Lodge
Kingsway, Hove, Sussex

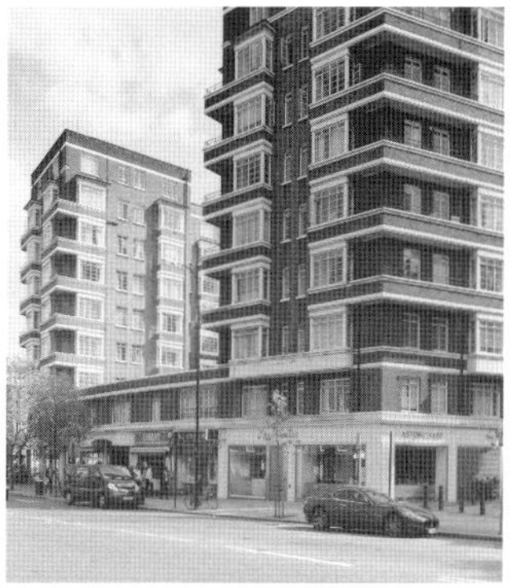

134

Rossmore Court
Park Road, St John's Wood, Westminster, London (F)

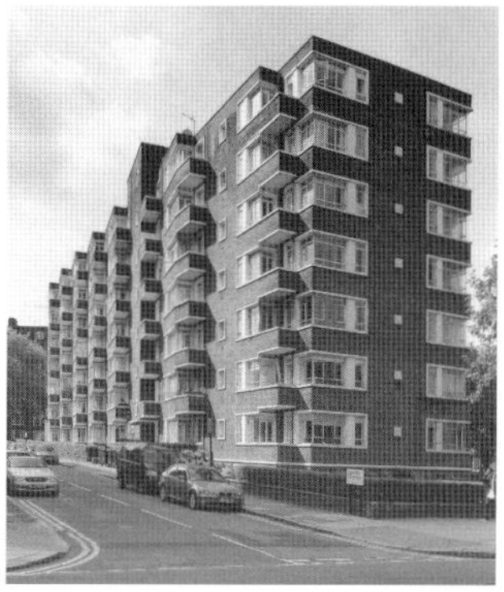

135

Oslo Court, 1938
Charlbert Street / Culworth Street, St John's Wood, Westminster, London (F)
Robert Atkinson

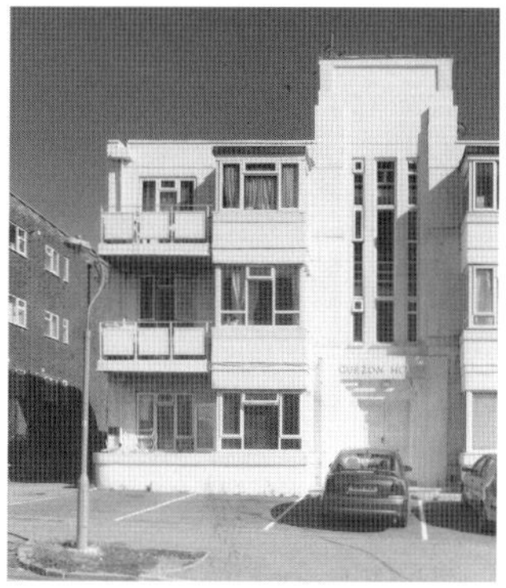

136

Curzon House, 1937?
Chichester Drive East, Saltdean, Sussex
R.W.H. Jones

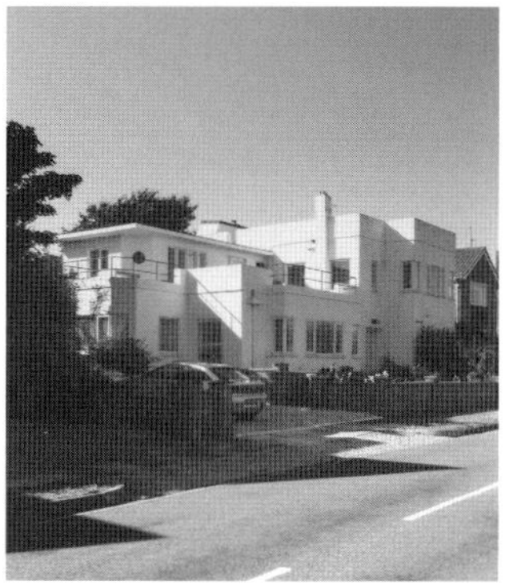

141

Bethany
Arundel Drive West, Saltdean, Sussex

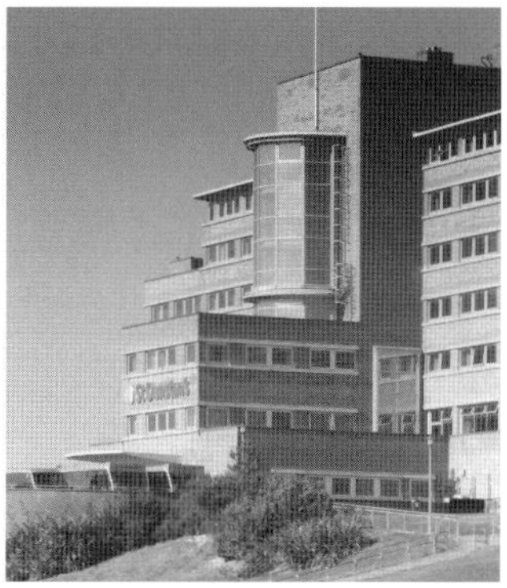

142

St Dunstan's, 1937–39
Greenways, Ovingdean, Sussex
Francis Lorne (Burnet Tait & Lorne?)

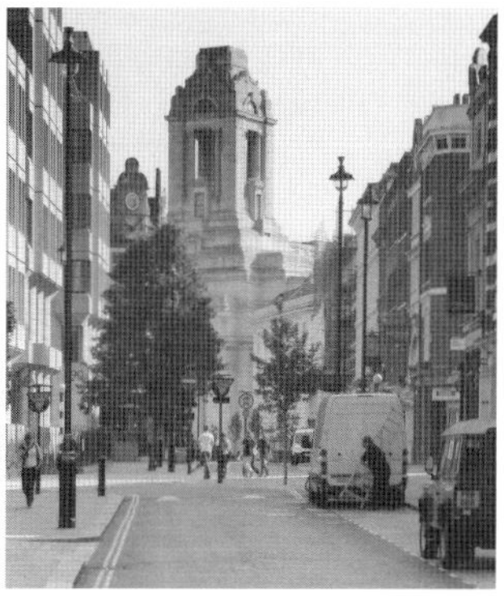

143

Freemasons' Hall, 1927–33
Great Queen Street, Holborn, Camden, London (K)
Henry Victor Ashley / F. Winton Newman

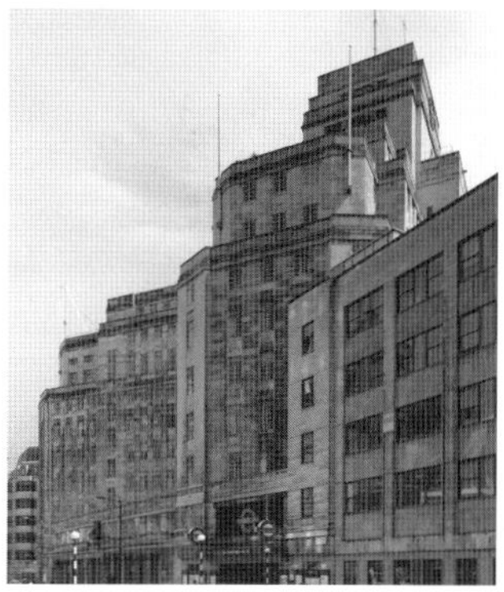

144

Broadway House
(London Underground Headquarters), 1927–29
Broadway, Westminster, London (K)
Charles Holden

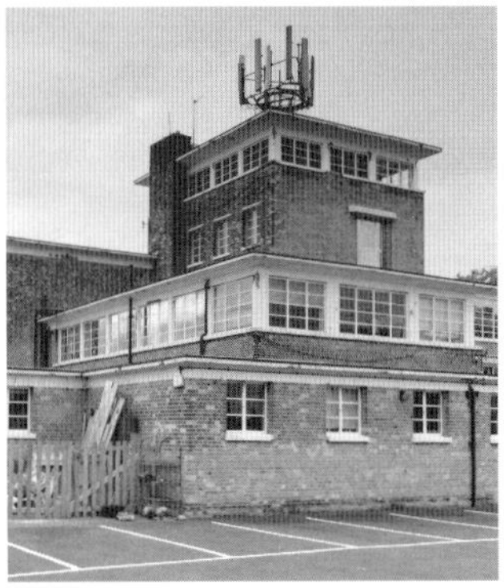

145

De Brohun Library and Clinic, 1939
Green Road, Enfield, London
W.T. Curtis / H.W. Burchett

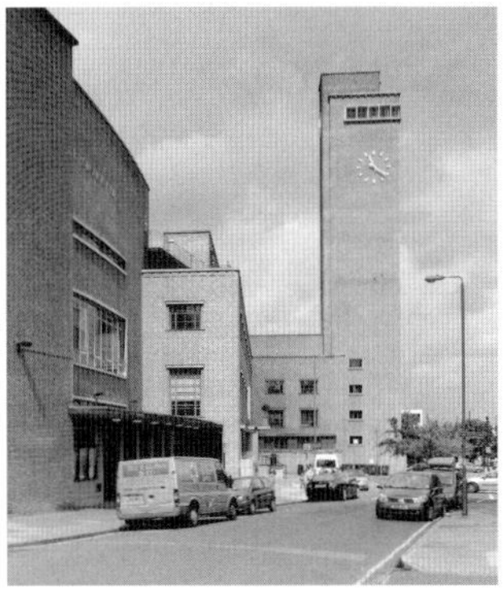

146

Greenwich Town Hall, 1939
Royal Hill / Greenwich High Road, Greenwich, London
Ewart Gladstone Culpin / Bowers

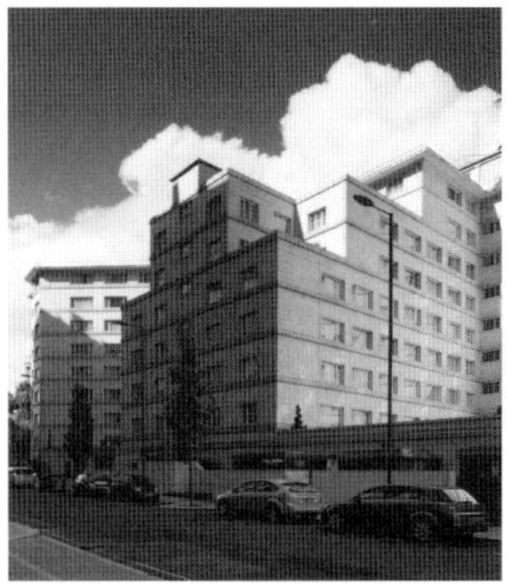

147

The White House Hotel, 1936
Albany Street, St Pancras, Camden, London (F)
Robert Atkinson

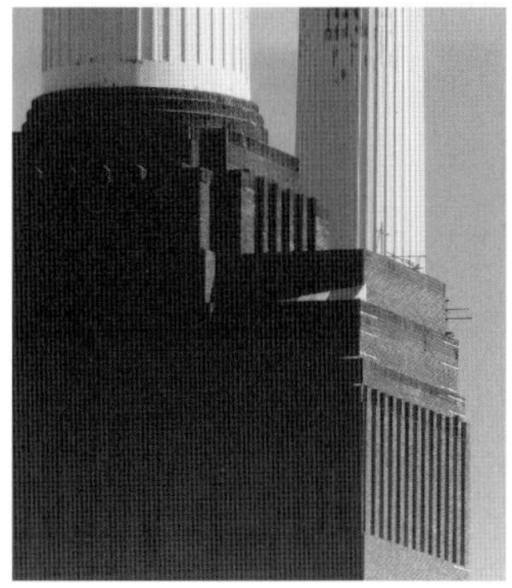

148

Battersea Power Station, 1929–35, 1929–55
Kirtling Street, Wandsworth, London (N)
S. Leonard Pearce / Giles Gilbert Scott

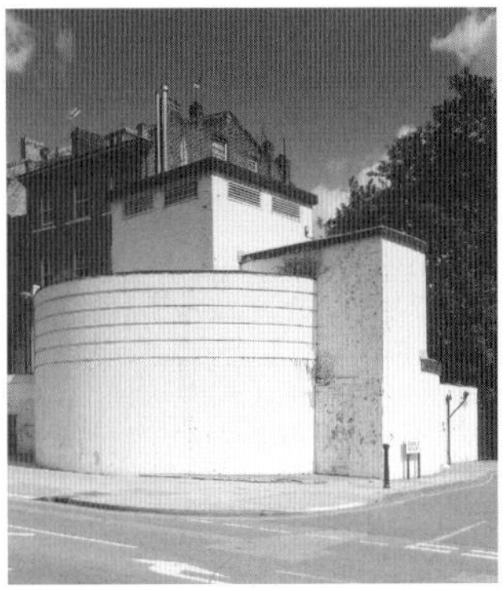

153

Belsize Park Deep Level Shelter, 1940–42?
Haverstock Hill / Downside Crescent, Belsize Park, Camden, London (F)

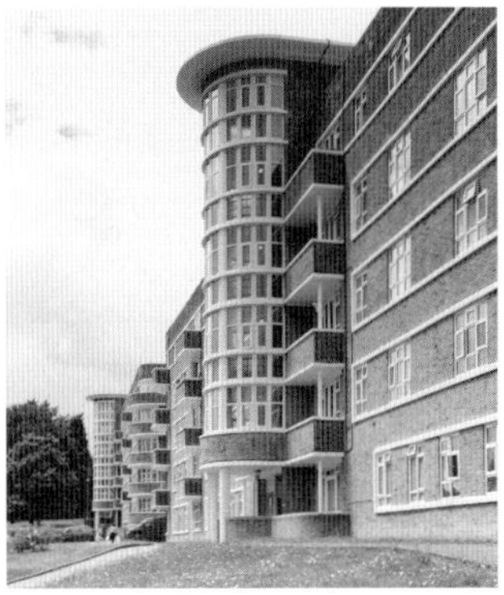

154

Flats Shackleton Close
Shackleton Close, Lewisham, London

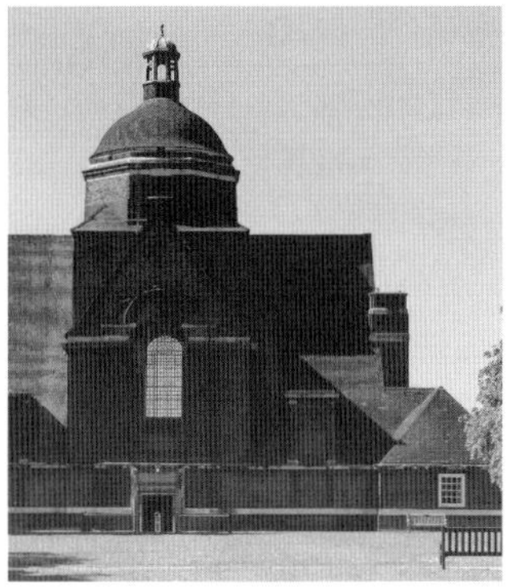

155

Hampstead Garden Suburb Free Church, 1911, 1960s
Central Square, Hampstead Garden Suburb, Barnet, London (A)
Edwin Lutyens

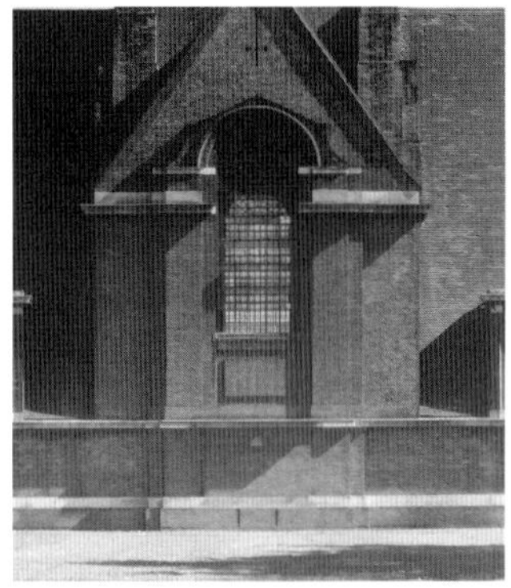

156

St Jude, 1909–11, 1915, 1935
Central Square, Hampstead Garden Suburb, Barnet, London (A)
Edwin Lutyens

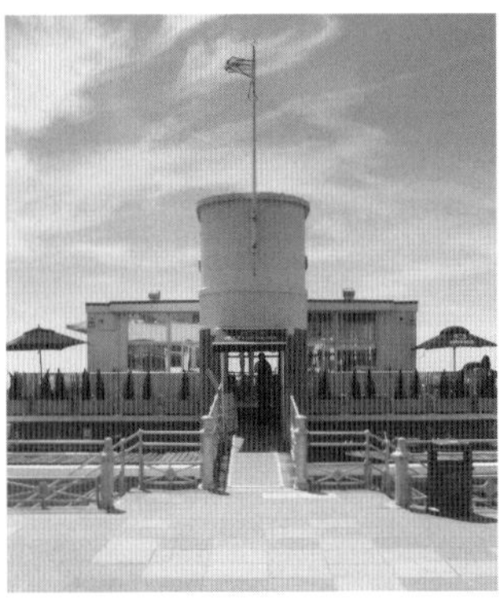

161

Milkmaid Pavilion (*Alfresco Restaurant*), 1950s
Kings Road Arches, Brighton, Sussex

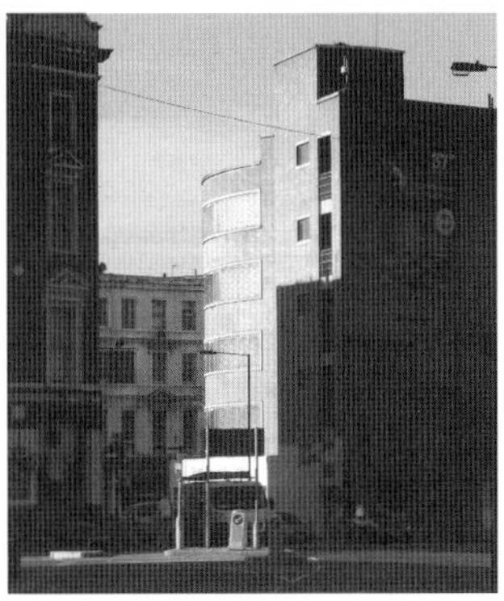

162

Olympic Garage, 1936
Maclise Road, Hammersmith, London (I)
Joseph Emberton

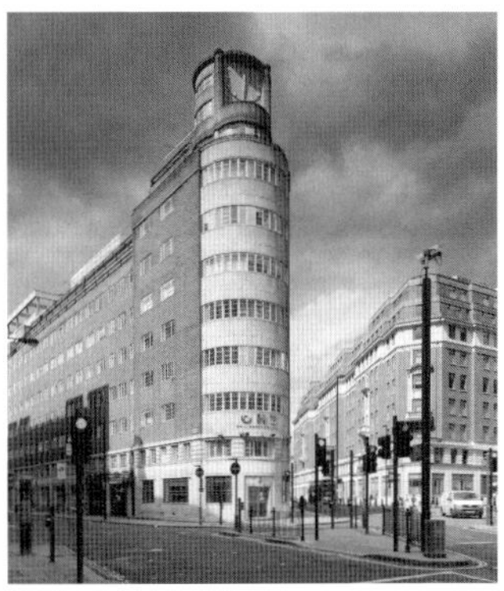

163

Commonwealth House, 1939
New Oxford Street / High Holborn, Bloomsbury, Camden, London (K)
H.P. Cart de Lafontaine

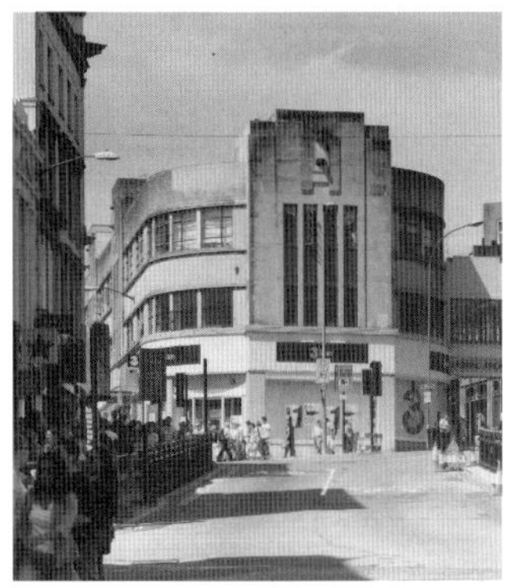

164

Imperial Arcade, 1934
Western Road / Dyke Road, Brighton, East Sussex
Garrett & Son

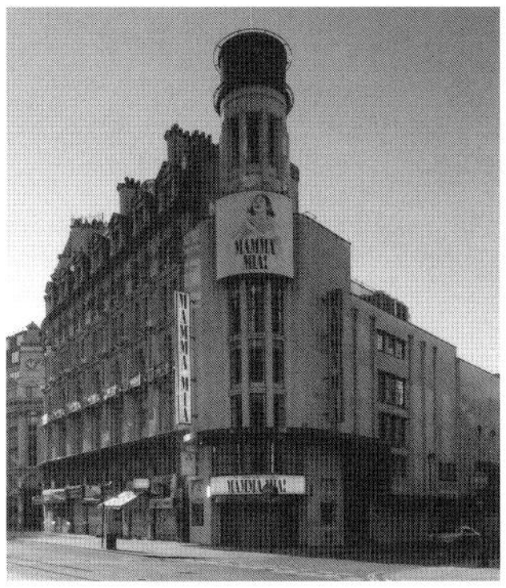

149

Prince of Wales Theatre, 1937
Coventry Street, Soho, Westminster, London (K)
Robert Cromie

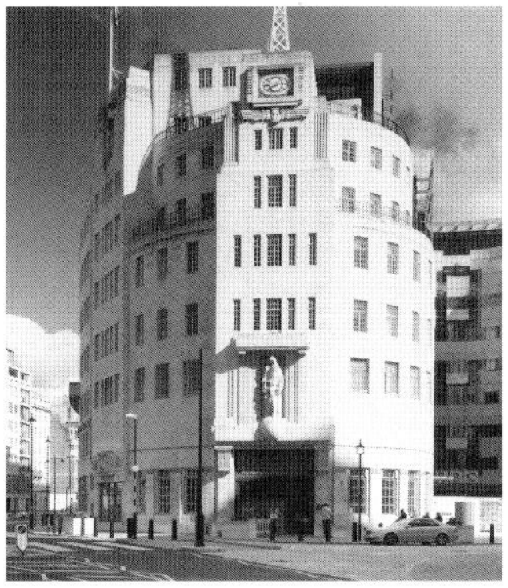

150

Broadcasting House, 1931
Portland Place, Fitzrovia, Westminster, London (J)
George Val Myer

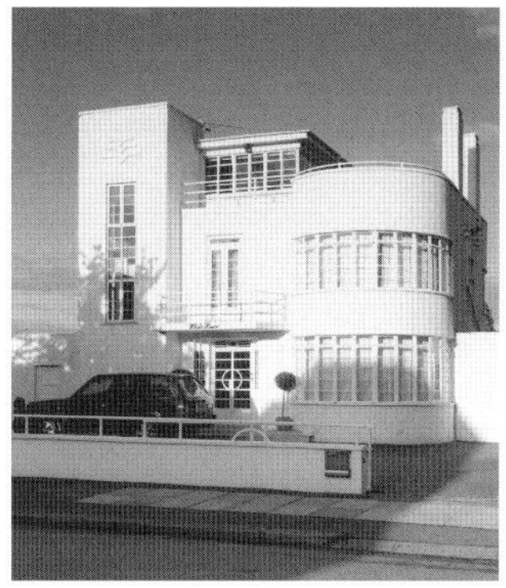

151

The White House, 1936
Downage, Barnet, London
Evelyn Simmons

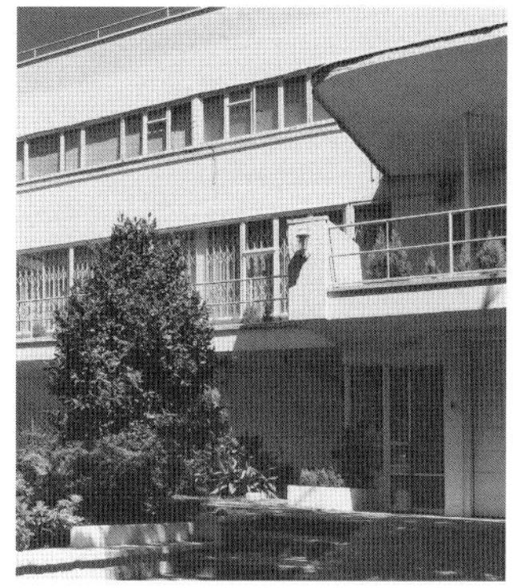

152

Sun House, 1934–35
Frognal Way, Frognal, Camden, London (F)
Maxwell Fry

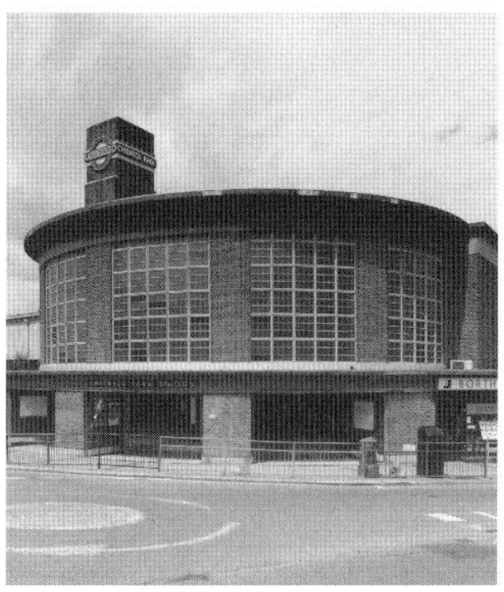

157

Chiswick Park Underground Station, 1932
Acton Lane, Hounslow, London
Charles Holden

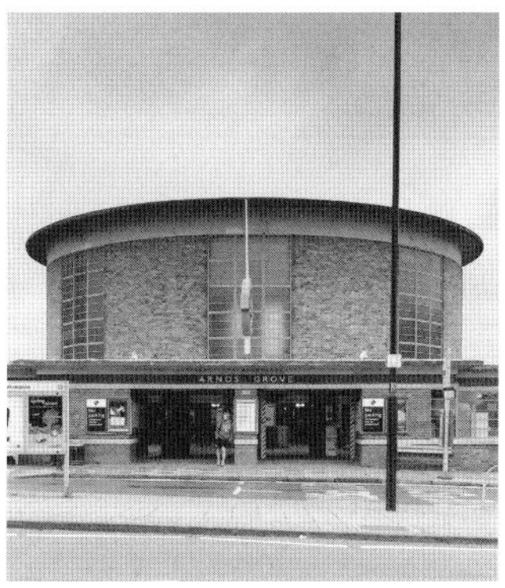

158

Arnos Grove Underground Station, 1932–33
Bowes Road, Enfield, London
Charles Holden

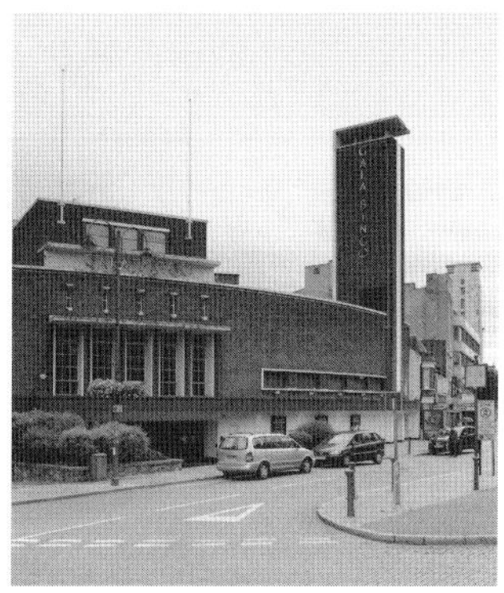

159

Granada Cinema Woolwich, 1937
Powis Street, Greenwich, London
Cyril Masey / Reginald Harold Uren

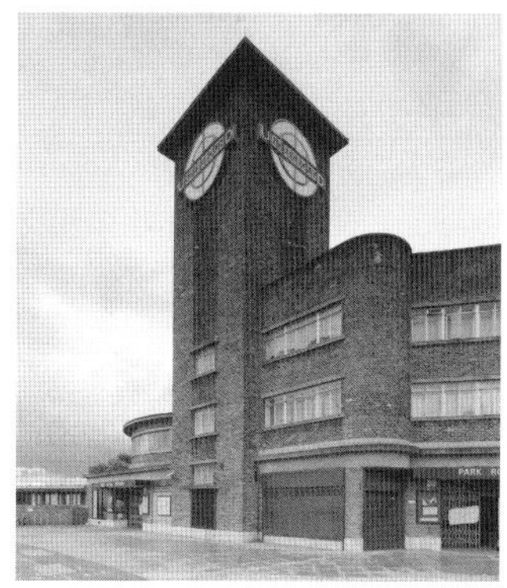

160

Park Royal Underground Station, 1935–36
Western Avenue, Ealing, London
Welch & Lander

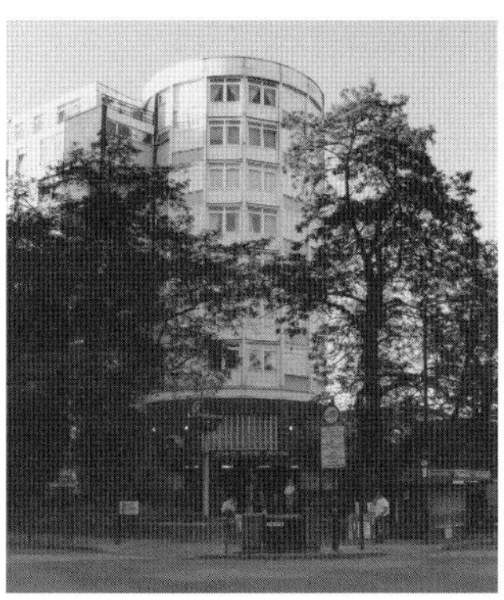

165

St John's Wood Underground Station, 1939
Finchley Road/ Acacia Road, St John's Wood, Westminster, London (F)
Stanley A. Heaps

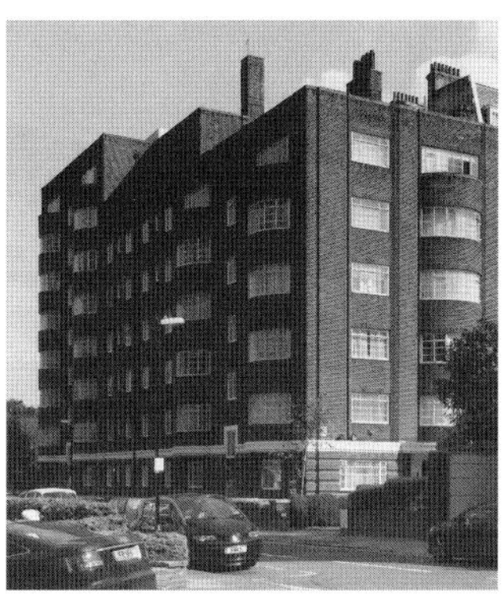

166

Northgate, 1936
Prince Albert Road / Culworth Street, St John's Wood, Westminster, London (F)
Mitchell & Bridgwater

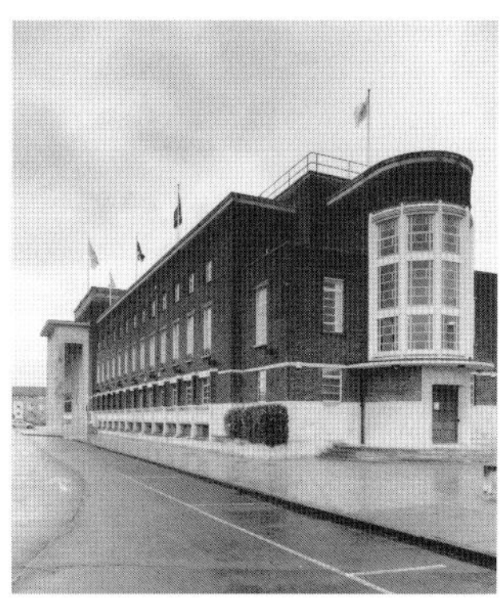

167

Dagenham Civic Centre, 1936–37
Wood Lane, Dagenham, Greater London
E. Berry Webber / F.C. Lloyd

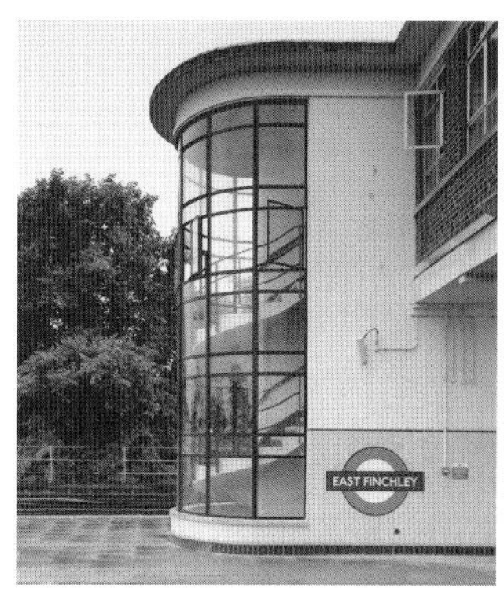

168

East Finchley Underground Station, 1939
High Road, Barnet, London (B)
Leonard H. Bucknell / Ruth Ellis / Charles Holden

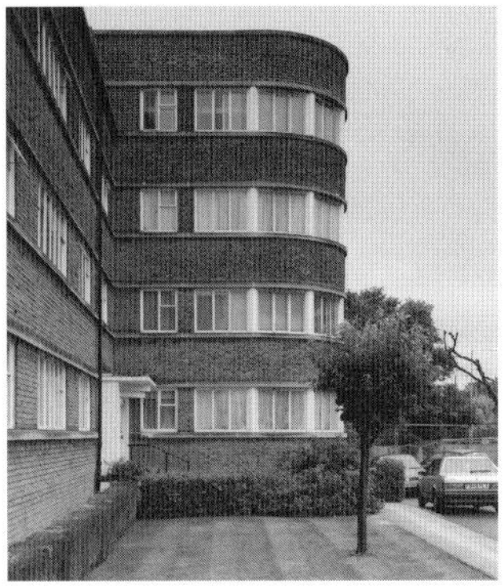

169

Belvedere Court, 1938
Lyttelton Road, Hampstead Garden Suburb, Barnet, London (B)
Ernst Ludwig Freud

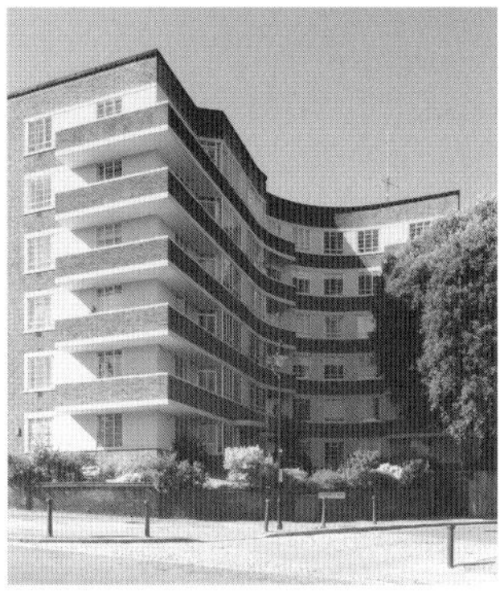

170

Cholmeley Lodge, 1934
Cholmeley Park, Highgate, Camden, London (B)
Guy Morgan

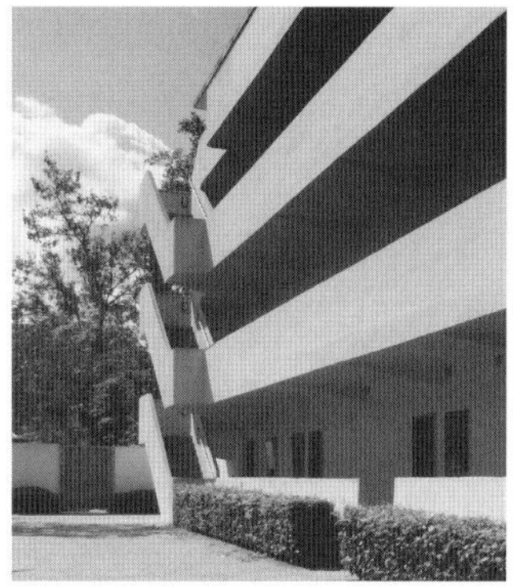

171

Isokon Flats (Lawn Road Flats), 1934
Lawn Road, Hampstead, Camden, London (F)
Wells Coates

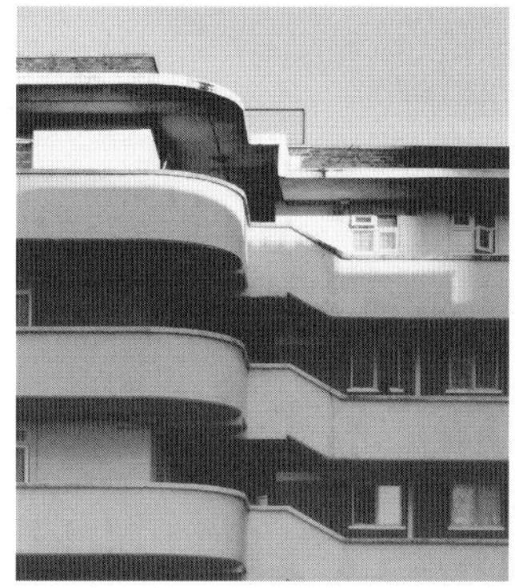

172

Wellesley Court, 1936
Wellesley Court, Maida Vale, Westminster, London (F)
Frank Scarlett

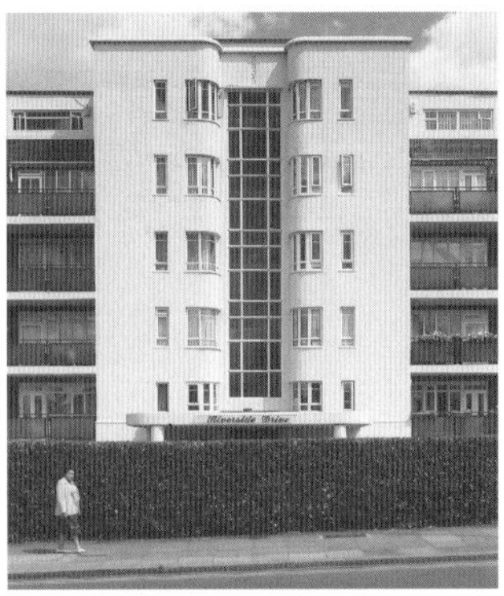

177

Riverside Drive
Golders Green Road, Barnet, London (A)

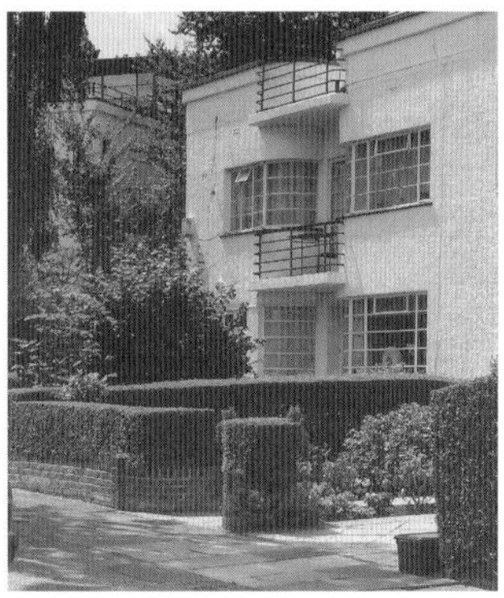

178

Terraces Lytton Close, 1935
Lytton Close, Hampstead Garden Suburb, Barnet, London (B)
C.G. Winburne

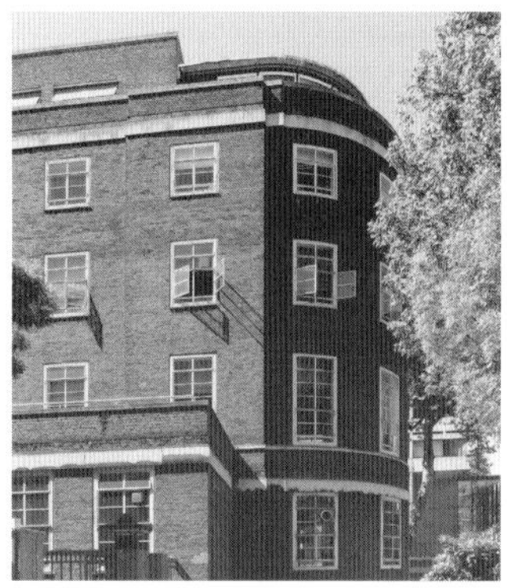

179

School of Oriental and African Studies, 1940
Woburn Square, Bloomsbury, Camden, London (K)
Charles Holden

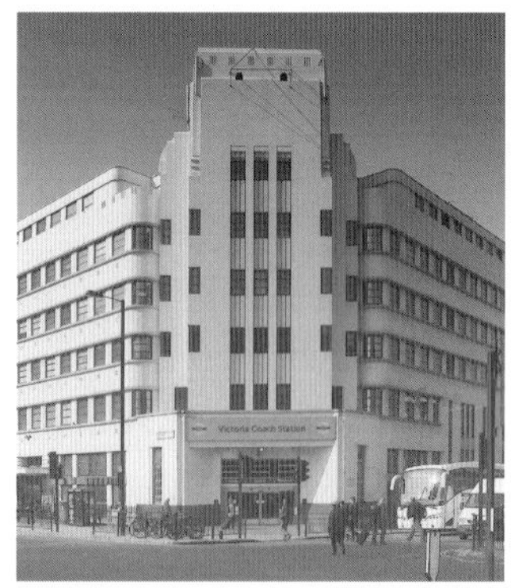

180

Victoria Coach Station, 1931–32
Buckingham Palace Road / Elizabeth Street, Westminster, London (J)
Wallis Gilbert & Partners

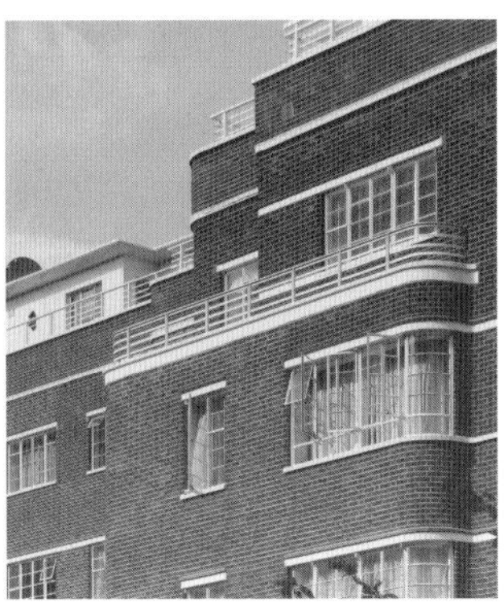

185

Stockleigh Hall, 1937
Prince Albert Road, St John's Wood, Westminster, London (F)
Robert Atkinson

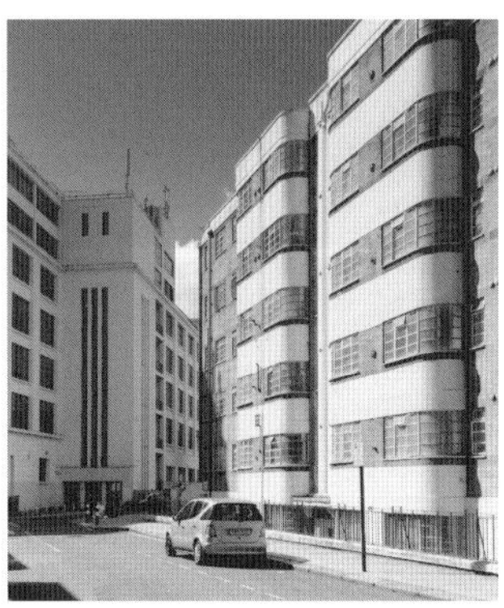

186

Mornington Court
Arlington Road, Camden Town, Camden, London (F)

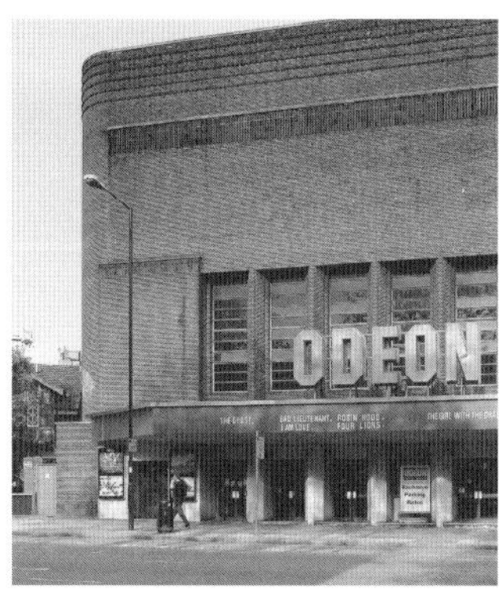

187

Odeon Cinema Swiss Cottage, 1937
Finchley Road, Swiss Cottage, Camden, London (F)
Harry Weedon

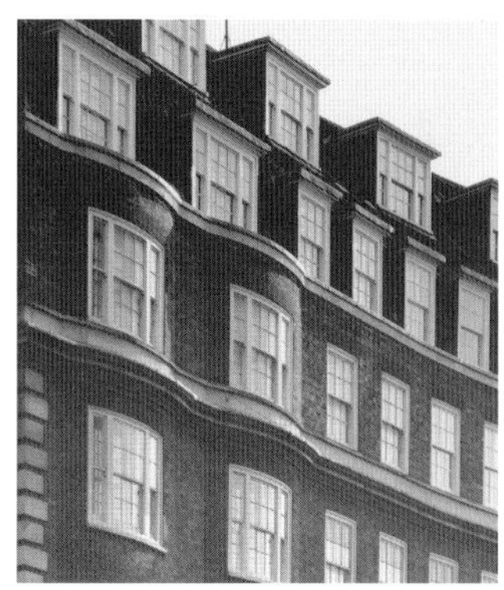

188

Newton Court, 1926
Kensington Church Street, Kensington, London (I)
Wills & Kaula

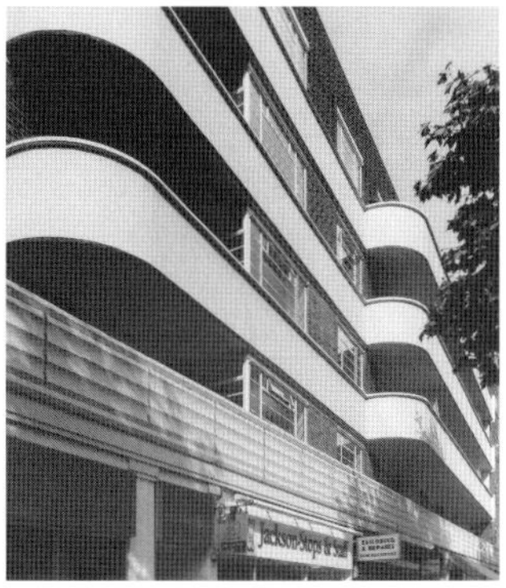

173

Lichfield Court, 1935
Sheen Road, Richmond, Greater London
Bertram Carter

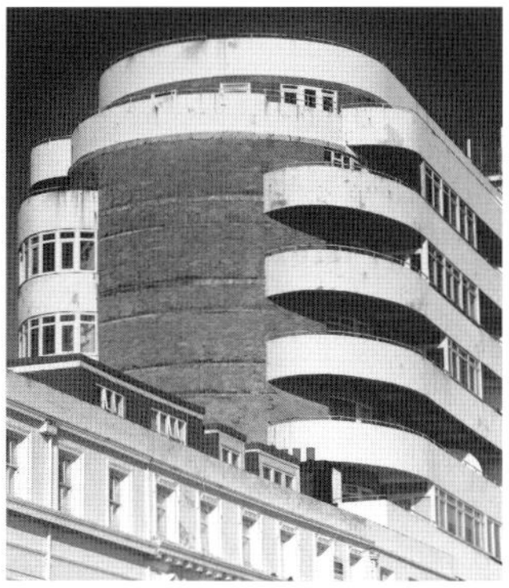

174

Marine Court, 1937–38
Marina, St Leonards, Sussex
Dalgliesh & Pullen

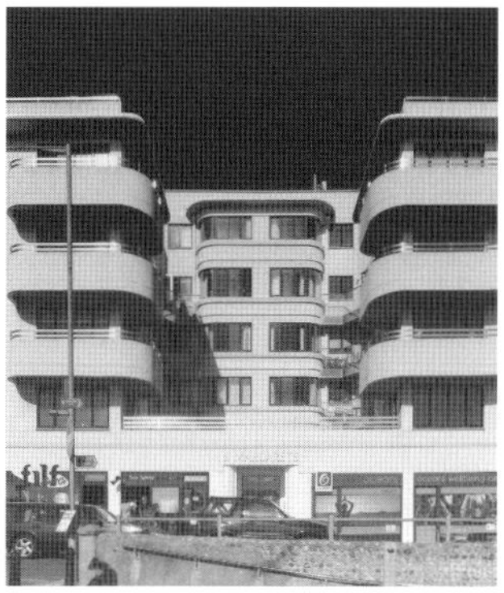

175

St Margarets
High Street, Rottingdean, Sussex

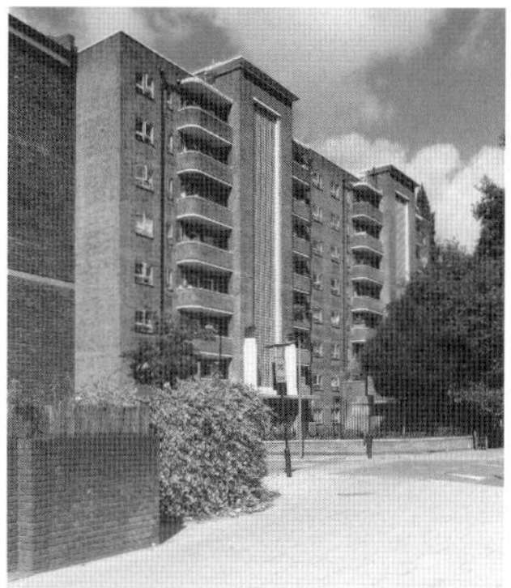

176

Cecil Rhodes House, c. 1948–50
Pancras Road, Somers Town, Camden, London (G)
Thomas Sibthrope

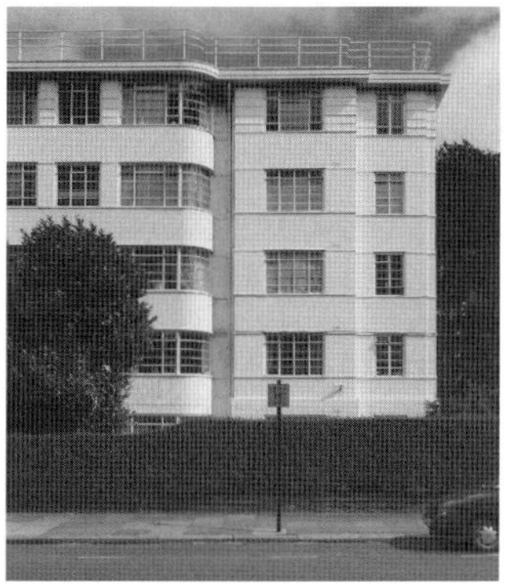

181

Stanbury Court, 1936?
Haverstock Hill, Belsize Park, Camden, London (F)

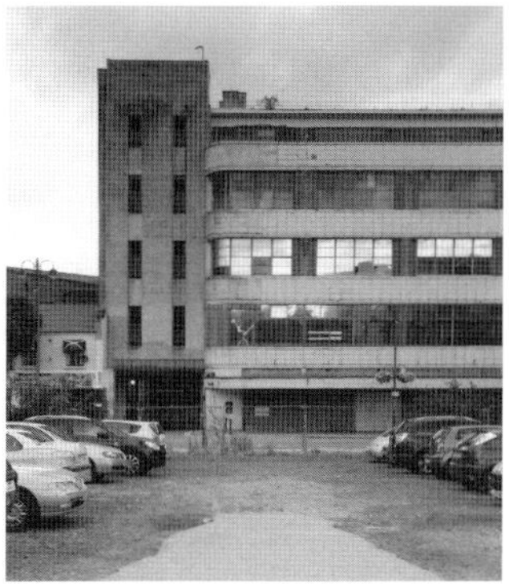

182

R.A.C.S. Store Powis Street, 1938
Powis Street, Greenwich, London
S.W. Ackeroyd

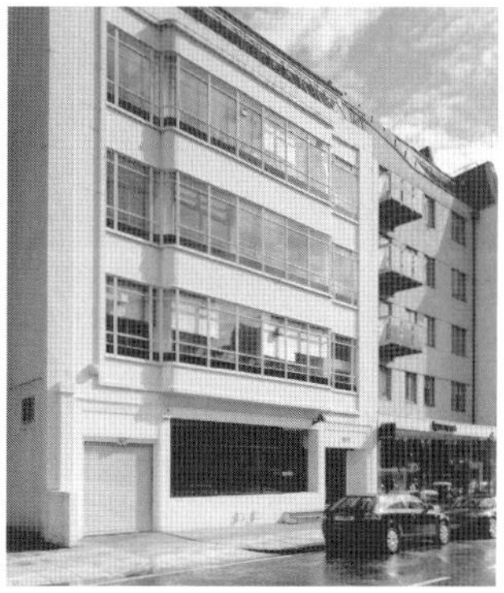

183

Flats Mortimer Street, 1933?
Mortimer Street, Fitzrovia, Westminster, London (K)

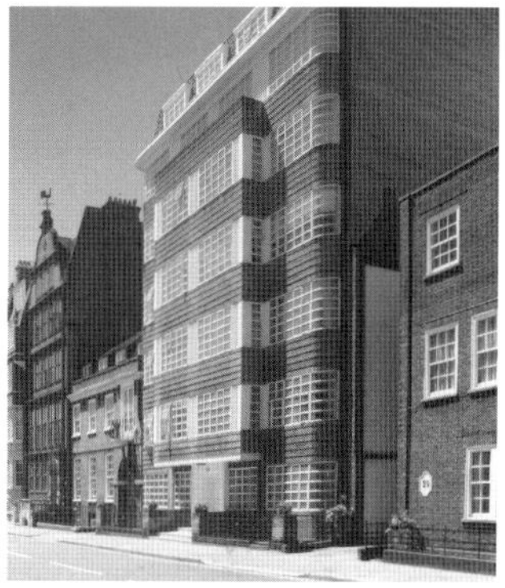

184

Flats Royal Hospital Road
Royal Hospital Road, Chelsea, London (N)

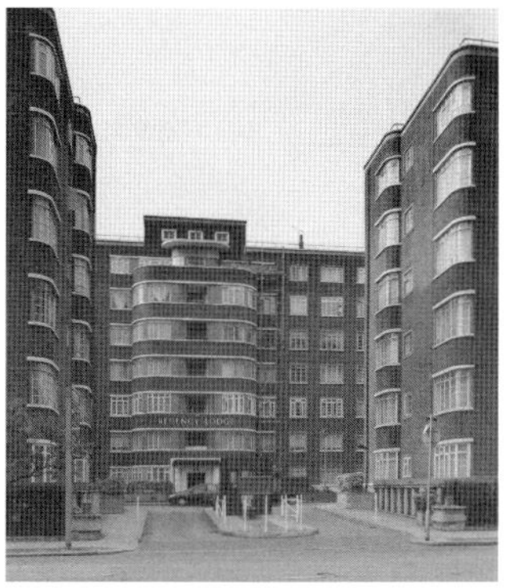

189

Regency Lodge, 1937
Adelaide Road, Swiss Cottage, Camden, London (F)
Robert Atkinson

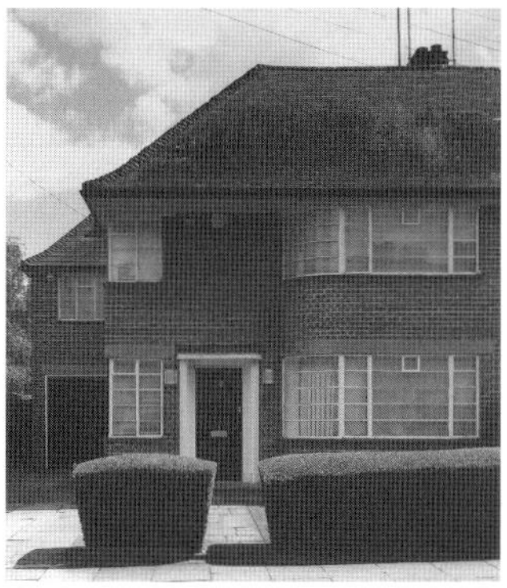

190

Semi-detached Houses Rowan Walk
Rowan Walk, Hampstead Garden Suburb, Barnet, London (B)

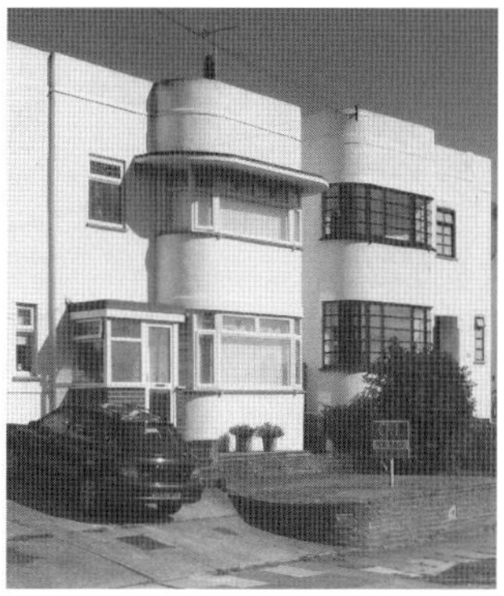

191

Semi-detached Houses Chichester Drive
Chichester Drive East, Saltdean, Sussex

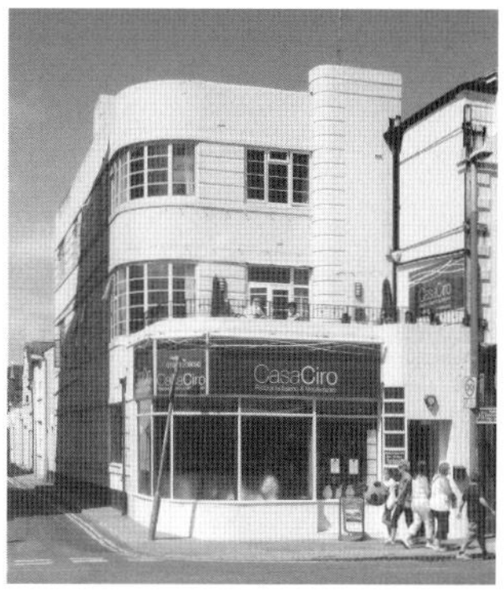

192

Flats Marine Parade
Marine Parade, Worthing, Sussex

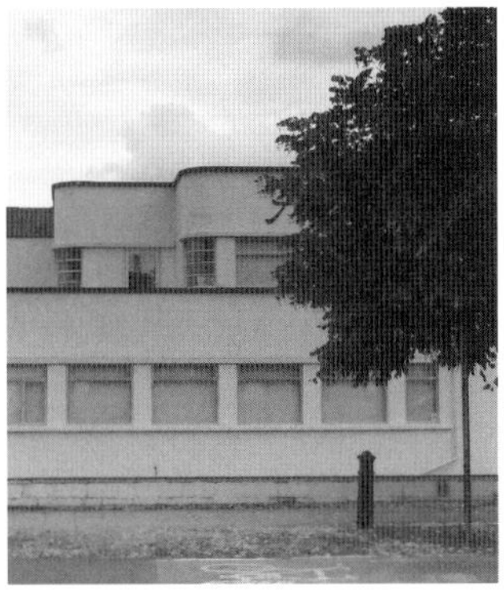

193

Adini Offices
Great West Road, Isleworth, Greater London

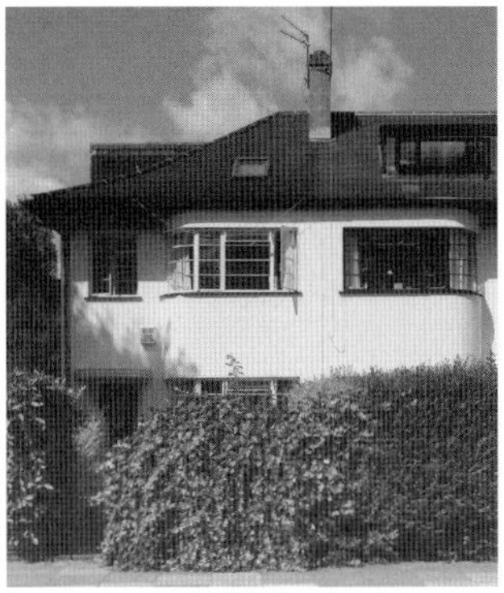

194

Terraces Garnett Road
Garnett Road, Hampstead, Camden, London (F)

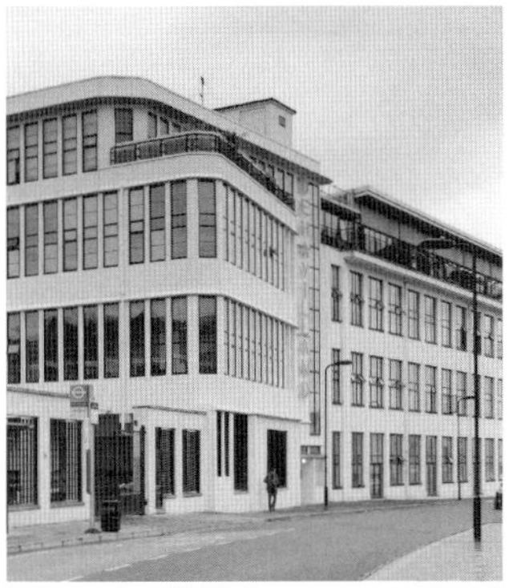

195

Hunt Partners Extension
(De Havilland Building), 1937–39
Theydon Road, Hackney, London (D)
Owen Williams

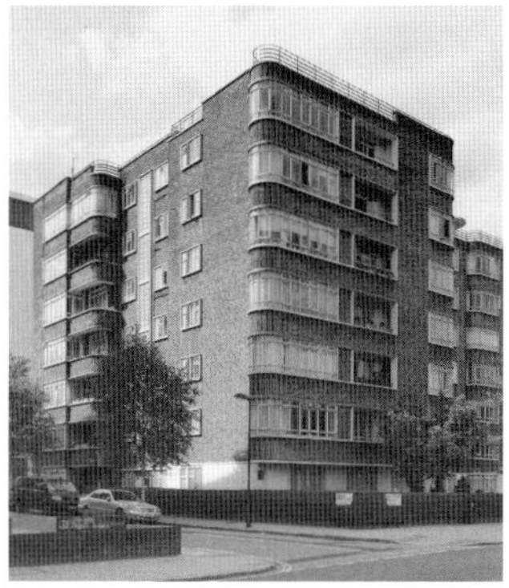

196

Viceroy Court, 1937
Prince Albert Road, St John's Wood, Westminster, London (F)
Marshall & Tweedy

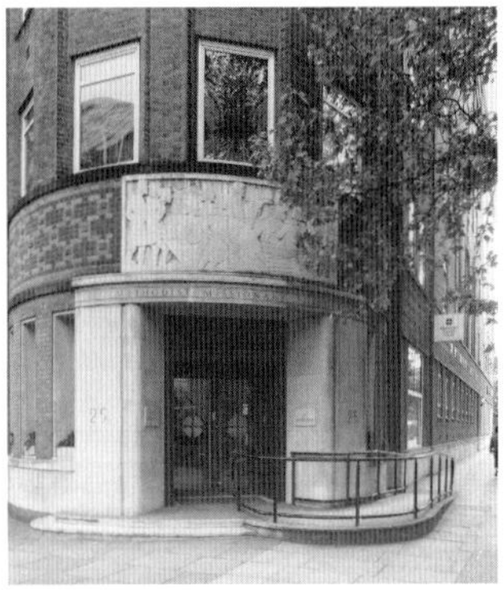

201

Methodist Missionary Society, 1939
Marylebone Road, Marylebone, Westminster, London (J)
Paul Manger / A.J. May / L. Sylvester Sullivan

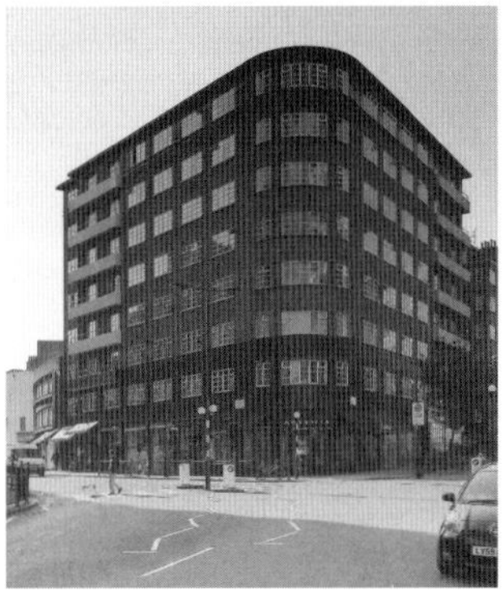

202

Winchester Court, 1935
Vicarage Gate, Kensington, London (I)
Donald F. Martin-Smith / D. Beswick

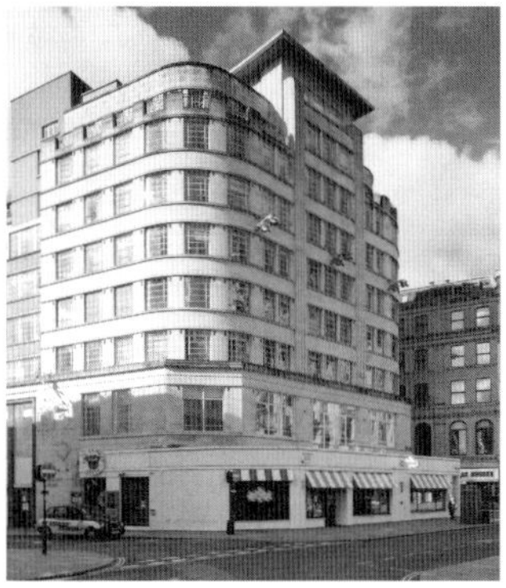

203

Haymarket House, 1939–55
Haymarket, Soho, Westminster, London (K)
Stone Toms & Partners

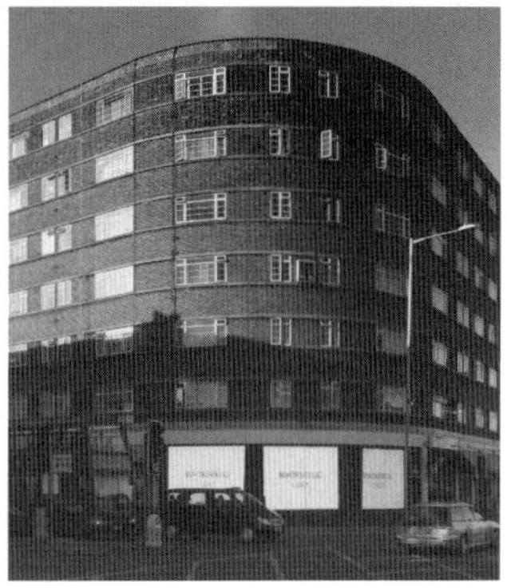

204

West Kensington Court, 1938?
West Cromwell Road, Hammersmith, London (I)

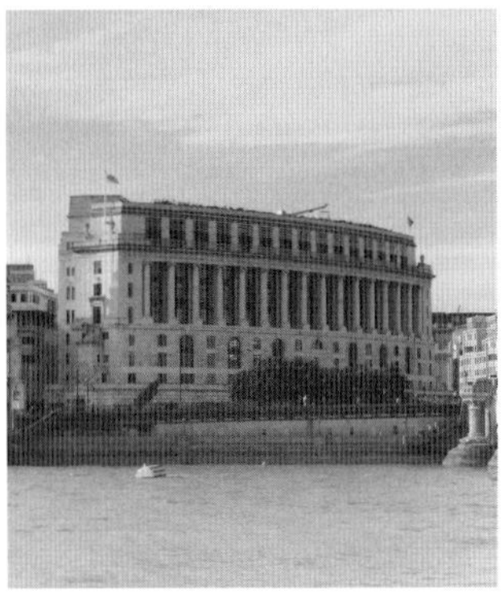

209

Unilever House, 1930–32
Victoria Embankment, City of London, London (K)
James Lomax-Simpson / Burnet Tait & Partners

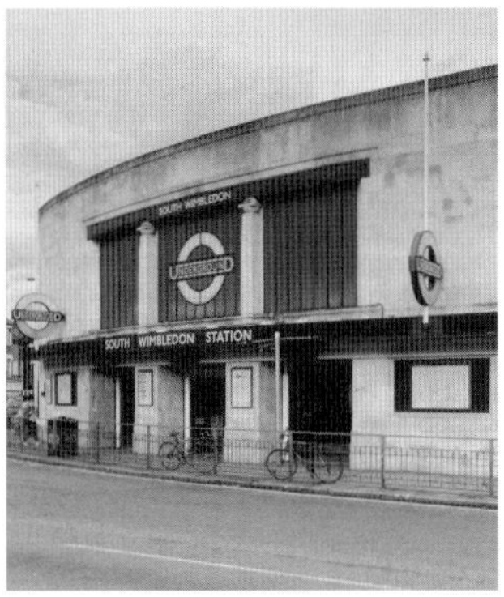

210

South Wimbledon Underground Station, 1926
Merton High Street / Morden Road, Merton, London
Charles Holden

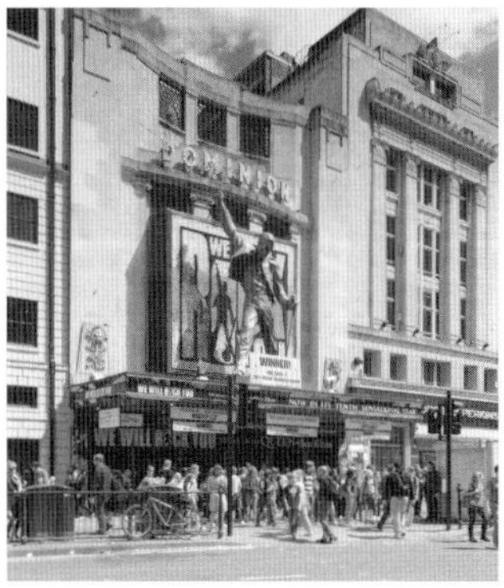

211

Dominion Cinema Holborn, 1928–29
Tottenham Court Road, Holborn, Camden, London (K)
William & Thomas Milburn

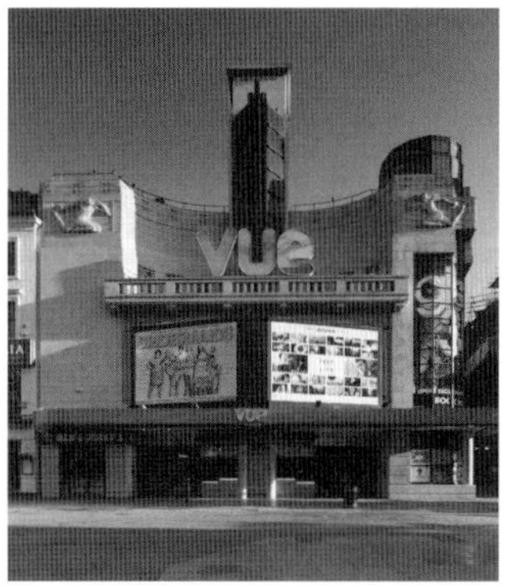

212

The Warner Cinema
(Vue Cinema Leicester Square), 1938
Cranbourn Street, Soho, Westminster, London (K)
E.A. Stone / T.R. Somerford

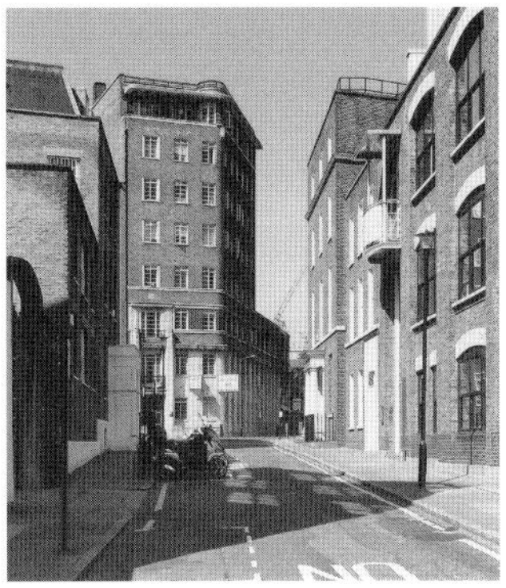

197

Mytre House (Haines House), 1937
John Street / Roger Street, Bloomsbury, Camden, London (K)
D.E. Harrington

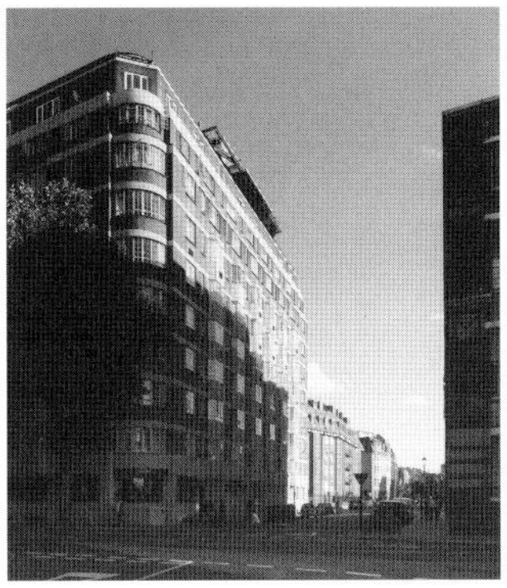

198

Chelsea Cloisters Mansions, 1937–38
Sloane Avenue, Chelsea, London (J)

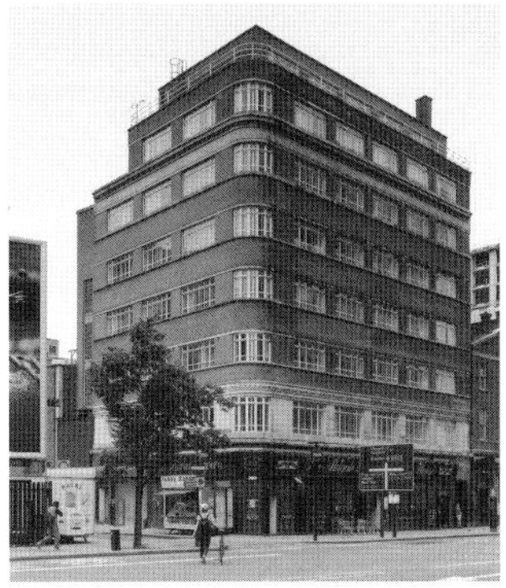

199

Students' Union Offices, London Metropolitan University, 1939
Whitechapel High Street, Tower Hamlets, London (L)
Philip S.B. Nicolle

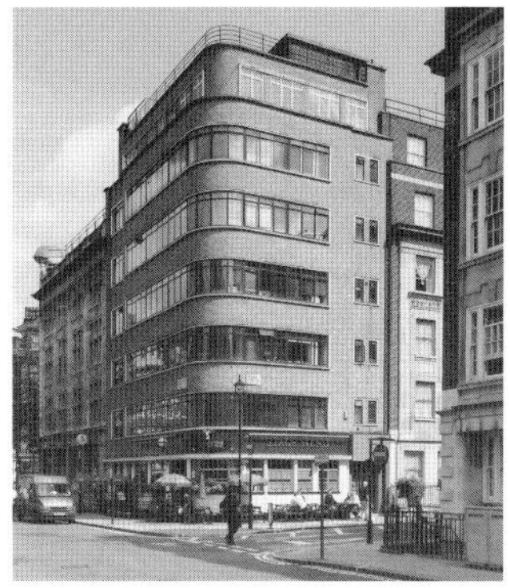

200

Offices Hallam Street
New Cavandish Street / Hallam Street, Fitzrovia, Westminster, London (J)

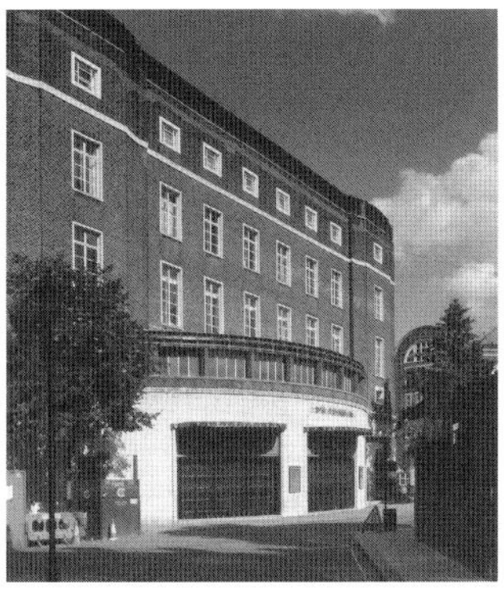

205

Lawrence Hall, 1923–28
Greycoat Street / Elverton Street, Pimlico, Westminster, London (K)
Howard Robertson / Murray Easton

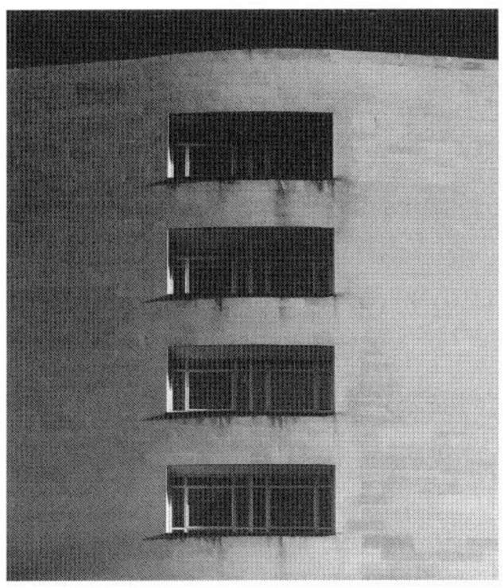

206

Lambeth County Hall, North Block, 1937–39
Chicheley Street, Lambeth, London (K)
Frederick Robert Hiorns / Giles Gilbert Scott

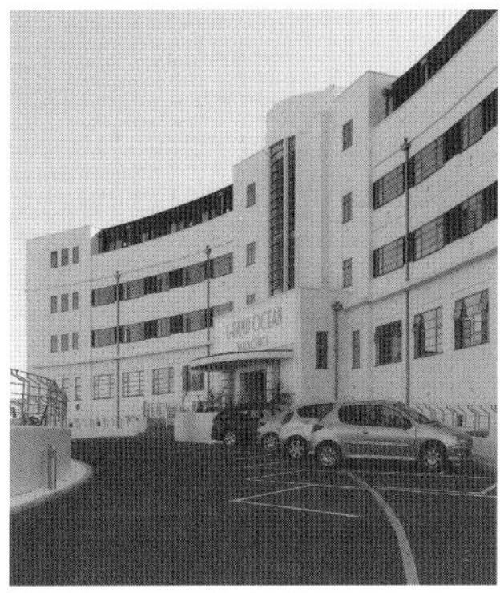

207

Butlin's Camp (Grand Ocean Hotel), 1938
Longridge Avenue, Saltdean, Sussex
R.W.H. Jones

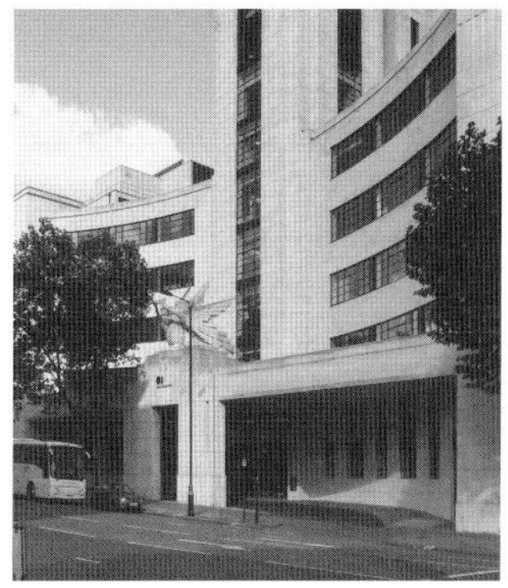

208

Imperial Airways Empire Terminal (National Audit Office), 1937–39
Buckingham Palace Road, Millbank, Westminster, London (J)
Albert Lakeman / W.H. Williams

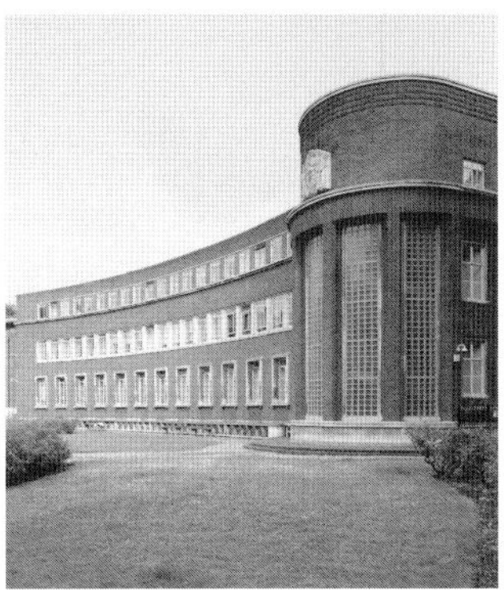

213

Laboratory Building, Metropolitan Water Board, 1938
Rosebery Avenue, Islington, London (G)
Howard Robertson

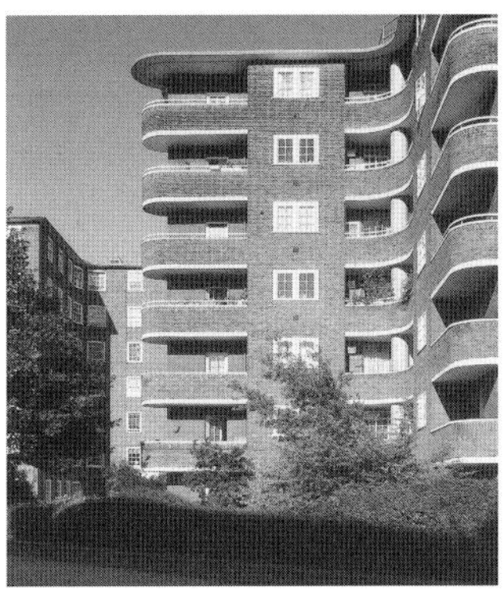

214

Flats Cundy Street, 1950–52
Cundy Street, Chelsea, London (J)
T.P. Bennett & Son

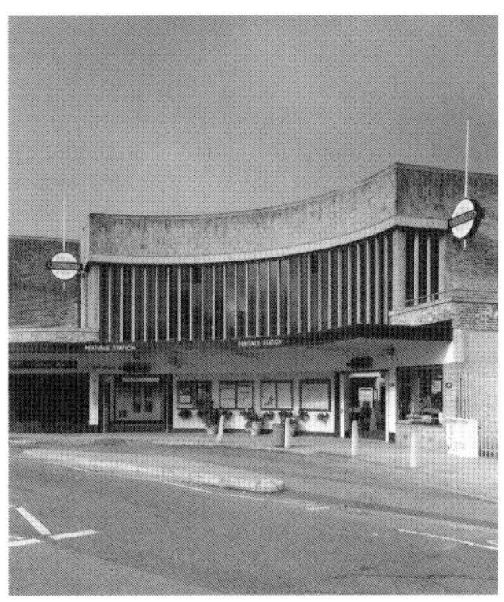

215

Perivale Underground Station (Perivale Halt), 1938–47
Horsenden Lane South, Greenford, Greater London
Brian Lewis / Frederick Francis Charles Curtis

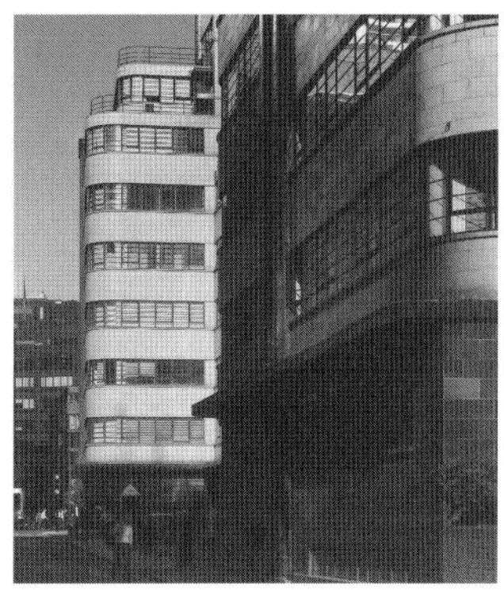

216

Ibex House, 1935–37
Minories, City of London, London (L)
Fuller Hall & Foulsham

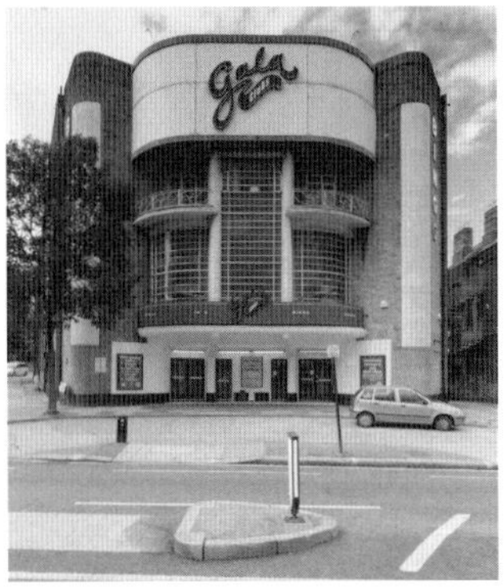

(217)

Dominion Cinema Acton (Gala Bingo Club Acton), 1937
High Street / Alfred Road, Ealing, London
Frank Ernest Bromige

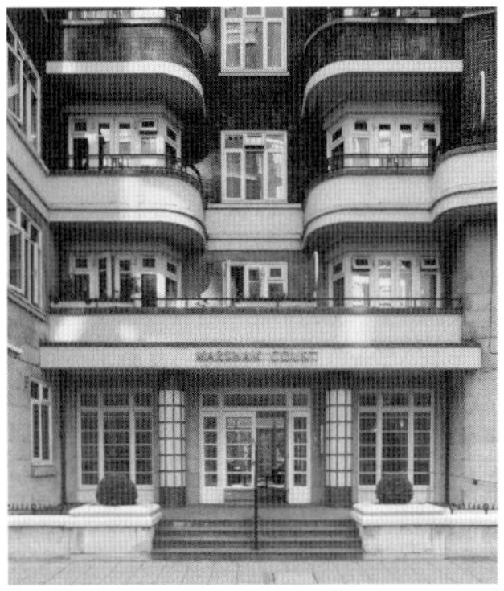

(218)

Marsham Court, 1934–36
Marsham Street, Millbank, Westminster, London (K)
T.P. Bennett & Son

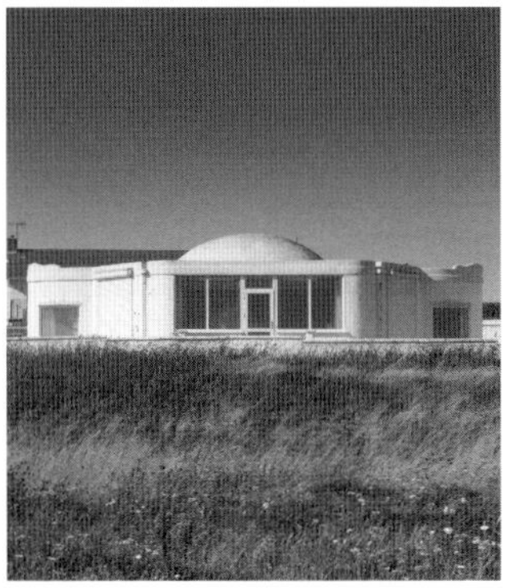

(219)

House Marine Drive
Marine Drive, Saltdean, Sussex

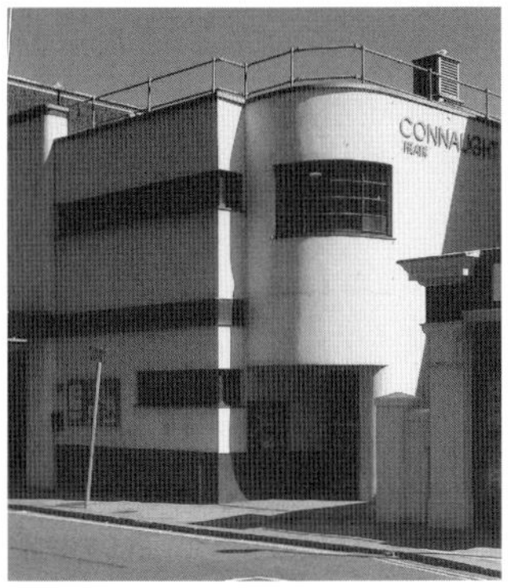

(220)

Connaught Theatre, 1935?
Union Place, Worthing, Sussex
A.T. Goldsmith?

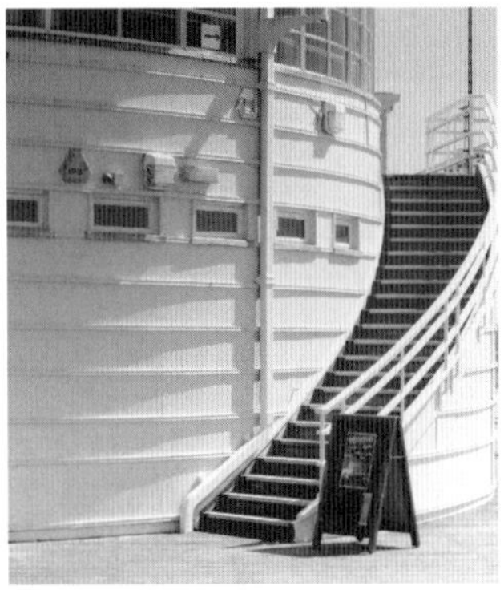

(225)

Worthing Pier Pavilion, 1935
Marine Parade, Worthing, East Sussex
(Borough Architect)

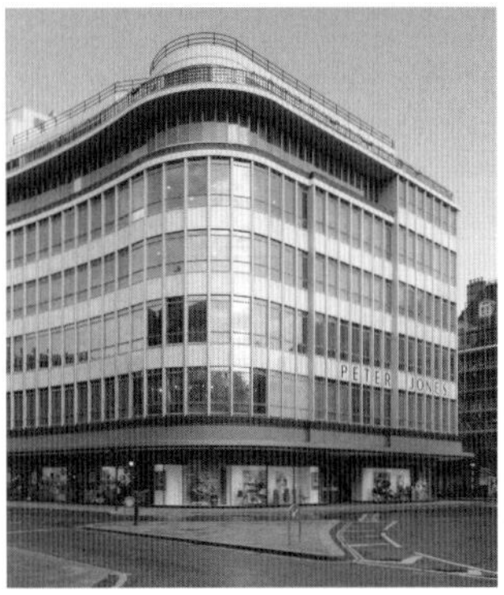

(226)

Peter Jones Department Store, 1935–37
Sloane Square, Chelsea, London (J)
J.A. Slater / A.H. Moberly / William Crabtree

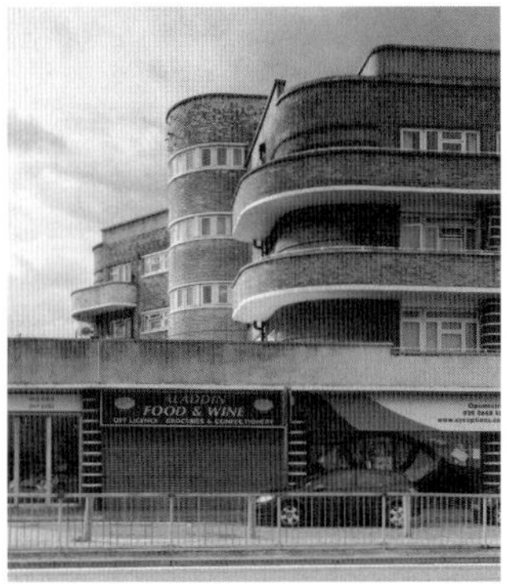

(227)

Rosehill Court, 1939–40
Rosehill Court Parade, Morden, Greater London
Carl Rudolph Jelinek

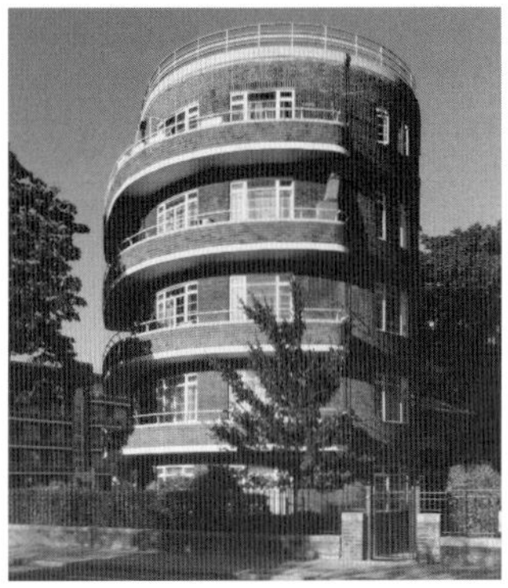

(228)

Barons Keep, 1930
Gliddon Road, Hammersmith, London (I)
Gunton & Gunton

All of the pictures were taken over the course of 2010 and 2011. The original names of the buildings are listed first, with current names following in brackets. In italics are names given to the buildings for reference purposes, where none could be found. The dates give the period of construction or the date of completion and those of any significant renovations or extensions. The capital letter in brackets refers to the respective map in this book. Dates were sourced and scrutinised with the greatest care. Uncertain entries are marked with a question mark. The architect and year of completion were not always available; the editor offers thanks in advance for any information submitted.

Sämtliche Bilder sind in den Jahren 2010 und 2011 entstanden. Historische Gebäudebezeichnungen werden zuerst genannt, heutige Namen stehen in Klammern, eigene Betitelungen sind kursiv gesetzt. Die Daten geben den Bauzeitraum oder das Fertigstellungsjahr der Gebäude beziehungsweise relevanter Um- oder Anbauten an. Der Großbuchstabe in Klammern verweist auf die entsprechende Karte in diesem Buch. Sämtliche Daten wurden mit höchster Sorgfalt erhoben. Unsichere Angaben sind mit einem Fragezeichen gekennzeichnet. Architekt und Baujahr waren nicht in allen Fällen zu ermitteln; der Herausgeber bedankt sich vorab für ergänzende Hinweise.

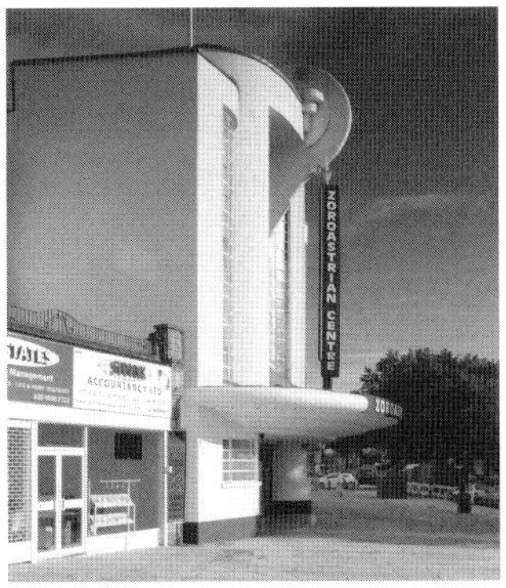

221

Grosvenor Cinema Rayners Lane (Odeon Cinema Rayners Lane), 1936
Alexandra Avenue / Rayners Lane, Harrow, Greater London
Frank Ernest Bromige

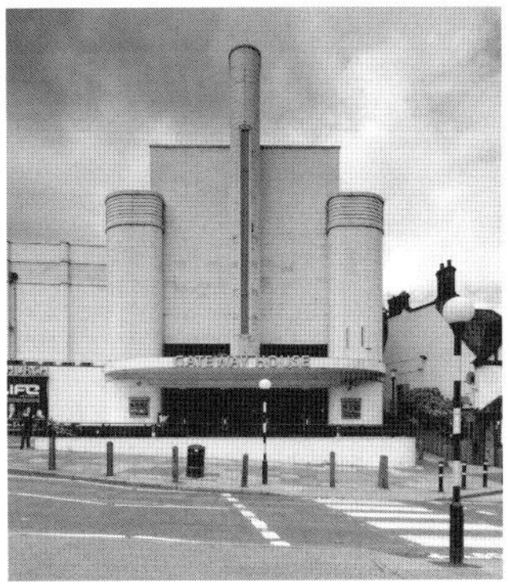

222

Odeon Cinema Woolwich, 1937
John Wilson Street, Greenwich, London
George Coles

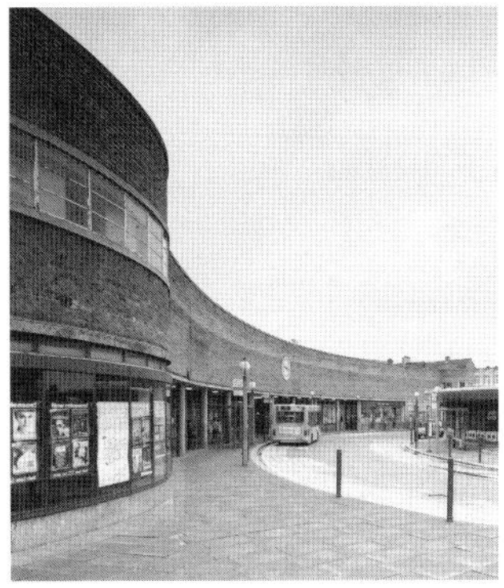

223

Southgate Underground Station, 1932–33
Station Parade, Enfield, London
Charles Holden

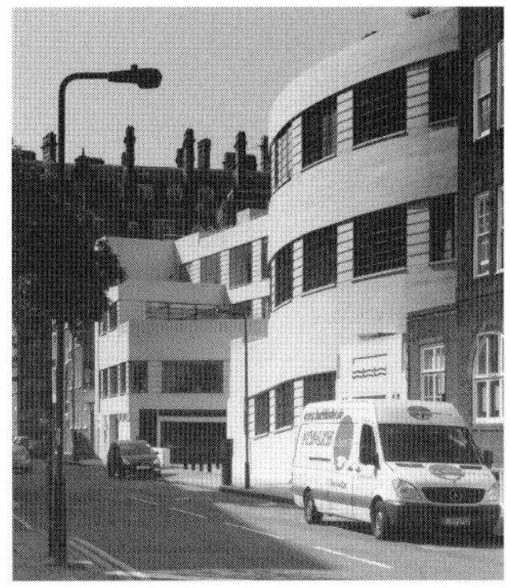

224

Daimler Car Hire Garage (*American Express Garage, McCann Erickson Offices*), 1931
Herbrand Street, Bloomsbury, Camden, London (G)
Wallis Gilbert & Partners

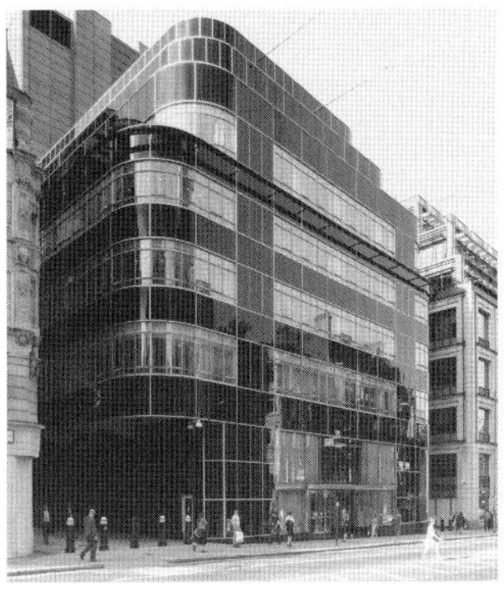

229

Daily Express Building, 1929–32
Fleet Street, City of London, London (K)
Ellis & Clarke / Owen Williams / Robert Atkinson

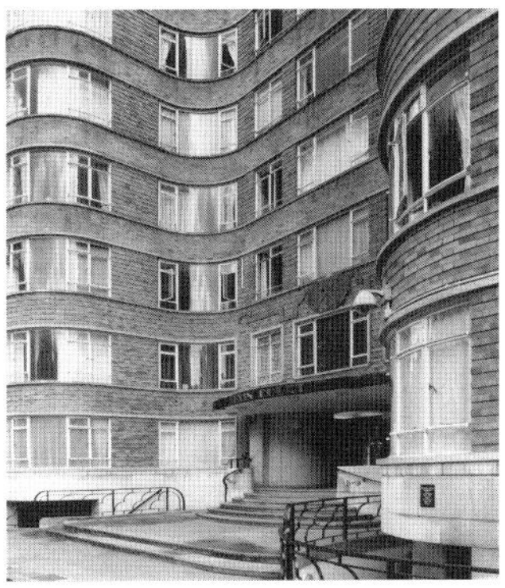

230

Florin Court, 1936
Charterhouse Square, City of London, London (K)
Guy Morgan

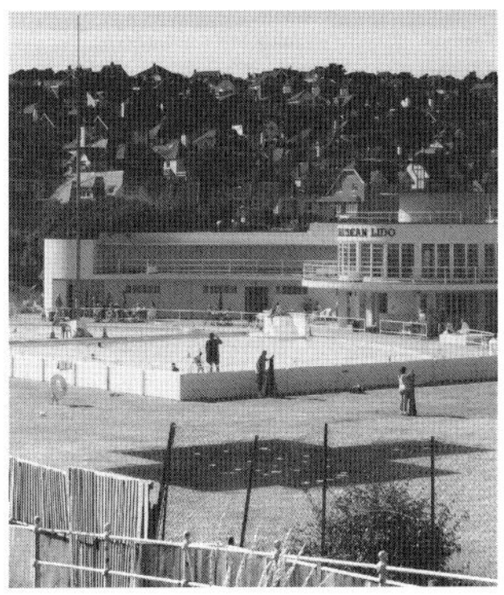

231

Lido Saltdean, 1938
Saltdean Park Road, Saltdean, Sussex
R.W.H. Jones

Bibliography (selection) Verwendete Literatur (Auswahl)

Bradley, Simon; Pevsner, Nikolaus (eds): The City of London (The Buildings of England, London 1). London, 1997; Cherry, Bridget; Pevsner, Nikolaus (eds): South (The Buildings of England, London 2). London, 1994; Cherry, Bridget; Pevsner, Nikolaus (eds): North West (The Buildings of England, London 3). London 1991; Cherry, Bridget; Pevsner, Nikolaus (ed.): North (The Buildings of England, London 4). London, 1999; Cherry, Bridget; O'Brien, Charles; Pevsner, Nikolaus (eds): East (The Buildings of England, London 5). New Haven/London, 2005; Bradley, Simon; Pevsner, Nikolaus (eds): Westminster (The Buildings of England, London 6). New Haven/London, 2003; Nairn, Ian; Pevsner, Nikolaus (eds): Sussex (The Buildings of England). Harmondsworth, 1973 (1st ed. 1965); Sharp, Dennis; Rendel, Dennis: Connell Ward and Lucas. Modern Movement Architects in England 1929–1939. London, 2008; Antram, Nicholas; Morrice, Richard: Brighton and Hove. New Haven/London, 2008; Jones, Edward; Woodward, Christopher: A Guide to the Architecture of London. 3rd ed. London, 2000; Atkinson, Clive et al.: A Guide to the Buildings of Brighton. Macclesfield, 1990; Cottam, David: Sir Owen Williams 1890–1969. Ed. by Gavin Stamp. London, 1989; Stamp, Gavin (ed): Britain in the Thirties, issue of: Architectural Design 49 (1979), No 10/11.

MAPS KARTEN

GREATER LONDON

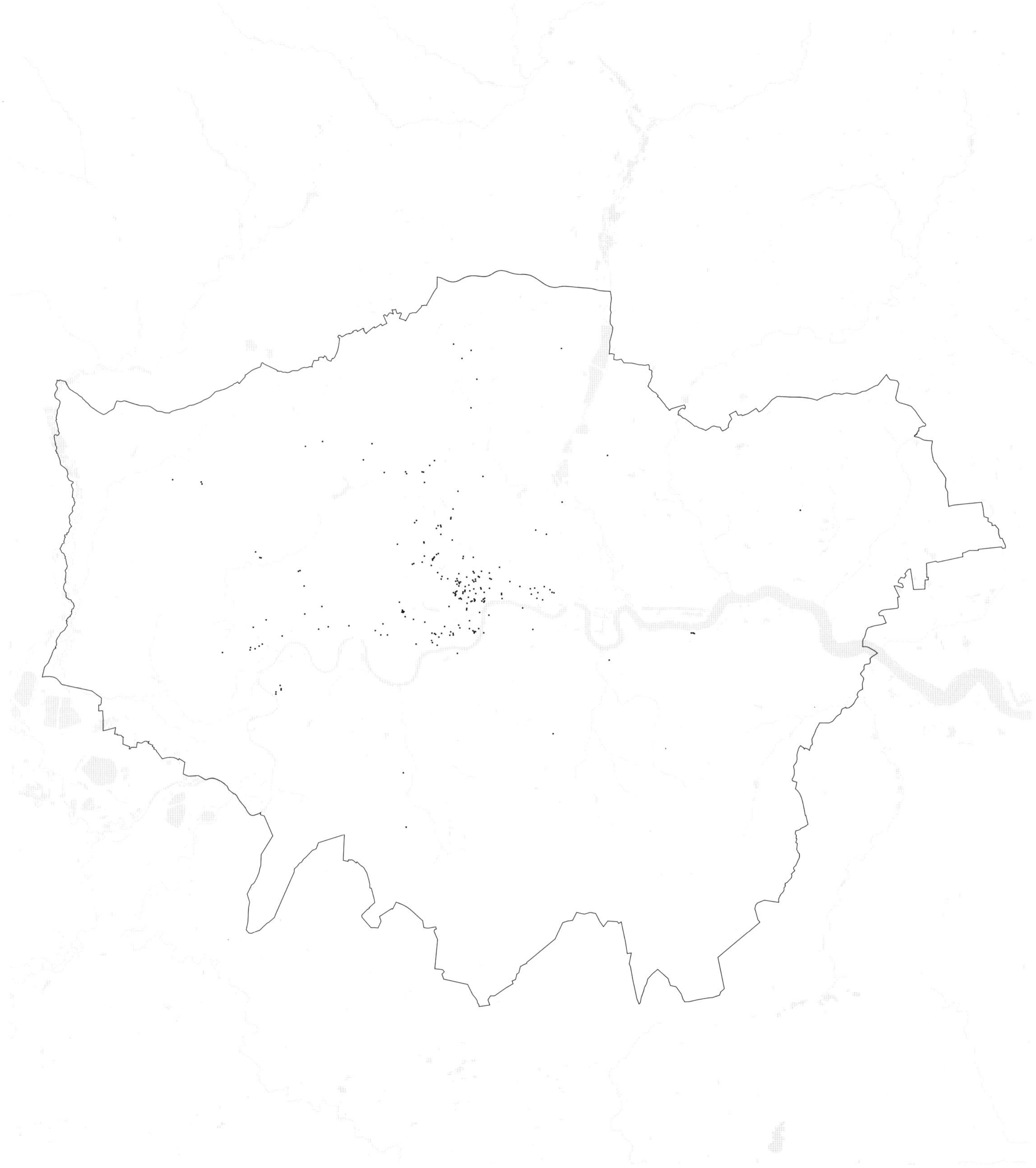

CENTRAL LONDON

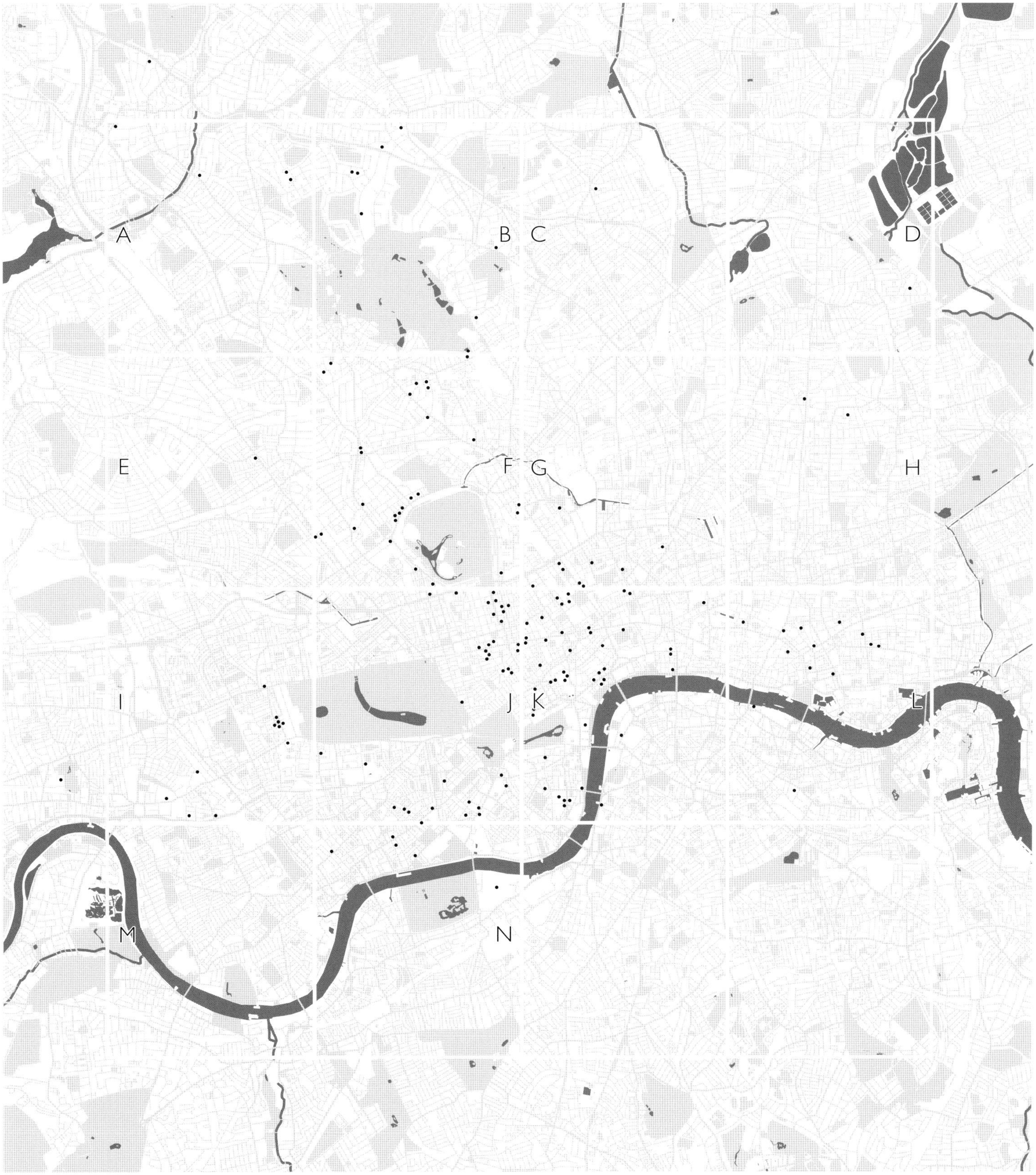

A

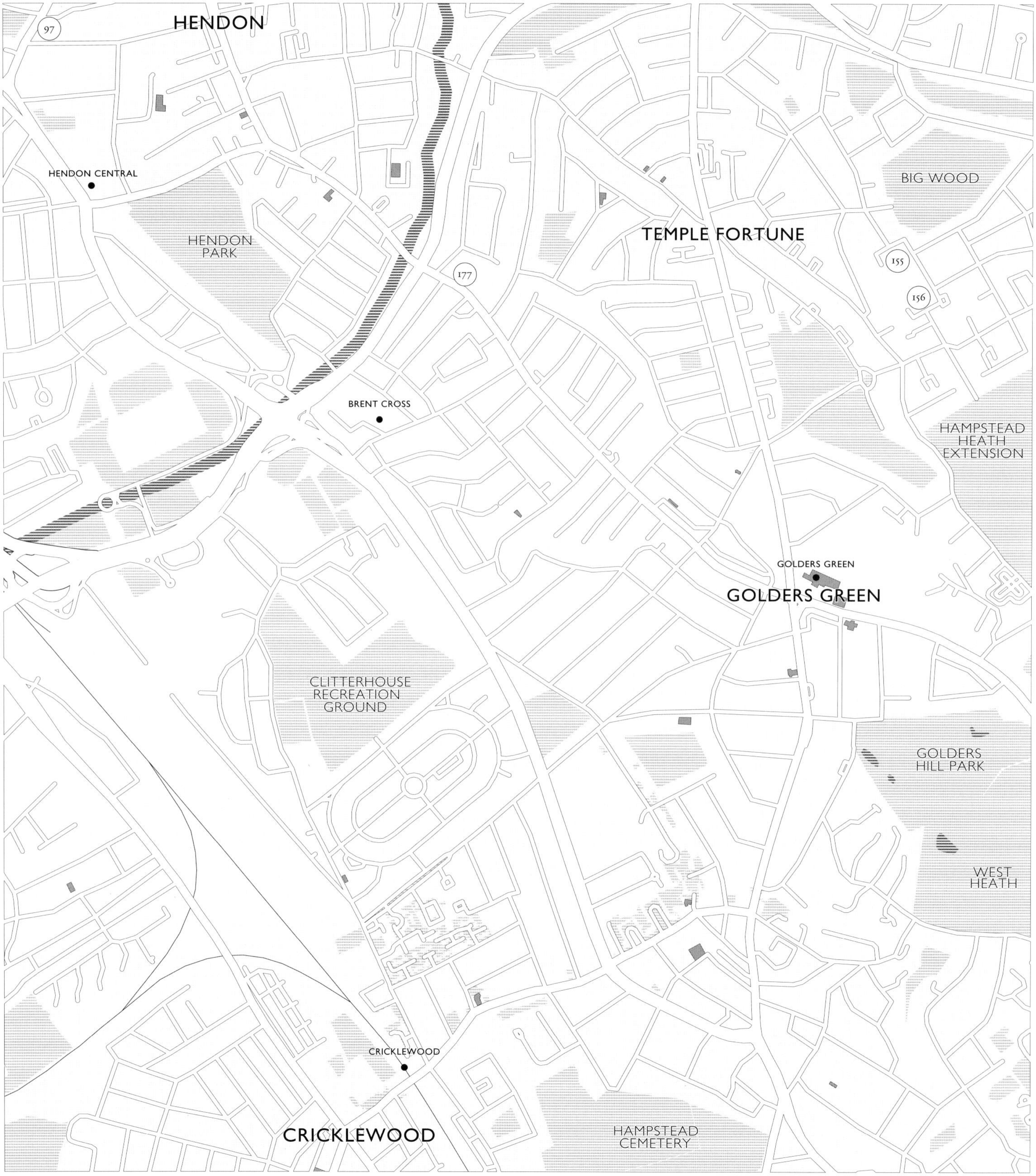
97
HENDON
HENDON CENTRAL
HENDON PARK
177
BRENT CROSS
TEMPLE FORTUNE
BIG WOOD
155
156
HAMPSTEAD HEATH EXTENSION
GOLDERS GREEN
GOLDERS GREEN
CLITTERHOUSE RECREATION GROUND
GOLDERS HILL PARK
WEST HEATH
CRICKLEWOOD
CRICKLEWOOD
HAMPSTEAD CEMETERY

B

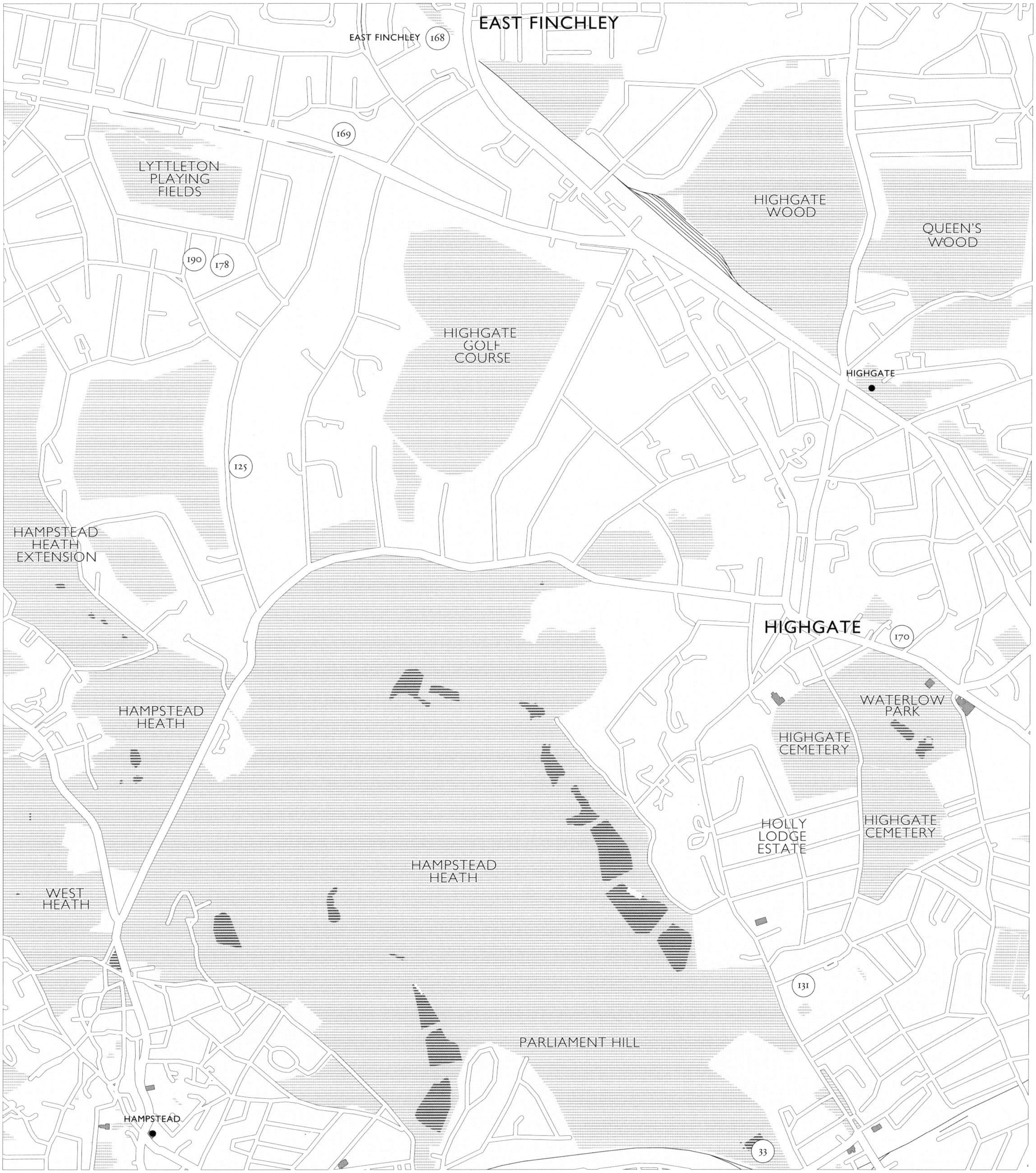
EAST FINCHLEY
EAST FINCHLEY
168
169
LYTTLETON PLAYING FIELDS
190
178
HIGHGATE WOOD
QUEEN'S WOOD
HIGHGATE GOLF COURSE
HIGHGATE
125
HAMPSTEAD HEATH EXTENSION
HIGHGATE
170
HAMPSTEAD HEATH
WATERLOW PARK
HIGHGATE CEMETERY
HOLLY LODGE ESTATE
HIGHGATE CEMETERY
HAMPSTEAD HEATH
WEST HEATH
131
PARLIAMENT HILL
HAMPSTEAD
33

C

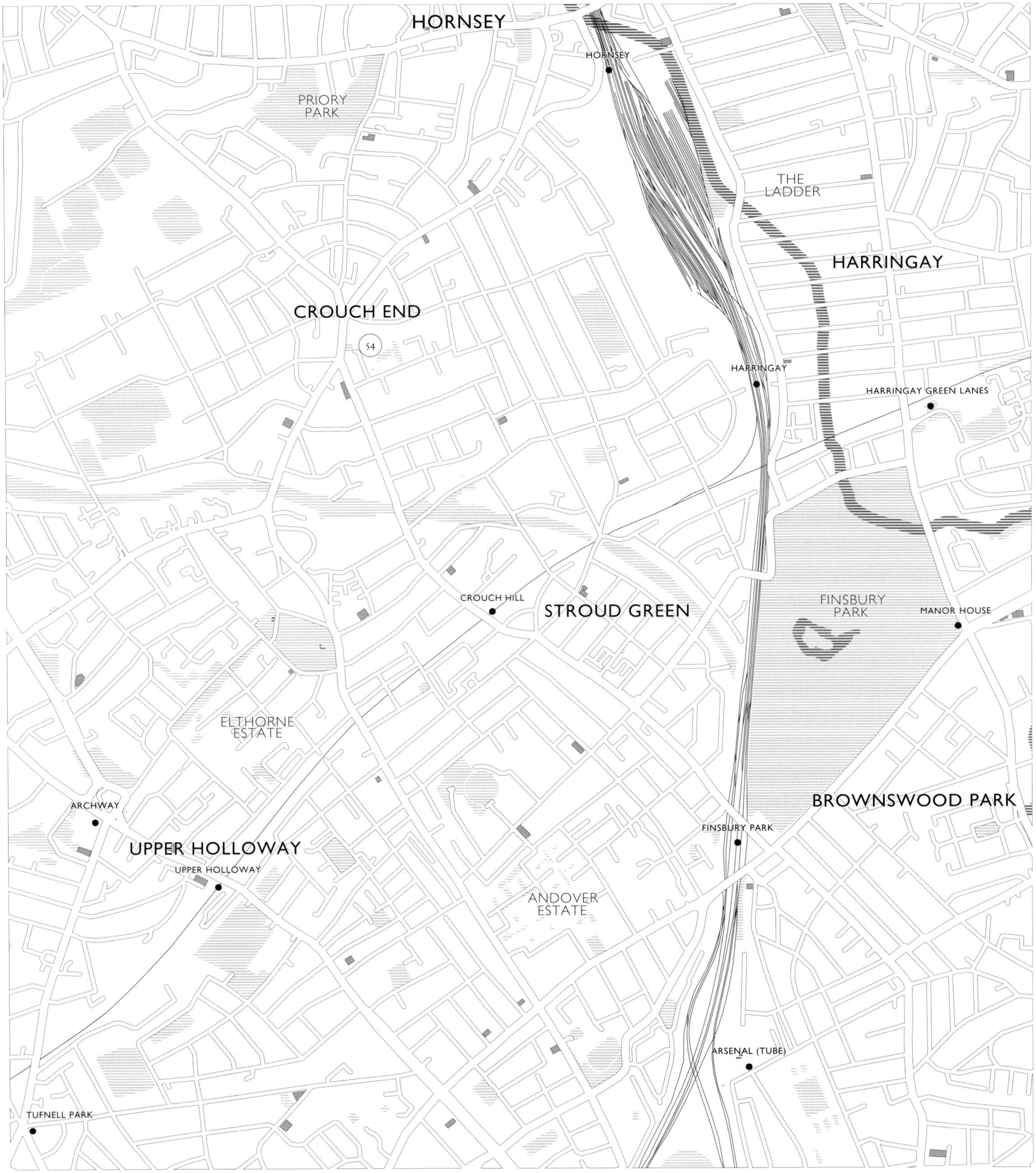
HORNSEY
HORNSEY
PRIORY PARK
THE LADDER
HARRINGAY
CROUCH END
54
HARRINGAY
HARRINGAY GREEN LANES
CROUCH HILL
STROUD GREEN
FINSBURY PARK
MANOR HOUSE
ELTHORNE ESTATE
BROWNSWOOD PARK
ARCHWAY
FINSBURY PARK
UPPER HOLLOWAY
UPPER HOLLOWAY
ANDOVER ESTATE
ARSENAL (TUBE)
TUFNELL PARK

D

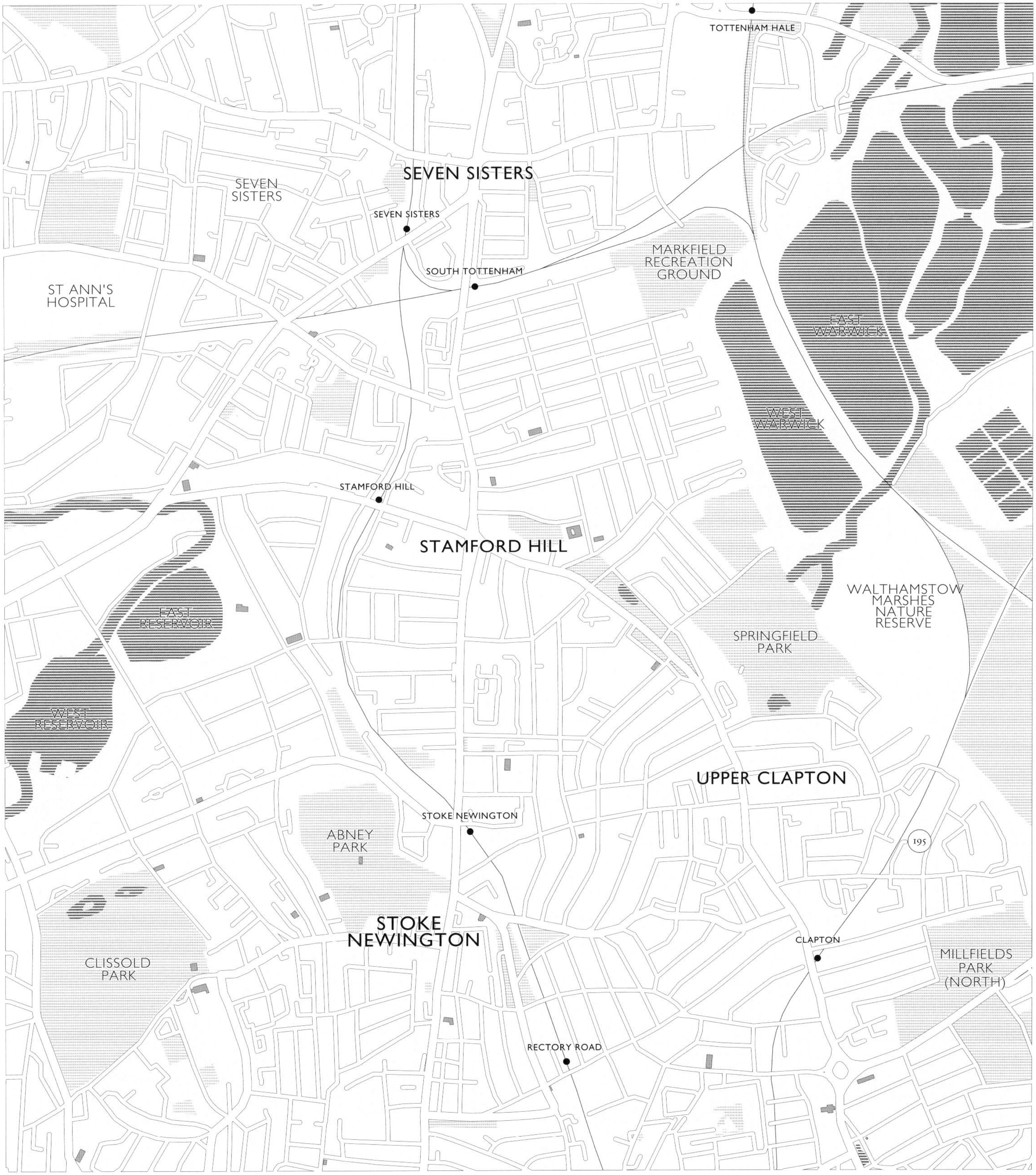
TOTTENHAM HALE
SEVEN SISTERS
SEVEN SISTERS
SEVEN SISTERS
MARKFIELD RECREATION GROUND
SOUTH TOTTENHAM
ST ANN'S HOSPITAL
EAST WARWICK
WEST WARWICK
STAMFORD HILL
STAMFORD HILL
EAST RESERVOIR
WALTHAMSTOW MARSHES NATURE RESERVE
SPRINGFIELD PARK
WEST RESERVOIR
UPPER CLAPTON
STOKE NEWINGTON
ABNEY PARK
195
STOKE NEWINGTON
CLAPTON
CLISSOLD PARK
MILLFIELDS PARK (NORTH)
RECTORY ROAD

E

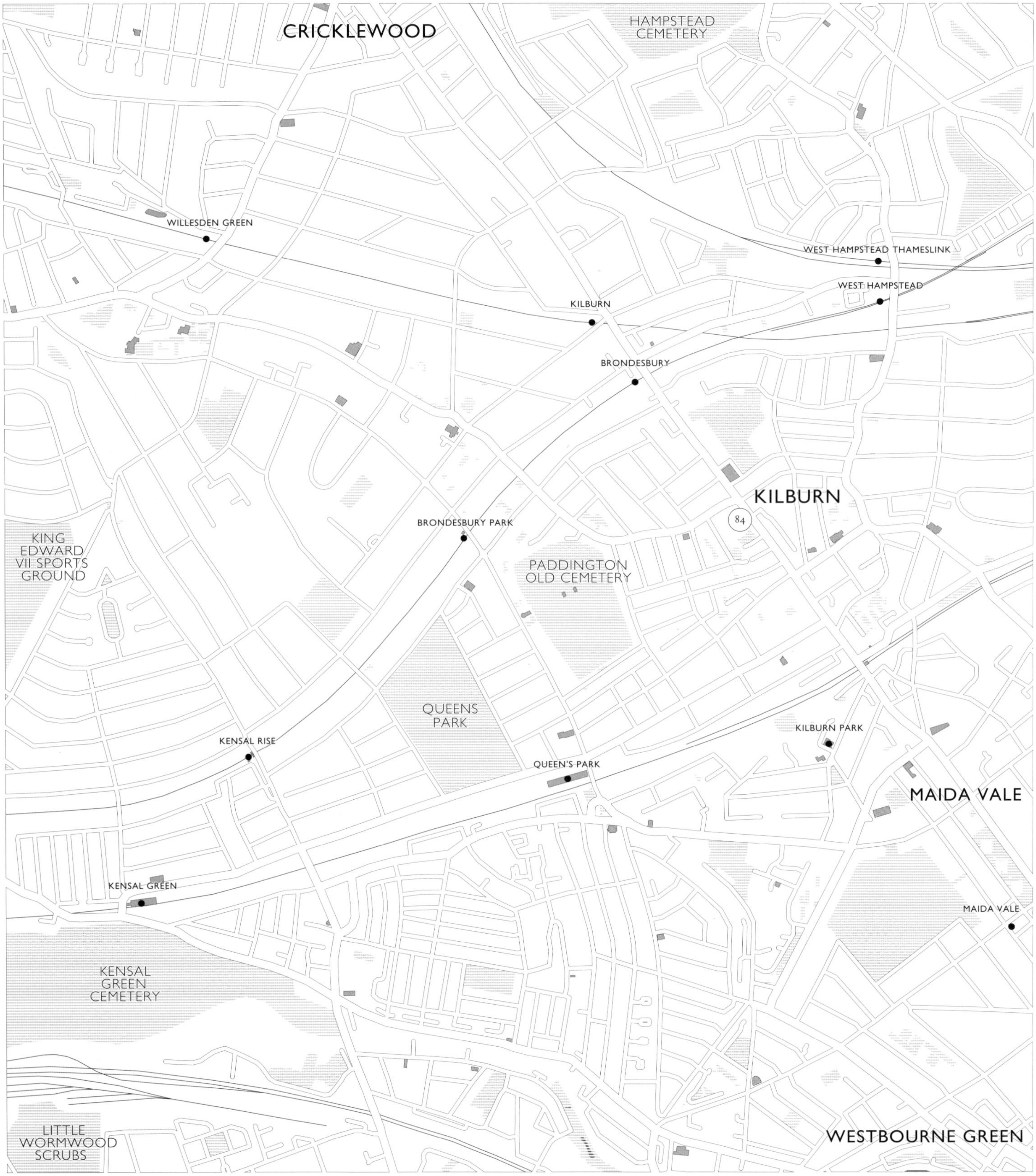
CRICKLEWOOD
HAMPSTEAD CEMETERY
WILLESDEN GREEN
WEST HAMPSTEAD THAMESLINK
WEST HAMPSTEAD
KILBURN
BRONDESBURY
KILBURN
84
BRONDESBURY PARK
KING EDWARD VII SPORTS GROUND
PADDINGTON OLD CEMETERY
QUEENS PARK
KILBURN PARK
KENSAL RISE
QUEEN'S PARK
MAIDA VALE
KENSAL GREEN
MAIDA VALE
KENSAL GREEN CEMETERY
LITTLE WORMWOOD SCRUBS
WESTBOURNE GREEN

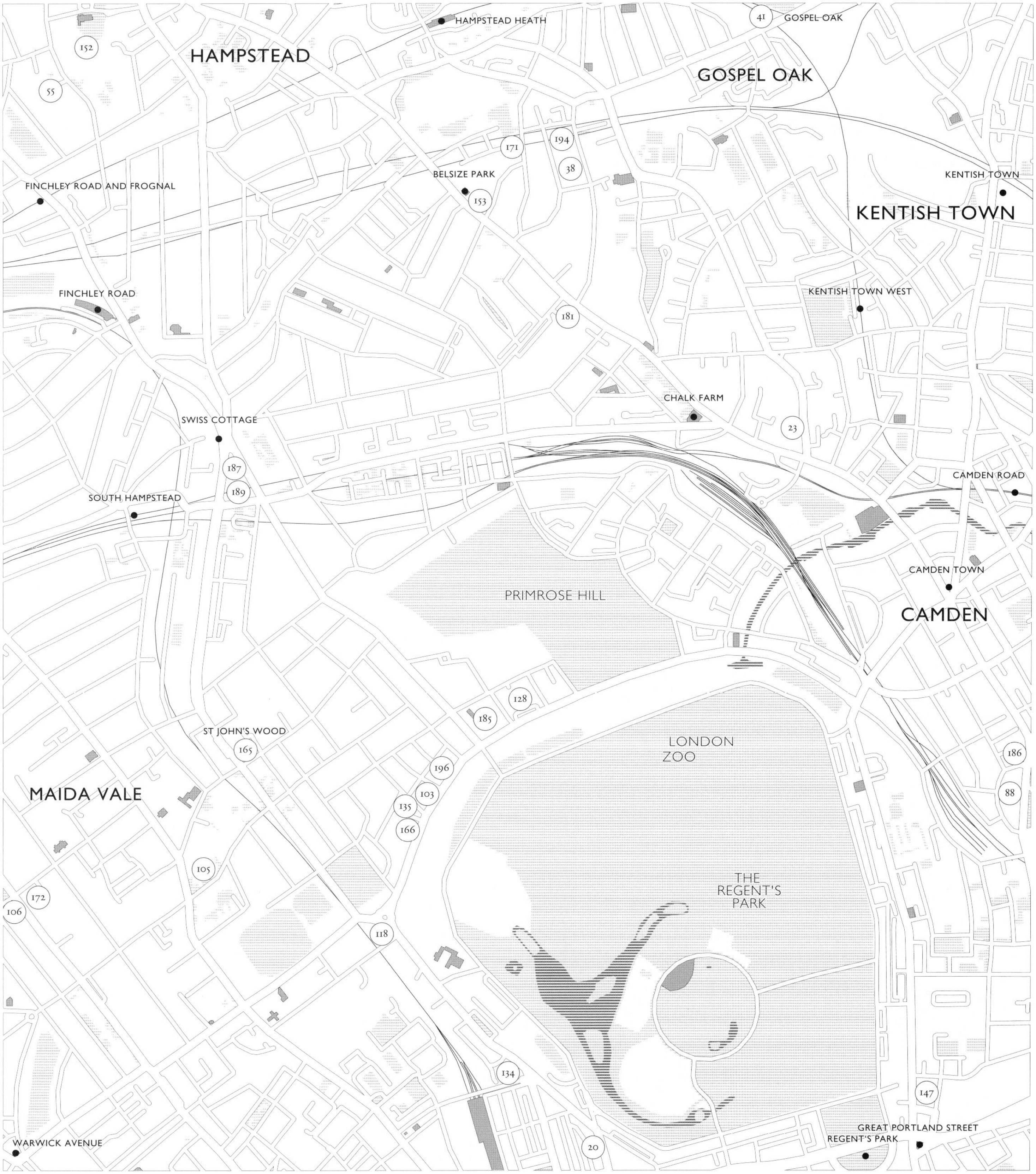
HAMPSTEAD HEATH
GOSPEL OAK
41
152
HAMPSTEAD
55
GOSPEL OAK
171
194
38
BELSIZE PARK
153
FINCHLEY ROAD AND FROGNAL
KENTISH TOWN
KENTISH TOWN
FINCHLEY ROAD
KENTISH TOWN WEST
181
CHALK FARM
SWISS COTTAGE
23
187
CAMDEN ROAD
189
SOUTH HAMPSTEAD
CAMDEN TOWN
PRIMROSE HILL
CAMDEN
128
185
ST JOHN'S WOOD
165
LONDON ZOO
186
196
MAIDA VALE
103
88
135
166
105
THE REGENT'S PARK
172
106
118
134
147
GREAT PORTLAND STREET
REGENT'S PARK
WARWICK AVENUE
20

G

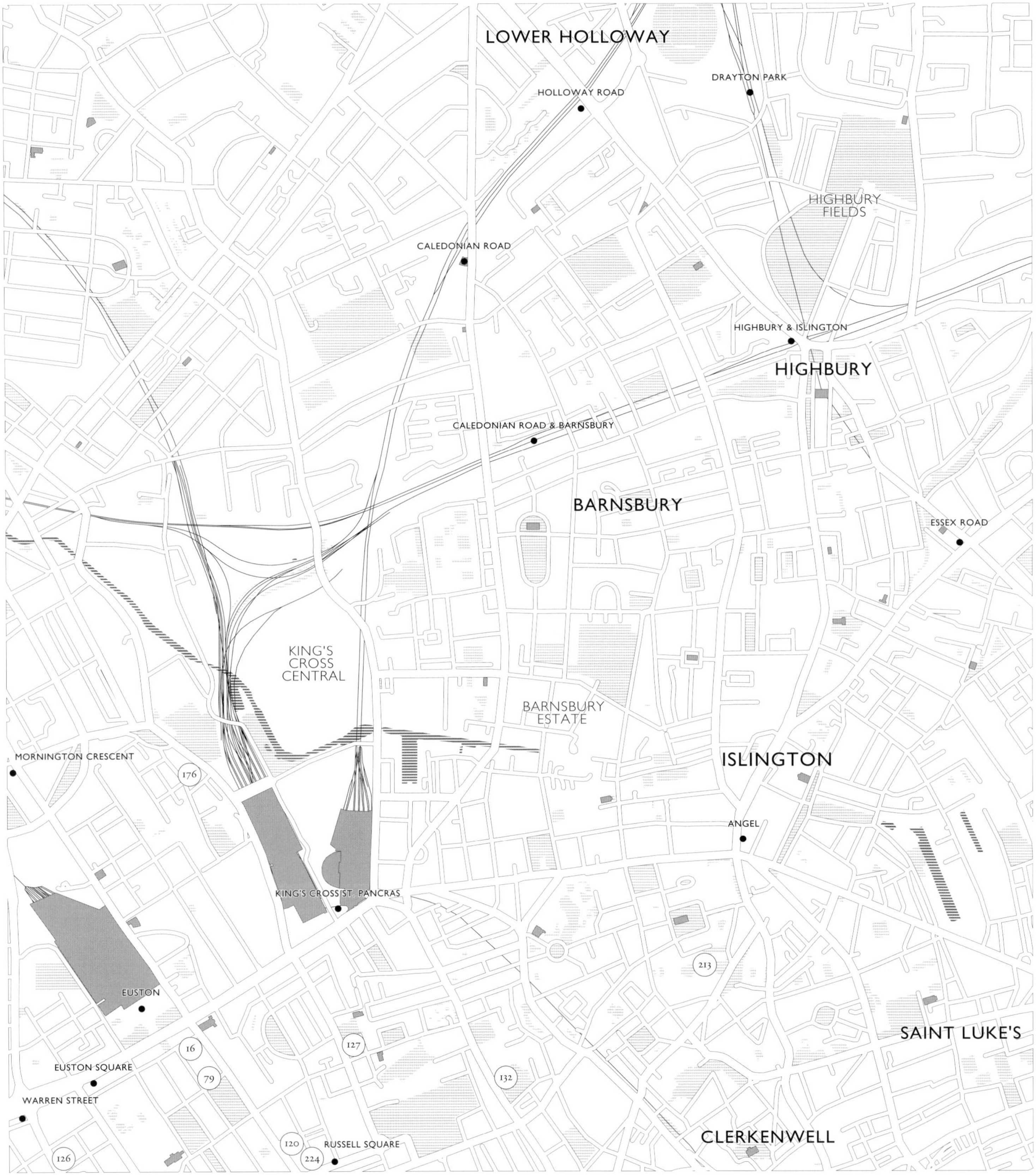

LOWER HOLLOWAY
HOLLOWAY ROAD
DRAYTON PARK
HIGHBURY FIELDS
CALEDONIAN ROAD
HIGHBURY & ISLINGTON
HIGHBURY
CALEDONIAN ROAD & BARNSBURY
BARNSBURY
ESSEX ROAD
KING'S CROSS CENTRAL
BARNSBURY ESTATE
MORNINGTON CRESCENT
176
ISLINGTON
ANGEL
KING'S CROSS ST. PANCRAS
213
EUSTON
SAINT LUKE'S
16
127
EUSTON SQUARE
79
132
WARREN STREET
120
RUSSELL SQUARE
224
126
CLERKENWELL

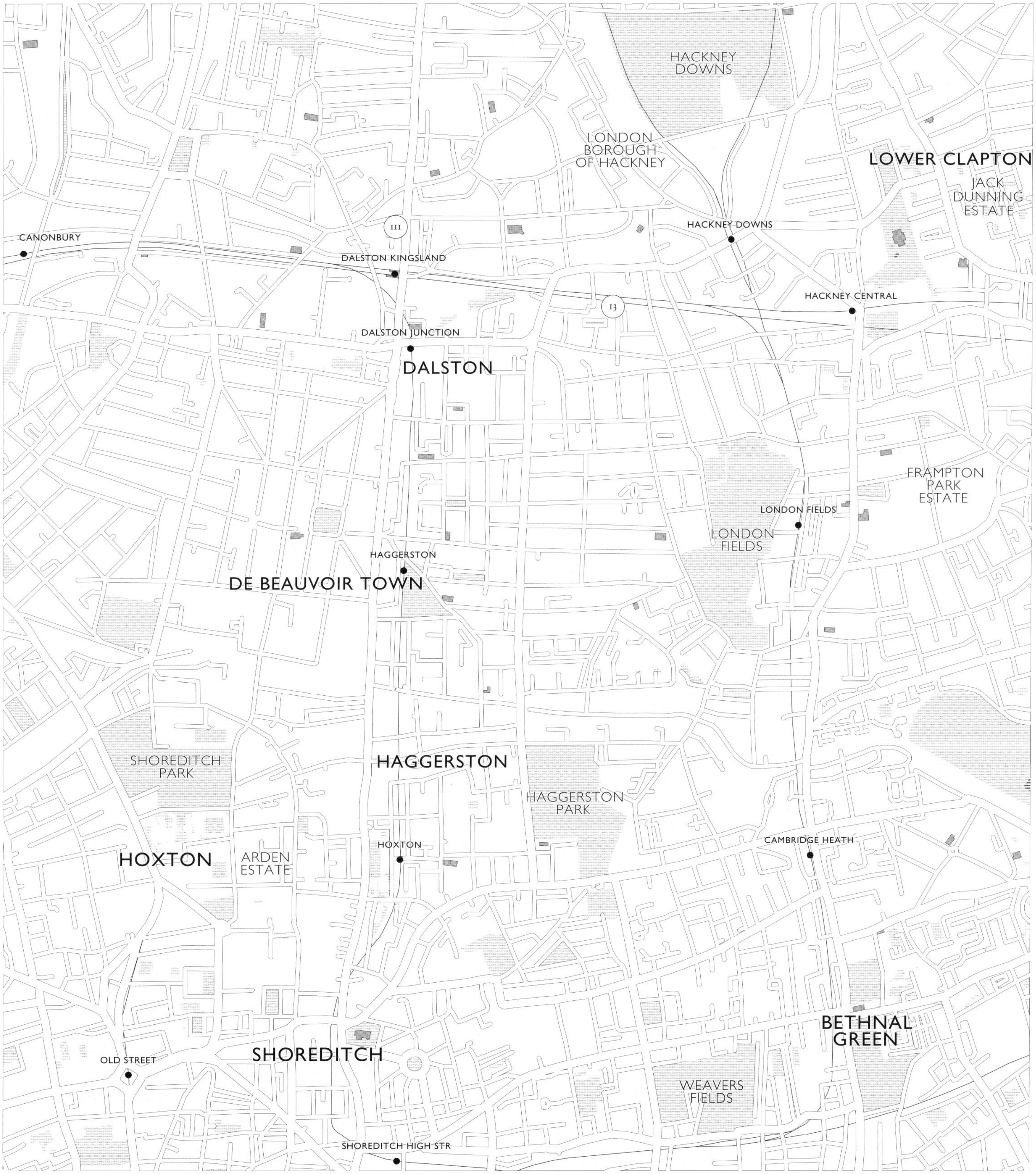
HACKNEY DOWNS
LONDON BOROUGH OF HACKNEY
LOWER CLAPTON
JACK DUNNING ESTATE
CANONBURY
III
DALSTON KINGSLAND
HACKNEY DOWNS
13
HACKNEY CENTRAL
DALSTON JUNCTION
DALSTON
FRAMPTON PARK ESTATE
LONDON FIELDS
LONDON FIELDS
HAGGERSTON
DE BEAUVOIR TOWN
SHOREDITCH PARK
HAGGERSTON
HAGGERSTON PARK
HOXTON
CAMBRIDGE HEATH
HOXTON
ARDEN ESTATE
BETHNAL GREEN
SHOREDITCH
OLD STREET
WEAVERS FIELDS
SHOREDITCH HIGH STR

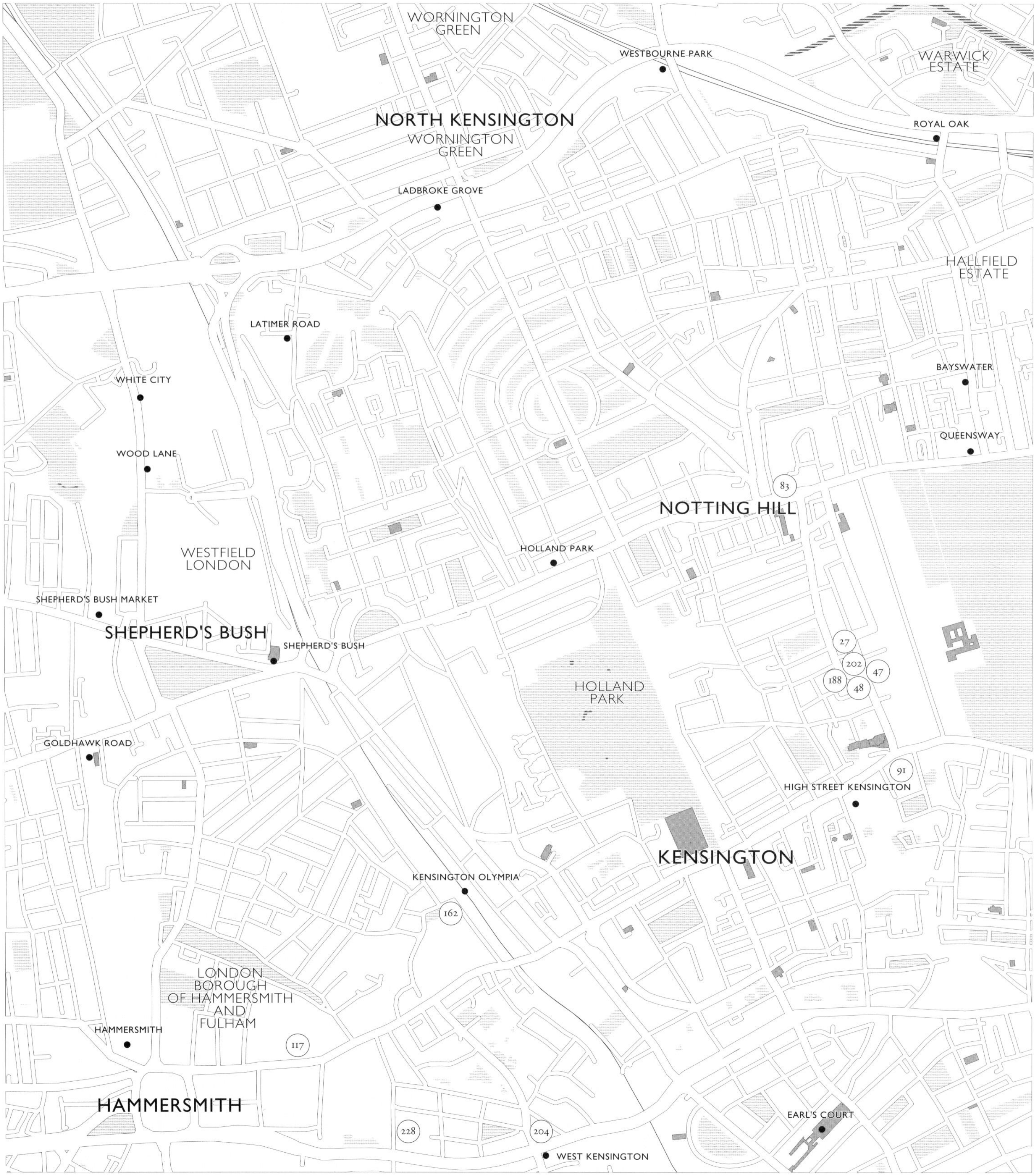
WORNINGTON GREEN
WESTBOURNE PARK
WARWICK ESTATE
NORTH KENSINGTON
WORNINGTON GREEN
ROYAL OAK
LADBROKE GROVE
HALLFIELD ESTATE
LATIMER ROAD
WHITE CITY
BAYSWATER
QUEENSWAY
WOOD LANE
83
NOTTING HILL
WESTFIELD LONDON
HOLLAND PARK
SHEPHERD'S BUSH MARKET
SHEPHERD'S BUSH
SHEPHERD'S BUSH
27
202
47
188
48
HOLLAND PARK
GOLDHAWK ROAD
91
HIGH STREET KENSINGTON
KENSINGTON
KENSINGTON OLYMPIA
162
LONDON BOROUGH OF HAMMERSMITH AND FULHAM
HAMMERSMITH
117
HAMMERSMITH
EARL'S COURT
228
204
WEST KENSINGTON

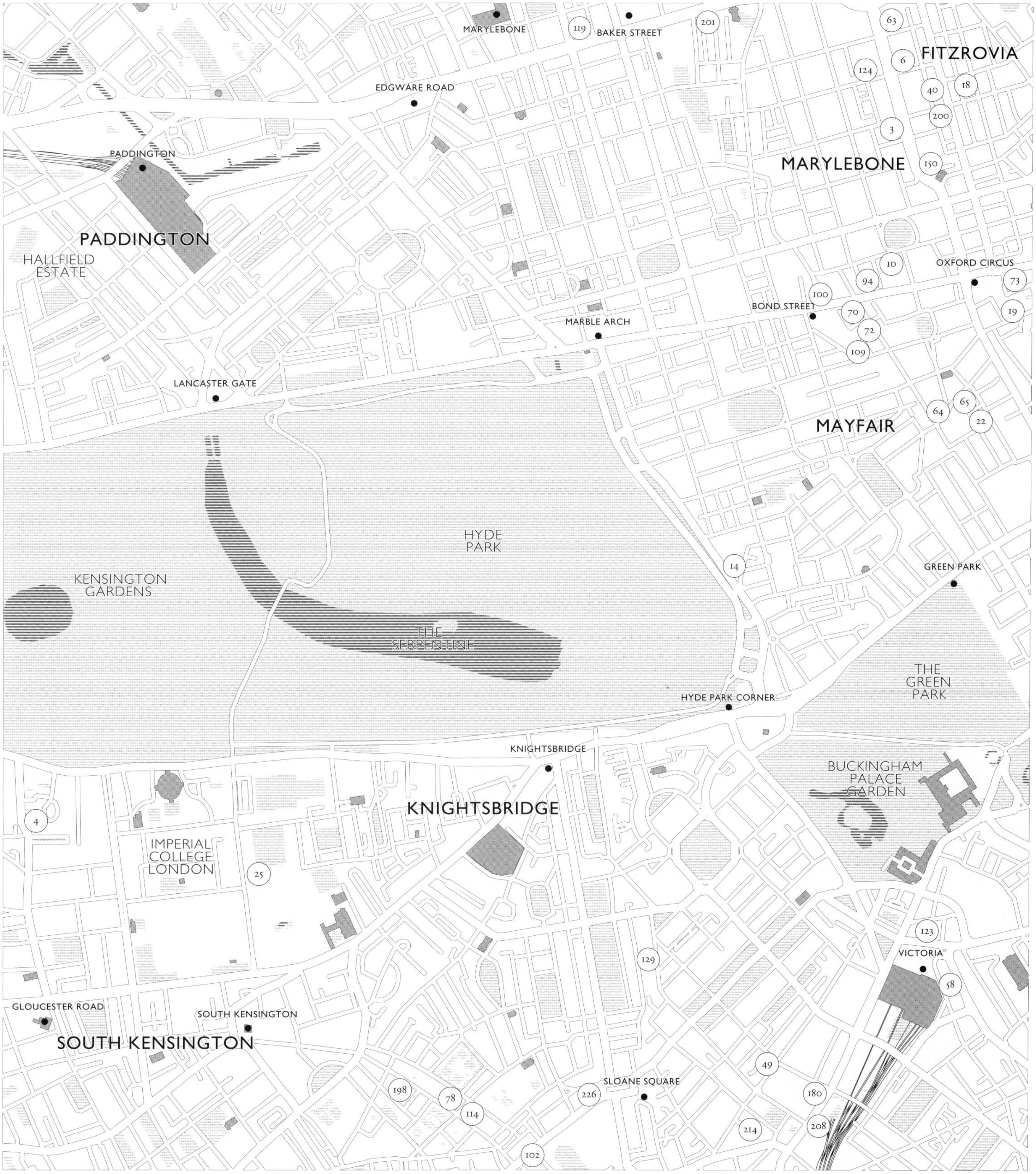
MARYLEBONE
119
BAKER STREET
201
63
FITZROVIA
6
124
40
18
200
EDGWARE ROAD
3
PADDINGTON
MARYLEBONE
150
PADDINGTON
HALLFIELD ESTATE
10
OXFORD CIRCUS
94
73
100
BOND STREET
70
19
MARBLE ARCH
72
109
LANCASTER GATE
64
65
22
MAYFAIR
HYDE PARK
14
GREEN PARK
KENSINGTON GARDENS
THE SERPENTINE
THE GREEN PARK
HYDE PARK CORNER
KNIGHTSBRIDGE
BUCKINGHAM PALACE GARDEN
4
KNIGHTSBRIDGE
IMPERIAL COLLEGE LONDON
25
123
129
VICTORIA
58
GLOUCESTER ROAD
SOUTH KENSINGTON
SOUTH KENSINGTON
49
SLOANE SQUARE
198
78
226
180
114
214
208
102

K

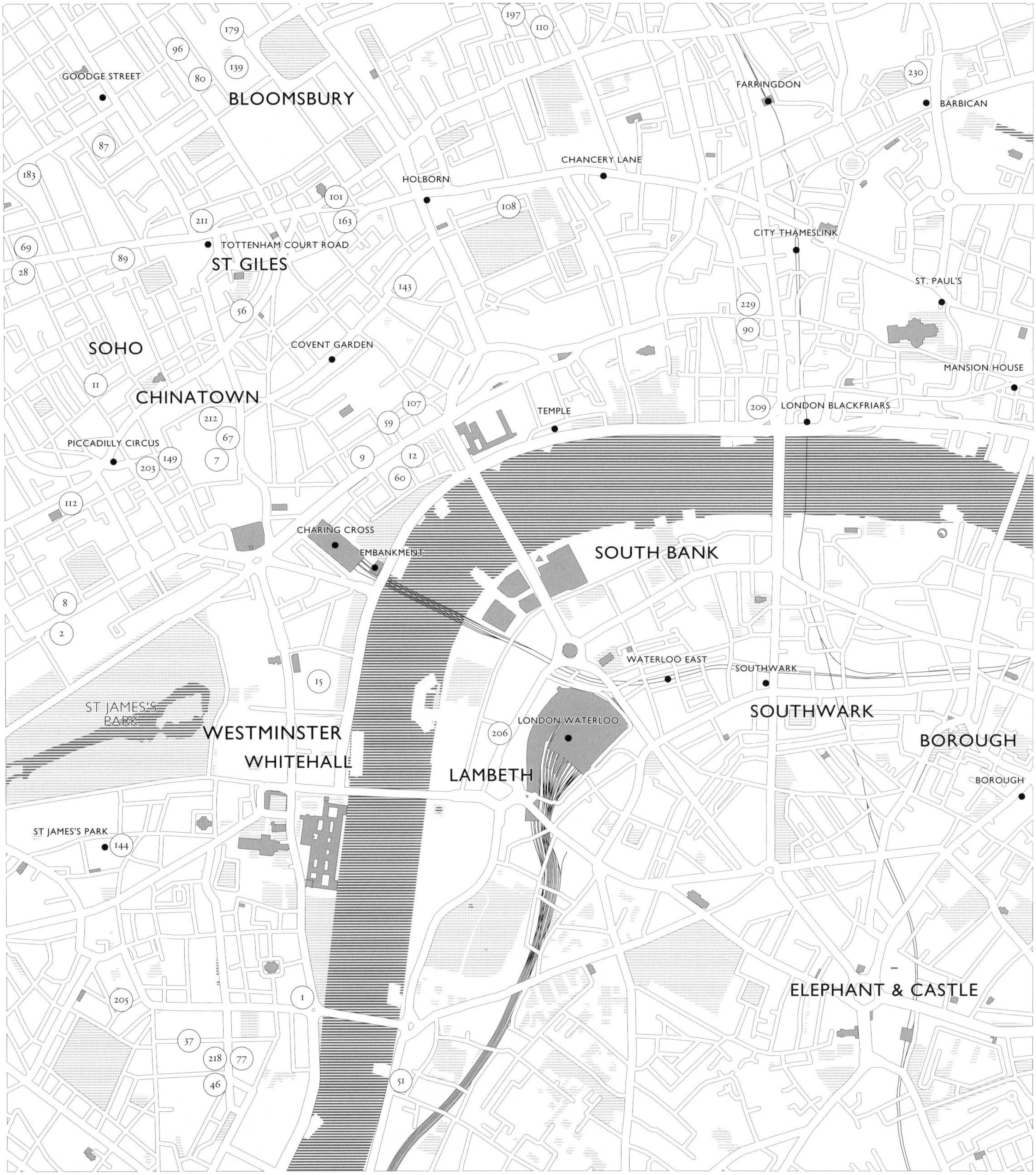

BLOOMSBURY
GOODGE STREET
FARRINGDON
BARBICAN
CHANCERY LANE
HOLBORN
TOTTENHAM COURT ROAD
ST GILES
CITY THAMESLINK
ST. PAUL'S
SOHO
COVENT GARDEN
MANSION HOUSE
CHINATOWN
TEMPLE
LONDON BLACKFRIARS
PICCADILLY CIRCUS
CHARING CROSS
EMBANKMENT
SOUTH BANK
WATERLOO EAST
SOUTHWARK
ST JAMES'S PARK
SOUTHWARK
LONDON WATERLOO
WESTMINSTER
WHITEHALL
LAMBETH
BOROUGH
BOROUGH
ST JAMES'S PARK
ELEPHANT & CASTLE
197
110
179
96
139
80
230
87
183
101
108
163
211
69
89
28
143
56
229
90
11
107
209
212
59
67
149
7
9
12
203
60
112
8
2
15
206
144
1
205
37
218
77
46
51

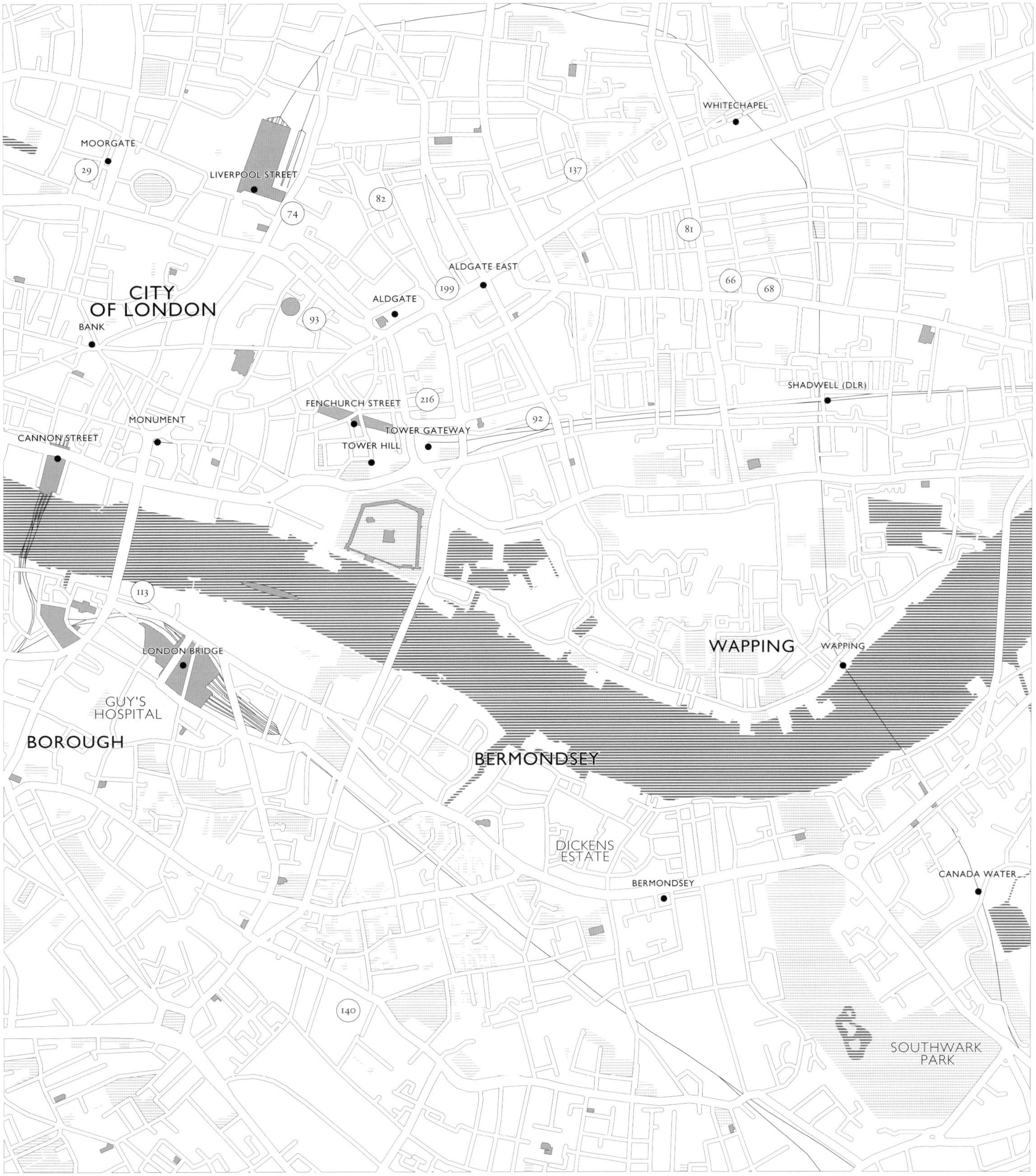
WHITECHAPEL
MOORGATE
29
LIVERPOOL STREET
137
82
74
81
ALDGATE EAST
66
68
199
CITY
OF LONDON
ALDGATE
93
BANK
SHADWELL (DLR)
216
FENCHURCH STREET
92
MONUMENT
TOWER GATEWAY
CANNON STREET
TOWER HILL
113
WAPPING
WAPPING
LONDON BRIDGE
GUY'S
HOSPITAL
BOROUGH
BERMONDSEY
DICKENS
ESTATE
BERMONDSEY
CANADA WATER
140
SOUTHWARK
PARK

M

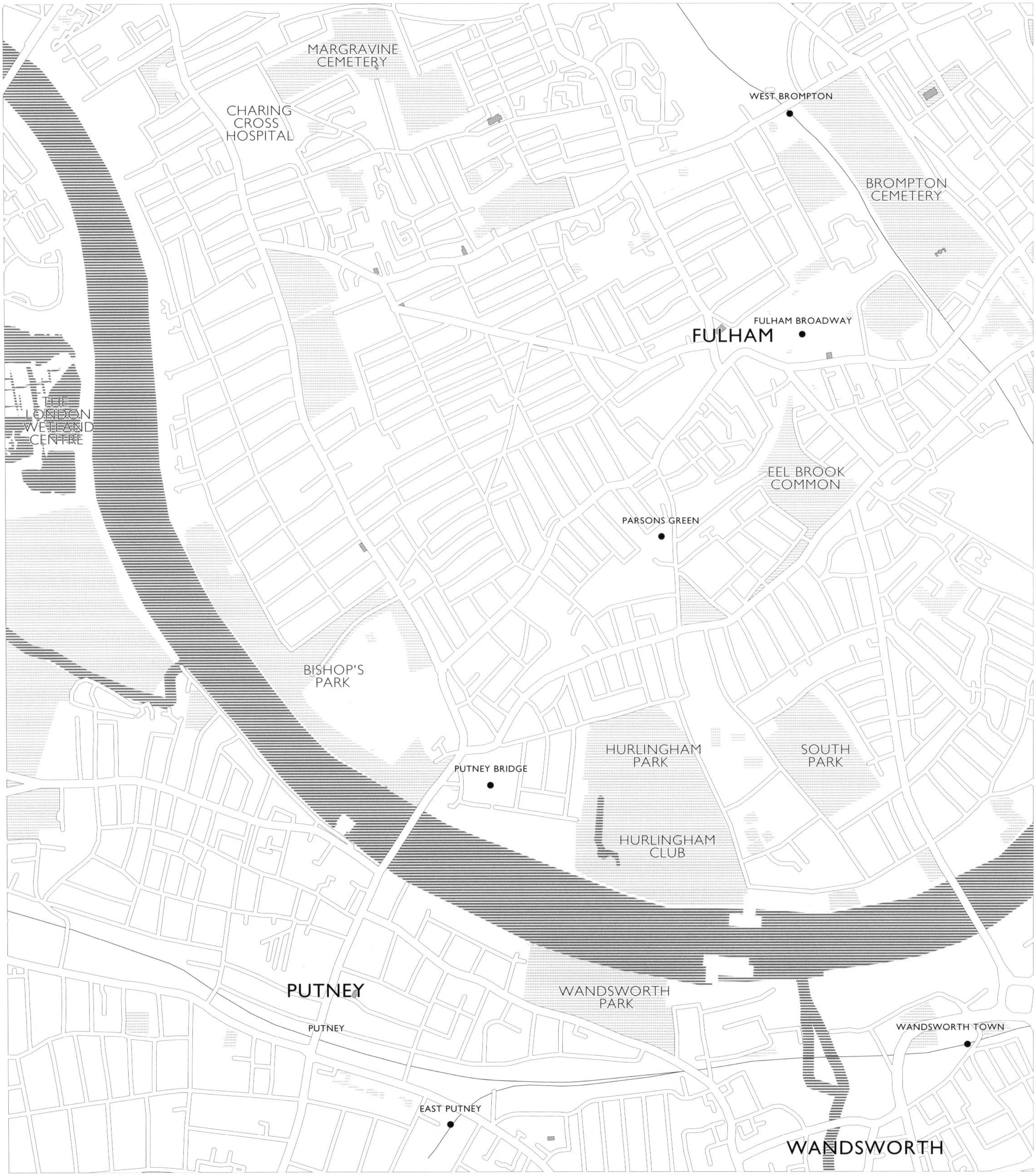
MARGRAVINE CEMETERY
CHARING CROSS HOSPITAL
WEST BROMPTON
BROMPTON CEMETERY
FULHAM BROADWAY
FULHAM
THE LONDON WETLAND CENTRE
EEL BROOK COMMON
PARSONS GREEN
BISHOP'S PARK
HURLINGHAM PARK
SOUTH PARK
PUTNEY BRIDGE
HURLINGHAM CLUB
PUTNEY
WANDSWORTH PARK
PUTNEY
WANDSWORTH TOWN
EAST PUTNEY
WANDSWORTH

N

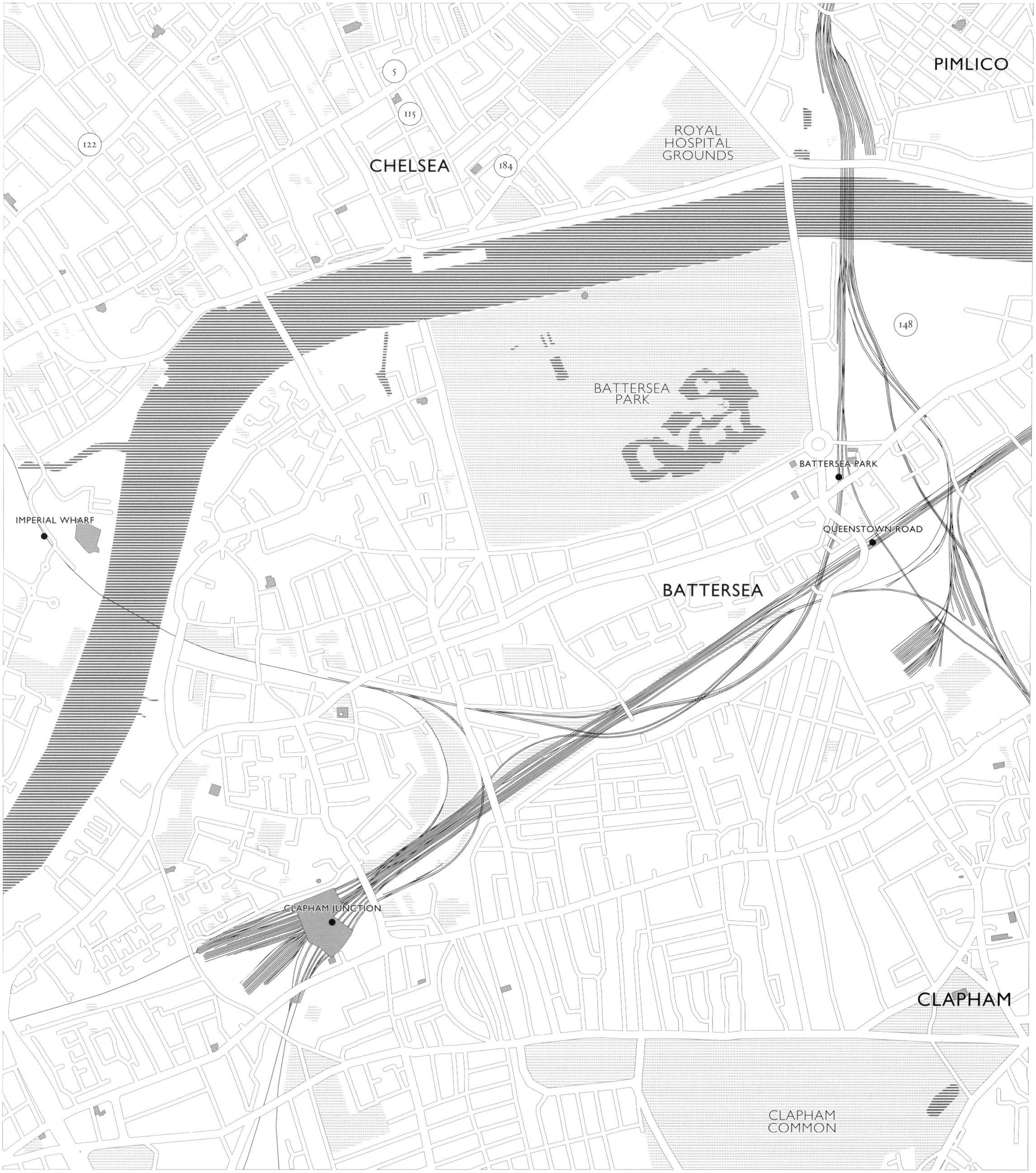
PIMLICO
5
115
122
ROYAL
HOSPITAL
GROUNDS
CHELSEA
184
148
BATTERSEA
PARK
BATTERSEA PARK
IMPERIAL WHARF
QUEENSTOWN ROAD
BATTERSEA
CLAPHAM JUNCTION
CLAPHAM
CLAPHAM
COMMON

BUILDING INDEX GEBÄUDEREGISTER

ARCHITECT INDEX ARCHITEKTENREGISTER

Modernism London Style would not have been possible without substantial support: the Erich Degen Foundation financed the first foray in London; the Department of Architecture at the ETH Zurich and Pensimo Management AG helped with the cost of printing, as did more than eighty other individuals and companies, notably atelier 10:8, Jürg Burger, Sebastian Claußnitzer, ee, Désirée Gmür & Bruno Fritschi, Ruedi Göldi, Dougie Hudson & Helen Southgate, Thomas & Ulla Katzorke, Friederike & Stephan Molls, Karin Molls, Petra & Olaf Lehmann, Jette Lehmann & Norman Seher, nightnurse images, Jason E. Olson, Michael Rabe, Ulrike Stangier, Nils Wagner and others, who would like to remain anonymous; meanwhile, Hochparterre and Archdaily helped to raise awareness of the project; whilst Julia Berger and Philip Shelley edited the text with the greatest precision and care; and Thomas Zuhr and Rainer Arnold of Hirmer, our publisher, showed their unwavering confidence in the endeavour. Our sincere thanks to everyone!

Ohne vielfältige Unterstützung wäre *Modernism London Style* nicht möglich gewesen: Die erste Exkursion nach London finanzierte die Erich Degen-Stiftung; bei den Druckkosten halfen neben dem Departement Architektur der ETH Zürich und der Pensimo Management AG über 80 weitere Personen und Unternehmen, von denen atelier 10:8, Jürg Burger, Sebastian Claußnitzer, ee, Désirée Gmür & Bruno Fritschi, Ruedi Göldi, Dougie Hudson & Helen Southgate, Thomas & Ulla Katzorke, Friederike & Stephan Molls, Karin Molls, Petra & Olaf Lehmann, Jette Lehmann & Norman Seher, nightnurse images, Jason E. Olson, Michael Rabe, Ulrike Stangier, Nils Wagner und weitere, die ungenannt bleiben wollen, als besondere Förderer hervortraten; indes halfen Hochparterre und Archdaily, das Projekt bekannter zu machen; und die Bearbeitung der Texte erfolgte mit kritischem und konstruktiven Blick durch Julia Berger und Philip Shelley; letztlich bewiesen Thomas Zuhr und Rainer Arnold vom Hirmer Verlag großes Vertrauen auch bei Unüblichem. Allen gilt unser Dank!

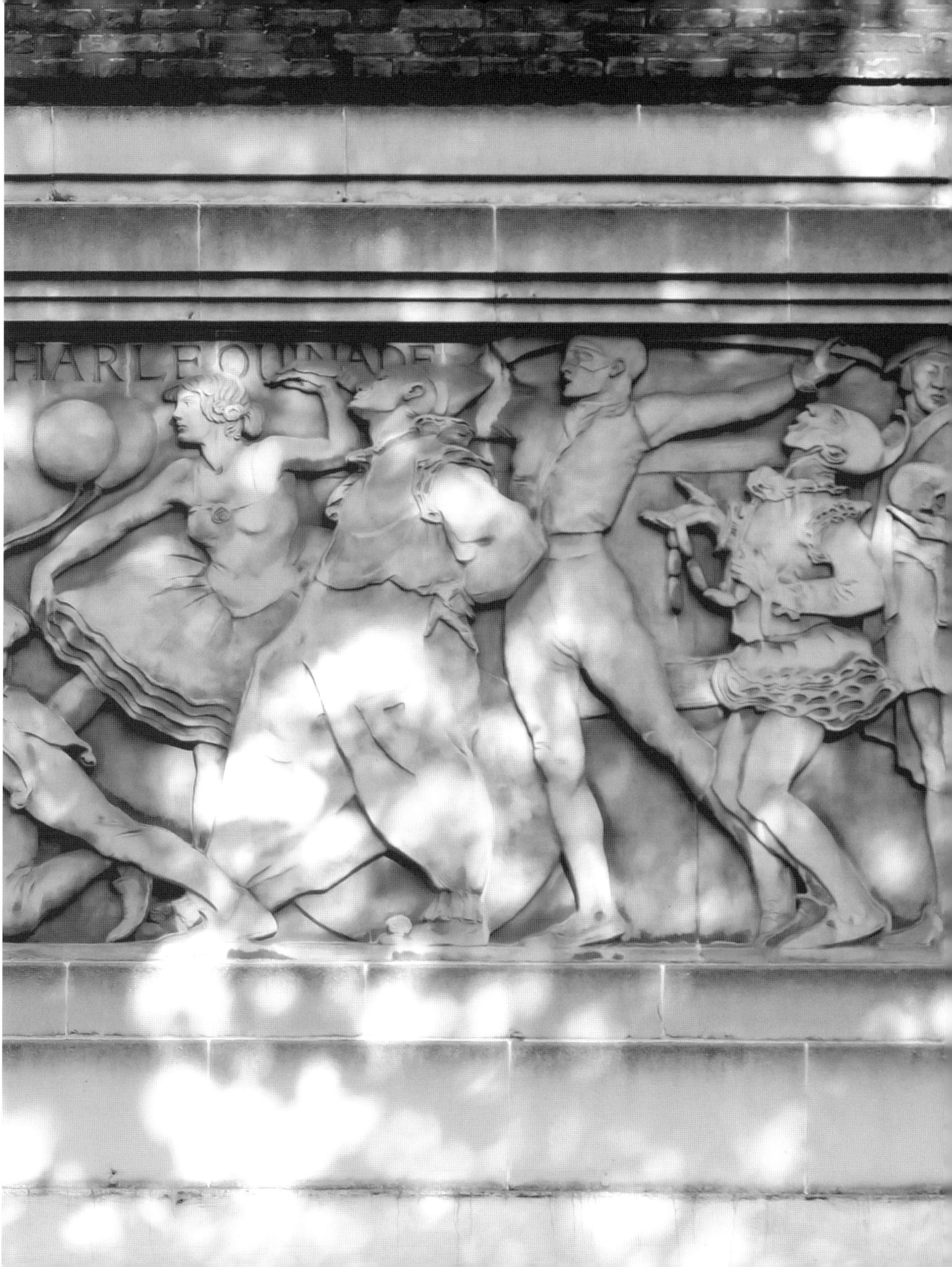
HARLEQUINADE

IMPRINT / IMPRESSUM

Hirmer Verlag GmbH
Nymphenburger Straße 84
80636 München

Christoph Rauhut (Editor / Herausgeber)

Layout / Gestaltung: Niels Lehmann, Christoph Rauhut
Translations / Übersetzungen: Christoph Rauhut (Deutsch), Philip Shelley (English)
Copy-editing / Lektorat: Julia Berger (Deutsch), Philip Shelley (English)
Proofreading / Korrektorat: Tanja Bokelmann (Deutsch), Susanna Rachel Michael (English)

Printing, Binding and Lithography / Druck, Bindung und Lithografie:
AZ Druck und Datentechnik GmbH

Paper / Papier: Profi matt 150g/qm
Typefaces / Schriften: Adobe Garamond Pro und Gill Sans

ISBN 978-3-7774-8031-2
2nd edition / 2. Auflage
www.hirmerpublishers.com / www.hirmerverlag.de

Credits / Bildnachweise
Text Rauhut: Fig. A: Scully, Vincent J.: The Shingle Style. Architectural Theory and Design from Richardson to the Origins of Wright. New Haven, 1955, inside title page; Fig. B: Rondelet, Jean-Baptiste: Theoretisch-praktische Anleitung zur Kunst zu bauen. Leipzig/Darmstadt, 1833–36, plate 1; Fig. C: Lindheimer, Otto: Aquarien, in: Durm, Josef et al. (eds): Gebäude für Erziehung, Wissenschaft und Kunst (Handbuch der Architektur, Part 4, Vol. 6, No 4). Darmstadt, 1893, fig. 547/548; Fig. D: Haeckel, Ernst: Kunstformen der Natur. Leipzig/Vienna, 1899–1904, plate 86; Fig. E: Darwin, Charles: On the Origin of Species by Means of Natural Selection (The World's Classics, XI). London/New York/Toronto, 1907, p. 1; Fig. F: Mebes, Paul (ed): Um 1800. Architektur und Handwerk im letzten Jahrhundert ihrer traditionellen Entwicklung. Munich, 1908, Vol. 1, pp. 138/139; Fig. G: [Anonymous]: Ausgeführte Bauten und Entwürfe von Arch. Otto Salvisberg. [n.p.], 1914 (Special print of: Moderne Bauformen 1914, No 3), unnumbered page; Fig. H: Vincentz, Curt R.: Bausünden und Baugeldvergeudung. Hannover, 1932, pp. 14/15.
Maps / Karten: © OpenStreetMap und Mitwirkende, CC-BY-SA
All other pictures / Alle weiteren Abbildungen: Niels Lehmann

Bibliographic information published by the Deutsche Nationalbibliothek
The Deutsche Nationalbibliothek lists this publication in the Deutsche Nationalbibliografie; detailed bibliografic data are available on the Internet at http://dnb.d-nb.de.

Bibliografische Information der Deutschen Nationalbibliothek
Die Deutsche Nationalbibliothek verzeichnet diese Publikation in der Deutschen Nationalbibliografie; detaillierte bibliografische Daten sind im Internet über http://dnb.d-nb.de abrufbar.